The Privilege of Crisis

Elahe Haschemi Yekani, Dr. phil., is a lecturer at the Department of English and American Studies at Humboldt-Universität zu Berlin.

Elahe Haschemi Yekani

The Privilege of Crisis

Narratives of Masculinities in Colonial
and Postcolonial Literature, Photography and Film

Campus Verlag
Frankfurt/New York

The printing of this book was facilitated by the generous financial support of the Research Training Group "Gender as a Category of Knowledge", funded by the German Research Foundation (DFG), and the Department of English and American Studies at Humboldt-Universität zu Berlin.

Bibliographic Information published by the Deutsche Nationalbibliothek.
Die Deutsche Nationalbibliothek lists this publication in the Deutsche Nationalbibliografie.
Detailed bibliographic data are available in the Internet at http://dnb.d-nb.de.
ISBN 978-3-593-39399-5

For further information:
www.campus.de
www.press.uchicago.edu

Contents

Acknowledgements

As any book that started out as a PhD thesis, this project could not have been completed without supportive supervisors. I want to thank Eveline Kilian and Stefanie von Schnurbein for always taking time and for having been incredibly kind and helpful throughout this process. Eveline Kilian has drawn my attention to the structures of narrative identity formation and Stefanie von Schnurbein has challenged me to ask what we might learn from the crises of writing. I could not have asked for better advice. Gabriele Dietze's help, especially in the early stages of the project, was crucial and I want to thank her for the encouragement. I enjoy our continued collaboration on queer intersectionalities to this day.

The Research Training Group "Gender as a Category of Knowledge", funded by the German Research Foundation (DFG), granted me a PhD scholarship that enabled the first two and a half years of this research, for which I am immensely grateful. My thanks extend to all my colleagues there who have contributed greatly with their critical comments to the development of the project. For the opportunity to work in this stimulating environment I would like to thank Christina von Braun, Volker Hess and Inge Stephan. I would also like to thank the coordinator of the Research Training Group, Viola Beckmann, for keeping up with the numerous requests of not always well-organised PhD students. I had the great pleasure and privilege to work with my friends and colleagues in several research groups on intersectionality, masculinity and queer theories. I want to especially thank Sven Glawion, Jana Husmann, Carsten Junker, Karolina Krasuska, Beatrice Michaelis and Simon Strick all of whom have offered valuable advice in my struggles with the crises of masculinity.

The Department of English and American Studies at Humboldt-Universität zu Berlin, my current academic home, offered me an equally stimulating surrounding to finish this project, and it is due to my colleagues Sabine Blackmore, Eva Boesenberg, Wolfram R. Keller, Eveline Kilian,

Martin Klepper, Stephan Lieske, Verena Lobsien, Helga Schwalm, among many, that I feel most welcome here. Jana Sodtke, too, has been more than helpful in organising my defence and other research activities. I also want to thank my students who helped me shape many questions raised in this book. The Center for Transdisciplinary Gender Studies (ZtG) at Humboldt-Universität zu Berlin has been a second departmental home, and I wish to thank Gabriele Jähnert, in particular, who has encouraged and supported this work from the earliest stages, as well as Kerstin Rosenbusch.

The Research Network "The Body in Cultural Studies", funded by the German Research Foundation, has offered another academic context in which I am constantly challenged regarding academic collaboration. This makes being part of this network a rewarding experience. Furthermore, I wish to thank the Queering the Humanities (2004) and Queer Again (2010) conference speakers, chairs and attendants with whom I shared wonderful and ongoing discussions. Moreover, I was able to present part of this research at the University of Sussex in 2010 and would like to thank my welcoming hosts for this opportunity.

My friends Katy M. Allen and Anson Koch-Rein have been more than generous in finding the time to proofread this manuscript despite their numerous occupations. Your help is greatly appreciated. The employees at the Staatsbibliothek zu Berlin and The British Empire & Commonwealth Museum have been most helpful in finding my visual material. I want to thank the Michael Stevenson gallery in Cape Town and especially Guy Tillim for generously granting me the right to reproduce his stunning picture as the cover of this book. Furthermore, I need to thank my editors at Campus, Rebecca Schaarschmidt and Friederike Fleschenberg, for their friendly assistance as well as Joachim Fischer for his help with the pictures.

Last, but certainly not least, I wish to thank my friends and family. Marie Schlingmann and Noemi Yoko Molitor have helped at numerous occasions to take my mind off colonial masculinity and enjoy a good deal of television. I thank my wonderful parents, Masoumeh Fateh Mohassel and S. Mohammad Ali Haschemi Yekani, my brother Ali, his wife Sabrina and their children, my cousins, Minu, Maryam and Mitra Haschemi Yekani, my uncles and aunts who have provided me with love, shelter and support whenever I needed it in many places around the world, from London and New York to Frankfurt and Berlin. My partner, Beatrice Michaelis, has been there from the start and has been my constant source of generous love and support. Thank you.

Introduction:
Contained and Exposed Crises

> "'Masculinity' is not a coherent object about which
> a generalizing science can be produced." (Connell 1995, 67)

The bemoaning of an alleged crisis of masculinity seems to be a cyclically recurring event, and given the still widely found adherence to the hegemony of the 'right kind of masculinity', must remain quizzical to all those who have been involved in counter-hegemonic practices for years. Currently, men in most Western societies are purportedly endangered as under-achievers in school, threatened by violence and/or unemployment and generally seen as 'less fit' to cope with the ever-increasing demands of capitalist societies and the changes this entails. While these are, in fact, issues that need to be debated more seriously, it is at least equally important to stress, as feminists such as Lynne Segal have done continually, that "it is men themselves, and their attachment to traditional ideas of 'manhood', which are very much part of the problem" (Segal 1997, xix). The realm of cultural texts has always been one of the prime arenas in which such "traditional ideas of 'manhood'" have been produced and negotiated. By focusing on the narrative patterns of colonial and postcolonial stories of male crises in this book, I want to highlight the discursive construction of crises rather than confirm that masculinity is, in fact, in crisis.

The recurrence of the discourse of masculinity in crisis in colonial and postcolonial narratives is no coincidence, and I deem it necessary to relate this discourse more strongly to questions of the construction of empire and nationality. The photograph on the cover links these colonial and postcolonial narratives. This picture by South African photographer Guy Tillim of the demolished statue of Henry Morton Stanley, which overlooked Kinshasa in colonial times, was shown at the 2004 exhibition *Leopold and Mobutu*. It points to fissures in the construction of masculinity. Stanley's statue is lying on a rusty boat, face to the ground and the lower parts of the legs shattered. A young Congolese is depicted casually urinating at the ruined monument of one of the most famous explorers of Africa and the embodiment of the fantasies of successful colonial masculinity.

Impressively, this picture visually captures a connection between old colonial myths of masculinity and the postcolonial present. The iconic image of the White[1] man as the benevolent 'father' overlooking 'his' land is no longer valid. Nonetheless, this fall of White masculinity continues to have an effect on how gender in general and masculinity in particular can be conceptualised. As the opening quote by Raewyn Connell emphasises, this book does not attempt to provide a meta-theory of masculinity or the concept of crisis. Rather, by providing readings of a selection of sources, it seeks to critically engage with English[2] narratives of male crises that were so prominent at the end of the nineteenth and again at the end of the twentieth century.

For the field of cultural production, the notion of 'crisis' is widely considered to be a driving force of works of fiction as well as an engine for aesthetic innovation. Joseph Conrad is celebrated as one of the many innovators of English literature. In his *Heart of Darkness*, the search for the mysterious Mr Kurtz sparks off an existential crisis for Marlow, the narrator of the tale. Conrad, who has been praised for his ability to delve into the abyss of the psyche of colonialism, conceived an intense and complicated journey that chronicles, in the words of the narrator, "[t]he dreams of

---

1 To underscore an understanding of both categories, 'Black' and 'White', as socially constructed rather than based on a conception of races as biological entities, both adjectives are capitalised in this book. However, as Jana Husmann-Kastein explains, it remains important to distinguish that Black, contrary to White, has been employed as a political marker of emancipative self-designation. In contrast, Whiteness is connected to socio-cultural dominance. (cf. Husmann-Kastein 2006, 44) Furthermore, to highlight the social construction of 'race' does not in any way negate or question the material effects of racism.

2 The term 'English' here refers primarily to the language of the texts and in this sense does not denote solely British literature but literatures in English. Nevertheless, the main focus remains on the British cultural context. I am very well aware that including authors, such as Conrad and Coetzee, in a text that focuses mostly on discourses of masculinity in Britain, might not do them justice as authors who were and are involved in a number of national contexts, and in the case of Coetzee it is surely more appropriate to speak of a South African writer or 'world writer'. Accordingly, his situatedness in these contexts will be thematised in the specific readings. In contrast, when the term 'Englishness' is employed in this book, it refers to an exclusive and nationalist assumption of a homogenous cultural identity. The discussion of Englishness will be important in the context of postcolonial writing that seeks to disrupt this clear-cut nationalist understanding of cultural identity. Consequently, the term 'Britishness', as opposed to Englishness, is employed as a more inclusive alternative that makes it possible to speak of Asian Britishness or Afro-Caribbean Britishness (cf. Kumar 2001; Wachinger 2003, 21–35) and will be expounded upon in the chapters on Kureishi and Smith.

men, the seed of commonwealths, the germs of empires" (HD 105). Despite Conrad's apprehensions concerning the rightfulness of the colonial endeavour, the *novella* also encompasses elements that are akin to a nostalgic yearning for male adventure and an unspoiled ideal of chivalrous masculinity which links this text to earlier colonial fiction.

Almost exactly one hundred years after Conrad's *Heart of Darkness*, a very different story of White masculinity in post-apartheid South Africa caused exuberant admiration as well as heated debates. J.M. Coetzee's award-winning *Disgrace* features the devastating story of the White male anti-hero David Lurie, a twice divorced academic who first loses his job after allegations of sexual harassment and who is then later confronted with the rape of his own daughter, Lucy, by Black farm workers. Coetzee has been applauded for his brutal honesty and his willingness to create this ambivalent character, Lurie, who provides the novel's point of view.

Despite the important differences in time of production and setting, there is a connection between these two texts. Their value as outstanding pieces of English fiction is often linked directly to the stories' capacity to reflect the plight of the whole of humanity through the failure of a single individual. Time and again, feminists, such as the philosopher Elizabeth Grosz, have emphasised that the construction of men as 'universal' and women as 'particular' is at the heart of much of Western philosophy and a foundation of male hegemony.[3] It is this very universalisation of the narratives of failing White masculinity in the context of post/colonialism[4] that I want to concern myself with. But it is not only these failing masculinities that are of interest here, as I will also analyse a range of different crisis narratives – narratives that focus on a celebratory overcoming of crisis or

---

3 Grosz explains that this universalisation is based on associating women with the 'body' and men with the 'mind' – a dichotomy that has become highly suspect: "If the mind is necessarily linked to, perhaps even part of, the body and if bodies themselves are always sexually (and racially) distinct, incapable of being incorporated into a singular universal model, then the very forms that subjectivity takes are not generalizable. Bodies are always irreducibly sexually specific, necessarily interlocked with racial, cultural, and class particularities." (Grosz 1994, 19)

4 The term 'postcolonial' is by no means unproblematic as McClintock (1995), Shohat (1996) and others have explained. It implies a temporal 'after' colonialism as well as an epistemological 'beyond' colonialism. While I make use of the term 'postcolonial', I agree with the cautionary attitude that critics who employ the term 'neo-colonial' advocate as a means to emphasise that colonial power relations are still in effect and that globalisation continuously produces new structures of dependence.

the ultimate collapse into despair, both from a hegemonic and marginalised perspective in English colonial and postcolonial fiction.

To lament the loss of male privilege in Britain was especially rampant at the turn of the nineteenth century and again at the end of the twentieth century. In the colonial context, the crisis of masculinity is linked to the still largely intact notion of universality, albeit a conception that begins to wane in the course of the late nineteenth and early twentieth century. These colonial narratives of masculinity are part of a contained conception of crisis and try to reinforce a model of phantasmatic White male heroism or, in Conrad's case, failure, and situate masculinity firmly at the centre. In the selected sources for this period, I will analyse different figurations of masculinity. *Gentlemen* and *hunters* populate Henry Rider Haggard's fiction and photographs in the newly-successful illustrated journals. These figurations of 'heroic masculinity' in general, seem to function as a nostalgic response to the growing crisis tendencies of male hegemony. The *hybrid* '*Sahib*' is a figuration that is specific for Rudyard Kipling's *Kim*, which stresses ambivalence in the encounter of coloniser and colonised. Finally, Joseph Conrad's tales often feature *failures*, men who, as has been briefly mentioned, threaten to despair over the atrocities of the colonial situation. However, in the texts' emphasis on the hegemonic perspective, they still adhere to what I call re-privileging[5] tendencies and the discursive privilege of masculinity in crisis.

Non-White masculinities in these works are reduced in terms of their role in the narratives. They frequently appear merely as a background effect, a foil for hegemonic masculinities. In *Playing in the Dark*, Toni Morrison speaks of "Africanism" as a vehicle by which America was able to imagine itself as 'superior' and 'White' at the expense of Black background characters: "black or coloured people and symbolic figurations of blackness are markers of the benevolent and the wicked; the spiritual […] and the voluptuous; of 'sinful' but delicious sensuality coupled with demands for purity and restraint." (Morrison 1993, ix) Following Morrison's reasoning, this background effect is also constitutive of European colonial literature.[6] African characters in colonial fiction often are "mere animal, if

---

5 Edgar Forster (1998) employs the term "re-sovereignisation" (*Resouveränisierung*) to connote a similar idea in a different context.
6 Morrison herself writes: "There also exists, of course, a European Africanism with a counterpart in colonial literature." (Morrison 1993, 38)

heroic" (Katz 1987, 141).[7] While the emphasis is on the construction of hegemonic masculinity in the colonial narratives, this also entails an analysis of non-White characters who are either constructed as 'noble savages' or 'animal-like' brutes, as in Haggard's adventure stories, or stand for symbolic Blackness, as will be explained with reference to Conrad's texts.

These figurations lend themselves to different narrative patterns. In colonial texts, in general, Blackness is often associated with the tropes of *superstition, polygamy* or *cannibalism*. Conversely, the figurations of hegemonic masculinity are connected to themes and motives such as the *quest into the unknown*, the *establishment of order*, or the *loss of control*, and as a consequence, the plots are shaped by a repeated reference to *loneliness* (as part of the quest), *struggle* (in the effort to establish order) and *hygiene* (as a means to maintain control). Given the different narratives' embeddedness in various genre traditions, some texts, such as Haggard's formulaic writing, are more prone to a repetitive use of these patterns while other writers, such as Kipling and Conrad, construct more ambivalent approaches to these patterns, as will become evident in the subsequent analyses.

In postcolonial narratives, other figurations of masculinity, which will be called *hybrid men, fanatics* and *anti-heroes*, render the clear distinction between hegemonic and marginalised masculinities at times more complicated. While Hanif Kureishi and Zadie Smith portray a new generation of so-called *hybrid men*, marginalised men who are now situated in the metropolitan centre, and who struggle to find their place in multicultural Britain, British films also feature spectacular hybrid characters, often in relation to both their ethnic background and their gender and/or sexual identity, as in *My Beautiful Laundrette* and *The Crying Game*. In addition, *The Black Album* and *White Teeth* depict men who could be described as *fanatics*, young Muslim men who, given their complicated position in racial, religious and gendered relations, resort to violence. The third figuration, *anti-heroes*, describes White men who have to come to terms with changed relations in postcolonial societies, as is the case in Coetzee's texts. The characters Fergus, in *The Crying Game* and to a certain extent – although much more optimistic in his outline – Archie Jones, in *White Teeth*, could be labelled anti-heroes as well. As can be seen in postcolonial narratives, the figurations cannot be

---

7 Frantz Fanon's writing was a crucial first step to examine the psychological effects of the continuous racist appellation, and he speaks of an "epidermalization of this [ascribed, E.H.Y.] inferiority" (Fanon 1967, 11).

clearly allocated to individual sources as in the colonial texts and the same holds true for the related narrative patterns.

In the selected postcolonial works, the narrative patterns of '*in-between-ness*' and *hybridity* as well as *guilt* relating to the after-effects of colonialism feature prominently. Generational conflicts and questions of assimilation and resistance play a crucial role in the novels of Kureishi and Smith, while Coetzee tries to come to terms with or negotiate White male hegemony. Additionally, films, such as *My Beautiful Laundrette* and *The Crying Game,* and their makers concern themselves with similar themes, linking these issues with questions of visual representation. In a postcolonial setting, the narratives address the crises of masculinities in a much more self-reflexive way. White masculinity can no longer be regarded as the unchallenged normative reference point in fiction. Nonetheless, the crises of hegemonic men still figure prominently in narratives of this time. Regarding these postcolonial texts, one could speak of exposed and more plural crises – as opposed to the contained colonial crises – given the more radical questioning as to what is 'universal' in literature.

I propose to analyse these figurations and tropes as part of a privileged narrative discourse that (re)produces the conception of masculinity in crisis. Rather than offering a systematic overview that seeks to provide an exhaustive list of 'figurations' and 'patterns', the reference to figurations and patterns functions as a hermeneutic tool that allows me to examine the repeated, yet heterogeneous narrative re-privileging of masculinity in crisis. The analysis of these various narrative strategies, which are entangled in a discursive web that privileges crisis as a distinctly masculine narrative, will be the focus of this book. As has been suggested with reference to the almost analogous reception of *Heart of Darkness* and *Disgrace,* both periods produce re-privileging tendencies which are typical of the discourse of masculinity in crisis.

Crisis as a Privilege

Within recent years, the field of masculinity studies[8] has broadened and one encounters the phrase 'crisis of masculinity' constantly. This discourse

---

8 For a good overview, cf. Berger, Wallice and Watson (ed.) (1996); Kimmel, Hearn and Connell (ed.) (2005) and with a strong focus on the German context, Erhart (2005).

of masculinity in crisis is now applied to vastly different historical or geographical locations of different masculinities. In fact, this terminology is employed so widely that Walter Erhart infers "that the so-called crisis is an implicit concept of masculinity itself, a narrative, which as its constitutive element so to speak, is inherent in every history of masculinity" (Erhart 2005, 222, my translation). Regarding this point, I disagree in part with Erhart's otherwise insightful account of the narrative construction of masculinity, and I will segue back to this later in the text. While crisis is a *privileged* narrative pattern of masculinity, it is, I argue, not *inherent* to the concept of masculinity. Accordingly, the title-giving "privilege of crisis" is intended as a point of rupture in the soaring naturalisation of crisis *as* male that we are currently witnessing. The ongoing (self-)fashioning of White masculinity under threat or in crisis, reinstalling 'him' over and over as the centre of attention, needs to be understood and read as a specific re-privileging narrative strategy that affects the comprehension of masculinity as a non-static concept reliant on iterative practices. Narratives do not simply reproduce White hegemonic masculinity, and masculinity does not intrinsically depend on narratives of crisis, but, as will be argued in greater detail, it is performatively constructed.

As a social norm, male hegemony is dependent on notions of immutability and universality that have been increasingly debunked in the context of both the modern and postmodern challenges to the so-called autonomous subject and male hegemony. In a poststructuralist understanding, processes of subject formation are reliant on what Judith Butler characterises as "the constitutive outside" (Butler 1993, 3). Consequently, the dichotomy of 'self' and 'Other' is constantly (re)negotiated. Butler links the normative position of hegemonic masculinity to a continuous oscillation between rationality and corporality. She makes out elements of stabilisation and possible destabilisation in this "figure in crisis" which is, paradoxically, to embody human reason:

[X]enophobic exclusion operates through the production of racialized Others, and those whose 'natures' are considered less rational by virtue of their appointed task in the process of laboring to reproduce the conditions of private life. This domain of the less than rational human bounds the figure of human reason, producing that 'man' […]. This is a figure of disembodiment, but one which is nevertheless a figure of a body, a bodying forth of a masculinized rationality, the figure of a male body which is not a body, a figure in crisis, a figure that enacts a crisis it cannot fully control. (ibid., 48–49)

Although the phantasmatic position of hegemonic masculinity at the centre is a construction, it remains dominant and powerful in the sense that it is still perceived as 'normal'.[9] Accordingly, it is important to clarify that men (as opposed to the construction 'Man'), too, can never fully enact this ideal of masculinity – a masculinity that alternates between the assertion of universality and the un-attainability of this idealised construct.[10]

Within this logic, the 'Others' of this idealised fiction of the autonomous subject cannot claim the position of fundamental crisis as they have never inhabited the place of universal humanity. Of course, models of narrating female or marginalised men's conflicts exist and prosper. However, it is the normative and unmarked position of White masculinity that lends narratives of hegemonic masculinity in crisis such a cultural momentum of standing for the whole of mankind. That is why, it can be argued, these texts are part of a discourse that re-privileges hegemonic masculinity. Proclaiming a crisis often entails a restorative impulse.

The term 'privilege' here connotes different facets of the discourse of masculinity in crisis. On a more general level, 'crisis' seems to have become the predominant mode of narrating hegemonic masculinity. In order to avoid the continued repetition of the by now much-criticised phrase 'crisis of masculinity', Connell introduces the term "crisis tendencies" (borrowed from Jürgen Habermas) to underscore that "[w]e cannot logically speak of the crisis of a configuration; rather we might speak of its disruption or its transformation" (Connell 1995, 84). Accordingly, one could argue that there is no crisis of masculinity but rather a continuing narrative production of crisis tendencies with specific privileging effects, which is what I seek to identify in the selected primary sources.

On a second, more textual level, privilege pertains to specific aesthetic strategies which construct masculinity as the principal frame through which agency is established in colonial and postcolonial fiction. Both facets of the privilege of crisis produce what I have called re-privileging tenden-

---

9 Sabine Mehlmann describes this paradoxical construction of modern men as simultaneously belonging to 'the superior sex' while also being seen as the 'gender-neutral representative of universal mankind' with reference to sexological, biological and psychological writings of the time. (cf. Mehlmann 2008, 37)

10 As Judith Jack Halberstam's influential book *Female Masculinity* (1998) has underlined, we need to be aware that masculinity is not a male prerogative. The diversification of male and female masculinities and the resulting severing of the seemingly unquestioned link between sex and gender can also be seen as one of the reasons why there is a new rise in the discourse of a crisis of masculinity at the end of the twentieth century.

cies of crisis as a slight modification to Connell's crisis tendencies. It is important to stress that these cultural constructions not only reflect social realities, but shape and produce them as well. In this context, Sabine Sielke links the discourse of the crisis of masculinity to the crisis of representation. (cf. Sielke 2007, 48–49) The question of who is privileged in terms of cultural representation and how this is achieved is connected to the more fundamental question of who is considered representative of the 'universal'. Who writes and who reads which kinds of stories, or what kinds of images and genres are produced at which point in time, has significance in how we understand race, gender and sexuality. Cultural texts are part of the social processes of negotiating masculinity.

Consequently, these general thoughts pertaining to masculinity need to be applied to the representation of the classic (male) 'hero' in literature whose story is also increasingly a narration of crisis. A pattern that emerges is the narration of masculinity as a (constant) crisis – a crisis that includes failure, restoration and processes of (re)negotiation. Therefore, as has been argued, crisis in fact paradoxically becomes the attribute of a privileged position – a narrative that can become quite appealing and a powerful strategy in the safeguarding of male privilege. Sally Robinson, for instance, has convincingly pointed out that the claim to the position of "being-in-crisis" has become a potent vantage point and "there is much symbolic power to be reaped from occupying the social and discursive position of subject-in-crisis" (Robinson 2000, 9). Further she explains that "[a]nnouncements of a crisis in white masculinity [...] perform the cultural work of recentering white masculinity by decentering it" (ibid., 12).

Focusing strongly on hegemonic masculinity, this book runs the risk of re-centring men and masculinity as well. While I am well aware of this danger, it is my understanding that it remains important to reflect how narrative patterns are shaped and possibly reproduce underlying masculine norms. How is the model of male crisis re-inscribed but also subverted in literary and visual texts? Within the crisis narratives that are the focus of this book one sometimes finds a nostalgic and sometimes a more radical process of negotiation of this assumed loss of male authority. In this sense, a look at modern and postmodern narratives of crises of masculinities still appears to be a productive venture, especially given the necessity to situate the discourse of the crisis of masculinity more explicitly within a contextualised colonial/postcolonial framework rather than read it as an ahistorical precondition of masculinity.

In terms of an intervention in the field of masculinity studies, I want to emphasise the need for a stronger focus on the *privilege* of the crisis of masculinity instead of propagating the *crisis* of masculinity time and again. Only by fundamentally severing masculinity from universality can there be a turn away from the perpetuation, rather than the dismantling, of the discourse of the crisis of masculinity. 'Crisis' should not become the 'universal' answer to the 'problem' of masculinity.

Especially at times when the normativity of White heterosexual masculinity *is* increasingly questioned, the assertions of assumed crises swell. However, although there is a continuity in linking masculinity to crisis (as a result of its failed adherence to an imaginary universality), crisis can have very specific implications at a given time and location that are not static.[11] One must not succumb to the idea that there is a teleology of progressiveness that will eventually undermine male privilege in due course. Rather, there is a need to continue to question narrative strategies which constantly normalise male hegemony. In light of this position, I want to briefly contextualise my historical focus on English colonial and postcolonial cultural texts which will be examined with regard to their entanglement in the discursive web of the privilege of crisis.

Colonial and Postcolonial Contexts

Even if it is important to emphasise the specificity of modern and postmodern crises of masculinity, they cannot be regarded as the solitary relevant periods of crises of masculinity. In fact, it is in question whether there has ever been a 'stable' male identity which was not constructed as being in crisis.[12] Again, at this point one has to be careful not to universalise this rhetoric of crisis since multiple and conflicting genealogies of an upsurge of crisis narratives can be established, and it is the construction of these high periods of crisis rather than crisis itself that is of interest here.

---

11 For more detailed accounts on how male hegemony is connected to perceptions of deliverance and salvation, cf. Glawion, Haschemi Yekani and Husmann-Kastein (ed.) (2007).

12 With reference to these nostalgic longings for earlier supposedly stable identities, Homi Bhabha has been immensely important criticising notions of intact national identities before colonialism and has highlighted the "production of the nation as narration" (Bhabha 1994, 209).

In Britain, the rhetoric of crisis becomes a prevalent discourse of masculinity at the *fin de siècle* and again from the mid-eighties to the present. While it is mainly the cultural interpretation of these crisis tendencies that is of interest here, several social and political factors, which comprise the backdrop of the growing concern around masculinity, have to be taken into consideration. In this context, cultural artefacts do not function merely as reflections of these events, but are part of and entwined in this larger discursive field that produces the privilege of crisis, which had one climax at the end of the nineteenth century.

That, which discursively emerges as a 'male identity' for the first time around the turn of the century, is constituted as being 'in crisis' from the very beginning. Until this moment, man was thought of as the universal representative of humanity, only woman was understood as a gendered subject. (Schnurbein 2001, 10, my translation)

An initial significant reason for this increased awareness of a crisis that has been widely noted is the impact of the suffragette movement[13] and the emergence of the so-called New Woman. In this context, Mrinalini Sinha, for instance, speaks of "the perception of a growing 'crisis' in British masculinity arising, from among other things, the feminist challenges of the 1880s" (Sinha 1995, 140). Victorian masculinity[14] not only faced the growing demands for women's rights but also, more generally, the debate on a dangerous 'feminisation of culture' loomed large and male privilege as well as a 'healthy' masculinity were perceived as endangered.

In addition, the impact of Britain's imperialism on the perceived crisis is not to be underestimated. Simon Gikandi importantly links the phases of colonial and postcolonial crisis of English national identity by reading together texts from both periods in his influential study *Maps of Englishness*. He examines the ambivalent relationship of coloniser and colonised and "the ways in which Englishness was itself a product of the colonial culture it seemed to have created elsewhere" (Gikandi 1996, x). However, al-

---

13 Only in 1918, did Britain finally grant women the right to vote (with women's voting age at thirty, which was only even later reduced to twenty-one in 1928). While the majority of men perceived these developments as a threat to their status in society, there was also a small minority of men voicing public support for the suffragette movement, such as Edward Carpenter. (cf. Tosh 2004, 103–125)

14 For a more general overview on masculinity in the nineteenth century, cf. John Tosh's *A Man's Place* (1999) in which he provides a differentiated look at the diverse roles of middle-class Victorian men and "the ideal of domesticity" which was both embraced and resisted in the course of the second half of the nineteenth century.

though Gikandi provides a helpful reading of imperial femininity[15], he to some extent misses out on focusing more extensively on the implications of masculinity in this context. The construction of male identity was crucially shaped by colonial expansion and processes of 'Othering' that pertain to aspects of race, ethnicity, nationality and religion. The renewed concern for colonial expansion and events such as the Great Exhibition of 1851 in London as an expression of this popular interest in the 'exotic Other' have to be regarded as a second important factor contributing to the discourse of masculinity in crisis. Britain's global imperialist activities had extended to a new height with the New Imperialism of the eighteen-eighties[16], culminating in the so-called 'Scramble for Africa', a direct result of the Berlin Conference of 1884–1885. Simultaneously, Britain's expansion acted as the catalyst for anti-colonial resistance, a prime example of this being the Indian Rebellion/Mutiny of 1857.[17] This became the most popularised event and a recurring reference point in cultural texts. The Rebellion/Mutiny had a long lasting effect as it was perceived as a treacherous act of irreverence against what many still imagined as Britain's 'gentlemanly' and 'benevolent' imperialism. Another important incident was the Morant Bay Rebellion of 1865 in Jamaica which aroused heated debates on the aftermath of slavery and the question of who counted as a British citizen. Other military conflicts connected to British imperial activities, such as the Zulu War (1876–1879) and the Boer Wars (1880–1881 and 1899–1902) in South Africa, influenced the public debate that was not univocally in favour of colonial expansion. Rather paradoxically then, as Tosh notes, "[d]uring the era of

---

15 Gikandi parallels Black and White colonial femininities. (cf. Gikandi 1996, 119–156) He focuses on Mary Seacole and Mary Kingsley and argues against a simplistic dialectic of complicity versus resistance in the analysis of the role of women in an imperialist system: "We want to read women as the absolute other in the colonial relation so that we can unpack the universalism of the imperial narrative and its masculinist ideologies, but the result (positing the white women as figures of colonial alterity, for example) can be achieved only through the repression of their cultural agency and the important role they play in the institutionalization of the dominant discourse of empire and the authority of colonial culture." (ibid., 122)

16 Hobsbawm, who speaks of "The Age of Empire", characterises this rise in colonisation as follows: "Between 1876 and 1915 about one-quarter of the globe's land surface was distributed or redistributed as colonies among a half-dozen states." (Hobsbawm 1989, 59) This, of course, included Britain as one of the leading nations: "[P]erhaps one-third of the globe was British in an economic, and indeed cultural, sense." (ibid., 74) Nonetheless, this was also a time that was perceived as a threat to English imperial rule.

17 As a consequence, the often mystified British rule over India, the Raj, was established in 1858 and Victoria crowned 'Empress of India' in 1877.

New Imperialism the empire was widely perceived to be in danger. [...]
The scale of colonial domination was now such that any failure to contain
insurgency or attack called into question the imperial resolve of the British." (Tosh 2004, 194) British imperialism was no longer the unchallenged
or unquestioned norm and the role of race became more important, a
factor that has often been underestimated when discussing the crisis of
masculinity, which refers to *White* masculinity, after all. Jayasena explains
that in the colonial context men had to "negotiate social and political
power *vis-à-vis* the 'imperial other' as well as through the 'domestic other' in
the figure of the New Woman" (Jayasena 2006, 8). Although true to a
certain extent, this reasoning tends to make a too strong separation of the
'male' public sphere and 'female' domestic sphere.

More recently, feminists have examined the conflicted entanglement of
imperialism and early feminism and the role of White women in colonialism. (cf. Ledger 1995; McClintock 1995; Walgenbach 2005) As Sally Ledger
comments, there is an element of complicity of mainstream feminism with
pursuits of the empire:

What is remarkable, and ironic, about the discursive constructions of the New
Woman as a threat to the 'race' is that the middle-class feminists of the 1890s
themselves had considerable ideological investment in notions of empire and in the
continuation of the 'race', with many of the New Woman writers championing
motherhood and ardently supporting purity campaigns. (Ledger 1995, 32)

The analysis of the construction of a rivalry of different emancipation
movements has become a central research field in light of debates on intersectionality in gender studies. (cf. Dietze 2011) Consequently, it is important to see 'gender' and 'race' as well as other factors not as separate
entities in the construction of a crisis of masculinity but rather as an entangled web that added to the perceived crisis. Therefore, Ledger proposes to
read the threat of the New Woman as part of a larger crisis of Victorianism. Gender relations were intertwined with the rise of trade unionism,
fears of colonial rebellion, urban poverty and homelessness as other destabilising factors.[18] (cf. Ledger 1995, 22) Accordingly, questions of race, gen-

---

18 Ledger also notes that many of the fissures that shaped these conflicts remain important
   factors in the way gender, class, race and sexuality are debated today, which underscores
   the importance to link the Victorian crisis of masculinity with the current discursive rise
   of male crisis narratives. "To the extent that the fissures remain today, the crisis of Victorianism at the *fin de siècle* is a crisis which persists in the final years of our own century." (Ledger 1995, 42)

der and class were conflictingly related to each other, in the discursive arenas of social comment, sexological writing and also in biological writing of the time.

In this context, the Darwinian revolution and growing secularisation can be considered yet another important cause contributing to the discourse on the crisis of masculinity, as will be further elaborated in the section on colonial writing. In his *The Origin of Species* (1859), Charles Darwin polarised and thoroughly shook Christian belief. 'Man' was degraded to the status of an animal that had to fight for its survival. 'Man' was no longer considered God's special creation – "his own image" (cf. Gen. 1.26–27 (KJV)). In addition, Darwin's monogenetic theory implied the kinship between all races – an argument that the so-called polygenetic thinkers of the time, who conceptualised races as entirely different species, contested. Again, what is at stake here is the notion of universality and difference – of 'self' and 'Other'.[19] This distinction constantly needs to be re-negotiated. Systems of knowledge structure narrative patterns and vice versa, i.e. masculinity as a concept shapes the way men's lives can be narrated and different narratives of men's lives change the perceptions of masculinity. These questions of who can claim subject status and what this means for an understanding of masculinity are for one thing related to and debated in the field of popular culture, a field in which the colonial novels of Haggard and Kipling as well as the press photography belong. But these queries also play a crucial part in Conrad's conception of colonialism's failure and the modernist re-invention of writing.

Finally, the modern technological revolution of the latter half of the century has significance too in this debate. The introduction of new media, such as photography and cinematography, new modes of communication, such as the telephone or telegraph, as well as faster transportation heightened the perception of a technological and economic acceleration of life. This related to the growing urbanisation, which sometimes was seen as a threat to traditional country life, indirectly threatening an idealised English identity. The orderly gentleman, who inhabits much of the visual repertoire from the British colonies at that time as well as colonial fiction, was already in many ways an image of the past compared with the advent of a new working-class masculinity in the large cities. As Ina Ferris (1994) points out, the older social category gentleman-by-birth was transformed in the

---

19 For more detailed accounts of how these processes of 'Othering' shaped the natural sciences, cf. Harding (ed.) (1993); Schiebinger (1993); Stepan (1982, 1993).

nineteenth century to the ethical category gentleman-by-virtue, and in this
sense, there was a middle-class appropriation of the concept. Given these
processes of negotiation, colonial masculinity existed in an uneasy relationship with the romanticised ideal of gentlemanly heroism and the growing
social changes within the 'mother country', a contrast only briefly hinted at
here and one which will be taken up and discussed at greater length in the
readings of the specific colonial sources.

For postcolonial Britain, new crisis tendencies emerge from what is
often connected to a postmodern questioning of fixed identities. After the
two world wars and by the late seventies, we find a bemoaning of men,
tagged as the great 'losers' of society, a discourse that continues to have an
impact at the beginning of the twenty-first century.[20] The resistance to
racial exclusion, women's emancipation and women's growing presence in
the work market as well as the increasing privatisation of state-owned industries in the Thatcher era (1979–1990) left their marks. Unemployment
affected the image of men as the sole 'breadwinners' and 'head of the family'. "As the twentieth century draws to its close, men appear to be emerging as the threatened sex; even as they remain, everywhere, the threatening
sex, as well." (Segal 1997, ix)

Second and third wave feminisms, gay liberation and queer the-
ory/activism have produced important critiques of traditional gender roles
and the nuclear family – notions which were promoted under Thatcher's
Conservative government in eighties Britain. Under Thatcher, ruthless
economic competition and renewal was encouraged while simultaneously
subscribing to a return to idealised Victorian conservative family ideals. In
other words, the mid-eighties and early nineties witnessed an individualistic
climate with increasing divorce rates, the rise of single-parent and patchwork families, while only very little change in idealised constructions of
gender, which no longer matched these new realities, coincided. (cf. ibid.,
xxv–xxxii) These contradictions still have an impact on our understanding
of gendered relations and the adherence to an idealised hegemonic masculinity that finds its expression in cultural texts as well.

From a hegemonic as well as a marginalised perspective, the after-effects of colonisation and changed gendered relations are now addressed in
global English literatures as in Coetzee's South African writing. In more

20 Schnurbein, for instance, notes that after a high period of the rhetoric of crisis at the last
turn of the century we find a new boom only at the end of the twentieth century. (cf.
Schnurbein 2001, 10)

general terms, globalisation challenges conceptions of identity that focus exclusively on national belonging.[21] Gender and race are challenged and a postmodern understanding of identities thrives both in a theoretical as well as political sphere. Again, what is at stake is the question of universality. Who counts as a 'real' British citizen is an ongoing political debate, which is shaped by questions of national inclusion and exclusion based on racialised markers of difference. As a result of the increased 'New Commonwealth' migration after World War II, the so-called Windrush generation, Britain in the eighties and nineties saw a growing number of second- or third-generation children with an Afro-Caribbean or Asian background who also increasingly altered the representation of marginalised masculinities in the cultural sphere. The fiction of writers such as Hanif Kureishi and Zadie Smith but also contemporary British cinema, negotiate these modes of simultaneously belonging and un-belonging to the United Kingdom.

When these texts are contrasted with the colonial period, we find a prospering spectrum of representation of marginalised masculinities, and it becomes increasingly difficult to maintain the overall hegemony of White masculinities. Cultural critic Kobena Mercer points out that in a postcolonial context there exist more and more narratives of the 'Others' talking back. He thereby, importantly, relates questions of modernity with colonialism and postmodernity with postcolonialism, respectively.

Indeed, if the period after the modern is when the Others of modernity talk back, what is revealed is the fictional character of Western universality, as the subject who arrogated the power to speak on behalf of humanity was nothing but a minority himself – the hegemonic, white, male, bourgeois subject whose sovereign, centered identity depended on the 'othering' of subordinate class, racial, gendered and sexual subjects who were thereby excluded from the category 'human' and marginalized from democratic rights to political subjectivity. (Mercer 1994, 271)

While there have always been voices of dissent (both from marginalised men and women), the problem of 'male hegemony' is one that is now much more exposed – so much so that hegemonic men themselves problematise masculinity. From a marginalised perspective one can claim crisis narratives and, of course, there have been powerful appropriations of male genres and storylines both from a postcolonial and/or female perspective.

---

21 Gikandi emphasises that much of the current "crisis of the national state" has its antecedents in colonialism and that these connections need to be addressed in any examination of Englishness or Britishness. (cf. Gikandi 1996, xvi)

However, while these narratives are influential in changing literary discourse, they often lack the grandeur that is associated with the universality of hegemonic crises – they are still perceived as particular crises. While from a marginalised perspective claiming crisis often means *gaining* a position to speak from, the crisis of masculinity entails the risk of *losing* everything. This dramatic height of fall – what in German is referred to as *Fallhöhe* – renders the crisis of masculinity all the more sublime and makes it a privileged reference point that is still associated with hegemony. Nonetheless, even as the discourse of the crisis of masculinity seems to prosper once more at the end of the twentieth century, there are also differences to the earlier colonial discourse of crisis that I wish to explore.

There is now a greater awareness of the paradoxical situation that by focusing on male domination as a problem *of* men, one risks to re-centre them. In the context of the gender relations in Western accelerating capitalist societies, Ines Kappert explains that "the discourse of masculinity in crisis is a mode of reproduction in the sense of a conservative revolution" (Kappert 2002, 254, my translation). Further, she writes, "[b]y focusing on himself as the victim and by excluding others from the economy of attention, he reasserts his position as representative centre of society once more" (ibid., 264, my translation). Within postcolonial accounts of masculinity, a struggle to find more appropriate forms of articulating masculinities other than by a conservative flight into crisis flourish and pave the way for a more complex understanding of masculinity.

Masculinity as an Interdependent Category

When one focuses on a concept such as masculinity, a range of problems arise. First of all, how can we speak of social constructs, such as masculinity and femininity, without reiterating and stabilising normative dichotomous gender models? By contextualising my readings of different masculinit*ies*, I hope to emphasise that it is a contingent as well historically specific understanding of masculinity and the notion of crisis that is of interest here rather than a static conception of a self-evident crisis that men face due to some alleged inherent predicament of masculinity. As Halberstam has explained with regard to the discrimination against female masculinities, there is a certain "conservative and protectionist attitude" (Halberstam

1998, 15) towards (male) masculinity. Whereas the performativity of femininity is much more readily accepted, masculinity draws a great deal of its discursive power from a conception of an alleged immutability. I explicitly use the now much more common plural, masculinit*ies*[22], which is further differentiated by the distinction between 'hegemonic' and 'marginalised' masculinities that will be expounded upon. Despite the variation of masculinities, it is this often underlying idea of an unchangeable masculinity, I would argue, that is connected with male hegemony, which, on the one hand, denigrates femininity and, on the other hand, creates hierarchies between various lived masculinities.

More generally, a second problem that occurs is that a category such as masculinity needs to be understood as an interdependent category. There is no 'pure' gender which is affected by other axes of stratifications only in a subsequent step. Rather, masculinity – like all genders – is simultaneously and interdependently produced within a complex web of power relations. It is this notion of interdependent categories – in contrast to an additive understanding of categories of difference – that structures my understanding of masculinity.

Intersectionality as a research paradigm was developed as a method to address the dilemma of the 'etc.' that follows any enumeration of categories of difference. African American theorists and activists, such as the Combahee River Collective (1981), Kimberlé Williams Crenshaw (1997) and Patricia Hill Collins (1999), have established the idea of intersectionality in a range of disciplines and theories ranging from political sciences, sociology, law, and history to critical race theory.[23] At the same time, one must not forget that the idea of interlocking or interdependent "systems of oppression" is not restricted to approaches which make use of the term intersectionality explicitly. Based on earlier feminist debates and interventions, feminist science studies[24], critical whiteness studies, postcolonial the-

---

22 The plural of masculinities points to different dimensions in the understanding of masculinity. On the one hand, there is a difference between the plurality of 'lived' masculinities (men) as opposed to the cultural construct of masculinity (Man) – on the other hand, and more fundamentally, any social category, such as gender, is also distinctly shaped by interdependencies with other categories.

23 For an overview on how the debate on intersectionality has been situated in the German context, cf. Haschemi Yekani, et al. (2008); Walgenbach (2007).

24 Within science studies, Donna Haraway most prominently combined postmodern notions of identity categories with a responsible and accountable way to deal with "situated knowledges" (Haraway 1991, 183–201) in the production of scientific knowledge.

ory and queer theory[25] have developed other models to address the issue of differences.

I have used the two terms 'intersectional' and 'interdependent' interchangeably in this study so far. However, Katharina Walgenbach (2007) has very productively suggested employing the term "interdependent categories" instead of the more common terminology of intersectional categories. In this way, the inseparability of distinct categories is emphasised and a category such as gender is understood as always already informed by other dimensions of difference such as race or age in a complicated web of power relations.

According to Michel Foucault (1998), however, careful attention must be paid in order not to relapse into a notion of linear power relations that suppress individuals from top to bottom. It is not enough to postulate a binary of privileged versus non-privileged. Sometimes the impression arises that too narrow an understanding of intersectionality, as a model, easily relies on such a conceptualisation of power, or on a notion of only selected intersections of axes of difference. Therefore, Wendy Brown warns:

We are not simply oppressed but produced through these discourses, a production that is historically complex, contingent, and occurs through formations that do not honor analytically distinct identity categories. (Brown 1987, 87)

It is my conviction that we need a more transdisciplinary framework that includes other models of criticising hegemony in order to understand the complexities of power relations and the interdependencies of categories. It is then within the field of critique of hegemony, which transdisciplinary

---

Others, such as Sandra Harding (1986, 1991), Anne Fausto-Sterling (2000) or Nancy Stepan (1993), have also formulated powerful critiques of the unquestioned processes of normalisation within the sciences. For a detailed overview of a critique of objectivity in the natural sciences, cf. Palm (2007).

25 Queer theories have emphasised not so much the interdependencies of different social categories, but the very instability of categorisations in the first place and question the need for fixed identity categories in a political context. However, a critique that focuses on hegemony often cannot do away with these markers of social stratification, and hence we have recently witnessed a rise in theoretical approaches such as Queer of Color Critique or Queer Diaspora Critique which seek to combine queer approaches with a critical perspective on racial and postcolonial formations. (cf. C. Cohen 2005; Ferguson 2004, 2005; Gopinath 2005, Manalansan 2006; Muñoz 1999; Puar 2007) For a more detailed overview of the differences and similarities of queer and intersectional analyses that also focuses more explicitly on the German context, cf. Dietze, Haschemi Yekani and Michaelis (2007) (in German); Haschemi Yekani, Michaelis and Dietze (2010) (in English).

approaches such as gender studies, queer and postcolonial theories provide that this book is situated.

The proposed framework of interdependent categories offers what can be called a "productive instability" – an idea mentioned by Butler in the chapter "Critically Queer" in her book *Bodies That Matter*. Laying claim to identity categories from a deconstructive point of view "ought not to paralyze the use of such terms, but, ideally, to extend its range, to make us consider at what expense and for what purpose the terms are used, and through what relations of power such categories have been wrought" (Butler 1993, 229). Together with Gabriele Dietze and Beatrice Michaelis, I have attempted to describe this as a "corrective methodology" (cf. Dietze, Haschemi Yekani and Michaelis 2007, 136–139, 2010). We will need to continue to develop new frameworks, test new terminologies to grasp the intricate processes of categorisation – a project that my narrative patterns of masculinity will in all hope support. Masculinity understood as an interdependent category provides a multifaceted perspective not only on gender *and* race *and* sexuality, but on the intricate ways in which these categories are interwoven. A reading can never be complete or focus extensively and equally on all axes of stratification (and, indeed, should not pretend it can be 'all-inclusive') as every reading is informed by a certain interest and situatedness of the researcher's point of view.

As has been initially stated, masculinity is not a singular or self-identical construct. These various interdependencies along the lines of race, class and sexuality in the construction of hegemonic masculinity in crisis have to come under scrutiny if we are to understand masculinity as a more diverse phenomenon. For this reason, I employ the labels 'hegemonic' and 'marginalised' masculinities as tentative indicators of differences among men and masculinities.

'Hegemonic' and 'Marginalised' Masculinities

My usage of the term hegemony is largely informed by Connell's definition which draws on Antonio Gramsci's writing:

Hegemonic masculinity can be defined as the configuration of gender practice which embodies the currently accepted answer to the problem of the legitimacy of patriarchy which guarantees (or is taken to guarantee) the dominant position of men and the subordination of women. (Connell 1995, 77)[26]

Consequently, hegemony is a historically mobile relation and also involves the disavowal of marginalised masculinities such as non-White and/or queer masculinities. Hegemony is further understood as a structural relation rather than being based on the acts of single individuals: "It is the successful claim to authority, more than direct violence, that is the mark of hegemony." (Connell 1995, 77) Stuart Hall has highlighted Gramsci's role in offering an emphasis on "relations" and "unstable balance". Hall explains that for hegemony to work it "is always the tendential balance in the relations of force which matters" (Hall 1996a, 423). Within a Marxist framework, Gramsci manages to convey a notion of hegemony – he speaks of the "apparatus of the political and cultural hegemony of the ruling class" (Gramsci 2005, 258) – which does not translate to simple top-down dominance.[27] Hegemony points to structural inequalities that are constantly stabilised and destabilised which is why it is appropriate to speak of hegemonic masculinity with regard to men's dominance over women and, at the same time, stress the stratification among men. Marginality and hegemony can never function along binary axes, as I have emphasised, and masculinity and femininity are stratified in relation to each other as well as intrinsically along the line of difference within.

Hegemonic masculinity is dependent on the racial marker of Whiteness as Whiteness is associated with 'normalness' and 'simply being human' in the West. Richard Dyer has emphasised this in his ground-breaking study *White* in which he writes: "The claim to power is the claim to speak for the commonality of humanity." (Dyer 1997, 2) Conversely, marginalised masculinity (which Connell calls "subordinated masculinities") is directly affected and stands in relation to hegemonic masculinity. Connell explains

---

26 In their revaluation of the concept, Connell and Messerschmidt respond to critiques arguing that the concept of male hegemony might actually reproduce male dominance. They suggest holding on to the concept stressing that "[h]egemonic masculinity was not assumed to be normal in the statistical sense; only a minority of men might enact it. But it was certainly normative" (Connell and Messerschmidt 2005, 832), and further they explain that "the conceptualization of hegemonic masculinity should explicitly acknowledge the possibility of democratizing gender relations, of abolishing power differentials, not just of reproducing hierarchy" (ibid., 853).

27 Cf. "State is the entire complex of practical and theoretical activities with which the ruling class not only justifies and maintains its dominance, but manages to win the active consent of those over whom it rules." (Gramsci 2005, 244)

that "[m]arginalization is always relative to the *authorization* of the hegemonic masculinity of the dominant group" (Connell 1995, 81, original
emphasis).[28] Masculinity remains contested ground and is constantly (re)-
constructed through different narratives. What marginalised masculinity is,
depends very much on the context. These juxtapositions are rendered
much more difficult if we take into account multiple categories of social
stratification such as class, ability or age – as has been explained in further
detail with reference to the concept of interdependent categories. By uti-
lising the terms 'hegemonic' and 'marginalised' relative structural locations
are implied rather than fixed positions.

In addition, postcolonial approaches demonstrate that a dichotomous
understanding of 'hegemonic centre' and 'marginalised periphery' falls
short of grasping ambivalences in this process, and it is literary critic Homi
K. Bhabha, coining concepts such as "mimicry", "hybridity" and the "third
space" who has been most influential here. However, the label hegemonic
masculinity is in so far helpful as it describes an idealised phantasmatic
position that is powerful in shaping the discourse of crisis and hinges on a
continuous process of 'Othering'.

It is within the logic of imperialism that hegemonic masculinity needs
to dissociate itself from the colonised – a process that, as Bhabha has
demonstrated in his essay "Of Mimicry and Man", produces what he calls
"slippage" (Bhabha 1994, 122). Following the colonial logic, the so-called
'natives' are meant to be 'enlightened' by the Englishman, to adopt his
ways, in short, they are to mimic him. Bhabha finds subversive elements in
this very mimicry of the coloniser by the colonised. What is at stake in the
'civilising mission' is *difference*, without which the domination of the latter
by the former would be (morally) challenged. Hence, "mimicry is at once
resemblance and menace" (ibid., 123). It is a subversive practice that

---

28 Similarly, Bourdieu (who employs the term "masculine domination" rather than "hegemonic masculinity") argues that: "Manliness […] is an eminently *relational* notion, constructed in front of and for other men and against femininity, in a kind of *fear* of the female, firstly in oneself." (Bourdieu 2001, 53, original emphasis) However, while both
   Bourdieu and Connell emphasise the relational and constructed character of masculinity,
   Bourdieu seems to highlight more strongly the naturalising effects that produce the
   bodily manifestations of the male "habitus". In addition, Bourdieu stresses the dominance of men over women, while Connell's concept points more to the differences between men which is why I find the concept of hegemonic masculinity more useful in my
   work which tries to acknowledge the differences between differently racialised, sexualised and classed masculinities.

threatens the binary between 'self' and 'Other'. This ambivalence or hybridity is an important facet in the way masculinity is perceived. Originally a racist term, 'hybridity' was positively re-conceptualised by Bhabha.[29] In his understanding of the term, hybridity figures as the "third space", a space for potentially subversive possibilities: "[T]he importance of hybridity is not to be able to trace two original moments from which the third emerges, rather hybridity to me is the 'third space' which enables other positions to emerge." (Rutherford and Bhabha 1990, 211) In this construction, identity and alterity are no longer understood as an opposing juxtaposition, rather there is an inextricable intricacy of the marginalised and the hegemonic. Hybridity in this case does not mean a blending of two opposite poles; rather hybridity is a sign of the very instability of two supposedly clearly distinguishable categories such as 'Black' and 'White', from their origination. This concept of hybridity is not only a feature of present-day postcolonial societies. As Robert Young points out, we have to be much more critical of supposedly coherent identities projected onto the past: "Today the Englishness of the past is often represented in terms of fixity, of certainty, centredness, homogeneity, as something unproblematically identical with itself." (R.J.C. Young 2005, 2) In accordance, hybridity proves a productive concept that connects colonial and postcolonial contexts. In so far as cultural texts stabilise and destabilise identities, the labels 'hegemonic' and 'marginalised' stand in a continuous (and unstable) relation to each other that involves the destabilising element of hybridity.

However, there are also problematic aspects of the concept of hybridity that various postcolonial critics have discussed. (cf. Brah and Coombes (ed.) 2000; Ha 2005; Huggan 2001) In an uncritically celebratory understanding of hybridity, in which there is an emphasis on 'mixture' (rather than the instability which Bhabha describes), hybridity figures as a privileged discourse of metropolitan elites[30], highlighting the consumption of difference that results in "hype of hybridity" (cf. Ha 2005). On a more conceptual level, the underlying politics of heterosexuality is another problematic assumption which Young, among others, criticises:

29 Other terms, such as syncretism and Creolization (cf. Ashcroft, Griffiths and Tiffin 2002) or mongrelization (cf. Rushdie 1988) are employed to denote a similar idea. For a discussion of the terminology of Bhabha, cf. Fludernik (1998).

30 In this sense, hybridity relies on the privilege of mobility that the 'Third World' subaltern has no access to. "[I]n our enthusiasm for migrant hybridity, Third World urban radicalism, First World marginality, and varieties of ethnographically received ventriloquism, the subaltern is once again silent for us." (Spivak 1993b, 255)

Whichever model of hybridity may be employed, however, hybridity as a cultural description will always carry with it an implicit politics of heterosexuality, which may be a further reason for contesting its contemporary pre-eminence. The reason for this sexual identification is obvious: anxiety about hybridity reflected the desire to keep races separate, which meant that attention was immediately focussed on the mixed race offspring that resulted from inter-racial sexual intercourse. (R.J.C. Young 2005, 25)

Bearing these reservations in mind, I try to analyse those facets of hybridity that concern the stabilisation as well as destabilisation of hegemony rather than focus on the cultural consumption of (exoticised) difference. I argue in my readings that, apart from posing a threat to the clear dichotomy of centre and margin, hybridity can also be employed as a stabilising element. Hybridity can be incorporated into a hegemonic white masculinity that usurps cultural difference and makes it its own, which will be expounded upon in the chapter on Rudyard Kipling's *Kim*. Hybridity can also be part of the failure to uphold difference. What it means to fail when facing the 'savage within' is epitomised in the figure of Kurtz in Conrad's *Heart of Darkness*. In a postcolonial context then, hybridity again has other connotations as the protagonists of Kureishi's and Smith's novels as well as the films of Frears and Jordan demonstrate. While Kureishi sees hybridity as a somewhat utopian marker of a new way of Britishness, Smith emphasises the 'everydayness' of hybridity as a crucial part of all expressions of Britishness. In contrast, Jordan focuses on the visual and erotic spectacle that is associated with hybridity. This book then hopefully provides a differentiated re-assessment of colonial and postcolonial masculinities that are variously positioned as hegemonic or marginalised. The role of ambivalence and hybridity in the construction of these identities need to be and will be interrogated accordingly.

Most of the cited theories on male hegemony (Connell 1995) and/or domination (Bourdieu 2001) are sociological rather than part of a cultural and literary studies framework. However, Ben Knights remarks, "masculine identities and (stereo)typically male ways of being and acting are constantly reinforced and re-enacted through social practices of communication among which narratives both oral and written, in speech, in films and on paper, figure prominently" (Knights 1999, 17). In this context, masculinity needs to be understood as a concept that relies on recurring narrative patterns which iterate the privileged discourse of masculinity in crisis.

The Narratability of Masculinity and Narrative Patterns

Within the postmodern preoccupation with identity, the view that identity is closely linked to narrative or narratability is emphasised. I employ the term narratability as the closest translation of the German word *Erzählbarkeit*.[31] Thereby I mean to trace shifting discursive rules that shape how gender can be conceived of in cultural texts – a framework of its possibility. Narratability connotes the very precondition of making certain identities 'narratable' which is linked to Butler's notion of intelligibility. (cf. Butler 1993) How we perceive of ourselves and others relates directly to cultural constructions of race, gender, sexuality and other (interdependent) categories of social stratification. Paul Ricœur has introduced the notion of "narrative identity" to describe these processes which cut across a range of different discursive fields. He explains:

a) knowledge of the self is an interpretation; b) the interpretation of the self, in turn, finds narrative, among other signs and symbols, to be a privileged mediation; c) this mediation borrows from history as much as fiction, making the life story a fictive history or, if you prefer, an historical fiction, comparable to those biographies of great men where both history and fiction are found blended together. (Ricœur 1991, 73)

While it is not so much the interpretation of the self or the genre of autobiography that is at the core of what is to follow, Ricœur's elucidations are of interest here insofar as they have become central to the postmodern formulation of how narratives shape identity, and consequently the narrative construction of social categories. As has been laid out by a range of literary critics, the concept of gender is linguistically conveyed. Erhart, for example, speaks of "narrative generating principles of masculinity and femininity" (2005, 170, my translation). Within the last few years, narratology has focused more explicitly on gender as a category. (cf. Fludernik 2000; Nieberle and Strowick (ed.) 2006; Nünning and Nünning (ed.) 2004) As Ansgar and Vera Nünning write in their introductory study, *Erzähltextanalyse und Gender Studies*: "Narrative here connotes a cultural practice across the borders of genre and media, which has far-reaching effects for the construction of gender and gender relations, because narratives not only reflect or fashion notions of 'gender', they construct them." (Nünning

---

31 Narratability clearly differs from the term 'narrativity' that Ruth E. Page (2003) and others employ. The term narrativity refers to the degree to which a text can be classified as a narrative in the first place.

and Nünning 2004 (ed.), 22, my translation) These critics also emphasise that every period has its specific culturally available plots and privileged techniques. In accordance, one has to maintain that the narrative construction of the self "draws on culturally available patterns and especially on literary narrative schemes" (Kilian 2004, 122, my translation), as Eveline Kilian has pointed out, and this is related to the notion of narrative patterns that I seek to develop.

In my understanding, a 'narrative pattern' signifies a recurring set of storylines or tropes that shape specific figurations of masculinity. With regard to the visual media herein selected, the term can also denote recurring stock images or a certain gaze structure. Consequently, this means that the range of texts I am going to focus on will be examined with regard to their distinct characteristics of verbal and visual modes of expression which inform specific colonial and postcolonial figurations of hegemonic and marginalised masculinities.

Narrative patterns are not fixed in their meaning; therefore, a text can induce pleasure and critique (and sometimes both simultaneously in conflicting ways) as the very act of reading produces each text performatively. Moreover, the term 'narrative pattern' is intended to clearly differ from a structuralist approach to literature which seeks to identify universal elements in narratives.[32] Indeed, the way in which I utilise narrative patterns is more closely associated with Foucault's well-known notion of discourse (cf. Foucault 1998, 2002) and the idea that gender depends on certain structures that shape the way masculinity and femininity can be narrated and/or visualised at a given historical time.

Butler has argued persuasively that gender is not a given but a performative practice which relies on an iterative system – a continual *doing* of gender. (cf. Butler 1999)

For if gender is constructed, it is not necessarily constructed by an 'I' or a 'we' who stands before that construction in any spatial or temporal sense of 'before.' [...] [T]he 'I' neither precedes nor follows the process of this gendering, but emerges only within and as the matrix of gender relations themselves. (Butler 1993, 7)

In accordance with these insights, Erhart calls for a "social, cultural and literary history, in which the signs and forms, the rhetoric and narrative patterns of the (dependently) 'first' or 'second' sex are put into perspective historically" (Erhart 2005, 169, my translation). Therefore, to be absolutely

---

32 Most notably Propp attempted this in *Morphology of the Folktale* (1973).

clear, patterns here do not signify structuralist morphology, but point to the iterative structures, which work in different genres and media, to produce specific constructions of masculinity.

Foucault explains that discourses are "practices that systematically form the objects which they speak of" (Foucault 2002, 54) and further elaborates that discourse "defines at the outset *the system of its enunciability*" (ibid., 146, original emphasis). With Foucault, patterns can be considered discursively recurring *énoncés*. Consequently, the narratives of masculinity produce and shape the way masculinity can be rendered intelligible, or the way it becomes *narratable*. These patterns are also dependent on a continuous 'Othering' of diverse femininities and marginalised masculinities.

Postcolonial critic Edward Said has introduced the by now widely discussed term "Orientalism" to refer to the self-centring of the Western imagination dependent on an Oriental 'Other'. With reference to Foucault he argues:

[W]ithout examining Orientalism as a discourse one cannot possibly understand the enormously systematic discipline by which European culture was able to manage – and even produce – the Orient politically, sociologically, militarily, ideologically, scientifically, and imaginatively during the post-Enlightenment period. [...] European culture gained in strength and identity by setting itself off against the Orient as a sort of surrogate and even underground self. (Said 2003, 3)

However, Said was also criticised (cf. Moore-Gilbert 1997, 40–53), for his too narrow understanding of Orientalism as a dominant discourse. In contrast, other postcolonial critics, such as Bhabha, emphasise more strongly ambivalences and slippages in colonial discourse.

Foucault himself stresses the discontinuities and fractures as well as the emergence of a possible "reverse discourse" that is always implied in any discourse.

Indeed, it is in discourse that power and knowledge are joined together. And for this very reason, we must conceive discourse as a series of discontinuous segments whose tactical function is neither uniform nor stable. To be more precise, we must not imagine a world of discourse divided between the dominant and the dominated one; but as a multiplicity of discursive elements that can come into play in various strategies. (Foucault 1998, 100)

In view of that, the privilege of crisis, too, is not to be confounded with a dominant discourse but must be seen as a privileged discourse when it comes to narrating colonial and postcolonial masculinities. Consequently, while I stress these inconsistencies, I maintain that narrative accounts of masculinity in crisis also have stabilising and re-privileging effects that reproduce an idealised notion of hegemonic masculinity. As has been explained with regard to Gramsci's influence on theories of hegemony, male hegemony must not be seen as a clear dominance from above but more as a normative construct that is stabilised by affirmative reiteration.[33] Again, I am not so much interested in whether, in fact, there is a crisis of masculinity but much more in how far cultural texts (un)relate to this privileged discourse.

In other words, it is these powerful and contradictory patterns and strategies which comprise our understanding of masculinity that are of interest here. Whilst very formulaic narratives, such as Haggard's adventure stories or the coming-of-age novel, are characterised by recurring plots, other texts included here do not follow such a clear outline. As has become a common understanding in the analysis of literary texts, textual strategies are also not to be confounded with a clear intention of an author. Foucault emphasises that:

> Power relations are both intentional and nonsubjective [...] there is no power that is exercised without a series of aims and objectives. But this does not mean that it results from the choice or decision of an individual subject; [...] the rationality of power is characterized by tactics that are often quite explicit at the restricted level where they are inscribed (the local cynicism of power), tactics which, becoming connected to one another, attracting and propagating one another, but finding their base of support and their condition elsewhere, and by forming comprehensive systems: the logic is perfectly clear, the aims decipherable, and yet it is often the case that no one is there to have invented them, and few who can be said to have formulated them: an implicit characteristic of the great anonymous, almost unspoken strategies. (Foucault 1998, 94–95)

Within narrative accounts, masculinity is not so much something one can claim; rather, it is a position that needs to be achieved often in terms of a heroic struggle. Plot structures are dependent on conflicts, and in this light, "being-in-crisis" is also a privileged position within a narrative in general. In this context, the hero's fall often functions as a catalyst for the plot and struggling emphatically with him generates our engagement as readers with texts. However, crisis narratives are also narratives about a crisis of these

---

33 This is not intended as a belittling of the devastating material effects which male hegemony has for both women and marginalised masculinities. On the contrary, it underlines the complexity of power relations which cannot simply be contested from a position 'outside' of power.

aesthetic conventions. The modern and the postmodern period are both concerned with the end of the classic 'hero' in fiction and the unaccountability of language. Schnurbein speaks of "crises of writing" (cf. Schnurbein 2001, 358–366) in this context, and this is a relevant point that needs to be addressed with regard to the so-called modern and postmodern crisis of authorship that can be best explored within the reach of this book in the writing of Conrad and Coetzee. In how far do these authors install a crisis of writing as a precondition of creativity that establishes a male ideal for both the modern and postmodern reinvention of authorship? In this way, the assumed crisis of masculinity influences *which* kinds of stories can be told and *how* they can be told.

Conceding that any choice of texts will always exclude others and reflects the researcher's situatedness, I have included literary texts as well as visual material as representative in their specific ways of adding to the cultural construction of masculinity in crisis. For both periods, popular and canonical sources were chosen as the discourse of masculinity in crisis affects writing across the (problematic) distinction of 'popular' and 'high' art.[34] Instead of reproducing the dichotomy of popular versus high art, the conception of genres as narrative frameworks proves helpful. When reading the different texts, their position within a specific genre tradition will be addressed as genres provide not an unchangeable or 'natural', static structure to which texts adhere but flexible "frames for producing knowledge" (cf. Junker 2010, 11–29) that negotiate literary conventions and reader expectations, and in this way, they also shape how masculinity is conceived.

In fact what needs to be stated is, on the one hand, a constitutive historicity of genres and, on the other hand, their constitutive hybridity. Genres change over time, they do not figure as transhistorical constants. [...] Every film [and literary text, E.H.Y.] refers to genre conventions but at the same time rewrites, modifies and *constructs* them. Genre (of which we think that it precedes the film [or literary text, E.H.Y.] hence is always an *effect* of those films, in which it manifests/substantiates/documents itself. (Liebrand and Steiner 2004, 7–8, my translation, original emphasis)

---

34 With reference to the importance of popular culture as a subject for cultural analysis, Hall maintains: "Popular culture is one of the sites where this struggle for and against a culture of the powerful is engaged: it is also the stake to be won or lost in that struggle. It is the arena of consent and resistance. It is partly where hegemony arises, and where it is secured." (Hall 2005, 71)

By focusing on a broad range of relevant canonical and popular texts, different genres, such as the imperial romance or the coming-of-age story, and different media, such as literary texts, photography and film, I want to emphasise that the discourse of the crisis of masculinity is not a homogenous field but a privileged narrative discourse which is not to be confounded. It is, for instance, interesting to parallel the coming-of-age story of Kim in colonial India with Kureishi's version of the coming-of-age narrative in seventies London in *The Buddha of Suburbia*. In this way, I aim at highlighting the continuities and discontinuities of these narrative patterns granted that I can only engage in small sections of the oeuvres of the writers and filmmakers.

As I stated initially, colonial crises – both in formulaic adventure fiction and in the context of modernist writing – can be seen as contained or enclosed crises that try to hold on to a universalist framework which is centred on White masculinity and cannot conceive of the 'Other's' crisis. Postcolonial crisis narratives function more self-reflexively. Here, the crises appear volitional, and plural crises of masculinities become conceivable. Nonetheless, it is not useful to assume a teleological 'overcoming' of hegemonic masculinity. Masculinity is stabilised *and* destabilised within the cultural and symbolic gender order in both periods.

Starting chronologically, I will consider Henry Rider Haggard's most famous imperial romances, *King Solomon's Mines* and *She*. Both share a formulaic structure which advances a nostalgic image of heroic masculinity and 'noble savages' and hence show the contradictions of the figurations of orderly gentlemen and hunters who seem to negate the emphasis on crisis at the time. Following the chapter on Haggard, I will focus on the visual archive of the popular press, most notably *The Illustrated London News*, and its repertoire of imagery which offers what I call a *spectacle of the 'self'* against the backdrop of rampant crisis tendencies. Processes of 'Othering' are shaped by a dual movement of disavowal and desire. Rudyard Kipling's character Kim perfectly embodies these ambivalences. His colonial coming-of-age story, *Kim*, the focus of the following chapter, rather paradoxically flirts with notions of hybridity while maintaining the concept of English superiority. Finally, Joseph Conrad and his writing of failing colonial anti-heroes come under scrutiny. His oeuvre, which is associated with modernist experimentation, more strongly includes crisis tendencies on the level of form: The genre of the colonial romance is not completely neglected by Conrad, but it can no longer provide the framework for his narratives of male failure. Conrad's fiction is contingent on a narrative re-centring and re-universalising of this very masculinity. This will be argued by reading *The Nigger of the "Narcissus"*, in addition to his most famous novella, *Heart of Darkness*.

My second focus is on the contemporary writings of authors such as Hanif Kureishi, Zadie Smith and J.M. Coetzee and the two films, *My Beautiful Laundrette* by Stephen Frears and *The Crying Game* by Neil Jordan. The protagonists in these texts are caught between the tensions of hegemony/marginalisation and identity in postcolonial societies. Authors such as Kureishi and Smith concentrate on the questioning of an elusive British identity in terms of race, ethnicity and nationality. The heroes of Kureishi's texts grow up caught between a striving for models of hegemonic masculinity and racialisation enhancing their feeling of crisis, which will be explained in relation to his novels *The Buddha of Suburbia* and *The Black Album*. Regarding the medium film, the spectacle of the interracial gay couple and the spectacular transwoman in *My Beautiful Laundrette* and *The Crying Game* will be addressed. In how far do the looking relations in these films correspond to or undermine the unmarked hegemonic male gaze? Zadie Smith's *White Teeth* contrasts the masculinity of the White British 'everyman' Archie Jones with a range of ethnically diverse characters. Smith seems to celebrate a "multicultural polyphony" that will be explored, especially with regard to its effects on the depiction of Britain as a "Happy Multicultural Land" and the role of humour in relation to the construction of masculinity in crisis. In a not strictly chronological order, this section closes with the third postcolonial author, J.M. Coetzee, who uses the postcolonial South African context as an allegorical frame to address questions of guilt, responsibility and agency from a hegemonic point of view in his novels *Waiting for the Barbarians* and *Disgrace*. Crisis becomes a volitional, if not the only possible subject position in Coetzee's narratives of hegemonic masculinity. The question whether this paradox of focusing on male hegemony and simultaneously interrogating this hegemony produces re-privileging tendencies in his oeuvre will be addressed in this closing chapter.

Questions of universality of 'self' and 'Other' are inseparable from the ways in which masculinity is conceived. Whereas it seems like the heroes of colonial fiction either overcome or despair over crisis, postcolonial male heroes often remain in crisis voluntarily and consciously reflect about being in crisis. While both these peak times of crisis narratives differ, they both can have re-privileging tendencies connected to the status of crisis which is still reliant on hegemonic assumptions about masculinity. In this understanding, 'crisis' has become a privileged mode of narrating both colonial and postcolonial masculinities, and it is only by contrasting these various and different crises of masculinities – the contained colonial and the exposed postcolonial crises – and their effects that we move away from a universalisation of crisis and hegemonic masculinity itself.

1. Colonial Masculinities: Gentlemen and Hunters, Hybrid 'Sahibs' and Failures

The paradoxical modern crisis of hegemonic masculinity is intertwined with the history of colonialism.[42] As has been suggested in the introduction, this colonial crisis can also be described as a contained crisis implicitly dealing with a phantasmatic adherence to the binary of 'self' and 'Other' – a binary that has been destabilised in the process of colonisation. Therefore, rather than understanding coloniality as coinciding with modernity, one has to see their mutual dependence. Walter Mignolo explains that "[c]oloniality [...] is the hidden face of modernity and its very condition of possibility" (Mignolo 2000, 722). In this way, social categories such as race but also religion and nation are established as preconditions or constitutive components of modernity (as well as literary modernism[43]). This is also – as Said has pointed out – a process of reciprocity which included resistance and opposition: "[M]any of the most prominent characteristics of modernist culture, which we have tended to derive from purely internal dynamics in Western society and culture, include a response to the external pressures on culture from the *imperium*." (Said 1994, 188)

Masculinity becomes an important realm of stabilising the construction of modern European superiority. "[T]he assertion of European supremacy in terms of patriotic manhood and racial virility was not only an expression

---

42 McClintock calls this "a crisis in male imperial identity" (McClintock 1995, 27) in her path-breaking study *Imperial Leather*.

43 Patrick Williams speaks of the "related but different temporalities and trajectories of modernism and modernity (and imperialism)" (P. Williams 2000, 31) to emphasise the complex relationship between modernism and empire. The relationship between the terms 'modernity' and the literary genre 'modernism' is explored in greater detail by Peter Childs. (cf. Childs 2000, 12–17) In his recent study, *Modernism and the Post-Colonial*, Childs takes the adventure writing of Haggard, Kipling, Conan Doyle and Conrad as a starting point to examine the later modernist writing of D.H. Lawrence, T.S. Eliot, Katherine Mansfield, Virginia Woolf and James Joyce and their "desire to move beyond the imperial visions of the previous generations" (Childs 2007, 19).

of imperial domination, but a defining feature of it." (Stoler 2002, 16) The role of popular imagery and narrative accounts of colonial virility are one factor contributing to this discourse, and in line with this argument Joseph Bristow speaks of an "imperialist genealogy of hegemonic masculinity" (Bristow 1991, 166) that can be traced in colonial literature[44] and photography.

In colonial adventure stories, one can clearly identify a nostalgic longing for as well as a restorative impetus of unchallenged norms of dominant masculinity.

In one sense the very pursuit of colonialism implied discontent with Europe. Those who were content with Europe stayed there, and behind each claim for colonial experience lay an implicit critique of European civilization. [...] Behind all these complaints and discoveries lay the basic attraction of primitiveness, the sense of dissatisfaction with an excessive and decadent civilization. Much colonial fiction was therefore concerned with regression – both social and personal – and with the re-establishment in the colonies of more authentic and more primitive ways of life. (Ridley 1983, 112)

Especially the fiction of Rider Haggard as well as popular photography portrayed colonial British gentlemanly masculinity as benevolent and superior.[45] The idealisation of the gentleman was connected to notions of fairness and restraint which were seen as particularly British achievements. The gentleman was unselfish, generous and committed to patient hard

---

44 The term 'colonial literature' is here employed as suggested by Elleke Boehmer. However, Boehmer also includes literature by creoles and indigenes, which was written in the colonial period, under this rubric. This section focuses exclusively on writing from the coloniser's point of view and consequently could also be described as "colonialist literature" or "writing of empire". (cf. Boehmer 2005, 2–3) The texts in this section are concerned both with settings in Asia and Africa and although there are important differences between these regions and their colonial histories, it is reasonable to compare these narratives because the differences have been systematically brushed over in colonialist discourse. Boehmer explains: "[T]ransference between very different colonial spaces was facilitated too by the horizontal distinctions which separated Europeans from others across the imperial world." (ibid., 52) According to her, the "travelling metaphor" created intertextual references between different writings of empire. (cf. ibid., 49–50) This is a process which is reliant on colonial narrative patterns and specific notions of masculinity which I will describe in the course of this section.

45 Another popular arena was the growing number of fiction for boys and boys' magazines which is excluded here. For an explicit focus on male juvenile or boy's fiction at the time, cf. Bristow (1991); Dryden (2000).

work.[46] "'Manliness' has almost always been a good quality, the opposite of childishness and sometimes of beastliness, counter not so much to womanliness as to effeminacy." (Vance 1985, 8) This heteronormative concept of manliness had to be dissociated from any suspicion of an 'inappropriate femininity', such as the homosexual. What is more, this conception was also connected to a hegemonic class position: "The rebellious working-class hooligan was just as much a figure of disapprobation as his middle-class counterpart, the dandy: both were seen as evidence of a morbid decline of manhood and as such a threat to ongoing imperial dominance." (Middleton 2002, 144) In this context, Tosh points to the difference between 'manliness' in general and the ideal of the gentleman in particular. (cf. Tosh 2004, 83–102) While the gentleman – as for example embodied by the Squire Sir Henry Curtis in Haggard's fiction – traditionally is of a higher (inherited) class background and stands for virtues such as politeness, the middle class concept of 'manliness' is seen as an asset that is acquired in a lifelong struggle and requires individual rigour and pertains to the new middle-class appropriation of the concept of the gentleman as described by Ferris (1994).

This idea of manliness as an acquired quality that is achieved in a struggle can be easily linked to the notion of evolution (which was often falsely equated with progress). Consequently, part of the colonial discourse on race and gender is a strong but often also very simplified reception of Darwin's theories at the time, which I want to expound upon at some greater length here as they become a recurrent reference point in colonial fiction in general and specifically in the narratives of Haggard, Kipling and Conrad discussed in this section. To a certain degree this recourse to a biological understanding of race, gender and sexuality is at odds with the strong emphasis on the cultural achievement that hegemonic manliness is supposed to be. Nevertheless, a certain paradoxical simultaneity seems to subsist that reads hegemonic masculinity as both the natural order of things as well as a cultural achievement. Darwinian narratives have become so thoroughly embedded in Western daily thinking that they tend to go unrecognised. Or, as Gillian Beer has formulated, "[p]recisely because we live in a culture dominated by evolutionary ideas, it is difficult for us to recognise their imaginative power in our daily readings of the world" (Beer 1983, 5).

---

46 For a discussion of the related ideal of "muscular Christianity" of Thomas Hughes and Charles Kingsley, cf. Mangan and Walvin (ed.) (1987); Vance (1985).

In his second major work *The Descent of Man* (1871), Darwin developed his idea of "natural selection"[47]. According to Darwin, a struggle for survival ensues. Yet, he does not postulate who will be the winner, as it is the case in Herbert Spencer's Social Darwinist writing. Evolution is connected to the ability of adaptation, not necessarily physical strength.[48] Nonetheless, Darwin alludes to the possible winner in this competition at several instances[49], and Victorian reception often favoured an understanding of his writing in this truncated manner. For this reason, 'civilisation' is identified as a necessary means of a successful adaptation and survival, and evolution is 'culturalised'. "The appeal to nature in deciding what was in reality a moral issue was fatal [...]. Nature was now the arbiter of morality." (Stepan 1982, xiii)

In his earlier *The Origin of Species* (1859), Darwin argues against the teachings of those who see the various races as independent species. He is an adherent of the monogenism-thesis, i.e. he believes that there is a common origin of the human species. Against this background there is a certain agitation which is rooted in the kinship, the so-called 'brotherhood of races'. If indeed all human races are related, the colonial project is in need of a biological rationale. Darwin suggests that the individual always acts in the benefit of the group because humans are social beings. However, this "social instinct" – as he calls it – is limited to the members of the group

---

47 Cf. "Man has multiplied so rapidly, that he has necessarily been exposed to struggle for existence, and consequently to natural selection." (Darwin 2004, 172)

48 Darwin's theory of evolution actually favours a linear and open understanding of development (i.e. one that is no longer conceptualised as theological-teleological). Therefore, his theory is not to be confounded with Social Darwinism of the kind Herbert Spencer proclaimed with his credo of the "survival of the fittest" which was immensely popular at the time. However, there was not only theological dissent with Darwin's writing, but also a lively inner-biological debate about the status of Darwin's theory at the turn of the century. (cf. Bowler 1992; Palm 2006)

49 Cf. "At some future period, not very distant as measured by centuries, the civilised races of man will almost certainly exterminate, and replace, the savage races throughout the world." (Darwin 2004, 183) However, from a biological point of view, how exactly "natural selection" proceeds remains ambivalent and Darwin, a supporter of the abolitionist movement, voices doubts himself: "We must remember that progress is no invariable rule. It is very difficult to say why one civilised nation rises, becomes more powerful, and spreads more widely, than another [...]. We can only say that it depends on an increase in the actual number of the population, on the number of the men endowed with high intellectual and moral faculties, as well as on their standard of excellence. Corporeal structure appears to have little influence, except so far as vigour of body leads to vigour of mind." (ibid., 166)

the individual belongs to: "[W]ith all animals, sympathy is directed solely towards the members of the same community, and therefore towards known, and more or less beloved members, but not all the individuals of the same species." (Darwin 2004, 130) Through this qualification the pursuit of the human species in colonialism appears quite natural, and is legitimised as a rivalry between groups, i.e. races. Equally, monogenism as a hypothesis is established while at the same time a temporal cleft is ascertained and difference is reintroduced once again through the backdoor legitimising the colonial endeavour as paradoxically humanitarian.

Were polygenetic thinking to prevail, the British public would have to understand the colonial enterprise as nothing more than ruthless competition for goods and territory in which Europeans were proving to be the superior predator. By coming up with a theory that opens a temporal gulf between primitive and modern man and yet includes all variations of man within a single species, Darwin's theory provided not only a scientific explanation for British superiority. It also offered a way for the British to consider themselves more humane than the people they dominated while profiting by their competitive superiority over colonial populations. (Armstrong 2005, 129)

Following this logic, travelling to Africa is constructed as a quest into the unknown, a journey into 'the past', a narrative pattern that prevails in both fictional as well as other accounts to this very day and constitutes Africa as this 'Other' without a history, which needs to be elevated and proselytised time and again.[50] In this context, McClintock has introduced the trope of an "anachronistic space".

According to this trope, colonized people – like women and the working class in the metropolis – do not inhabit history proper but exist in a permanently anterior time within the geographic space of the modern empire as anachronistic humans, atavistic, irrational, bereft of human agency – the living embodiment of the archaic 'primitive'. (McClintock 1995, 30)

Bringing 'civilisation' to the less privileged 'savage races', establishing order, was consequently seen not as harmful but conceptualised as 'humane' and as a moral prerogative of the British. The White man is installed as the father who – due to his greater "vigour of body and mind" (Darwin 2004, 166) – is in charge of the inferior and 'primitive races'. These conceptions are far-reaching as Beer comments: "But the metaphor of European man as the adult parent, and other races as caught somewhere on the scale of

---

50 For further elaboration of missionary work in the colonies, cf. Etherington (ed.) (2005).

childhood and adolescence, was only occasionally glimpsed as implying the future dominance of that second generation." (Beer 1983, 119) Racism is hidden behind the assumed benefaction – *la mission civilisatrice* – that the 'White father' bestows on the 'Others'.

Darwinism as well as Social Darwinism influence the way White masculinity can be narrated. In Rudyard Kipling's famous poem, "The White Man's Burden", from 1899, he talks of the exertions for the coloniser when speaking of the imperial mission.[51] To take up the task is the White man's responsibility:

Take up the White Man's burden—
Send forth the best ye breed—
[…]
Comes now, to search your manhood
Through all the thankless years,
[…]
(Kipling 2006, 257–258)

This search for masculinity is reliant on the "best of the breed", which again emphasises a biological understanding of masculinity. In this evolutionary framework, both femininity and non-Whiteness are considered more 'primitive'; the most civilised status is connoted as male and White. Concerning the interdependencies of race and gender in this context, McClintock states: "The white race was figured as the male of the species and the black race as the female." (McClintock 1995, 55) Consequently, relations of dominance in the Darwinian project rely on a gendered logic as Gabriele Dietze has shown in her book, *Weiße Frauen in Bewegung*:

A more detailed look at the analogy of women with lower 'races' shows that female qualities are not regarded as cultural achievements, but as an unvaried inheritance of earlier stages of evolution. […] The analogy of lower races with weaker genders at the same time justifies the subjugated status of both groups. (Dietze 2011, n.p., my translation)

Hegemony of men therefore was not restricted to the domination of men over 'weaker races' but included the authority over all women.[52] Within this theoretical framework, the role of the woman is limited to the passive

---

51 The poem coincided with the beginning of the Philippine-American War, and Kipling urges the United States to take up its imperial responsibility.

52 Darwin stresses the active role of males in sexual selection when he writes, "there is a struggle between the males for the possession of the female" (Darwin 2004, 246).

"opportunity of selecting one out of several males" (Darwin 2004, 246).[53] Again, we find a paradoxical translation of Darwin's biological explanations into a cultural heteronormative conception of gender. On the one hand, women can be seen as the 'possession' of men and the 'prize' for manly endeavours, and on the other hand, women also hold the symbolic power of choosing between men. In this sense, femininity is encoded as both powerful and powerless at the same time.

The urge to explain 'true manhood' as something of an achievement (which femininity is not) can still be found today. Even though there is a certain consensus that gender is a cultural construct, this does not do away with the recurring wishful recourse to a 'biological foundation' of the normative gender order.[54] It is these processes of performatively constructing hegemonic masculinity – today and in the nineteenth century – that need to be analysed in light of their paradoxical celebration of masculinity as biologically grounded *and* culturally elevated.

Cultural texts are one of the discursive arenas in which gendered constructions are negotiated, and they are part of these complex interrelations

---

53 There have been some attempts of a more positive feminist re-reading of Darwin. (cf. Grosz 1999)

54 In his – for masculinity studies quite influential book – *Manhood in the Making*, David Gilmore, for instance, advocates a problematic "non-sexist" and universalist interpretation of rituals of manhood and by doing so often ignores structural hierarchies. While he maintains that this is not due to some 'biological programming', his argument appeals to a universality of men as protectors of dependants. In this anthropological study on manhood, he explains that masculinity figures as an "elusive status": it is constantly under threat and needs to be reasserted (mostly at the cost of others): "Among most of the peoples that anthropologists are familiar with, true manhood is a precious and elusive status beyond mere maleness, a hortatory image that men and boys aspire to and that their culture demands of them as a measure of belonging." (Gilmore 1990, 17) He further argues that "manhood ideologies always include a criterion of selfless generosity, even to the point of sacrifice. Again and again we find that 'real' men are those who give more than they take; they serve others." (ibid., 229) This interpretation seems to fall prey to the idea of a 'benevolent role' of men as devoted spouses. It neglects the structural privilege of masculinity and is caught up in a heterosexist logic. It also bears an uncanny resemblance to the notion of the benevolent White father referred to earlier. Gilmore fails to see that it is men's structural position in society that allows them "to give more than they take". Rather than seeing hegemonic masculinity as an effect of social structures, Gilmore naturalises it as the origin of these structures and in this sense acts against his better intention of not grounding gender in the biological trap of 'anatomy is destiny'.

between scientific and aesthetic texts.[55] (cf. Street 1985) Much of colonial writing is characterised by a constant reference to struggle, which encompasses accounts of incredible success as well as failure – and both these narratives indicate ideals of heroism. It seems as if the male body in colonial fiction is at risk at all times and the already mentioned themes and motives of the *quest into the unknown*[56], the *establishment of order*, or the *loss of control* structure the plots of colonial adventure fiction. These tropes shape the way hegemonic masculinity, in its various figurations, such as *gentlemen* and *hunters* but also figures like Kipling's *hybrid 'Sahib'* or Conrad's *failures*, become imaginable and narratable.

Marginalised masculinity for that matter is seldom more than a part of the scenery: it serves what I have called a background effect with reference to Morrison, and the deaths of numerous Black characters remain incidental. They are portrayed as either childlike 'noble savages' who serve the White coloniser or as brutal enemies who need to be destroyed due to their 'backward' ways most commonly represented by the tropes of *superstition*, *polygamy* or *cannibalism*. (cf. Dryden 2000, 40) Sometimes, however, the Black man is elevated by the White man and learns to abandon his 'uncivilised' ways. If he is an active part of the adventure plot, his success is linked to his alleged superhuman physical strength or to his enormous capacity to endure pain, or as Dyer has put it: "Black people can be reduced (in white culture) to their bodies and thus to race, but white people are something else that is realised in and yet is not reducible to the corporeal, or racial." (Dyer 1997, 14–15) Consequently, the status of Black masculinity is overwhelmingly linked to bodily capacities, never to intellect. Marginalised masculinity can be related exclusively to biology while hegemonic masculinity becomes a culturally elevated version of this biological masculinity.[57]

---

55 In her pioneering study *Darwin's Plots* (1983), Gillian Beer, for instance, has documented how Darwin's writing is shaped by plot structures of nineteenth-century fiction. Cf. also Levine (1988) in this context.

56 Boehmer identifies the "quest beyond the frontiers of civilization" (Boehmer 2005, 2) as one of the most recurring patterns in colonial fiction.

57 In his analysis of colonial literature, Abdul JanMohamed (1985) focuses on the recurrent trope of the Manichean Allegory. He assesses how the relationship of 'self' and 'Other' is differently addressed in a number of central texts. JanMohamed roughly distinguishes two types, namely the "imaginary" and "symbolic" colonialist text. Whereas the former clearly sticks to a logic of attributing evilness to the 'native' (and Haggard's fiction would fall in this category), the latter is more ambivalent. In symbolic colonialist texts, the 'native' functions as a mediator of European desires and JanMohamed further distinguishes

In this section on colonial masculinities, I will first focus on the heroes of Haggard who always master the hazardous quests triumphantly. The visual representation of hunters and orderly gentlemen as a *spectacle of the 'self'* in *The Illustrated London News* concerns the chapter on colonial photography. Next, I will read Kipling's *Kim* as an Orientalist coming-of-age story with an ambivalent desire for 'Otherness'. The final chapter deals with Joseph Conrad who in many ways serves as a transitionary figure for my purpose of connecting the earlier modern discourse of containing masculinity in crisis with the later postmodern discourse of exposing masculinity in crisis.

---

two subtypes. (cf. JanMohamed 1985, 66) In the first kind of text, syncretism and openness toward the 'Other' are demonstrated (and here *Kim* is his prime example), whereas the second kind of fiction completely avoids the focus on the 'native'. In these texts, syncretism is seen as impossible and the focus is on the pitfalls of colonialist discourse and the hegemonic 'self'. *Heart of Darkness* is one of the examples for this type. While I do not deny the narrative differences between the more celebrative colonialist texts, such as Haggard and popular colonial photography, and the more ambivalent texts of Kipling and Conrad, I will argue that both the attempt to create syncretism in Kipling's *Kim* and Conrad's recourse to failure in *Heart of Darkness* are more entrenched in a male-centred colonialist discourse than JanMohamed concedes.

Henry Rider Haggard: Nostalgic African Adventures

As a young man, Rider Haggard was part of the colonial endeavour when he served on the staff to Sir Henry Bulwer, Lieutenant-Governor of Natal in South Africa, and in 1877, Haggard even helped to raise the British flag in Pretoria during the celebrations of the annexation of the Transvaal. On his return to England, he started to work as a lawyer, but with increasing success, Haggard was enabled to support his family and himself as a full-time writer. In 1912, having been a Tory all his life, he was knighted for his contributions to agricultural reforms and his service to a number of Royal Commissions for which he composed exhaustive reports.[58]

Though at times he voiced criticism of the capitalist British ventures overseas, he was a prominent proponent of jingoistic imperialism, and he sternly believed that the presence of the White man was elevating for the 'native':

> [O]n only one condition, if at all, have we the right to take the black men's land; and that is, that we provide them with an equal and just Government, and allow no maltreatment of them [...], but, on the contrary, do our best to elevate them from savage customs. (Haggard, *Cetywayo and His White Neighbours*, quoted in Etherington 1984, 8)

Of the three selected colonial writers, Rider Haggard is certainly the one writing most generically, producing more than fifty volumes of fiction, often composing his formulaic stories at full speed, at times finishing a novel in a few weeks – a lack of careful craftsmanship that admirers and critics alike have attested. However, his fiction had strong mass appeal and earned him record-breaking sales. Haggard was part of the "romance re-vival" of the eighteen-eighties which was seen as an antidote to the more feminine encoded domestic novel and the genre of realism, and most espe-cially to Émile Zola's French naturalism. "The romance could at once purify British fiction of foreign contaminants and *remasculinize* it." (Daly 1999, 19, original emphasis) Apart from his well-known adventure stories or *romances*, as they were called at the time, Haggard also wrote more realis-tic fictions set in England which he labelled *novels*. However, none of these ever achieved success comparable to his African fictions. To this day, *King*

---

58 For more comprehensive biographical accounts, cf. M. Cohen (1960); Etherington (1984); Pocock (1993).

Solomon's Mines and *She* have never been out of print and enjoy ongoing popularity. What is it about these 'yarns' that captures the imagination? His romances in general do not deal with the daily life in the British colonies. Rather, they depict fantastic journeys into Africa's still 'undiscovered' heartland. They reflect an escapist longing for an unspoiled past, where 'men were still men', without the perturbance of a growing urbanisation and industrialisation, and certainly not with women's suffrage. Rebecca Stott speaks of a longing "to act without cultural restraints", which is characteristic of imperialist fiction.

Haggard's African romances and the genre of imperialist fiction thus appealed to the 'schoolboy imperialist' fantasizing about his initiation into manhood out in the African bush and to the British man, fantasizing about the freedom to act without cultural restraints […]. Africa becomes the testing ground for white male adventure, the landscape of adolescent fantasy. (Stott 1989, 70)

Hence, for Stott it is most notably the depiction of a foreign territory as a "testing ground for White male adventure" that renders Haggard's stories so appealing. McClintock similarly identifies Haggard's description of an unchallenged powerful masculinity as a reason for his fame: "Much of the fascination of Haggard's writing for male Victorians was that he played out his phantasms of patriarchal power in the arena of empire." (McClintock 1995, 233) Moreoever, Lindy Stiebel notes the contradictory desire for scientific exploration and mapping as well as the urge to explore the mysterious and unknowable, which includes the impulse to leave 'civilised society' behind. These desires were satiated by the imperial romance: "Certainly, the romance with its grand dreams of wish fulfilment, its deeds of heroism and its binary opposite, the fear of failure, of dark menace from without, suited the late nineteenth-century British mood well." (Stiebel 2001, 37)

John Cawelti has argued that it is the common narrative structure, or what he calls formulas, in popular fiction which causes the readers' excitement and lets them share the same fantasies. (cf. Cawelti 1976, 1–36) With reference to Northrop Frye's influential structuralist model, critics emphasise that the mode of romance is seen as conveying wish-fulfilling fantasies and dreams closely connected to the motif of the *quest*. (cf. Frye 1973, 186–206) Graham Dawson writes: "Narrative pleasure derives from the contrast between the conserving familiarity of well established generic conventions made stable through endless repetition and offering the comfort of a known reading experience [...] carrying an intense charge of interest and excitement."[59] (G. Dawson 1994, 54)

In this vein, Richard Patteson provides a structuralist analysis of *King Solomon's Mines*, which details the narrative framework of this nostalgic genre. He classifies Haggard's writing as "African romances", which he specifies as a subgenre of the "imperialist romance". In his reading, *King Solomon's Mines* serves as one of the prime examples for this subgenre.[60] He identifies the twelve most recurring "plot functions" with recourse to Propp's terminology (cf. Patteson 1978, 112–113), among them, for example, the fact that "a series of preliminary adventures take place, during which the heroes triumph over numerous adversities" (ibid., 112).

Frye's and Cawelti's elucidations concerning genre, in general, and Patteson's notion of "plot functions", in particular, on first sight appear similar to what I have called narrative patterns since they both describe recurring elements of the narrative. However, as I explained in the introduction, I do not seek to identify universalist elements of a narrative in a structuralist understanding. Whereas the mentioned studies on the genre of the adventure novel emphasise the common narrative structure, I focus on the relation these narrative patterns have to a discourse on masculinity in crisis. Hence, while I agree that genre conventions produce recurring patterns, it is the reciprocity between these patterns and a discursive field that shapes ideals of hegemonic masculinity which is of interest here. By naturalising narrative structures in a structuralist framework, one fails to see the hegemonic investment that goes along with how stories about gender, race and sexuality can be told. In his study that focuses on the figure of the "soldier hero" Dawson explicates such a conception of narratives that understands

---

59 As Etherington (1984) and Stott (1989) note these escapist fantasies still haunt our cultural imagination a century later in the form of adventure movies, such as *Romancing the Stone* (1984) and *The Jewel of the Nile* (1985) both starring Michael Douglas, *Allan Quatermain and the Lost City of Gold* (1987) which is very loosely based on Haggard's *Allan Quatermain* and features Richard Chamberlain and, last but not least, the immensely popular *Indiana Jones* quadrilogy (1984–2008) starring Harrison Ford. All of these films take up the successful generic convention of the colonial adventure novel while trying to blank out, or at least modify, the nowadays more offensive characteristics of colonialist discourse.

60 Patteson gives a broad definition of the genre: "[I]mperialist romance chronicles the adventures of European explorers who travel into previously uncharted territory and establish their benevolent influence among the dark-skinned natives." (Patteson 1978, 112)

cultural texts as a product of both the unconscious and the culture industries.

[P]owerful hegemonic constraints [...] ensure that some forms are installed as more appropriate than others. They exert at best a pressure of conformity upon potential alternatives or, at worst, render unspoken and invisible that about which these alternatives would speak. (G. Dawson 1994, 24)

In this sense, the *quest into the unknown* is not simply a universally recurring narrative, but one that is linked to the way male heroism is imagined and at the end of the nineteenth century intertwined with the notion of a Darwinian temporal cleft that established the colonies as antecedent to European civilisation. Genres in this understanding do not exist prior to narrative structures but it is narrative structures that produce and change generic conventions and as a result conceptions of hegemonic masculinities. Haggard's adventure tales need to be understood as both conforming to and producing genre conventions as well as the ideal of hegemonic masculinity.

King Solomon's Mines: "We are men, thou and I"[61]

King Solomon's Mines, dedicated to "all the big and little boys who read it" (KSM 3), tells the fantastic story of the first adventure of Haggard's celebrated trio, big game hunter Allan Quatermain, Squire Sir Henry Curtis and Captain John Good. At the onset of the tale, the men make each other's acquaintance on a boat where the two gentlemen hire Quatermain as a guide on their quest to find Curtis's younger brother, George Neville, who had gone missing on his expedition to find the fantastic treasures of King Solomon in one of Africa's supposedly unexplored regions. After these introductory events, the journey into the great unknown can begin. First, however, the White men need to prepare for their adventure by outfitting their expedition. These preparations are told meticulously by Haggard, detailing exactly the number of oxen, provisions, medicines and last but not least guns. Before they can finally set off, they need 'native' support so they hire two servants as well as a third Black man, Umbopa, who from the beginning seems to stand out and of whom the White men are suspicious.

---

61 Parts of this reading have been published in an earlier and shorter German version which focuses on the gentleman-hero as a character who is simultaneously both the saviour and is being saved in *King Solomon's Mines* in contrast to Conrad's *Heart of Darkness* and has been published as Haschemi Yekani (2007c).

He is described as "a very tall, handsome-looking man, somewhere about thirty years of age, and very light-coloured for a Zulu" (KSM 46). Interestingly, those marginalised men who are sympathetically drawn are nearly always 'Zulus' (as opposed to the evil 'Masai' or 'Hottentots'), and in general lighter in their complexion. Their willingness to be *enlightened* by the White man is literally transferred to the colour of their skin, symbolically linking moral superiority with lightness/Whiteness – a common strategy of the time.[62]

With the company finally complete, the journey can begin. Along this trail the near death of the protagonists is repeated in manifold variations. As Patteson's plot function, mentioned earlier, reminds us, many small obstacles need to be overcome before the climax of the story can be reached. Part of the heroes' struggle is the danger of fever in the tropics as well as the threats of a landscape encoded as feminine.[63] "The white man must explore and penetrate this foreign territory, but he must also resist or be threatened with absorption into otherness: cultural otherness and sexual otherness." (Stott 1989, 77) Africa, imagined as a female body, thus, is rendered enticing and threatening at the same time, a test for the men's virility and their capacity to remain in control.

The main plot is repeatedly interrupted by smaller 'exotic' episodes such as an elephant hunt. During one of these sequences, one of the 'Zulu boys' throws himself in front of his master to save him from a sure death from the fast approaching animal. The always clumsy and, therefore, comic character Good stumbles on his unsuitable garments. "Good fell victim to his passion for civilised dress." (KSM 61) Good's mishap is really just a funny little incident, and the death of the boy is commented on only succinctly by Umbopa: "'Ah well,' he said presently, 'he is dead, but he died like a man'." (KSM 62) With this deed of self-sacrifice in order to protect the White man the Black boy is awarded the status of masculinity, a privi-

---

62 In this context, Dyer remarks: "Nineteenth-century racialist thought repeatedly intertwined science and aesthetics." (Dyer 1997, 71) For a discussion of the gendered symbolic meaning of the colours black and white in early European race theories, cf. Husmann-Kastein (2006).

63 For a more detailed discussion of the feminine landscape in Haggard, cf. Low (1996); McClintock (1995, 241–245); Stiebel (2001); Stott (1989). Stiebel, for instance, speaks of "Africa as sexualised bodyscape" (Stiebel 2001, 80) in Haggard's fiction, and Low writes, "[t]he quest for treasure is enacted upon the female body, so that the quest for treasure is erotically charged. [...] [M]asculinity is confirmed through overcoming a feminised nature." (Low 1996, 50)

lege that is constantly withheld from most of the adult Black men. As a general rule, the adventure is a bodily trial only for the White men, an example of which is the subsequent arduous march through the desert, which Quatermain describes: "We were literally being baked through and through. The burning sun seemed to be sucking our very blood out of us." In contrast to these White men is Ventvögel [one of the Black servants of the expedition], "on whom, being a Hottentot, the sun had no particular effect" (KSM 79). *King Solomon's Mines* is full of passages which contrast the English men's civilised refinement with the biological bodylines of the African men. While the walk across the desert for the African is no more than a cinch, the White men after the journey are "utterly worn out in body and mind" (KSM 80). Again, after struggling through the deadly desert, their water supplies have reached an end, and they give up all hope when suddenly Ventvögel comments that he "smells" water. Instantly, they realise that they are saved as they "knew what a wonderful instinct these wild-bred men possess" (KSM 84). Over and over, marginalised men will be readily at the rescue of their White masters. Gail Ching-Liang Low is right to point out the "privileged status of the narrator" (Low 1996, 51) in this context. "The structure of the text enables the unreflexive and authoritative white voice to scrutinise, define and pin down its black subjects." (ibid., 51) These kinds of pseudo-scientific racialised attributions are repeated with reference to both Black and White subjects although, of course, only White men are cultured enough to 'overcome' their 'natural' shortcomings in the African landscape.

Within the logic of the narrative, the apparent bodily shortcoming of the White men needs to be reinterpreted as in fact a sign of superiority. Their stamina in the face of immense physical exertions lets them stand out and is interpreted as a sign of their virility. "On one level, the journey is an arduous physical one in which several African helpers may lose their lives, and on another level it is a psychological test of nerves for the Englishman." (Stiebel 2001, 66) However, their superiority first and foremost is of an intellectual nature. They are smart enough to use guns and 'hire' servants. With regard to their bodily capacities, the alleged refinement of the White civilised males renders them all the more susceptible to the dangers of the wild: they need clothes, medicines, provisions and of course guns to protect themselves.

Nonetheless, there is a certain narrative strategy to consolidate White masculinity that can be identified in the writing of Haggard behind which fractures and doubts about the righteousness of the imperial mission loom. In a letter to his son Harry, who lives in England and studies to become a doctor, hunter Quatermain addresses these doubts early in the novel:

[A]m I a gentleman? What is a gentleman? I don't quite know, and yet I have to do with niggers – no I'll scratch that word 'niggers' out, for I don't like it. I've known natives who *are*, […] [gentlemen, E.H.Y.] and I have known mean whites with lots of money and fresh out of home, too, who *ain't*. (KSM 9, original emphasis)

The incommensurateness with the claim of one's own moral superiority – a claim that does not allow for a defilement of the White gentleman's clean record – with the brutal colonialist struggle is a recurring theme.[64] Notwithstanding these quandaries, a real critique of the imperialist project is never articulated.[65] Only a certain kind of colonialism – the one too keenly interested in the ungentlemanly capitalistic profit – is identified as roguish and unjustly taking advantage of the 'native'. In Dyer's words:

This is a logical conclusion of the civilising mission, which did not question the presence of the British in the empire, but did challenge the actual behaviour of the rulers towards the ruled, either in terms of Christian principle or because such rudeness and cruelty itself set a bad example of moral refinement. (Dyer 1997, 186)

The imperialist's idealised engagement in the colonies is supposed to be an earnest and enduring one and not just a quick hunt for profits. This is linked to the described notion of the Darwinian temporal cleft. The 'good imperialist' (the gentleman) is genuinely interested in the land and people and benevolently wants to lift the 'native' from his 'uncivilised backwardness'. On a stylistic level this is for example evident when Haggard's fictionalised Zulu speech is characterised by English archaisms and in this

---

64 Bernhard Reitz (1996) emphasises that Haggard's conception of gentlemanliness is based on the Christian notion of deliverance which accounts for imperialism as a teleological progress narrative.

65 In his book-length study on Haggard, Norman Etherington is quick to vindicate Haggard's romances against any charges of racism on the grounds that Haggard allegedly "does not make statements about race [which he, in fact, repeatedly does, E.H.Y.] but offers statements about us, about our psychology, our past. […] In […] *King Solomon's Mines*, white men discover their own interior savage selves" (Etherington 1984, 46). Though I disagree with this statement for many reasons, it is not my intention to prove or disprove a distinct racist affiliation in the *individual* author such as Haggard, Kipling or Conrad. Rather, I am interested in a discourse that establishes White masculinity as the only human norm over and over again and which is, hence, as part of a Eurocentric *structure*, reproduced, for instance, when Etherington describes White men's "going native" as "our psychology, our past".

way the alleged 'backwardness' of the African characters in terms of (evolutionary) development is mirrored in their speech.[66] After the successful passage through the desert, the heroes reach the mountains that tellingly are called Sheba's breasts.[67] Unfortunately, there is also a rapid change in climate, and it is suddenly freezing, which makes their situation dire: "What this meant to us, enervated by hardship, want of food, and the great heat of the desert, any reader can imagine better than I can describe. Suffice it to say that it was something as near death from exposure as I have ever felt." (KSM 95) In this direct address to the readers, a common device in Haggard's fiction, Quatermain appeals to the reader's empathy in his exaggerated claims. This kind of sympathy again is only directed at the White men and when Ventvögel logically dies of the cold – one must not forget that, in the racist logic of the text, as a 'Hottentot' he can stand heat, but, of course, not cold –, they can quickly recover from the shock of the "poor fellow's" (KSM 96) death.

On their way to the mythical Kukuanaland and the mines, the want of proper food compels them to eat raw food – a threat to the boundary of 'primitive' and 'civilised'. However, it is the gentlemanly behaviour and insistence on proper clothing that upholds their civilised status in this brutish environment. In *Imperial Leather*, McClintock analyses colonial advertising for soap and other commodity goods and concludes that these also function at a symbolic level: "Domestic hygiene […] purifies and preserves the white male body from contamination in the threshold zone of Empire." (McClintock 1995, 32) After having taken a bath in a river, Good is "actively employed in making a most elaborate toilet. He had washed his gutta-percha collar, thoroughly shaken out his trousers, coat, and waistcoat, and was now folding them up neatly till he was ready to put them on." (KSM 109) These elaborate and detailed descriptions of the efforts to keep up a 'civilised hygiene' signify the protection from the loss of control and

---

66 This is a device that James Fenimore Cooper had also employed for the speech of Native Americans in his series of so-called *Leather-Stocking Tales* (1823–1841) influenced by the Romantic notion of the 'noble savage'.

67 The sexualisation of the landscape here is hardly subtle: "These mountains standing thus, like the pillars of a gigantic gateway, are shaped exactly like a woman's breasts. Their bases swelled gently up from the plain, looking, at a distance, perfectly round and smooth; and on top of each was a vast round hillock covered with snow, exactly corresponding to the nipple on the female breast." (KSM 85) Stott links this kind of description (to be repeatedly found in Haggard's fiction) directly to the language of late nineteenth-century pornography. (cf. Stott 1989, 85)

might seem odd in a 'male genre' such as the adventure novel. This pattern is exaggerated in Good's comic insistence on these rituals at the most improper occasions. "He was, as usual, beautifully shaved, his eyeglass and his false teeth appeared to be in perfect order, and altogether he was the neatest man I ever had to do with in the wilderness." (KSM 54) When asked about his emphasis on cleanliness, Good responds, "I always like to look like a gentleman" (KSM 54). However, there also seems to lurk a danger connected to a masculinity that is ironically *too* civilised, which risks losing its manly characteristics. Masculinity in contrast to femininity, which was always reliant on 'artificial' means, was at best to come 'naturally' to men. As has been noted earlier, while it is important to dissociate oneself from savage 'backwardness', the dandy 'effeminate' masculinity of the turn of the century was also not an appropriate masculinity for heroes.

Hegemonic masculinity is further differentiated by class. Whereas Sir Henry's upper-class background clearly links him to the ideal gentleman tradition, the middle-class hunter Quatermain sees himself more as a timid and simple man, someone who is practical, not very cultured and knows his way better wielding a gun than a pen. In sharp contrast to Curtis' and Quatermain's physical fitness Good is short and stout. After a rather unsuccessful career, the good-hearted retired Captain of the British Royal Navy now accompanies his friend Curtis on his adventures, though his described unmanly behaviour lands Good in trouble time and again, and it is the more matter-of-fact masculinity of Curtis and Quatermain that more often than not rescues Good. At one point in the story, Good's foolishness regarding his cleanliness for once is to the benefit of the heroes. When they are ambushed by 'natives' on their way to Kukuanaland, Good's appearance – only half shaved, wearing a shirt with his pants down and showing his false teeth – is enough to convince the 'natives' that the White men come from another world. As a drawback, he will have to hold on to this look, an extremely embarrassing occurrence for him, throughout his stay in the kingdom.

The way masculinity is and can be imagined is in close connection to the perception of women and femininity. Adventure heroes in their homosocial[68] environment cherish only the company of other men while at the

---

68 I use the term as defined by Sedgwick: "'Homosocial' is a word occasionally used in history and the social sciences, where it describes social bonds between persons of the same sex; it is a neologism, obviously formed by analogy with 'homosexual,' and just as obviously meant to be distinguished from 'homosexual'." (Sedgwick 1985, 1)

same time any homosexual desire is strictly taboo. (cf. Sedgwick 1985) Tosh explains how the empire offered a space distinctly different from the Victorian household, where masculinity was tied up in domestic arrangements. At home, men had to fulfil their roles as husbands and fathers and marriage was indeed quite obligatory. In contrast then, "[t]he empire was run by bachelors; in the public mind it represented devotion to duty or profit (and sometimes pleasure), undistracted by feminine ties" (Tosh 1999, 175).

Obviously, the genre of adventure fiction – suitable for the education of young boys – demanded a chaste depiction of any sexual contact. It does, however, seem striking that there is no White 'sweetheart' waiting at home for any of the men, nor any reference made to romantic love throughout the story.[69] Both the imagined perils of homosexuality and 'miscegenation' loom large in this genre.[70]

In all this celebration of manhood, one can easily detect homoerotic undertones. In *King Solomon's Mines*, it is especially the magnificent body of, on the one hand, the White 'Viking' Curtis and, on the other hand, the Black Zulu Umbopa whose physical strength is admired. Henry Curtis' fine body is praised repeatedly in the story and in the beginning, Quatermain remarks that Curtis is "one of the biggest-chested and longest-armed men I ever saw. He had yellow hair, a big yellow beard, clear-cut features, and large grey eyes set deep into his head. I never saw a finer looking man, and somehow he reminded me of an ancient Dane." (KSM 11) Curtis and Umbopa are envisioned as an ideal pairing of White and Black masculinity,

---

69 While Haggard seldom features White women in his stories, White femininity in the colonies represents the ultimate danger to both the colonies and femininity in the larger context of imperial fiction. This is excellently worked out by Dyer in his discussion of so-called "end-of-empire fictions" of which E.M. Forster's *A Passage to India* (1924) is the prime example. Dyer focuses on the popular TV series *The Jewel in the Crown* (1984) and convincingly argues that the appearance of White women in the colonies and their characteristic depiction as helpless and paralysed was used as symbol (as well as a cause) for the decline of the empire. Haggard's narrator implicitly makes the same connection when he repeatedly cautions his young male readers that women are trouble. Concerning the role of White women in the colonies in general, cf. Strobel (1987).

70 This was also the time of the Labouchère amendment to the Criminal Law Amendment Act of 1885, which outlawed sexual relations between men and which was also known as the 'blackmailer's charter' under which Oscar Wilde was infamously tried and sentenced in 1895. So obviously, this threat of sexual relations between men (in contrast to sexual relations between women which were never outlawed in Britain but, of course, also remained a social taboo) was conceived as a public ailment.

and further to this idea, Haggard also describes the Danes[71] as "white Zulus" (KSM 11) thus emphasising the link between the two men. This fantasy of master and servant carries a huge erotic charge that is reinforced during the initial meeting of these two characters, which I will hence quote at some length:

> Sir Henry told me to ask him to stand up. Umbopa did so, at the same time slipping off the long military great coat he wore, and revealing himself naked except for the moocha [loin-cloth, E.H.Y.] round his centre and a necklace of lions' claws. He was certainly a magnificent-looking man; I never saw a finer native. [...] [H]e was broad in proportion, and very shapely. In this light, too, his skin looked scarcely more than dark, except here and there where deep black scars marked old assegai wounds. Sir Henry walked up to him and looked into his proud face. 'They make a good pair, don't they?' said Good; 'one as big as the other.' 'I like your looks, Mr. Umbopa, and I will take you as my servant,' said Sir Henry in English. Umbopa evidently understood him, for he answered in Zulu, 'It is well;' and then with a glance at the white man's great stature and breadth, 'we are men, thou and I.' (KSM 48–49)

What is at first sight implying a kinship between these men is, nevertheless, constructed hierarchically. In this context, the revelation of the naked Black body – only marked by even darker scars – for the pleasure of the White spectators is a feature of the imperial gaze. The claim for 'real' manhood here is a connecting and possibly homoerotic link between these two fine warriors. However, the 'noble savage' can become the 'brother' (when it is understood that the 'elder' White brother holds all the power, of course) of the White man, but certainly not his lover. In the context of the homosocial male adventure, male homosexuality remains a strict taboo and as White women are not present within the story, the heroes are tempted by the beauty of the 'native' women. In this way, the luring queerness of male bonding is evaded and heterosexuality is naturalised as the only proper albeit also policed sexuality.

On the White men's arrival in Kukuanaland, they admire the 'native' soldiers and behold the women: "These women are, for a native race, exceedingly handsome." These women are further described as "well-bred" because "the lips are not unpleasantly thick as is the case in most African races" (KSM 129). Again, whenever an African character is described as righteous or beautiful, his or her features are also linked to a more Euro-

---

71 The recurring reference to the 'Danes' in Haggard's writing functions as a hyperbole of phantasmatic Whiteness and virility.

pean appearance. In Kukuanaland, the White men and their companion Umbopa also meet the despotic king, Twala, and his trusted advisor, the witch Gagool. The lack of morality is immediately symbolically linked to the outer appearance of the Black characters. It is written on the body and so the sight of Twala is quite frightful to behold. He is

an enormous man with the most entirely repulsive countenance we had ever beheld. The lips were as thick as a negro's, the nose was flat, it had but one gleaming black eye (for the other was represented by a hollow in the face) and its whole expression was cruel and sensual to a degree. (KSM 141)

Back in their quarters on their own, Umbopa finally reveals his secret identity as the long-lost rightful heir to the crown. The party now settles on a scheme to overthrow the despot during their stay.

First however, they have to overcome another threat. In the colour-coded logic of the text, the 'native' women are immediately drawn to Good's "beautiful white legs". The adventurers are offered any of the women they desire for marriage, an offer to which Quatermain hastily replies, "'Thanks, O king, but we white men wed only with white women like ourselves. Your maidens are fair, but they are not for us'" (KSM 178), though he fears Good will be tempted. Here, race is crucially linked to (reproductive) heterosexuality. In this understanding, as Dyer mentions, "[h]eterosexuality is the means of ensuring, but also the site of endangering, the reproduction of these [racial, E.H.Y.] differences" (Dyer 1997, 20). The possible off-spring of a liaison between the White hero and a Black 'native' woman is a clear threat and boundary violation in terms of the unambiguousness of race and the maintenance of difference. 'Miscegenation' is to be avoided by all means.[72] (cf. Dryden 2000, 48) "Inter-racial heterosexuality threatens the power of whiteness because it breaks the legitimation of whiteness with reference to the white body." (Dyer 1997, 25) For this reason, a convenient way to simultaneously describe and render impossible an affair for the White man is to have his 'native' love interest die before they are in any danger of actual sexual contact. In *King Solomon's Mines*, this motif, the liaison of the White man with a sacrificial Black

---

72 While this was a taboo theme in literature, the reality of 'mixed race' offspring in the colonies is proof of the often consummated sexual acts between White colonisers and 'native women'. Etherington even speculates about Haggard having had affairs with Black women in South Africa during his youth. (cf. Etherington 1984, 5) For an insightful discussion of so-called 'mixed-race' offspring in French Indochina, cf. "Sexual Affronts and Racial Affronts" in Stoler (2002, 79–111).

woman, is represented by the couple Good/Foulata and the same pattern will be repeated in the depiction of the pair Leo/Ustane in *She*. The Black woman not only dies; she is actually "glad to die" as this is in service to her White master.

As part of the 'savage' dance that embodies the superstition of the 'natives', the White men are to witness how the fairest and most beautiful woman is to be sacrificed. The White men cannot passively watch such a 'barbarous' act. The heroism of White masculinity is constructed as benevolence towards the 'native' woman who needs to be rescued from the Black man's depravity.[73] Good saves the gorgeous Foulata, who is now inseparably attached to him. She will later lovingly nurse Good who, after the epic battle (which describes the loss of some several ten thousands of lives), is injured.

In the course of the story, the heroes triumph against great odds and successfully reinstall their companion as the rightful king of Kukuanaland. The evil witch Gagool, in consequence, is spared from the death sentence because she can now lead the men to their original goal, King Solomon's mines. Deviously, Gagool attempts to trap them into the cave, but Foulata is attentive enough to the situation to try to stop her. In her attempt, she is fatally wounded by Gagool, who, in turn is crushed by the massive stone that now seals the chamber. Good bemoans Foulata and starts kissing her to which the dying girl responds: "I love him, […] I am glad to die because I know that he cannot cumber his life with such as me, for the sun cannot mate with the darkness, nor the white with the dark." (KSM 281)

With this climactic fight which leaves both female characters dead and the threat of 'miscegenation' banned, the men are again left to their own devices. Trapped with all the riches of the world, they now lament their oncoming sure death. It is only the capable Sir Henry who does not give up hope:

Laying my head against Sir Henry's broad shoulder I burst into tears; and I think I heard Good gulping away on the other side, and swearing hoarsely for doing so. Ah, how good and brave that great man was! Had we been two frightened children, and he our nurse, he could not have treated us more tenderly. (KSM 288)

This "tender masculinity" of Sir Henry, who in no situation loses his countenance, can motivate the others to find that saving shaft which hides

---

73 Most famously Gayatri Chakravorty Spivak has coined the phrase of "White men are saving brown women from brown men" (Spivak 1988, 296) to describe this conception.

a passage to freedom. Not forgetting to take as many diamonds as they can, they heave away the stone that blocks their rescue. Sir Henry's prowess is again of great help: "Sir Henry's strength had done it, and never did muscular power stand a man in better stead." (KSM 291) At this point, class again distinguishes the three men. Whereas Curtis and Good really are not interested in the money, Quatermain, the hunter and trader, has to think about how to provide for his son.[74] Finally free, they struggle through the underworld and tunnels of King Solomon's mines to emerge (or, symbolically to be reborn) into the African daylight. "Gaunt-cheeked, hollow-eyed wretches, smeared all over with dust and mud, bruised, bleeding, the long fear of imminent death yet written on our countenances, we were, indeed, a sight to frighten the daylight." (KSM 299) After this frightful journey, Quatermain comments on the incredible – even unbelievable fact – that all along the way Good never lost his single eyeglass which he leaves to the 'natives' as a parting gift.

Upon the heroes' departure, Umbopa (now called by his real name Ignosi) promises to establish just rule in Kukuanaland as well as to shield it from the bad influences of White civilisation such as alcohol, trade and guns. Kukuanaland thus will forever remain the hidden untouched paradise in an Africa that is imagined by the White men as a retreat from the ills of, on the one hand, 'backward barbarisms' and, on the other hand, corrupted British civilisation.

On their journey back home, the protagonists perchance meet the long lost brother of Sir Henry, George – the search for whom had been the initial objective of the quest – living in an oasis with his servant. It turns out they had been there for two years when during their attempt to find the mines George's leg was crushed by a boulder. Quatermain compares George and his servant to another famous literary couple: they had lived "like a second Robinson Crusoe and his man Friday" (KSM 316), thereby,

---

74 The service in the colonies was often the only opportunity for many men and women – the "ragbag surplus of men and women to whom an industrializing Britain could offer no place" (McClintock 1995, 238) – to earn their living (which is not meant as a justification of the endeavour in any way). Haggard himself shared this experience. His parents would not spend money on his university education (as they did for all the other sons of the family, because they did not think him intellectually fit for such a career) and sent him instead abroad to earn his livelihood in South Africa. On his return, he was still not able to support himself and was dependant on the fortune of his newly married wife. Ironically, only writing his romances, which condemn such a capitalist understanding of colonialism, ultimately secured his financial success.

paying tribute to one of the major imperial texts of British literature and a forerunner to the adventure tradition. (cf. Green 1980)

The men leave together and embark on a ship to England while Quatermain initially stays behind and bids farewell directly to the reader. The novel ends with a letter from Curtis who is now back in England reunited with the other two men: "You should have seen what a swell Good turned out the very next day, beautifully shaved, frock coat fitting like a glove, brand new eye-glass, &c &c." (KSM 318) Quatermain passes final judgement telling the reader that he, too, will leave for England with the next ship in order to be finally reunited with his son.

Even though they were met by critical obstacles along their way, the White men have succeeded in accordance with the tradition of the adventure tale to establish order at home and abroad. Consequently, Patteson is quite right when he writes that "the effort to establish order is perhaps the *sine qua non* of the imperialist romance" (Patteson 1978, 118). A rightful king, who has renounced the 'barbarous' ways of his forefathers, has been secured to the throne and, what is more important, brothers have been reunited as have father and son. The continuation of male hegemony once again is (at least fictionally) secured. Haggard's tale – although published at the height of the discourse of the crisis of masculinity – is a fantastic securing of masculine norms. In his next work, *She*, the threat of the New Woman is transferred yet again to the African landscape which functions as a utopian space of withdrawal from the demands of modernity.

She: "Heat, misery, and mosquitoes"

Following the immense success of *King Solomon's Mines*, *She*, published two years later in 1887, sold a nearly record-breaking 30,000 copies within only a few months. (cf. Gilbert and Gubar 1989, 6) This time the well-known hero of *King Solomon's Mines*, Allan Quatermain, appears only as the fictional editor (a literary device to be found in numerous of Haggard's novels) of the extraordinary story of a quest of the protagonists Ludwig Horace Holly and his foster son Leo Vincey. To complete this new adventurous trio, they are accompanied by the male attendant to Leo, Job. The three men set out from a famous fictional college in England on Leo's twenty-fifth birthday to Africa to unravel the mystery behind Leo's ancestry. When Leo was only five years old, his father gave Holly from his death bed a chest revealing the strange family history. The contents suggests that the Vinceys can trace back their family's origins more than 2,000 years to an Egyptian priest of Isis (of Grecian extraction) named Kallikrates who was murdered by a mighty Queen of a 'savage' people, a White woman of peculiar loveliness. This complicated background is however only the excuse for the fantastic adventures to follow. As is typical of the genre, Haggard's fiction is action-driven and does not focus too closely on details and character's psychology. Consequently, Andrea White argues that:

Adventure fiction celebrated, in its various 'exotic' settings, a pre-industrial past, and [...] fulfilled the industrialized reader's desires [...] for an arena for manly, heroic action, uncomplicated by the complex moralities of a modern, democratic world. (A. White 1993, 63)

She is an excellent example of this kind of fiction. After a shipwreck and a wearisome journey through unknown territory, the three men, now escorted by an Arabic servant named Mahomed, finally arrive at the ancient city of Kôr, where the above-mentioned mysterious and immortal queen Ayesha – or, as she is called by her servants "She-who-must-be-obeyed" – lives. 'She' is a descendant of an ancient White race and has bred her own (Black) slave race – the Amahagger. This notion of the ancient White race was popular at the time and is connected to the idea of the temporal cleft already described. Whenever there was an archaeological discovery hinting at great accomplishment to civilisation in Africa, it was quickly attributed by Western scientists to some ancient and supposedly White race as the Egyptians, Persians or Phoenicians, and references to all these are rampant in Haggard's writing.[75]

The Amahagger of Kôr are not only depicted as the servants of such a mythical White queen but are also a matriarchal society in which the women can freely choose their husbands and possess as much power as the men. They are now confronted with White men for the first time and are obviously immediately taken by the good looks of the youngest of the White men, which gives the narrator the opportunity to praise Leo's physique emphatically: "Leo's tall, athletic form and clear-cut Grecian face, however, evidently excited their attention." (S 80) Ustane, one of the Amahagger women, falls in love with Leo and kisses him, which according

---

75 In the nineteenth century, classical civilisation, especially ancient Greece but also Egypt was unquestionably linked with Whiteness. These assumptions have been identified as relying on racist conceptions and Martin Bernal's work *Black Athena. The Afroasiatic Roots of Classical Civilization* (1987) has sparked off a heated and ongoing debate on the subject.

to their custom means that she has selected him as her husband. However, Leo later is recognised by Ayesha as the rebirth of the ancient Kallikrates, his ancestor whom Ayesha had murdered 2,000 years ago in a fit of jealousy because he would not return her love. Now she dreams of a reunion and wants to bestow eternal life on him. This is the reason for her cruel murder of Ustane who she saw as her rival for Leo's affections. Following the murder, 'She' shows the men the "Pillar of Light", a magical flame that can give eternal life. Since 'She' had received eternal life once already, stepping into the light a second time finally destroys her. After her gruesome death, the men are free to leave and in the end, they arrive safely in England exactly two years after they initially left.

She offers a rich account of a battle of the sexes which heroically restores the men as the 'natural' leaders in the end. The older Holly appears in sharp contrast to his beautiful foster son Leo. Holly's ugliness is only matched by his superhuman strength. He describes himself as:

Short, thick-set, and deep-chested almost to deformity, with long sinewy arms, heavy features, deep-set grey eyes, a low brow half overgrown with a mop of thick black hair, [...] such was my appearance nearly a quarter of a century ago, and such, with some modification, is it to this day. Like Cain, I was branded – branded by Nature with the stamp of abnormal ugliness, as I was gifted by Nature with iron and abnormal strength and considerable intellectual powers. (S 7–8)

But his intellectual powers are of no use when it comes to meeting women. "Women hated the sight of me" and he continues to recount how he supposedly had converted one woman to the "monkey theory" (S 8) which of course refers directly to Darwin's, at the time, enormously controversial *The Origin of Species* and the idea that humans and apes have a shared ancestry. In contrast, Leo

was very tall, very broad, and had a look of power and grace of bearing that seemed as native to him as it is to a wild stag. In addition his face was almost without flaw – a good face as well as a beautiful one, and when he lifted his hat, [...] I saw that his head was covered with little golden curls. (S 1)

Leo, whose beauty is admired repeatedly throughout the novel and who is compared to Apollo – an ideal of White muscular masculinity (cf. Dyer 1997) – several times, is immensely strong but not very bright and ironically seems to miss most of the adventure. After their initial shipwreck, he catches a bad fever and thus, is sleeping most of the time while also being nursed by the angelic Ustane, his Amahagger 'wife'. However, this couple's relationship is – apart from the first kiss – completely chaste. As I have pointed out in greater detail with regard to the couple Good and Foulata in *King Solomon's Mines*, such a relationship is not intended to thrive and the narrative pattern of the self-sacrificing Black woman is repeated. Conceived as shy and nearly asexual, Ustane is harmless and completely devoted to Leo. In a battle, she throws herself in front of him which saves Leo's life. Stott notes that "the native woman is usually dispensed with to avoid the complications of miscegenation. [...] Furthermore, romantic complications with native women threaten male camaraderie." (Stott 1989, 70) In *She*, the two main female characters are sharply contrasted, the irresistible *femme fatale* Ayesha versus the angelic Ustane: both of them, however, are not meant to survive.

The only time Leo attempts to stand up against 'Her' in order to protect Ustane he fails miserably. Leo tries to attack Ayesha who stretches out her hand and stops him magically. As a consequence, Leo remembers feeling as if he had received a violent blow in the chest: "utterly cowed, as if all the manhood had been taken out of him" (S 228). The evil woman deprives him of his strength in this symbolical castration. He cannot protect his woman as heroes are meant to, but Ustane's sacrifice is also in his own best interest as their relationship could never be approved of back in England.

The more experienced Holly, however, is not quite as easily vanquished as his protégé. When he is introduced to 'Her', he is ordered to bow, an act he refuses to do: "I was an Englishman, and why, I asked myself, should I creep into the presence of some savage woman as though I were a monkey?" (S 140) There is apparently no greater humiliation for an English gentleman than to obey a 'savage' woman. Although 'She' is of White descent, 'She' is clearly still marked as 'savage' or at least, oddly in-between.[76]

Later in the story, the men must pass an abyss on a narrow plank in order to reach the magical "Pillar of Light". Ayesha can literally float over the plank and mocks the hesitant men. Holly decides to follow quickly because "it is better to fall down a precipice and die than be laughed at by such a woman" (S 275). In the presence of the supernatural power of 'Her', the male characters' masculinity is constantly threatened, a belittling of which is worse than death. Job is the one character who is less secure in his manhood and simply not 'fit enough' and consequently, eliminated in the

---

76 Tamar Heller describes Ayesha as having a "tripartite identity" (Heller 2007, 56) that combines codes of Blackness, Orientalism and Whiteness.

struggle to achieve 'true' masculinity. Instead of walking the plank upright, as the other two men did, he suddenly hesitates. Leo cries: "'Come, be a man, Job [...] it's quite easy'" (S 276) to encourage him. But this feat is not as easy for Job. His profession as a male attendant connects him to femininity and also his appearance is less virile than that of the other men who have earned the 'native' names, Lion (Leo) and Baboon (Holly). Job, in contrast, is called Pig "on account of his fatness, round face, and small eyes" (S 121). In this instance, heroic masculinity explicitly becomes a bodily ideal of muscularity. It is permissible to be ugly as Holly as long as he can display 'manly' strength. To be weak and fat as Job is to be fatally feminised. Accordingly, Job fails to master this critical situation and crawls for the remaining part face down along the plank. When he eventually reaches the other side, Job drops the plank they will need for their return, and he can only be saved by Leo's superhuman powers.

In their influential reading, Gilbert and Gubar interpret *She* as a reaction to the threat the New Woman poses at home in England.[77] The debate is transferred to the colonies and to the realm of adventure fiction wherein gender relations can still safely be restored. In both of Haggard's texts, the urge to thwart an emerging female supremacy in favour of the 'rightful' male hegemony takes on a sense of urgency, most dramatically illustrated by the character of Ayesha in *She*, but also by Gagool, the evil witch in *King Solomon's Mines*. Restoring this male order in adventure fiction seems to always involve violence and usually enormous battles that cost thousands of (Black) lives as one of the consequences.

As I have argued so far, the gender identity of the heroic male is conceptualised as a struggle to attain and to maintain. But does this struggle affect their sexuality? Although the protagonists leave their home country, where the only suitable mates, i.e. White English ladies, are to be found, there is no word of complaint. Back in England – the reader is told – it is only the women who are all magically drawn to Leo, not vice versa. Also, his affection for Ustane is somewhat limited and her loss only shortly grieved. The two years of abstinence pose no difficulty for the chaste he-

---

77 Similarly, Elaine Showalter reads the "male quest romance" of Haggard, Kipling and Conrad as "a complicated response to female literary dominance as well as to British imperialism and fears of manly decline in the face of female power" (Showalter 1990, 83). Nonetheless, with her very strong focus on gender, Showalter does not comprehensively analyse the influence of British imperialism or other socio-cultural factors contributing to the discourse of masculinity in crisis, as Ledger (1995), for instance, has criticised.

roes. Once more, while heterosexual manliness is naturalised as a Darwinian struggle, it is also presented as a cultural accomplishment of men who are able to 'master their sexual appetites'.[78] As many critics have noted, part of the appeal of colonial fiction was to be relieved from the burden of dealing with women. (cf. Mangan and Walvin (ed.) 1987; Tosh 2004) With recourse to Sedgwick's *Between Men* (1985), Shannon Young (2006) and Madhudaya Sinha (2008) speculate about an erotic triangle involving Leo, Ayesha and Holly. Holly fondly comments on his close relationship to his foster son numerous times, but when he learns of Ayesha's unstoppable love for Leo, the power of Ayesha's beauty becomes a source of uncontrollable envy in him. "Holly's jealousy as he imagines Ayesha and Leo together sexually could be not only about his desire for her, but his sublimated desire for him." (S. Young 2006, 138) Read as homosocial or homoerotic bonds, meaningful relationships are exclusively possible between men in the logic of this narrative. Women are portrayed as more of an obstacle rather than a reward for adventurous men. The 'native' women in the novel are either beautiful maiden-like girls who will most likely die in the course of the story or they are the evil witches who will also meet their justice in due course. As in *King Solomon's Mines*, White British women are only rarely part of the plot.[79] Nonetheless, masculinity relies on the feminine foil from which it can dissociate itself.

Throughout the novel, misogyny informs the men's common sense. Holly comments on how women hate him because of his ugliness and that he really is afraid of them. Job, who is in fact depicted as 'effeminate', seems altogether woman-hating and is the character in the story who most freely expresses his resentments against women and 'natives'. He serves as the novel's mouthpiece for misogynist and racist stereotypes. Holly, the narrator, distances himself from Job's crude judgements and even uses the term 'brothers' to refer to Black men, but, in general, he seems disproving

---

78 Cf. "A man who would have authority over others must first master himself." (Tosh 2004, 73)

79 Consequently, if there is an exception such as the young and tomboyish character of Flossie Mackenzie in the novel *Allan Quatermain*, Quatermain himself insists on her being sent home to a place where she will grow into a proper English lady: "'[Y]ou owe a duty to your wife and daughter, and more especially to the latter, who should receive some education and mix with girls of her own race, otherwise she will grow up wild, shunning her kind." (AQ 99) The sexuality of the character is stabilised by restoring her to her 'natural environment'.

more of the language than of the content of Job's racial slurs.[80] Similar to
Leo's experience, one of the Amahagger women approaches Job and kisses
him to claim him as her husband. This strikes him with "terror and disgust.
Job, [Holly comments,] is a bit of a misogynist" (S 88), which is an admissible and even normal character trait in an Englishman.

In this novel, the heroes can only be drawn to women seemingly by
magic. The queen, Ayesha, is veiled all of the time for whenever 'She' unveils herself, every man with his eyes upon her becomes enchanted by her
supernatural beauty. Holly, sadly, is the first to fall prey to 'Her' powers: "I
am but a man, and she was more than a woman." (S 190) His male superiority is dismissed by this evil woman, and he is forever marked by this love
spell. This unbalance even threatens the relationship to his foster son.
When he wakes up the following day, he muses over the power of 'Her'
spell, specifically in how it affected him: "Why cannot man be content and
live alone and be happy, and let the women live alone and be happy too?"
(S 159) It is in fact heterosexuality – the need to make contact with the
'Other' sex – that is frightening and somewhat undesirable for him.

As has been argued with reference to *King Solomon's Mines*, the quest
narrative unfolds as a sequence of dangerous episodes that need to be
mastered. In the exotic settings of adventure stories, the male hero is persistently on the verge of losing control over himself or his environment.
Therefore, in all of Haggard's fiction the hero needs to place a great emphasis on hygiene and clothes in order to keep his integrity and poise.[81]
Consistently in *She* the protagonists seem to find enough time in between
their trials and tribulations to take care of their appearance. The reader can
rest assured that between the shipwreck and the shooting of lions, these
men still manage to put on a clean white shirt and shave themselves, as the
following quote illustrates:

The first care of Job and myself, after seeing to Leo, was to wash ourselves and put
on clean clothing. [...] Never shall I forget the comfort of the 'wash and brush-up,'

---

80 When the men first arrive in Africa, Job comments on meeting 'natives' for the first
   time: "'[T]hese blackamoors and their filthy, thieving ways. They are only fit for muck;
   and they smell bad enough for it already.' Job, it will be perceived, was no admirer of the
   manners and customs of our dark-skinned brothers." (S 51)
81 In his historical study *Reizbare Maschinen* (2003), Philipp Sarasin, for instance, has analysed the discourse of hygiene in the nineteenth century and shown how this new belief
   in individual responsibility for health and well-being helped to establish the ideal of the
   modern bourgeois body.

and of those clean flannels. The only thing that was wanting to complete my joy was a cake of soap, of which we had none. (S 134)

McClintock argues aptly that "Victorian cleaning rituals were peddled globally as the God-given sign of Britain's evolutionary superiority, and soap was invested with magical, fetish powers" (McClintock 1995, 207).[82] When at some point in the story the men suddenly have to depart from their camp and leave behind some of their equipment, tellingly clean clothes are indispensable: "Our preparations did not take us very long. We took a change of clothing apiece and some spare boots into my Gladstone bag, also we took our revolvers and an express rifle each [...]. The rest of our gear [...] we left behind." (S 257) The only equipment the male adventure hero needs in central Africa is guns and clean clothes. The bodies of the White men noticeably need protection, and the cleansing rituals are a means of controlling boundaries between the 'savage' and the 'civilised'. The guns hint at the systematic violence that is implied in these ventures. These recurring intermissions are not necessarily part of the central plot; nonetheless, describing how the men wash and rest after the tiresome quarrels is constitutive of the way a civilised masculinity is imagined and celebrated. The emphasis on products, such as soap or manufactured clothes, in this context also links the adventure novel with commodity capitalism. There is now a market for products that cater to this cultured conception of masculinity. Consequently, another fundamental feature of these stories is the constant stress of the refinement of the heroes.

In comparison to the 'savage', the refined White male is so highly civilised that his greater sensitivity makes him in fact more vulnerable. However, as in *King Solomon's Mines*, this vulnerability is interpreted as something of an (evolutionary) accomplishment and is contrasted with the brute, callous and animal-like 'native'. This superiority can even be identified by simple animals, such as mosquitoes, that can distinguish 'native' from 'civilised' blood:

For, whether they were attracted by the lantern, or by the unaccustomed smell of a white man, for which they had been waiting for the last thousand years or so, I know not; but certainly we were presently attacked by tens of thousands of the most bloodthirsty, pertinacious, and huge mosquitoes that I ever saw or read of. (S 67)

---

82 These fetishistic rituals are abundantly present in *She*. In the 'wilderness', Job is "shaking out [...] clothes as a makeshift for brushing them, which he could not do because there was no brush" (S 167) and later the heroes go "through a perfunctory wash" (S 267).

Their 'native' companion, the Arab Mahomed, conversely, is completely unaffected by this peril: "as for Mahomed the mosquitoes, recognising the taste of a true believer, would not touch him at any price" (S 70). In a Darwinian sense the White men are endangered and are in this situation not exactly biologically 'the fittest'. But it is their ability to overcome a dangerous situation that is interpreted as their true heroism. In this way, Darwinian thinking could be reinterpreted and stretched to serve the imperial project and these enthralling plots.[83]

The White men prove their steadfastness: They survive the brutal attack of the mosquitoes while the African character simply is immune to this danger – a pattern common in colonial fiction. In contrast to *King Solomon's Mines*, however, where there is at least the Black hero Umbopa, the Africans in *She* are never fully realised characters and simply serve as a foil on which White accomplishment can be proliferated. Wendy Katz further explicates that the "dehumanization succeeds in placing the non-white outside the bounds of the white reader's sympathy [...] [because he or she] lacked sufficient sensitivity to qualify for even minimal human compassion" (Katz 1987, 133). The reader is clearly meant to identify with the superior, truly heroic, White characters. In *She*, this marginalised non-White masculinity is epitomised by Mahomed. Again, he is not to be compared with the somehow sympathetic description of the proud Zulu warrior Umbopa. Mahomed is described as being just a "stout swarthy Arab" (S 48). Mahomed's racial difference is emphasised and intertwined with religious attributions and his 'wrong' faith as a Muslim. He is the target of ridicule by Job, and when he is killed in the course of the story, this is portrayed as really just a tragic little incident comparable to the deaths of the servants in *King Solomon's Mines*. In the course of a barbaric ritual, Mahomed is supposed to be cooked and eaten by the cannibalistic Amahagger. Cannibalism becomes probably the single most important marker to connote lack of civilisation in the White imagination. When one of the women attacks Mahomed, Holly fires a gun at her, but unfortunately, the

---

83 The later novel *Allan Quatermain*, for example, is dedicated to Haggard's son, Arthur John (Jock) Rider Haggard, and in his dedication Haggard once more identifies manhood, in general, as an achievement and the English gentleman, in particular, as the greatest evolutionary success of humankind: "In the hope that in days to come/he, and many other boys whom I shall never know, may,/in the acts and thoughts of Allan Quatermain/and his companions, as herein recorded,/find something to help him and them to reach/to what, with Sir Henry Curtis, I hold to be the/highest rank whereto we can attain –/the state and dignity of English Gentlemen." (AQ 3)

bullet kills Mahomed, in addition to the Amahagger woman. Holly remarks sardonically that: "It was an awful and yet a most merciful accident." (S 100) Here, the 'civilised' death through a firearm is apparently far more merciful than the 'savage' ritual of being cooked and eaten.

Although lacking many of the more literary qualities, Gilbert and Gubar (1989) identify *She* as a precursor to Conrad's more sombre tale *Heart of Darkness*. Interestingly, Haggard called the abyss the men cross on their way to the Pillar of Light "the heart of the darkness" (S 273). In how far Conrad was inspired by Haggard's fiction (which he actually detested) is contentious. (cf. A. White 1993, 105–106) At the climax of Haggard's story, the men stare in disgust at the sight of Ayesha dying in the fire and exclaim: "*horror of horrors*" (S 293) – again foreshadowing "The horror! The horror!" of Conrad's *Heart of Darkness*. At first, 'She' seems incredibly beautiful but as the fire blazes, 'She' becomes more and more disfigured. "Smaller she grew, and smaller yet, till she was no larger than a baboon." (S 294) Realising her own imminent death, Ayesha shrieks like an animal and calls out Kallikrates' name one last time. "Overcome with the extremity of horror, we too fell on the sandy floor of that dread place, and swooned away." (S 294) The fact that 'She' is linked to a monkey of all animals is no coincidence. Her death is the evolutionary process turned upside down or, as Stiebel puts it, "[S]he shrivels up into a Darwinian nightmare of man's origins, a monkey." (Stiebel 2001, 86) Job is not destined to survive this final and most demanding test of his masculinity after having only accomplished the other tasks with the help of the other two stronger men. He cannot recover from the shock of Ayesha's gruesome death: "His nerves already shattered by all he had seen and undergone, had utterly broken down beneath this last dire sight, and he had died of terror, or in a fit brought on by terror. One had only to look at his face to see it." (S 296)

To put it somewhat bluntly, in this narrative, the excessive femininity of evil women needs to be punished while even fainting men can seem heroic. The success of the heroes appears superhuman in the light of all this danger and some must die during this journey. But it is exactly this quality to reinterpret even fainting as heroic which restores a powerful White hegemonic masculinity in the end. "As always the Englishmen are good sports, react spontaneously in the face of adversity, combat evil, and restore order." (Katz 1987, 43) Again, the restoration of order stands at the end. They can return to England, back into the famous English college, at this time still a safe homosocial environment that continues to ban women from entering its institution.

Haggard's popular and formulaic adventure stories were part of a discourse that re-established White masculinity as superior and heroic, incorporating among other elements the quest romance and Darwinian thinking. A vital aspect of this venture was the denigration of femininity and Blackness. In the context of the many social changes at the end of the nineteenth century this male hegemony was not at all timeless or unthreatened as the authors of adventure fiction would have liked their readers to believe. Claudia Breger in her reading of *She* emphasises how the members of the ruling class are themselves subjected to Foucauldian disciplinary processes. The success in establishing control at least implicitly entails a crisis to begin with. With regard to the production of White hegemony Breger refers to

its inevitable instability in the process of its complex performance. 'White masculinity' is a delicate process of negotiation because too much 'dark drive' threatens its imaginary whiteness, too little its imagined masculinity. (Breger 2005, 83, my translation)

Establishing White hegemonic masculinity continues to be a circuitous narrative strategy, albeit still a very powerful one. The precariousness of this masculinity – its crisis so to speak – becomes the very privileged condition for its narrative self-fashioning as heroic and successful as part of the exuberant and exciting plots these stories provide. This is a position that neither marginalised masculinities nor female characters (White or of Colour) can inhabit in this genre (at that time). Adventure fiction becomes what Martin Green calls the "energyzing myth of English imperialism" (Green 1980, 3) and an imaginary realm unspoilt by the dangerous feminised domestic sphere.[84] Here most clearly the crisis of masculinity is a contained crisis and in many ways even abrogated on the level of plot where the superiority of the heroes is never seriously challenged. A re-

---

84 The idealised evangelical doctrine of 'separate spheres' of the female 'angel in the house' and the public realm of gentlemen was, of course, often much more contradictory in real life than Haggard's fiction suggests. Consequently, G. Dawson is right to point out the contradictions this caused for men who tried to live up to the ideal of "'manly sensibility' – integrating 'robust manliness with refinement'" (G. Dawson 1994, 65). Nonetheless, Tosh is also correct to remind us that "we are imposing an artificial contradiction if we suppose that [there was] [...] an accepted principle of 'separate spheres'. The point is rather that men operated at will in *both* spheres; that was their privilege." (Tosh 2004, 71)

privileging of masculinity is achieved by a narrative emphasis on successful heroism that can be read as a restorative impetus in relation to the discourse of the crisis of masculinity. This discourse functions as the foil for the success of these 'yarns' but is not addressed directly.

In his later fiction Haggard can be linked to the problematic tradition of primitivism[85], not usually associated with colonialist fiction, which, on the whole, celebrated the idea of civilised progress unquestioningly.

Imperialist that he was, Haggard found himself advocating increasingly unpopular positions. His ideas on the primitive would be echoed by such anti-imperial modernists as Lawrence and Yeats, who also rejected the liberal idea of progress with its emphasis on commercialism and enlightened self interest and saw more to be hoped for from tapping back into our more intuitive, 'primitive' natures than from modern civilisation. (A. White 1993, 99)

While 'going native' is usually not connected to the conventional adventure tale, one of Haggard's later romances *Allan Quatermain* – originally serialised in *Longman's Review* from January to August 1887 – explores this theme. Here the reader witnesses the happy reunion of his famous trio Quatermain, Curtis and Good. But this story differs decidedly from their shared earlier adventures. First, there is a more sombre tone than was evident in *King Solomon's Mines*. Second, ending with the death of the ageing protagonist Allan Quatermain, sixty-three years of age in this adventure, the genre convention of the happy ending is somewhat off balance. What is more, the other men, too, decline to happily return to England and choose instead to stay behind in Africa. This marks a decisive shift from the conventional adventure plot that usually ends with the heroes safely restored to England and as a consequence more thoroughly questions the distinction between coloniser and colonised.

Can the white male imperialist or explorer, with the restraints of civilization removed, retain his whiteness, his manhood, in the face of barbarism? To 'go native' is to regress, to revert to a savage past, it is to descend the ladder of evolutionary progress, but it is also to release the repressed self. To explore Africa is to explore oneself, to test the strength of the veneer. (Stott 1989, 77)

However, unlike Conrad's Kurtz, who really loses his civilised status, Haggard's heroes maintain their poise and manly qualities. Moreover, while Kipling's Kim blends into 'native' society, Haggard's heroes retain all the

---

85 Cf. Torgovnick who analyses "primitivist discourse, [as] a discourse fundamental to the Western sense of self and Other" (Torgovnick 1990, 8).

characteristics of the English gentleman. Their ideal masculinity is simply transferred to the utopian African landscape. While Kim's India is a place full of different cultural influences (almost too many), Haggard's Africa is simply blank – waiting to be culturalised by the White men. (cf. Poon 2008) In *Allan Quatermain*, Africa becomes an Arcadian safe ground, a retreat from the corruption of English society. In the story, Sir Henry reflects on why he should return to a country where squires have lost their influence when he can rule as a White king in Africa. Low terms this the "pastoral politics" (37) of the novel. By the end, they have (re)established a wonderful (White) reign in Africa. This includes "the introduction of true religion in the place of this senseless Sun worship" (AQ 281), which was characteristic of the 'natives' before the British influence of the protagonists. Even though the Zu-Vendi people they rule were initially conceptualised as a White race – which allowed for the exceptionally happy relationship between Curtis and the 'native' woman Nyleptha –, it is the White man's blood/semen that promises perfection. Curtis proudly comments on his male first born in the end:

He is a regular curly-haired, blue-eyed young Englishman in looks, and, though he is destined, if he lives, to inherit the throne of Zu-Vendis, I hope I may be able to bring him up to become what an English gentleman should be, and generally is […] the highest rank that a man can reach upon this earth. (AQ 282)

In this way, the novel provides an escapist fantasy that allows Englishmen to restore their power. Africa serves as a projection for a longing for a safe and sound adventurous masculinity voicing Haggard's criticism of the decline of established power structures in England. The metropolis of London, with its new working classes, the demand for women's suffrage and industrialisation are seen as evils of civilisation. In accordance, Dawson sees the adventure quest "as a strategy of containment for underlying anxieties and contradictions, the key to which should not be sought only in the public world, but in the masculine relation to the domestic sphere" (G. Dawson 1994, 76). This ambivalent notion of civilisation is persistent in Haggard's writing, as has become evident in the readings of these novels. On the one hand, civilisation and English superiority are considered God's gift to the 'natives'; on the other hand, the same civilisation proves to be damaging when the ideal of hegemonic masculinity is threatened. Popular adventure fiction consequently can be read as a restorative response to the discourse of hegemonic masculinity in crisis.

Even within a formulaic genre such as the imperial romance, there is a complex way to address and construct different masculinities. Hegemonic masculinity clings to its status as civilised and enlightened. However, too much cultural refinement might prove to be harmful as well. The yearning for a heroic and 'pure' masculinity is felt in these accounts. Marginalised masculinities are either portrayed as evil and 'backwards' or as childlike and noble, but never truly heroic – a status that is steadfastly reserved for and connected with the efficacy of hegemonic White masculinity.

Colonial Photography: The Spectacle of the 'Self'

This chapter is concerned with the visual representation of White colonial masculinity in the popular press that started to flourish in the late eighteen-eighties. The strategy of containing the crisis of masculinity and the effort to re-establish masculinity as the successful universal bears strong resemblance to the hyperbolic language of the adventure novels of Haggard. However, it is the specific visual strategy of staging a *spectacle of the 'self'* that is of interest here. In how far do the images of successful hunters and soldiers flaunt an unfailing colonial masculinity and in how far can these pictures be seen as a response to the discourse of masculinity in crisis? I will argue that there is an effort to contain the crisis of masculinity both on the level of the picture itself and as a reaction to broader socio-cultural discourses. Firstly, in the staging of masculinity in these pictures there is an attempt to freeze masculinity in a certain pose which avoids objectivation/feminisation and secondly, these pictures can be read as a nostalgic reaction to the discourse of imperial decline and changing gender relations at the turn of the century.

From the beginning, the fascination with the British empire was reliant on the visual representation of this vast geographic territory and its various 'exotic' inhabitants – in its height it covered one quarter of the world's surface and counted more than 340 million inhabitants. The East India Company trained its employees to use the camera in order to document the steady rise of this territory:

The East India Company developed a style of photography which was documentary, recording military expeditions as well as topographical surveys, public works projects, famine relief works, archaeological surveys and diplomatic embassy commissions. (Worswick and Embree (ed.) 1976, 5)

Coinciding with the new emphasis on biological explanations of racial difference, photography became the visual medium of the turn of the century that was used to 'prove' these differences. Dyer writes, "photography was the means for both scrutinising human physiognomy and demonstrating variations (and superiorities/inferiorities) in human types" (Dyer 1997, 105). In this context, Worswick and Embree discuss the connections of the rise of commercial photography and the large-scale ethnographic eight-volume project *The People of India* which was edited by John Forbes Watson and John William Kaye (1868–1875) and supposedly provided 'visual proof' of various types and races.

When the publication […] was completed, the volumes contained 468 photographs and had the distinction of being one of the first major ethnographic studies produced by the camera. (Worswick and Embree (ed.) 1976, 7)

Initially, providing the British public with these much sought images was still a venture that was reserved to those who were part of the military imperial apparatus and that is why Hershkovitz speaks of the "the photographer as artist-hero" (Hershkovitz 1980, 88) in this period.[86] The first colonial photographers were considered chroniclers of progress rather than independent artists and the discussion whether photography was to be considered an art form was only begun at a later time. (cf. Kemp 1980; Newhall 1964, 97–110)

In general, the literature on colonial photography has largely focused on the representation of the 'Other', especially in the context of ethnography, the World's Fairs or the Orientalist stereotypes in colonial postcards (cf. Edwards 1992; Förschler 2005; Hight and Sampson (ed.) 2002; Maxwell 1999; Stam and Spence 1999), while the visual production of the 'self' often only comes second.[87] Similarly, in discussions of visual codes it is usually the eroticised depiction of the female body that has been at the centre of attention.[88] Psychoanalytic film theory has utilised the term "male gaze" (cf. Mulvey 1997) as a means to theorise these gendered looking relations – and this will be expounded upon in greater length in the chapters in which I discuss postcolonial British films. While there have been attempts to analyse visual regimes of both gendered and racialised 'Otherness', the interdependence between the two was, until more recently, rarely the centre of attention. Already in 1988, Jane Gaines formulates this critique in her essay, "White Privilege and Looking Relations", where she

---

86 But even up to the eighties collections such as Jan Morris' *The Spectacle of Empire* (1982) were still generally celebrative of the empire's 'fine features' such as fair play and bravery and as a result, it includes nostalgic pictures of the opulence of Indian elephants and the like, while downplaying racism and violence connected to imperial rule.

87 The anthology *Weiße Blicke* (Schmidt-Linsenhoff, Hölz and Uerlings (ed.) 2004), focuses on White self-construction through the appropriation of 'Otherness' and racialised looking relations. That is why the visual (self-)representation of White masculinity is not a primary focus of the collection with the exception of Birgit Haehnel's contribution which analyses the construction of the desert as an arena of 'authentic masculinity'. However, her visual repertoire consists of landscape painting and not photography.

88 However, there have also been discussions of the male body as a spectacle – often in advertising or as part of gay imagery, where the naked or semi-naked male body can increasingly become an eroticised spectacle as well. (cf. Neale 1992; Solomon-Godeau 1997)

points out the missing analysis of race in many feminist theories of the gaze.[89] Ann Kaplan responds to this criticism in her book *Looking for the Other* and examines interracial looking relations in films about travelling. Here she employs the term "imperial gaze" which she defines as "gaze structures specific to representing the ethnic Other [...] and the colonial habits of thought that underlie this gaze" (E.A. Kaplan 1997, 60). Although I analyse photography and not film here, the term "imperial gaze" seems fruitful to describe what Stuart Hall has called a "regime of representation" which shapes gendered and racialised looking relations in the colonial sphere. According to his Foucauldian analysis of power and knowledge in looking relations, "the whole repertoire of imagery and visual effects through which 'difference' is represented at any one historical moment [can be described] as a *regime of representation*" (Hall 1997a, 232). Such a conception of regimes of representation or the notion of the cultural screen, which Kaja Silverman proposes and which I will come back to in the course of the chapter, understand imagery and looking relations as historically and regionally encoded rather than postulate intrinsic and unchanging gendered and racialised conceptions of 'the gaze' for which psychoanalytic gaze theories have come under scrutiny.

Figuratively speaking then, this chapter is concerned with changing the direction of the "imperial gaze" and looking at the construction of the 'self' in a specific context. Hall has coined the phrase of the "spectacle of the 'Other'" in order to describe the Western urge to look at Black and other racialised bodies. This spectacle of the 'Other' relies on negative racial stereotyping which "reduces, essentializes, naturalizes and fixes 'difference'" (Hall 1997a, 258). Part of this fixing of difference is also positive stereotyping connected to the fetishising/sexualising of the 'Other' body. However, in order to fix difference, as Hall says, "typing" is also involved in the representation of the 'self', and the popular images of heroic White masculinity contributed to a large degree to this spectacle of the 'self'. These types, such as the hunter, which will be discussed later, are recurring patterns in the spectacular staging of White bodies in colonial photography and become part of the visual representation of the empire at the turn of the last century.

McClintock characterises this visual colonial spectacle in the following terms:

---

89 bell hooks, too, emphasises these shortcomings in theories of the gaze in her chapter "The Oppositional Gaze" in *Black Looks* (hooks 1992, 115–131).

Victorian forms of advertising and photography, the imperial Expositions and the museum movement – converted the narrative of imperial Progress into mass-produced consumer spectacles. (McClintock 1995, 33)

With reference to Foucault's concept of the disciplinary gaze, Tony Bennett examines the expansion of this regime of spectatorship which revolves around what he calls "the exhibitionary complex". In the growing spectacle of museums and exhibitions a new 'we' that was constituted by looking at 'foreign' objects and bodies was established as a counterweight to the practices of surveillance that Foucault describes, and in this way "provided a context for the *permanent* display of power/knowledge" (Bennett 1988, 79, original emphasis). Hence, while photography and other exhibitionary practices, were employed to visualise and prove 'abnormality'[90], as has often been noted, this visual spectacle was also employed to highlight and produce the assumed grandeur of White masculinity that found a growing audience at the beginning of the twentieth century. However, this photography of the norm had to follow other staging conventions. While the 'Other' body is objectified, the manly body must retain his subject status in the shot. There is a crisis of masculinity implicit in the act of becoming the object of the camera that has to be transformed and avoided.

Roland Barthes speaks of the desire to pose once one is aware that a picture is going to be taken: "I transform myself in advance into an image. This transformation is an active one: I feel that the Photograph creates my body or mortifies it [...]." (Barthes 1994, 10) Consequently, this transformation of oneself into an image is linked to losing one's sense of self and is compared to death by Barthes. In this way, the pose can function as both exaltation or objectification. (cf. Braun 2001) In accordance, Sekula calls photography "a system of representation capable of functioning both *honorifically* and *repressively* [...]" (Sekula 1986, 6, original emphasis). While photography "mortifies", in Barthes' terminology, it also provides "for the ceremonial presentation of the bourgeois self" (Sekula 1986, 6). However, this notion of 'death' or objectification is especially problematic in association with the representation of masculinity and remains highly ambiguous, and in order to achieve a visual language that works "honorifically" rather than "repressively" certain rules must be adhered. Accordingly, as Patricia

---

90 In addition to the depiction of 'exotic' types abroad any form of deviance, such as ill and 'mad' people as well as criminals at home quickly became the object of this 'scientific look' of the camera. Cf. Sekula (1986) for the importance of police photography in this context.

Vettel-Becker maintains, it follows from the conventional understanding of photography that "to objectify the body is to feminize it. Consequently, the male body must be inscribed with ritual frameworks of masculine-coded violence, such as war, sports, crime, gunfighting, and cattle roping." (Vettel-Becker 2005, 118) In this sense, photography of hegemonic masculinity must attempt to contain the crisis of objectification by focusing on a 'manly' display of capability often enhanced by the display of 'props', such as guns.

Despite these arguments for a need to counter feminisation by adopting certain poses of successful masculinity, there is also another aspect of why the spectacle of the 'self' flourished at the turn of the century. If one were to follow the strict and binary logic that the objectified body that is shot is *always* feminised *per se*, it would become increasingly hard to account for the male desire to have one's picture taken and one risks re-inscribing an essentialist (bi)gendered logic into looking relations and the medium itself.[91] Thus, while one can agree that there have been cultural codes that have fostered and privileged the objectification of the female body in photography, there is also a visual fashioning of masculinity that turns having one's picture taken into a desirable position. Therefore, I understand photography and other visual media as cultural practices and part of the historical and culturally specific production of gendered, racialised and sexualised looking relations that are not inherent in the medium. (cf. Gestrich 2008) In line with this understanding, David Bate has argued convincingly to be more skeptical of this clear opposition of the 'masculine' position of the bearer of the gaze and the juxtaposed position of the 'feminine' object of the gaze. Bate maintains that colonial photography becomes the site of a new male "colonial fantasy" in which not the object of the picture is eroticised/feminised but the picture itself; having one's picture taken as a successful hunter, for instance, becomes the site of desire:

The look is to court the scopic drive as a site of desire where the spectator may occupy a multiplicity of positions in relation to the image: as subject, object or outside of the camera's look. The photograph, then is the setting not the object of desire. […] [A] spectator's imaginary identification might very well be with the subject of the photograph as self-image. (Bate 1993, 90)

---

91 In a work that focuses on FtM-transgender photography, Anson Koch-Rein (2006) has described the mechanisms by which photographic conventions can also be employed and queered to establish powerful images of trans masculinities.

In this way, there is a desire for a spectacle of the 'self'.[92] Masculinity must not be presented as an eroticised object of the gaze; it must represent itself as authoritatively in control, which influences the visual imagery immensely. Gaines emphasises privilege with regard to axes of the gaze and explains how the privilege of looking is connected to Whiteness, what she calls a "licence to 'look' openly" (Gaines 1988, 24). I would add that White male privilege is also connected to the notion of being looked at without becoming objectified. In the colonial pose there is an urge to self-fashion oneself as the spectacular centre of the image in a way that allows White masculinity to look *and* be looked at.

Visual imagery can be understood as part of what Silverman calls the cultural screen. In her understanding, the screen functions as a cultural existing "image-repertoire". It limits "what is at a given moment representationally 'possible.'" (Silverman 1996, 204) It shapes the understanding of hegemonic masculinity and conversely what images of masculinity become available. "How we are 'photographed,' and the terms under which we experience our specularity, are the result of another agency altogether, as are the values which we impute to the gaze. They are the result of the cultural screen." (ibid., 168) Moreover, those coordinates of the cultural screen that are culturally dominant are "given-to-be-seen" (ibid., 221). The spectacle of the 'self' stages what is 'supposedly already there': White male supremacy, and in this way the pose of successful colonial masculinity becomes part of the most recurring narrative patterns, or "dominant fictions" (ibid., 178). The specificity of the medium confers the photographic image with the promise of subjectivity and selfhood while also implying the very ephemeral nature of this status:

Whereas the moving image consigns what it depicts to oblivion, the still photograph gives us access to a stable and durable image of self. [...] The still camera simultaneously 'kills' and affirms; it lifts the object out of life and into representation, and psychically and socially actualizes it. (ibid., 198–199)

92 Despite the fact that these photographs implied a White audience, Whiteness can also become a spectacle of 'Otherness' from a Black standpoint as bell hooks has argued. (cf. "Representations of Whiteness" in *Black Looks* (hooks 1992, 165–178)) By emphasising this, hooks points out that it is the assumed privilege of universality that renders it so hard, in the words of Dyer, to make "whiteness strange" (Dyer 1997, 4). It is this privilege of universality that works in these photographs: Although they are the object of the photograph, the men in the staging of their heroic masculinity attempt to remain successful subjects and not the objectified aberration from subjectivity.

Accordingly, the pose, as an aspiration to the cultural ideal, bestows subjectivity while implying failure as well, as I will point out in the reading of the specific images.

In contrast to narrative fiction and especially the escapist hyperbolical adventure stories that have been at the centre of attention of the previous chapter and which clearly incorporated the element of the fantastic, the medium of photography is still linked to the idea of authenticity and evidence – the depiction of the 'real'. Despite the fact that photographs were manipulated from the medium's earliest stages, pictures are still widely seen as a proof that something 'really' has happened. Most prominently, Barthes has theorised this when he writes:

> Painting can feign reality without having seen it. Discourse combines signs which have referents, of course, but these referents can be and are most often 'chimeras.' Contrary to these imitations, in Photography I can never deny that *the thing has been there*. (Barthes 1994, 76, original emphasis)

In the context of emerging photojournalism, Beaumont Newhall introduces the idea of the photographer as the "faithful witness". Roger Fenton, one of the first war photographers during the Crimean War in 1855, as well as James Robertson and Felice Beato, who took pictures of the aftermath of the siege of Lucknow in 1858, became photojournalist pioneers. News coverage suddenly included imagery from all over the world. (cf. Newhall 1964, 67) Understood in this way, the prospering photographic journalism becomes the witness and proof of White men's ability and achievement to enter and control 'foreign' territories, peoples and animals. This imperial pretence is seen by Susan Sontag as constitutive of the medium: "There is an aggression implicit in every use of the camera. […] From its start, photography implied the capture of the largest possible number of subjects. Painting never had so imperial a scope." (Sontag 2001, 7) Mass pictorial journalism contributed to Britain's self-understanding as the leading imperial power at the turn of the twentieth century. In this sense, these pictures were both part of the technical advances and the growing ephemeral information industries at the turn of the century and had a continued effect on the cultural image-repertoire of how a 'real' man was to appear.

The Illustrated London News was the world's first ever illustrated weekly newspaper that offered engravings of current events and later one of the first newspapers that championed the photographic half-tone process.[93] Up until then mainly wood engravings were used as illustrations in newspapers and were produced from photographs. (cf. Newhall 1964, 176) However, the amelioration and changing or editing of unwanted details was a regular part of creating the drawings from the pictures. Therefore, it is explicitly photography and not the also popular illustrations or advertisements[94] that are discussed here as they do not have the specific 'verifying' qualities of photography that I have mentioned.

With the professional evolution of pictorial journalism, the visual repertoire of heroic White British masculinity whose 'accomplishments' were represented became accessible to large audiences in Britain. This new visual presence brought the empire 'back home' with extended coverage on Britain's imperial campaigns all over the world. Within a year of its first publication in 1842, the circulation of the ILN, at a price of sixpence, had risen to 60,000 and by 1856 had reached 200,000.[95] Among the authors for the newspaper were such illustrious literary names as Robert Louis Stevenson, Thomas Hardy, Joseph Conrad, Arthur Conan Doyle and Rudyard Kipling, which calls to mind some of the colonial writing that is the focus of other chapters in this section.

When writing about photography, there is no implicit 'correct reading' of a picture as its meaning always remains highly ambiguous and subjective. There is no concomitant narrative in a picture in its own right, and the meaning of it can easily be manipulated according to the context in which it is placed. However, regarding the interpretation of pictures, Hall employs the term "preferred meaning" (cf. Hall 1997a, 228), which bears resemblance to Silverman's aforementioned concept of "dominant fictions". This type of reading largely depends on the context of a picture presented as captions, texts surrounding the image, placement etc. Of course, this meaning can also evolve over time. In my reading of colonial pictures, I will focus on the depicted body, the pose and clothing, while

---

93 Due to this popularity *The Illustrated London News* is the source for most of the pictures discussed in this chapter while some are also taken from the resource *Pictures of Empire*, which is the online collection of the British Empire and Commonwealth Museum.

94 For an analysis of Victorian advertisement and racial stereotypes, cf. Hall (1997a, 239–249); McClintock (1995, 207–231).

95 Facts regarding the history of *The Illustrated London News* are taken from the website of the ILN Picture Library: <http://www.ilnpictures.co.uk/> (accessed 01 October 2007) which is no longer available. The ILN Picture Library itself is now included in the Mary Evans Picture Library.

also paying attention to the original captions and in this sense try to reconstruct how 'heroic' masculinity as a preferred meaning was implied in the staging of these pictures. Moreover, I will try to emphasise the more ambivalent aspects that this self-fashioning or spectacle of the 'self' entails.

The cultural construction of masculinity depends on patterns that differ in narratives and visual representations. Even though I highlight this difference here, I will continue to employ the term narrative patterns. Visual representations are part of an archive that informs the discourse of masculinity in crisis, and photography is often embedded in narrative contexts. "In general, it is patterns in the photographs that are being looked for, evidence of repeated visual conventions whose implications can then be assessed." (Scherer 1992, 35) Furthermore, James Ryan writes in his seminal study, *Picturing Empire*: "It is this narrative component of photographs; their relation to other images and texts, both visual and verbal, just as much as their contents, which determines their meanings." (Ryan 1997, 225)[96]

I will focus my discussion on two specific narrative patterns: firstly, *heroic hunters* and secondly, on a group of pictures which depict what I have called *establishing order.*[97] These pictures in a sense fall into two different genres: the staged shot of the hunter and his prey and the more documentary shot of "work in the colonies" mostly taken during military campaigns. However, all images clearly stage the depicted men as keeping their poise while mastering difficult and dangerous situations. Similar to Haggard's adventure novels, these pictures seem to attest to heroic unfailing masculinities that are not connected to the discourse of the crisis of masculinity at first glance. However, as I explained, by becoming the object of the shot, there is also a risk involved of being objectified. Therefore, the visual code that is needed to highlight the poise of White masculinity is reliant on the pose of the hunter, the spotless white clothes or the attributions of

---

96 The relationship between text and photograph is intertwined in the process of creating meaning as both feed back into each other: "Thus the photograph elevated the credibility of the narrative, while the narrative, in turn, reinforced the preconceived notions that were to be illuminated through gazing at the accompanying images." (Harris 1998, 22)

97 I explicitly exclude ethnographic and scientific imagery as well as pictures that have been used in anthropometric contexts (cf. Edwards 1992; Maxwell 1999) which worked in the construction of 'different races' but which also have drawn a fair amount of critical attention. Landscape photography (cf. "Framing the View" in Ryan (1997, 45–72)), too is excluded as the focus is on (journalistic) imagery of the White male body in the colonial setting.

civilisation in the 'wilderness'. Even if these images are seen as 'truthful' presentation of 'life in the colonies', White masculinity works as a frozen pose. Relating back to Barthes's thoughts on 'death', they can then also be seen as implying the decline of the pictured ideal – an image that has been, an image of the past.

Heroic Hunters

With his book *The Empire of Nature*, John MacKenzie has provided the most useful study on the history of the 'Hunt in Britain' to date. He not only traces the historical roots of the hunting cult back to ancient times, he also recognises hunting as a pursuit that glorified masculinity.[98] Hunting as a civilised pastime of an elite ruling class followed strict rituals and was clearly set apart from the unadorned killing of animals for human consumption. "The 'sporting code' was a crucial identifier not only of the ruling race but of class, training and breeding within that race." (MacKenzie 1987, 183) The hunt was not undertaken primarily for the meat but for trophies, although a diet including a lot of meat was seen as the privilege of the hunter. Hunting was first glorified in the Romantic period and later came to influence Victorian decoration styles when the display of trophies became immensely popular. The connected practice of taxidermy formed the basis of today's natural history museums but also zoology and later wildlife preservation policies are connected to the history of the hunt.[99] Both hunting and the scientific display of animals were, however, intertwined with colonial endeavours and often coincided with the infamous 'ethnic shows', where people from various colonial backgrounds were displayed as part of exhibitions. Many of the individuals who were dis-

---

98 In the late nineteenth and early twentieth century, women were largely not present during (imperial) hunts although there were exceptions. However, when women took part they were seen as crossing some sort of border. "The Hunt has always been a masculine affair, though there has never been any taboo, in Europe at least, on high-born women being present as spectators as well as, occasionally participants. [...] Many hunters stressed the fact that the imperial hunt was no place for [...] women, though some women did participate and some turned it into a powerful expression of female emancipation of sorts." (MacKenzie 1987, 179)

99 Cf. "It was indeed that scientific dimension, the acquisition of zoological, botanical, meteorological and ballistic knowledge, and the associated ordering and classifying of natural phenomena which helped to give hunting its supreme acceptability among late Victorians." (MacKenzie 1988, 51)

played in these shows died due to maltreatment and/or the contracting of diseases from Europeans. (cf. Edwards 1992)

Hunting pictures from the colonies usually show orderly men in their hunting gear presenting their trophies and directly facing the camera. These images in many respects remind one of the stories of Haggard with his big game hunter hero Allan Quatermain.[100] When talking about hunting imagery, the analogy of gun and camera comes to mind immediately. The prey can be hunted and 'shot' as the double meaning of the word underlines either by the camera or by the gun. Other connections, such as 'pulling the trigger', come to mind. With regard to this analogy, Sontag states:

> The camera/gun does not kill, so the ominous metaphor seems to be all bluff – like a man's fantasy of having a gun, knife, or tool between his legs. Still, there is something predatory in the act of taking a picture. [...] [I]t turns people into objects that can be symbolically possessed. (Sontag 2001, 14)

However, possessing a picture of oneself killing something else might also be seen as a very powerful subject position. As I explained initially, the object of desire then is not so much the object of the shot but the shot of oneself as a successful hunter itself becomes the object of desire. "[H]unts began to be undertaken primarily for purposes of photography."[101] (Ryan 1997, 100) So that increasingly, the image itself, more than the animal, becomes the prey. "Photography is a special prey: it does not kill, quite the opposite it provides new life to the shot subject and only in the picture provides him with a voice." (Stiegler 2006, 52, my translation) As a result, the hunter becomes the active subject, embodying a manly colonial ideal.[102]

In plate one, the perspective of the riflemen is almost matched by the position of the camera behind the men's backs. The invisible prey is in effect aimed at by the gun as well as by the camera which directs its look right between the shoulders of the two huntsmen who take aim in the front of the boat. The viewer becomes a first-person witness of the immi-

---

100 MacKenzie points out that the real life model for Quatermain was the famous hunter F.C. Selous. (cf. MacKenzie 1987, 191) For a discussion of the role of hunting in Haggard's *She*, cf. Madhudaya Sinha (2008).

101 Later even, the original hunting safari is replaced entirely by the still popular photo safari. (cf. Sontag 2001, 15)

102 As Dietze (2006) has pointed out, it seems as if instead of the big game hunter today's visual (post)colonial fantasies are based on the image of the 'heroic' environmental activist protecting endangered wild life often in a visual code similar to the one discussed here and currently very prominent in German TV productions.

nent shot while the backs of the hunters are included in the framing. The hunt is for the animal (a hippopotamus as the caption explains) but also for the best shot that demonstrates the men's ability and control. This photograph captures the strain and expectation during a hunt. Everything is still possible: the animal might escape or even attack the men of whom we only see their backs. So in a sense, this picture as an 'action shot' departs from the more common pose of the successful hunter next to the already killed prey. The three men (one of whom is only partly visible in the frame) are not individualised heroes. We do not see their faces or learn their names in the caption. Nonetheless, they embody colonial masculinity as an abstract concept; their pith helmets and jackets are as prominent as their rifles – a sign of their eagerness and virility – and part of the visual code that denotes colonial masculinity.

Plate 1: Shooting Hippopotamus On Lake Victoria
Original Caption: "Victoria Nyanza Shooting Hippos From Launch"
Date: 1906

In its attempt to capture the action of the kill, the image reveals detail while anything surrounding the hunters is excluded. The colonies become devoid of other (non-White) people – who were most likely present as hunting auxiliaries on the boat –, and the life in the colonies is depicted as a confrontation of the neatly clothed and well-equipped White man with nature in an 'empty' land whose nature he is about to tame or kill.

In contrast to this 'action shot', the big game hunter posing next to his dead prey becomes one of the most recurring and stereotypical images of colonial masculinity and shows the accomplished deed. In terms of aesthetics, these pictures are clearly characterised by adopted frozen poses. The eighteen-nineties were shaped by radical improvements in film and paper as well as optical lenses, and especially the invention of dry plates, which made it possible to greatly reduce exposure times and produce finely detailed images. (cf. Newhall 1964, 85–93) Nevertheless, the easy to use Kodak hand camera only found wide distribution after World War I (which also initiated widespread amateur photography). (cf. Sachsse 2003, 71–73) Before World War I, the cameras used for press photography still required a fixed underground. These cameras normally had to be mounted to a tripod, which usually a 'native' auxiliary had to carry, and despite the reduced exposure times, the pictures required careful control and composition. For these reasons, these images cannot be compared to quickly taken snapshots. Press photographers at that time had already professionalised in the sense that they worked for agencies, which sold their pictures to the magazines. They accompanied expeditions, soldiers and prominent politicians around the world during their colonial missions in 'hunt' for their prey of the spectacle of the 'self' which would then be sold to consumers in Britain.[103]

These hunting stories – often presented as a series of several photographs documenting different stages of the hunt – regularly feature prominent colonial leaders. On plate two and three, the then current viceroy of India is depicted during his hunting trip, which was considered a newsworthy item and worth the effort to have photographers (and their heavy equipment) accompany the trip. The captions in both cases point to the connection of political leadership and success as a hunter. Especially the original page heading of plate two, "As Well And As Strong As Ever: The Viceroy of India Shooting", is to underscore the association of an able hunter with a successful leader. The picture shows Lord Hardinge (viceroy of India 1910–1916) kneeling down to inspect a buck he shot. He is sur-

---

103 I have included information on the photographer/agency when this information was available, which is not always the case in the pictures from the ILN at the time.

rounded both by White and 'native' members of the hunt who are kept at a respectful distance surrounding the victorious huntsman, which essentially acts as a frame for the viceroy and his prey at the centre of this photograph.

Plate 2: Original Caption: Examining Part Of The Bag: Inspecting A Buck Shot By Lord Hardinge
Original Page Heading: "As Well And As Strong As Ever: The Viceroy of India Shooting"

The Illustrated London News, Nov 29, 1913, p. 882
Photographs by Herzog and Higgins
Detail from a Series of Photographs

This *mis-en-scène* is to also cast away any doubt which man might have been the successful shooter. But despite this strategy of 'verifying' the event by posing next to the dead animal, the picture is, of course, by no means proof of the actual deed of killing it. The text states that there has been rumour of Lord Hardinge's retirement due to his failing physical health after an unspecified bomb attempt on his life, which refers to the attack by the so-called "Indian revolutionary underground" which took place 23 December 1912 on the occasion of the transfer of the capital of British India from Calcutta to New Delhi. A crisis in colonial leadership is hence present in the text but rigorously absent in the imagery, which is used to counter these rumours of weakness. Accordingly, the accompanying text passage reads: "Such photographs as these, which show the Viceroy on sport intent, seem to go a good way to prove that his Excellency is at last not particularly unfit." Although not entirely convincing, the pictures are at least seen as possible proof of fit rule despite other indications. Successful political leadership is transferred to the visual spectacle of hunting, and pictures such as these become part of a visual repertoire to ensure manly colonial composure despite crisis tendencies in colonial rule.

Plate three documents an even more impressive tiger hunt, or *shikar*, and again features the most important shot of the series, the individualised hero next to his prey in the central position. Interestingly, this detail seems to be a drawn illustration[104] based on the photograph printed to the right (number five), where the viceroy is still surrounded by a number of other men whose faces are indiscernible. But in the successful extraction in the middle piece, his individuality is more pronounced; he holds his gun stretched out a little further to the left than on the photograph and has enough space to prove his individualised achievement, which, as the photograph shows, involved the work of several White members of the expedition and even more 'native' helpers. The series of pictures on plate three includes different stages of the hunt. First, the equipment needs to be transported laboriously to the place of action; pictures one, two and six depict this effort. Picture three in the series is of special interest, as it represents the typical refinement of the imperial hunt. It shows the leisurely posture of the hunters sitting on chairs in front of a lavishly filled lunch table or lying smoking in the middle of the wilderness, while being waited on by the 'native' servants, sparing no effort, the table is even decorated with a white tablecloth.

---

104 There is only a reference to the photographers of the series and the caption for this picture does not specify this image as a drawing or the name of an artist. But the extraction from the background and especially the 'sketchy' quality of the tiger, suggest that it is, in fact, an illustration.

Plate 3: Original Page Heading: "Lord Curzon As Sportsman: The Returned Viceroy On A Tiger-Hunt"
Caption 1: The Guns Crossing A River Bed
Caption 2: The Jungle Folk Keeping Cool At Midday
Caption 3: Tiffin
Caption 4: Lord Curzon And One Of His Trophies
Caption 5: Lord Curzon And Party At The Shikar, Or Tiger-Hunt
Caption 6: The Guns Entering the Jungle
Caption 7: Waiting for the Tiger

The Illustrated London News, June 04, 1904, p. 843
Photographs by Johnston and Hoffman, Calcutta

This achievement of civilised refinement proves to be almost as admirable as the successful kill. What is rendered out of frame is the effort that this undertaking entailed. The White men can lie back as they do not have to do any of the menial carrying, which sets their sport clearly apart from the need to kill for a living: The "'sporting' hunter diverged from the native hunters whom he invariably used as his auxiliaries" (MacKenzie 1987, 183). It is the White hunter in his nearly always spotless white clothes and pith helmet who is at the centre of attention. Black bodies are de-individualised, and this is part of the visual strategy of re-centring and individualising the needed White masculinity.[105] The hunter had to be presented in the right light, and whenever 'natives' are present, they are merely ornamental or serving and assisting the White man. Their part in the hunting mission is not acknowledged and their efforts rendered invisible, often literally out of frame or pushed to the margins of the frame.

The *shikar* of the viceroy, in particular, was seen as a symbolic display of the strength of the Raj, which at the time was already challenged by the emergent militant Indian nationalism. Nonetheless, the original page heading "Lord Curzon As Sportsman: The Returned Viceroy On A Tiger-Hunt" promotes an image of undisturbed British rule over India, and there is no text accompanying this series except for the page heading and captions. Lord Curzon (viceroy of India 1898–1905) is presented as successful sportsman – a staging of virile political leadership. A lurking crisis of imperial power was visually contested in this display of manly sportsmanship. "The adoption of a codified shikar was important to imperial display and the myth of power. This too required that indigenous hunting was frustrated." (MacKenzie 1988, 303) Keith Booker explains that, rather paradoxically, there existed nostalgia for 'innocent rule' by the colonial leaders already during this time of British rule which he posits is related to the theatricality of the Raj with its lavish visual displays of colonial might.

After all, the official beginning of this empire can be placed at the post-Mutiny transfer of colonial India to direct British government control, a move already informed by nostalgic visions of colonial innocence prior to the violence of the Mutiny. (Booker 1997, 171)

---

105 Another aspect pertains to privilege on the level of the medium itself. Photography has been called the medium of light and Dyer analyses how Whiteness was already privileged in the earliest stages of the development of the medium. "[P]hoto and film apparatuses have seemed to work better with light-skinned people, but that is because they were made that way, not because they could be no other way." (Dyer 1997, 90)

So while Curzon ruled at a time when the Indian national movement started to gain momentum, these pictures of the Raj are marked by an increased theatricality of virile colonial masculinity, and herein, one can detect the visual answer to a crisis in colonial rule that was especially felt at the close of the nineteenth century.[106] Here a visual stabilising strategy is at work: colonial unrest and political turmoil are not depicted, yet, an undisturbed colonial officer in the wildlife is. It is especially the spectacular nature, rather than the people, in the colonies that provides the perfect backdrop to stage colonial masculinity.[107] The containment of crisis can be linked to both the political context and the visual display of colonial masculinity in the pose of the hunter.

Similar to plates two and three, which point to the connection of successful gunmanship and political leadership, plate four shows the spectacle of the British monarch hunting. The King cannot only shoot foxes and deer in Scotland; he also partakes in a shikar in his colonies. "The Hunt, in short, constituted propaganda: it showed emperor, king, or lord exhibiting power, enjoying the privilege that went with it and asserting prestige within widespread territorial ground." (MacKenzie 1988, 10) The third Delhi Durbar of 1911, which was held to commemorate the coronation of a new emperor or empress of India, was the first at which the monarch was actually present. King George V not only came to visit 'his subjects', he also famously took part in a prominently staged and widely covered[108] hunt in Nepal following the coronation.

The intent of the picture is to frame the glorious political leadership by portraying the king shooting from atop an elephant.[109] However, aristocratic masculinity is staged as so refined that, in effect, the manliness is presented rather ambivalently. The visibility of assistance, on the one hand, points to his aristocratic privilege of not 'dirtying' his hands with the menial work. He holds the power that allows him to act without having to move: *rex non pugnat*. On the other hand, it implies a certain lack of manly

---

106 Wurgaft (1983), for instance, explains that Curzon's unsuccessful attempt to divide the Punjab in effect strengthened 'native' resistance.

107 Mary Louise Pratt has called this spectacular staging of nature in travel literature the "monarch-of-all-I-survey scene" (Pratt 1992, 205).

108 The Durbar itself was turned into a silent film titled *With Our King and Queen through India* filmed in the early colour process Kinemacolor and was released on 2 February 1912.

109 According to the information provided by *Images of Empire*, this picture is taken from an album of official photographs of the royal tour, many of which were reproduced in John Fortescue's *Narrative of the Visit to India of King George V and Queen Mary* (1912).

ability that usually characterises the hunter. The three 'native' auxiliaries, visually clearly set apart by their turbans, are outside of the howdah and lead the animal and only a correctly dressed White Englishman can be shown in the very proximity of the monarch. The White man in the back of the howdah assists the king in reloading his rifle and has to stretch out his arm all the way in order to insert the bullet.

Plate 4: Assisting King George V
Original Caption: "Loading."
Date: 1911

The spectacle again is not so much the killing of the animals but the pompous display of colonial splendour that can only be found outside of England in the colonial space. The public can marvel at their monarch on top of an elephant, who allegedly shot twenty-one tigers during this trip. It is this 'exoticness' of the setting, the foreign wildlife, but also the 'correctness' of this display that attests to colonial grandeur. The demure servants of empire, the royal emblem and initials on the howdah and the clothes all add to this staged effect. On other pictures of the hunt, more elephants carrying other members of the expedition as well as journalists and photographers are visible. In this shot, an outstretched arm of another member of the hunt can be seen on the left of the frame, and the shadow on the howdah in this picture might actually be the shadow of the photographer who took this picture. Hence while the visual strategy of the photograph is to display the monarch hunting in the 'wilderness', the 'civilised' technical effort to stage this spectacle is reinserted in the picture.

These photographs of various hunters at first sight figure as a rather undisturbed spectacle of the 'self' and, as has been noted, are reliant on visual strategies that turn the images themselves into 'proof' of the manly ability of the depicted subject. This strategy can be linked to both the crisis of colonial rule in the colonies but also the crisis of masculinity in more general terms since masculinity 'at home' was more challenged than the imperial spectacle suggested. Ryan explains that "the domestic and the imperial were interlinked through practices of representation" (Ryan 1997, 174). He elaborates that

[t]he rise of big-game hunting on the outskirts of Empire, and its presentation as a manly occupation, might thus be partly seen as one response to the increasingly assertive visibility of particular groups of women in late Victorian society, notably the suffragettes. Many hunters celebrated the 'outdoor life as absolute freedom' as a refuge not only from modern, industrial Britain but also from women. (ibid., 110)

The colonial space becomes the site of a visual stabilising of colonial masculinity in crisis, a crisis that is felt from political turmoil in the colonies and also the challenges of modernity and changing gender conceptions at home. The photograph as a medium is employed as a visual proof to contain or counter these crisis tendencies and re-privilege masculinity as an unchallenged norm by its inclusion in illustrated newspapers. The crisis paradoxically becomes the occasion to re-assert a manly ideal and in this sense can be connected to privilege. For this purpose, the colonial setting is often imagined as an empty space, one that is contrasted to the urban and crowded metropolis of London. Whereas Britain is more and more industrialised, women demand their right to public participation, and the empire is challenged, these pictures purport a nostalgic image of successful hunters and political leaders. This ability to uphold moral and political refinement is also visually present and points to the second narrative pattern of *establishing order.*

Establishing Order

While the images of the imperial hunter often depict the splendour of the empty imperial landscape and focus on exotic animals, the image of the gentlemanly soldier demands slightly different staging conventions. Photographers also accompanied military campaigns in order to document Britain's success in 'bringing civilisation' to the remote spaces of its empire. Rather than focusing on an individualised hero, it is the ability to establish order and master difficult situations in distant and inhospitable places all over the world that marks the manly achievement, which finds documentation in these 'shots from the front'.

Plate five is part of a series that documents the building of a bridge in Southern Nigeria. According to the text, this is the first bridge in the "hitherto unexplored country". The newness and emptiness of the territory again needs to be emphasised. The British are not taking land away; they are the first to really cultivate and make the most of the natural resources that the 'natives' ignorantly have left undeveloped. The scene depicts two White British officers monitoring the barely discernable African workers in the middle of the picture. To the British officers' left and right, we also see 'native' soldiers superintending the labourers; one is standing behind a tree to the left while two more are sitting to the right, and one is holding a rifle, which underlines the military nature of this undertaking and the possible resistance of the workers who need to be held at gunpoint.

Plate 5: Original Caption: Officers Superintending The Making Of A Road Through The Bush
Original Page Heading: "Opposed By 'Doctored' Cannibals: The Mysterious Nigeria Expedition"

The Illustrated London News, Jan 30, 1909, p. 155
Photographs by a Member of the Expedition
Detail from a Series of Photographs

In the centre of the photograph a chair is seen, on which one of the White men is sitting. As I have argued so far, the display of accurate clothes and chairs and tables in these shots from the 'wilderness' function as fetishised 'props of civilisation'. Being part of the visual display, these objects and clothes are 'transformed' from their everyday meaning to the category of 'costume' and 'display' as Silverman explains:

The pose also includes within itself the category of 'costume,' since it is something 'worn' or 'assumed' by the body, which, in turn, transforms the other worn or assumed things into costumes. When included in the pose, even a sensible winter coat ceases to be a source of protection against the cold, and becomes part of the larger 'display.' (Silverman 1996, 203)

These props are not accidentally part of the scenery but become visual markers of refinement. The poor quality of the picture makes it hard to identify the faces of the men, and there are no names mentioned in the captions. In their posture, the men are clearly aware that they are being photographed. They pose for the camera. The one man standing faces the camera directly, while the other man sitting on the chair is turning his head sideways to face the camera. Once more, White bodies are centred, and Black bodies are pushed to the background and the margins of the frame. The White presence is normalised, and Black bodies only become the focus if their 'abnormality' or 'exoticness' is to be highlighted. These pictures underscore White rule. The White gaze controls the Black workers, and the gaze of the camera documents this imperial gaze asserting order.

Again, while the pictures stress the accomplishment of this control, the text explains that: "Opposition was expected from the Munshi, Okpoto, and Ibi tribes, all of them addicted to slave traffic and cannibalism." The White man's ability is staged in the picture; the Black man's 'depravity' of slave trafficking and cannibalism needs no visual proof. It is simply 'their nature' and again, cannibalism is one of the most recurring stereotypes to define 'Otherness'. In addition, the claim that the 'natives' had been "doctored for war" – as the page heading explains – depoliticises 'native' resistance and ascribes it to the evil sorcery, which the White man came to abolish. Popular journalism at the time can rely on ready-made conceptions and stereotypes about 'native depravity' and sensationalist references, in this case to cannibalism, which is in no way connected to the actual event in the image. The picture only shows the construction of the road and bridge. This sensationalist mood is furthered by the 'exotic' ameliorations that surround the whole series.

While White men can bring civilisation to these remote places all over the world, they have to be on guard not to lose their sense of control or 'go native'. Consequently, the emphasis on refinement and hygiene is not only present in the adventure novels, but it is also to be found in the visual representation of colonial masculinity. Plate six, again a picture taken from a series documenting a military operation in North Somalia (Somaliland), features a photograph entitled "A Campaigner's Toilet". Next to other shots which show the transportation of camels and other military equipment, this photograph, interestingly, is part of the military operation as well. The two men in the photograph are not splendid military heroes in glorious poses. Both men are sitting back-to-back, one on the ground and the other one on some sort of box. They are occupied with their travelling kit and are performing their daily toilet routine facing a mirror, possibly shaving with other equipment such as bottles lying on the ground. As I explained with reference to McClintock (1995), hygiene is seen as a central accomplishment that attests to White supremacy, and *The London Illustrated News* is full of advertising for the commodities of empire, such as soap and travellers' leather cases. This again underlines the links of colonialism and capitalism.

Plate 6: Original Caption: "A Campaigner's Toilet: Preparing To Enter Berbera"
Original Page Heading: "The British Expedition To Somaliland: Preparations For The Advance"

The Illustrated London News, Feb 21, 1903, p. 267
Detail from a Series of Photographs

Proper hygiene, the picture seems to suggest, is part of military success and as important as other stages in the campaign. The soldiers can still find the time to accomplish these routinely tasks which stabilise their 'civilised' status.

Plate seven also depicts Berbera in North Somalia. It was taken in the same year as plate six. In this series, pictures of the consulate, a hospital and a Röntgen ray apparatus are featured. Colonial masculinity is not only linked to the successful care of oneself, it is also associated with the care for others, and this recalls the idea of benevolence as a constitutive part in the construction of gentlemanly masculinity. British imperialism was always reliant on the notion of 'just rule', and the idea that only the one showing self-restraint was able to rule accurately and ideally without the exertion of cruelty and violence. It is this constraint and control which finds its expression in the pictures of the military campaigns. In plate seven, a soldier oversees the distribution of new saddlery to 'native' recruits.

Plate 7: Original Caption: "Issuing New Saddlery To Recruits For A Fresh Move Against The Mullah"
Original Page Heading: "The Operations In Somaliland: Scenes At Berbera"

The Illustrated London News, Aug 29, 1903, p. 311
Detail from a Series of Photographs

The commanding officer does not even have to carry a gun; he has an armed 'native soldier', whom he seems to instruct, standing to his left to attend to the recruits. The only White man in the picture is at the centre of the gaze, and he emanates control over the situation while the Black men follow his orders and tend to the menial labour. Whereas there clearly is a stronger Black presence in terms of numbers in this picture than in others, it is Whiteness that is centred and bestowed with the subjectivity to control the scene. The possible crisis of being a White minority in the same space with a majority of Black bodies, which implicitly also challenges White universality, is countered by the visual strategy of singling out these White bodies and bestowing them with subjectivity opposed to the de-individu-alised Black bodies. These function as a backdrop of the centred White man. It seems to be the air of 'natural authority' rather than violence or brute force that is a characteristic of this spectacle of White British control.

Plate eight is part of a series of photographs documenting the close of a victorious military campaign in Northern Nigeria. The accompanying text mentions that the town Burmi had successfully been attacked and most of the chiefs as well as seven hundred men had been killed while the town had almost been destroyed completely. The pictures, however, do not document these violent events or their after-effects at all, as one would expect from a journalistic coverage of a military campaign. Part of the series is a small round portrait commemorating Major Marsh, who died on the side of the British, and in this way, his subjectivity is established in opposition to the unnamed seven hundred dead on the side of the enemy. Instead of picturing the enemy, innocent pictures of street scenes and drawings of 'native dance' and 'fishing methods' are included. Characteris-tically, the British are depicted in their peaceful effort to establish order rather than in any actions connected to violence or warfare.

In plate eight, two White men are sitting on chairs with their backs to the camera and facing a crowd of 'natives' in a typical scene that denotes their capacity rule justly. As the caption explains, the acting high commis-sioner, Mr Wallace, proclaims a new emir. While one Black man is holding a document that probably entails the official appointment of the emir, the White men serve as witnesses of this civilising ritual. Their elevated posi-tion is firmly established as they are the only ones sitting on chairs which almost function as thrones in this context. The man on the left is wearing a more civilian outfit and a hat while the man on the right displays the colonial uniform and a pith helmet.

Plate 8: Original Caption: "Mr. Wallace [The Acting High Commissioner] Proclaiming A New Emir"
Original Page Heading: "The Close of the Campaign in Northern Nigeria"

The Illustrated London News, Aug 29, 1903, p. 310
Detail from a Series of Photographs

Again, it is this prominent display of clothes and props that turns this scene into a colonial spectacle of the 'self'. The viewer can identify with the elevated position of the White men as the White perspective is matched by the gaze of the camera in this photograph. The viewer can watch the crowd of crouching 'natives' through the shoulders of the men and imagine him- or herself in this elevated and benign position of bringing civilisation to the most remote places in the world.

This spectacle of the 'self' in many ways is connected to the larger discourse of masculinity in crisis and can be read as an attempt to re-centre White masculinity as an unchallenged position of subjectivity. Hence somewhat paradoxically and similar to the appeal of Haggard's adventure writing and the boom of the 'manly' imperial romance, the talk about the crisis of masculinity triggers an even greater demand for heroic images, and in this way, re-privileges White masculinity. These photographs are informed by nostalgia for 'manly' freedom. On the one hand, the colonial space serves a male arena uncontested by the 'domestic demands' of femininity or the suffragettes, and on the other hand, the 'empty' lands and wilderness of the colonies figures as an antidote to the increasing industrialisation in the urban metropolis.

These photographs become the object of colonial desire of both the depicted subjects but also a larger British audience that could partake in this nostalgic and ostentatious display of the spectacle of the 'self', which helped to hold on to the myth of White supremacy. This supremacy is in need of establishing an uncontested subject status and must manifest the difference between 'self' and 'Other', and in the spectacular staging of the 'self', it reaffirms the claim to universality once more.

Rudyard Kipling: The Ambivalence of Empire

In contrast to other authors of colonial fiction, Rudyard Kipling was born in the colonies and lived in India for an extended period of time. However, he was educated in boarding schools in England during what he considered an unhappy period of his life and in his youth, Kipling felt quite torn between his alleged home, Britain, and his actual home, 'British India'. Kipling can be considered a typical Anglo-Indian who even spoke Hindustani, and it is his ability to present insights into the 'native' ways of life that were considered one of his greatest literary achievements. In 1882, Kipling returned to India where he worked as a journalist for *The Civil and Military Gazette* in Lahore and *The Pioneer* in Allahabad. Seven years later, in 1889, he was able to settle in England – already a well-known writer of short stories, and was quickly able to establish his place in the literary circles of the time.[110] When he married his American wife, Caroline Balestier, the couple moved to the United States for a few years, but feeling unwelcome, they returned to Sussex in 1896. Kipling also travelled to South Africa before the Boer War and resided as a guest of Cecil Rhodes. There he wrote fervent articles in support of the British troops. In his fiction, Kipling combines the feeling of the privilege of the colonial class with a suffering from (self-afflicted) separation from 'home'. Like no other writer of empire, he is seen as capturing the ambivalent and painful processes of maturing estranged of one's own cultural background, a 'hardship' of the colonial class abroad. At the beginning of the twentieth century, this was also a declining class as the resistance to the empire in the colonies grew and the support for colonial expansion in Britain waned. Kipling "is a man projecting fantasies of omnipotence onto a world that bears less and less resemblance to his dream" (McClure 1981, 81). Despite the fact that Kipling was the first Englishman to be awarded the Nobel Prize in literature in 1907, his literary reputation suffered immensely during his lifetime. Kipling's fame abated from being considered the foremost chronicler of British India to being slightly ridiculed for his jingoistic attitudes towards the end of his life. Nicholas Daly calls this a fall "from Nobel Prize to children's author" (Daly 1999, 120) as it is his short stories, such as "Baa Baa,

---

110 During this time, Kipling and Haggard met which was at the height of Haggard's success when he was thirty-three and Kipling twenty-three. The two men established a close friendship that lasted until Haggard's death in 1925 (for the surviving letters, cf. M. Cohen (ed.) (1965)).

Black Sheep" and, of course, the *Jungle Books* for which he is remembered best today.

However, the novel *Kim* has been reassessed and has become a central reference point in postcolonial studies of empire, especially given Edward Said's renewed focus on the novel in his essay *"Kim*, The Pleasures of Imperialism" which was first published in 1987 and reprinted in *Culture and Imperialism* (1994). While many of the short stories adhere to the colonialist logic rather clearly, *Kim* is considered to be his most complex piece of longer writing, and therefore, it is the sole focus of this chapter that concerns itself with the question of ambivalence in the colonial encounter. It is especially Said's discussion of the notion of pleasure, but also the interest in ambivalence in light of Bhabha's later criticism, that makes *Kim* such an appealing object of study.[111] On the one hand, Kipling's text clearly privileges a model of hegemonic self-restraint which stabilises the coming of age into the right kind of British masculinity and is reliant on the continued recourse to Orientalist stereotypes. But, on the other hand, and in contrast to Haggard's adventurous African stories, which do not focus on a depiction of life in the colonies, Kipling is considered one of the first writers who presented a view from within that also captured the fascination with the 'Other's' culture. Kim is a new ambivalent imperial hero, "the 'country-born' imperialist" (McClure 1981, 64) or a hybrid 'Sahib' as I call it.

While the British majority at home followed events such as the 'Indian Mutiny' from a safe distance, the Anglo-Indian community often felt that their fears and concerns were neglected and belittled in Britain. It is this view from the inside of the colonies, the 'Anglo-Indian' perspective, which includes both a fascination with Indian culture and Orientalist stereotypes as well as the belief in British hegemony that is characteristic of Kipling's writing.[112]

---

111 Janet Montefiore argues that there are also stronger affinities to modernism in Kipling's writing than often granted in criticism on Kipling. (cf. Montefiore 2000, 113) Jesse Oak Taylor (2009) links Kim's interest in artefacts and his wandering through the city to modernist conceptions of masculinity such as the dandy or the *flâneur*.

112 Moore-Gilbert (1986) has analysed the difference between what he calls "metropolitan" and "Anglo-Indian" Orientalism and Kipling's role in this discursive field.

Kim: An Orientalist Coming of Age

In *Kim*, Kipling's only successful full-length novel, the author presents a hero who is utterly immersed into colonial India. It is not a coincidence that Kipling chooses such a young protagonist. Childhood here functions as a liminal phase which renders (temporary) hybridity permissible from a hegemonic point of view. In contrast to the grown men in Haggard's and Conrad's writing, who are always endangered by the threat of 'going native', the colonial setting is not a hostile place for Kim. On the contrary, India figures as a playground full of pleasurable adventures that are aborted only in the end. The tale of Kim culminates in the process of growing up, which is deemed necessary from an Anglo-Indian perspective. While ambivalence, as will be argued, is a tolerable flaw in a colonial boy, the colonial man, who is to 'lead the natives', must assert his distance from and authority over 'native' life. *Kim* is a novel in which the crisis of colonial masculinity is not given, but must be learned and puerile hybridity mastered as part of adolescence.

Kim's coming-of-age story includes elements of the picaresque (cf. McClure 1981, 71; Schefold 1999, 41), such as Kim's travelling along the Grand Trunk Road through the vast Indian landscape and his meeting of the various 'exotic' inhabitants of different backgrounds. In this sense, the novel can be described as a generic mixture of the *Bildungsroman* (moving toward incorporation to society) and the picaresque (moving toward radical rejection of social restraints). (cf. Booker 1997, 144) As has been often noted, the vividness of the narrative of *Kim* rests on the young protagonist's ability to enter 'native' society and return. Kim is one of the first fictional characters who can be described to embody the hybridity of the colonial encounter that destabilised the clear allocations of coloniser and colonised. (cf. Suleri 1992, 2) In the text, Kim's hybridity is characterised as follows:

Kim was English. Though he was burned black as any native; though he spoke the vernacular by preference, and his mother-tongue in a clipped uncertain sing-song; though he consorted on terms of perfect equality with the small boys of the bazaar; Kim was white – a poor white of the very poorest. (K 49)

A number of contradictions are negotiated in this quote. For example, Kim's physical appearance needs to be 'whitened' in order to assert a distance from the 'native' boys with whom he socialises. Despite being "burned black", Kim is also undoubtedly "white". Notwithstanding the fact that in this quote his skin colour is described to actually match that of the 'natives', he repeatedly puts on make-up in order to pass as 'native'.[113] In the course of the story, Kim assumes the dress and colour (by wearing brown dye) of a "low-caste Hindu boy" (K 175) or a Mohammedan (K 179), but he is always careful not to look "too black" because he would appear "a *hubshi* [nigger]" (K 174). Here an Orientalist fascination with Indianness coincides with a simultaneous degradation of Blackness. Patrick Williams and others argue that the character is presented as culturally Indian and naturally British. (cf. Randall 2000, 17; P. Williams 1989, 50) Although there is a strong emphasis on Kim's 'in-betweenness', his 'natural' privilege is never contested. (cf. McClure 1981, 72) In this sense, "the colour 'white' functions as a residual 'truth' which cannot be erased despite Kim's appearance and behaviour" (Low 1996, 213).

Nonetheless, as is evident in the quote, Kim's hegemonic status is still endangered by a number of other factors, and "Kim variously represents white superiority *and* white subordination" (Bristow 1991, 198). While his Whiteness is not challenged, he might be considered the 'wrong' kind of White – after all he is, "a poor white of the very poorest". The poor Whites in the colonies were seen as the most vulnerable class of colonisers who too easily associated with the 'natives' and threatened the clear distinction between the rulers and the ruled as the menace of 'miscegenation' but also cultural decline were suspected. (cf. Mohanty 1991, 325)

At the beginning of the story, the reader learns that Kim's mother was an Irish nurse-maid in a Colonel's family and his father was Kimball O'Hara, an Irish soldier. Both died, which left Kim an orphan. A "half-caste woman" (K 49) now looks after Kim, a woman who had lured his father into a fatal opium addiction causing that he died "as poor whites die in India" (K 50). The Indian woman claims that she was the sister of Kim's mother – so the possibility of 'miscegenation' is hinted at, but immediately, the narrator assures the reader that his mother was, in fact, an Irish

---

113 In the 1950 film version of *Kim* (directed by Victor Saville), this contradictory visual politics becomes plainly evident. Dean Stockwell, who plays the young Kim is already wearing 'brown face' to connote his 'Indianness' but he puts on extra make-up when he is supposedly disguising himself as a 'native'. Even more tellingly all major parts, such as that of Mahbub Ali (Errol Flynn) and the lama (Paul Lukas) are also played by White actors who are visually 'blackened' to fit their parts, and one must attest that Errol Flynn in his display of Hollywood heroic masculinity at no point is a convincing "big burly Afghan" (K 66), as the character is described in the novel.

woman. Although Kim is not the offspring of such an illicit affair[114], he also is not hegemonically English but poor *and* Irish. Many critics have noted the significance of Kim's Irishness (cf. Ellis 1995, 316; Nagai 2006; T. Watson 2000, 106).[115] Tim Watson, for example, writes that "the hybrid Irish, who are both colonizer and colonized [...] will defend the borders of the Empire at the same time as they challenge its integrity and must themselves be contained" (T. Watson 2000, 110). While Kim's Irishness endangers his Whiteness to a certain degree, the reference to the Irish as part of the colonial British army abroad also produces the fiction of unity in light of imperial crisis.[116] The text enacts a double strategy of continuously stressing Kim's hybridity – his immersion into Indian society, his unclear Irish ancestry, his poverty – while simultaneously adhering to Kim's access to race superiority.

As has been mentioned, the fact that Kim is still a child allows for a temporary suspension of rules that have to be reinstalled in the course of the story. Don Randall argues convincingly that the concepts of adolescence and hybridity developed interdependently in the nineteenth century. Both hybridity and childhood are considered states of 'in-betweenness' that demand careful regulation. The young colonisers abroad were perceived to be especially at risk and therefore many – like Kipling himself – were sent back home for their proper education. Following this reasoning, the "child becomes a focal representative of the imperial enterprise, a precarious investment in the national and imperial future" (Randall 2000, 7). Despite all the playfulness, the narrator bestows order time and again, and this is evident in the disruption between the voice of the narrator and the statements of the character. For instance, "while Kim insists that he is Indian, the narrator adamantly asserts Kim's British origins" (JanMohamed 1985,

---

114 The first school of the Military Orphanage that Kim attends and where he is beaten and unhappy is described as being for the sons of "Sahibs – and half-Sahibs" (K 159). This shows that among the Anglo-Indians the offspring of British soldiers and 'native' women was a known fact that had to be institutionally taken care of. In the short story "Beyond the Pale", Kipling famously presents the tragic outcome that must result from 'miscegenation'. (cf. Behdad 1994, 239)

115 As McClintock and others have shown, in the nineteenth century the Irish were often conceptualised as a 'darker race' in comparison to the English. Hence, there is a long tradition of anti-Irish sentiment that finds expression in racialised language. (cf. McClintock 1995, 52–61; Street 1985, 101)

116 Kaori Nagai also mentions that Kipling's Irish characters in India are generally depicted as immigrants who settle in the colonies for good while the English characters eventually return home. (cf. Nagai 2006, 18)

79). The reader, at various points, is informed – in statements that McBratney characterises as "authorial ventriloquism" (McBratney 2002, 114) – that Kim could "lie like an Oriental" (K 71) and "[w]here a native would have lain down, Kim's white blood set him upon his feet" (K 94). Consequently, I argue, JanMohamed is slightly too optimistic in his assertion that the novel provides "a positive, detailed, and nonstereotypic portrait of the colonized that is unique in colonialist literature" (JanMohamed 1985, 78). Granting that the text is more ambivalent than a univocal colonialist master narrative, it is, as the quotes illustrate, filled with ubiquitous recourse to stereotypes that are provided by the narrator. (cf. P. Williams 1989, 42–43)

The authoritative voice of the intrusive narrator[117] tries to manifest the dichotomy of 'self' and 'Other' that the hybrid character Kim threatens to undermine. In this sense, the narrative appears quite contradictory at times. In terms of the language employed by Kipling, the novel presents the "heteroglossia of British India" (Randall 2000, 149) and Kipling includes a whole range of un-translated words. Randall links this inclusion of 'alien terms' to the fact that by "mimicking the forms and figures of subcontinental languages, the dialogue recalls that English is very rarely the spoken language of *Kim*" (ibid., 150). This again underscores the mentioned separation of the voice of the narrator – which is clearly English, addressing an English-speaking audience – and Kim who first has to learn to speak and write English properly in the course of the story. The narrator seems to have the privilege to have access to both 'worlds'. But, in order to function as a figure of omnipotence and omniscience, the narrator is reliant on the fact that the character Kim possesses the 'magical power' of invisibleness within 'native' culture – as it is Kim's insights that are supposedly narrated – and always critically assessed. (cf. Low 1996, 236)

Another important aspect of Kim's process of growing up is his relation to religion. India is presented as a country of numerous and 'exotic' religious customs that attract the young protagonist who is initially not interested in following one prescribed creed: "India was awake, and Kim was in the middle of it, more awake and more excited than anyone, […] for he borrowed right- and left-handedly from all the customs of the country

---

117 Lyon calls a "gossipy familiarity, a tendency to digress" (Lyon 1989, 124) characteristic of Kipling's narrators.

he knew and loved." (K 121)[118] Religion is not a fixed reference point in the child's life, and while the Christian missionaries, like the Anglican Reverend Bennett and Roman Catholic Chaplain Father Victor, appear as suspect characters and are divided by "an unbridgeable gulf" (K 133), the Tibetan lama is constructed as a more positive, but somewhat naïve, source of inspiration for Kim. He decides to join the Buddhist lama to help him on his journey as his *chela* (disciple). Nonetheless, Kim is not really interested in the spiritual journey of the lama, but takes care of his worldly needs by finding shelter and food in his typical roguish fashion.[119] The lama is depicted rather paradoxically as a wise man and source of inspiration, and at the same time, he seems utterly helpless to find his way around in India without Kim. Typically, the British are constructed as 'natural' authorities who can even teach the 'natives' about their own land and customs. Kim cannot only pass as Indian, he even knows India better than the Indians.

> The Lama, symbol of the traditional India, needs the protection of Kim, his British *chela* – a word which means both acolyte and bodyguard. This gives rise to a fundamental irresolution in *Kim*. While Kipling seeks complementarity between the compassionate transcendentalism of the Lama and Kim's ethic of action and belief in the reality of the material world, their visions, though parallel, can never meet. (Moore-Gilbert 1986, 135)

While Kipling presents a plurality of different religious creeds, "discomfiture of the Buddhist-Imperialist contact" (Hagiioannu 2003, 105) remains in *Kim*.[120] Similar to Kipling's presentation of 'race' as an unshaken natural foundation, the narrator time and again affirms that there are inborn characteristics of the White man pertaining to his religious beliefs that no disguise can eradicate, and in this sense, Whiteness and Christianity become

---

118 Kipling himself also borrows rather freely concepts from Hinduism when it suits his narrative purposes. (cf. Parry 1998, 213) In this sense, India is imagined as 'overflowing' with mysterious cultural artefacts and traditions. This differs from Haggard's Africa which is depicted as empty and 'uncultured'. If there are cultural artefacts described in Haggard's stories, they are connected to an ancient White race, as has been explained.

119 Green (1980) as well as Meyers (1973) compare the couple to Huck and Jim in Mark Twain's *Huckleberry Finn* (1884), which both describe as a literary predecessor to Kipling's *Kim*.

120 Additionally, and despite the fact that Kim's friend Mahbub Ali is a Muslim, Kim also at times displays a condescending attitude towards Muslims: "Kim seems to respect the lama's status in a way that starkly contrasts with his lack of respect for the religious beliefs of the Muslim farmer whose child he helps cure." (Booker 1997, 38)

inseparably concurrent. While the character is open to a range of religious practices, the narrator apodictically proclaims – even before Kim will himself come to the realisation in the course of his education – that "[n]o native training can quench the white man's horror of the Serpent" (K 91), and in this way, foreshadows Kim's ultimate return to the 'right religion', which, paradoxically, becomes a natural rather than cultural attribute, as well. The snake in the Indian landscape is immediately translated into the Biblical Serpent and the danger of seduction, which Kim naturally abhors.

As is typical for both the coming-of-age story and the adventure tale, travelling or the quest is a significant trope in *Kim*. The plot of the novel centres on the journey of Kim and the lama through India. The lama is on a spiritual mission to find the "River of the Arrow", and Kim seeks his father's regiment and their banner of a "Red Bull on a green field" to learn more about his ancestry on his quest. When the two protagonists finally meet the regiment of White soldiers, Kim is at first mistaken for a 'native boy'. His disguise, but also his lack of English education, causes concern, but once more, his biological Whiteness is seen as the most important foundation for his future reformation: "He is certainly white, though evidently neglected." (K 134) At first, Kim is reluctant (cf. K 155) to accept the missionaries' credo of "once a Sahib is always a Sahib" (K 136), and he attends a *madrissah* (school) grudgingly. However, even the lama is now persuaded of Kim's 'Sahibness' (cf. Low 1996, 214) and parts from his *chela* for the time being. As a sign of his gratefulness for Kim's help, the lama pays for Kim's Catholic public-school education. Father Victor is not happy "takin' a heathen's money to give a child a Christian education" (K 160) but, in his mind, this is better than to leave Kim to the Anglican Bennett, and Kim receives the Catholic education that was provided especially for the Irish troops. Despite the "Asiatic side of the boy's character" (K 161), the missionary is committed to "'make a man o' you, O'Hara, at St Xavier's – a white man, an', I hope, a good man" (K 165). Making Kim a White Englishman is the most important mission of the book, and it is not always easy to persuade the boy himself why this is indeed an appealing position other than, of course, that it entails hegemonic privilege and corresponds to his 'true nature'.

Kim has to be educated about his rightful place in colonial society, and education is seen as an indispensable part of the colonial mission: "In major works such like *Kim* and *The Jungle Book* he [Kipling, E.H.Y] tries to imagine a system of education that will produce the instinct of domination without the corollary fears of isolation and deep conviction of inadequacy." (McClure 1981, 33) However, in *Kim* this transition is not achieved as smoothly. Kim does not even speak or write English properly, and he has been so utterly absorbed into 'native' society that he is struggling to find his identity. "'I am a Sahib.' [...] 'No; I am Kim. This is the great world and I am only Kim. Who is Kim?' He considered his own identity, a thing he had never done before, till his head swam." (K 166) The original childlike easiness and the label "Little Friend of all the World", as he is repeatedly called in the novel, begin to be questioned. In school, Kim learns to accept that as a future coloniser, he must show a 'strong hand' towards the ruled. "One must never forget that one is a Sahib, and that some day, when examinations are passed, one will command natives. Kim made note of this, for he began to understand where examinations led"[121] (K 173), and he acknowledges that soon he will be "altogether a Sahib" (K 178) – a fact that again the narrator already knows.

However, while Kim has to attend school, the holidays are a time to resume his old lifestyle. For that time, he can go back and forth between his "libidinally charged liminality" (Randall 2000, 123) of the masquerade as a 'native' and his new life as a future colonial officer. Emphatically, he states that the holidays are a time when he must be "free and go among my people. Otherwise I die!" (K 184) Kim can, probably for the last time, resume his adventures and complete his mission of helping Mahbub Ali and Colonel Creighton to play "the Great Game" of espionage as he had completed little tasks for the men along his journey with the lama. After passing his school exams and before entering into Government appointment, he is reunited with the lama and gets half a year leave in order to "make you de-Englishized" (K 232), as his companion on his last mission, Hurree 'Babu' calls it. Hurree 'Babu' is the stereotypical Bengali who pronounces his own inferiority in alignment with Social Darwinist sentiment and calls himself a "good enough Herbert Spencerian" (K 272) to know the 'shortcomings of his race'. While it is permissible for Kim to become immersed into Indian society, the 'Babu', the colonial subject who has adopted English language and culture, is harshly ridiculed, called "the monstrous hybridism of East and West" (K 288). Hurree becomes the ludicrous and failing "mimic

---

121 Montefiore points out that the education in *Kim* is primarily focused on arithmetic and the making of maps which seem to be the most relevant faculties of future colonial officers rather than the humanistic ideals of public-school education in Britain. (cf. Montefiore 2000, 124–129)

man" who is characterised by his lack of manly courage. In the novel and in accordance with Social Darwinist thought, this is explained not as his own fault – but like Kim's superiority – as a part of his nature. McBratney, however, argues that by becoming a 'successful' hybrid of East and West, Hurree also functions as a subversive "mimic man" in Bhabha's sense who threatens to undermine the dichotomy of coloniser and colonised. (cf. Bhabha 1994, 132) While this is true to a certain extent, Hurree's adoption of English cultural codes is also continually ridiculed in the novel, even by himself, and cannot be compared to Kim's mastery of 'native' ways. In the logic of the novel, the 'weakness' of Hurree's race will always re-surface and is inferior to Kim's privileged hybridity.

But before Kim can finally claim the position of the 'Sahib', he nonetheless has to overcome the crisis of hybridity – that is, he first has to accept that hybridity is, in fact, a crisis for his male colonial identity. And his acceptance of this fact marks a considerable change in tone in the novel. The playful ambivalence of Kim's childhood has turned into adolescent confusion about his cultural allegiance. Ambivalence and hybridity have turned into problematic aspects of his identity. "Each long, perfect day rose behind Kim for a barrier to cut him off from his race and his mother-tongue. He slipped back to thinking and dreaming in the vernacular [...]." (K 261) Repeatedly, the question of his identity haunts him, and he keeps asking, "'Who is Kim – Kim – Kim?'" (K 233) or tries to assert, "'I am Kim. I am Kim. And what is Kim?' His soul repeated it again and again."[122] (K 331) While he initially was happy to flaunt his belonging to 'native' society, which included a playful multitude of different identities, he now yearns for a stable place.

At the height of the story, Kim can overcome this identity crisis, and he can rely on his natural superior faculties suddenly. In the climactic fight with the Russians[123], Kim is suddenly confronted with the "Irish devil" in his blood (K 291) and 'remembers' that he is a White man after all. (cf. K 293) In this passage, both Irishness and Whiteness are reconciled and become part of Kim's heroic qualities. He does not have to learn to become a 'Sahib' – he was always already a 'Sahib' deep down, and Schefold argues

---

122 Lane argues that the question "what is Kim" refers to his crisis of racial identity, while the question "who is Kim" is linked to his social identity. (cf. Lane 1995, 41)

123 Due to its portrayal of British Russophobia, Booker considers *Kim* one of the first Cold War texts (cf. Booker 1997, 181), which in terms of genre can also be seen as one of the first spy thrillers.

accordingly that Kim's crisis is based on his 'subjective' quest for an identity that 'objectively' existed all along in the logic of the narrative. (cf. Schefold 1999, 44) Irishness – as long as it serves the British empire – can be
reconciled with hegemonic masculinity. During Kim's journey, all the 'natives' with whom he socialises, instinctively recognise this 'natural' authority – even before Kim can. Lane argues that the "brevity of Kipling's fictional endings indicates the urgency with which he tried to disband the
shattering chaos of desire" (Lane 1995, 18). Accordingly, on the last pages
of the novel, the lama, for Kim's sake, somewhat abruptly abdicates nir-
vana, and the search of both the lama and Kim, who is finally addressed as
a man, has come to an end. Ironically, by maturing into a stable 'Sahib'
identity, Kim "will find himself less able to impersonate Indians successfully and function effectively as a spy" (McBratney 2002, 127).

As has been argued, this male coming-of-age story negotiates the narrative patterns of the quest and the threat of the loss of control. But while
the adventure heroes of Haggard can overcome the danger of losing control and Conrad's protagonists fail, Kipling's hero is never really threatened
because he can rely on inborn characteristics. Paradoxically, Kipling, on the
one hand, stresses ambivalence and hybridity, but on the other hand, he is
also one of the colonial authors who rely most explicitly on essentialist
recourses to race.

The notion of adolescence as a liminal phase, in which rules and regu-
lations are temporarily suspended, was restricted to young men and excluded girls and young women who had to comply with Victorian ideals of
femininity from an early age. In this sense, it is important to emphasise that
Kim is a male coming-of-age story. Or, as Said writes: "It is an overwhelmingly male novel, with two wonderfully attractive men at its centre –
a boy who grows into early manhood, and an old ascetic priest." (Said
1994, 136) Accordingly, the story is reliant on male bonding and coincides
with both homoerotic undertones (in the relationship of Kim and the
trader and agent for the British army Mahbub Ali) and a strong emphasis
on celibacy (in the relationship of Kim and the lama). Kim easily connects
with male characters in the story, and the older men seem to function as
surrogate father figures for the orphan Kim. (cf. Sullivan 1993, 154–155;
Wegner 1993–1994, 150–152) This variety of different male bonds is made
possible because Kim initially is a boy "who is not yet marked by the name
of the father not entirely subjected to paternal law" (Randall 2000, 117).
Kim seeks the company of men, and the text presents a "deferred hetero-

sexuality" (Arondekar 2002, 74) that is characteristic of colonial tales in general and also plays an important role in both Haggard's and Conrad's fiction. In *Kim*, there are no White women but a number of 'native' women that Kim meets along his journey. Although still quite young, Kim is described as irresistibly attractive to these women: "Kim is allowed sexuality so that he may triumph over it, in the unacceptable shape in which it presents itself, as part of his rites of passage to (proper) manhood." (P. Williams 1989, 47) He has overcome the weaknesses of his father who was guilty both of the use of drugs and a too close association with the 'natives'. This also pertains to the relationship with the lama, who due to his 'wrong' creed and race cannot be considered an adequate father figure for Kim. Growing up is constructed as a struggle that involves some pain and the surrender of the affections of a child. After the fight with the Russians, Kim has to overcome his illness – and this is the only time he cries in the story – and begin to sever his ties with the lama.

In the end, it is the English Colonel Creighton the "ethnographer-scholar-soldier" and "the main figure of worldly authority" (Said 1994, 151) who will initiate Kim into adult manhood independent from other men. Although Kim is a poor White, he resists the temptation of 'miscegenation'. By refusing sexual invitation of the 'native' women, most importantly the Woman of Shamlegh, "he has passed a crucial test of colonial manhood – the denial of sexuality" (Sullivan 1993, 175). The process of maturing is strongly linked to restraint, an imperative to keep control, and Kipling constructs in *Kim* the perfect boy hero who can overcome all these temptations. The 'native' women are depicted as either wicked temptresses or, as the Kulu woman, as a caring mother figure. (cf. Wegner 1993–1994, 151) In this sense, Kim can rely on the manly English authority of Creighton and the loving affection of the Kulu woman who figures as 'Mother India', who is according to Kipling's logic more than happy to care for her own colonisers. In this constellation, the stereotypical Orientalist trope of the feminised colonies and the virile manly colonisers is reaffirmed.

The much-mentioned threat and ambivalence in the relationship of 'self' and 'Other' is only implicitly evident in other characters. While the 'good' colonised subject – like Hurree 'Babu' – will imitate the English, he cannot become English. According to Bhabha, "colonial mimicry is the desire for a reformed, recognizable Other, *as a subject of a difference that is almost the same, but not quite.*" (Bhabha 1994, 122, original emphasis) Conversely, the coloniser must assert and continually produce this difference. Kim's father, for example, is the embodiment of failed colonial masculinity which figures as a subtext and warning in the novel. Despite Kim's unclear status in the beginning and his 'challenged' Whiteness, he can still become the vehicle of colonial fantasies of omnipotence. Kipling is aware of ambivalence and constructs Kim in a way that he can enjoy the pleasures of imperialism for a time and then return to a strict binary order. Adolescence, in this sense, becomes a phase of increased regulation of the 'self'. Kim accepts that he has to adhere to rules, and accordingly, all the depicted 'natives' seem more than happy with this 'natural order'.

> Just as there are no sexual women in the book, there are also no nationalists, or natives who would prefer to be freed from imperialist control. The desexualizing and disembodying effect in Kim's attitude towards his own sexuality is a sort of colonization of the self and of one's own desires. (Sullivan 1993, 176)

There are two competing British attitudes toward India, both finding expression in *Kim*. On the one hand, there is a strong attraction to a land unknown, mysterious, seductive, and on the other hand, the novel stresses self-mastering and self-sacrificing repression involved in the commitment to govern. (cf. Wurgaft 1983) Kim displays rational links with the British and emotional links with the Indians, and it is this "contradictory pattern of desire – to be loved and to control –" (Sullivan 1993, 2) with which the boy has to cope.

According to the logic of the text, while Kim is culturally Indian, he is inherently British, and nothing can do away with that fact. "Indeed, this novel brings into play a complex series of connections between class, race, and gender that, curiously, make the ideal boy adventurer the one who thrives at the furthest remove from what might be thought to be his proper place in the world." (Bristow 1991, 195) Hence, somewhat paradoxically, it is his rootedness in India that makes Kim the perfect colonialist. This strong attachment to India is evident in Kim's display of entitlement to be considered an inhabitant of India. Kim assumes that this is his natural place, but it is also a place of privilege. It is his people and his land. In the very beginning of the novel, Kim pushes the Muslim and Hindu children off the canon Zam-Zammah, the symbol of the conquest of the Punjab, which stands in front of the Lahore Museum.[124] That is to say that

---

124 Kipling thereby also links military and scientific elements in the British Raj. (cf. McBratney 2002, 113)

from the very outset of the story, Kim makes, as Randall phrases it, "his own success a 'rule' of the game" (Randall 2000, 120), and he only has to realise this in order to succeed.

While it is true that the character presents a more compassionate insight into Indian life and customs than the authoritative voice of the narrator, this episode in the beginning points to inconsistencies in the construction of voice in this novel. Whereas throughout the story, the character Kim seems to be more hesitant regarding his hegemonic entitlement, which the narrator emphasises, this display of authority in Kim's action in the very beginning hints at his 'Sahibness', which he only attains at the end of the plot. Consequently, there is a strange, and at times, illogic drifting apart and converging of the perspectives of character and narrator.

The fact that Kim can mingle within 'native' society and display cultural hybridity in his looks and manners does not do away with or threaten his hegemony. In this context, one can argue, that "the white man [...] [is] simultaneously invisible, or at least capable of invisibility in a context that renders him eminently spectacular" (Mohanty 1991, 315). Behdad calls this process of reinventing the colonial self "self-exoticism", which is reliant on "a split between the mimetic identification with the Oriental and the differential construction of identity through a disavowal of the Other's subjectivity" (Behdad 1994, 234–235).

Different from the spectacle of the 'self' in photography, which renders the 'selfness' of the White man – the display of virility and order in the exotic environment – spectacular, Kim in his mimicking of the 'native' turns his very ability to blend into 'native' society into his most spectacular feature. In Kipling's microcosm, hybridity is absorbed into hegemony and becomes a decisive benefit in the rule of the 'natives', and there is no doubt about the righteousness of British rule in India. (cf. T. Watson 2000, 99) Kim incorporates 'Otherness' and becomes a hegemonic hybrid figure while the marginalised hybrid figure Hurree is ridiculed and linked to inferiority. In addition to and unlike the character of Kurtz in *Heart of Darkness*[125], Kim does not 'go native' in the sense of losing his superiority. As he is still a child, Kim has not fully developed his superior moral skills, and consequently, he cannot lose them. Adolescence becomes the privileged time that is open to hybridity and a playful, unthreatening version of colonialism that ends in successful self-regulation. Kipling's India is not like

---

125 For a more detailed direct comparison of Kipling's and Conrad's fiction, cf. Lyon (1989); McClure (1981).

Conrad's 'dark Africa', a place of despair, or Haggard's Africa that serves as a retreat from civilisation, his version of India is a mystical and unknowable playground that the right 'Sahib' can successfully master – in mastering himself. By linking these practices to 'fun' and 'games', Kipling downplays militaristic aspects of British rule. "The boyish presence thus dehistoricizes and depoliticizes." (Randall 2000, 144)

Kim, in which the aspects of 'hybridity' – the emersion into Indian society – are combined with notions of 'Sahibness' – the unquestioned entitlement to rule – is a coming-of-age story that has at its central conflict the coming to terms with hegemonic responsibilities. The narrative is shaped by the commanding gaze of Kim, who can name and explain 'natives' and their behaviour even better than the 'natives' themselves, and the voice of a narrator, who seems to re-assure the reader of Kim's intact Englishness.

Kipling's India is a land of great natural beauty where young men can pursue adventure free of the constraints of polite European society. It is a land where one can dispense with most of the constrictive formalities of life in England, where one need not deal with women, where all politics is reduced to the status of a game played out against the backdrop of the Indian landscape as a panoramic game board. (Booker 1997, 41)

But despite the fact that Kim grows to claim colonial manhood in the end, hybridity still implies a crisis in the formation of a stable colonial masculinity – and, as has been argued, Kim's challenged Whiteness and his absent father seem to represent such a threat of failure as a subtext. In comparison to Haggard's escapist adventures, in which the implicit crisis of colonial masculinity is met with a nostalgic recourse to almost unchallenged and fantastic supremacy, Kipling admits to "the fissuring impact of colonial, cross-cultural confrontation upon British imperial subjectivity" (Randall 2000, 169). However, it is the privilege of the adolescent boy to become immersed into the ambivalence of the colonies as long as his 'true' racial superiority is restored in the end. The novel's narrative pleasure rests on its questioning of boundaries and its display of exotic hybridity combined with a hegemonic entitlement that is never seriously doubted. "Though the novel appeared sixteen years after the formation of the Indian National Congress, it cannot admit to the possibility of native resistance." (Boehmer 2005, 42) Consequently, Kipling's hybrid 'Sahib' can be seen to occupy the middle ground between fantastic omnipotence and utter failure in colonial fiction.

Joseph Conrad: Masculine Modernism

In contrast to Haggard and Kipling, Joseph Conrad's writing is generally acclaimed for its stylistic innovation, and he is often referred to as the harbinger of modernism. His life was shaped by the crossing of borders and the imperialism of the late nineteenth century. Born in the Russian part of Poland in 1857 as Józef Teodor Konrad Korzeniowski, it was by no means likely that he was to become one of the most influential writers in the English language. All his life, Conrad struggled with writing and perceived it as a slow and painful process (cf. Raval 1986, 3), and he remains one of the few authors who have been incorporated into the canon of a language that is not their mother tongue.

As a result of his parents' involvement with Polish nationalist activities, he left for France where he started his career in the British merchant navy in 1874. Similarly to Haggard, he was deeply influenced by his voyage to Africa. In 1890, he travelled through the Congo and witnessed many of the atrocities committed under the despotic rule of the Belgian King Leopold II which caused outrage even at the time. Only after nearly twenty years as a sailor did he succeed in living as a full-time writer and eventually became a British citizen in 1886. In contrast to Haggard, he declined knighthood which was offered to him in 1924. This reflects his skepticism towards the imperial project which is developed in his writing. As Terry Collits writes, the "appearance of Conrad's novels […] coincided with an epistemological crisis as well as a crisis of empire" (Collits 2005, 24). Contrary to the celebratory depiction of heroic masculinity of Haggard and Kipling, *failure* of White masculinity is one of the central themes in his oeuvre. In this regard, Etherington notes that "[w]hereas Haggard's characters emerge shaken but refreshed from their encounter with the savage within themselves, Conrad's characters recoil with horror" (Etherington 1984, 113). Nonetheless, I will argue in my readings that Conrad's writing takes part in the tradition of the narratives of male crisis that re-establish the White man as the sole representative of humanity time and again – albeit focusing on a failing masculinity, instead of the more triumphant adventure heroes of earlier writing. Kenneth Bruffee sees Conrad as a precursor for a new genre, which he calls "elegiac romance", a "twentieth-century version of quest romance" (Bruffee 1983, 37). According to Bruffee, a characteristic of this genre is the coming to terms with the loss of the nineteenth-century ideal of heroism, although he does not address the underlying implications this has for the construction of masculinity. Somewhat foreshortened Bruffee declares heroism and hero-worship as nineteenth-century delusions that the twentieth century has outgrown and he writes that there is no "modern hero" (ibid., 15). However, as the analysis of Conrad's colonial (as well as later Coetzee's postcolonial) anti-heroes shows, these developments are closely linked to notions of masculinity being in crisis as well as aesthetic crises of writing that call for re-invention and thereby often implicitly rely on a male artistic ideal that can also have re-privileging tendencies, even in the light of a recourse to failure.

My analysis is selective of a small part of Conrad's oeuvre although failure is a repeated theme in all his writing.[126] I chose two texts from the beginning of what many critics consider his major phase. These two tales extensively address notions of male failure in the colonial context. The first example has a contested status within Conrad's work, centring on marginalised masculinity in an allegorical framework. In contrast, the second selected text has become probably the single most famous account of White men's 'going native' or losing control to this day. By now, there exists a vast and unmanageable amount of criticism concerned with *Heart of Darkness* whose qualities of criticising imperialism are seen as outstanding at the time of its writing.[127] In contrast, *The "Narcissus"* remains – not only due to its offensive title, but also to its much more conservative outline – one of the more obscure Conrad texts that, consequently, has received much less critical attention. While *Heart of Darkness* backgrounds marginalised masculinities and centres on the failure of hegemonic masculinities, *The "Narcissus"* is striking for its time as it features a Black male character in a central narrative role. However, in the somewhat atypical case of James Wait, it is the allegorical link to death as a 'dark presence' onboard that the White

---

126 Tellingly, Suresh Raval calls his book-length study in the major works of Conrad *The Art of Failure* (1986). Especially *Lord Jim* is another interesting narrative of failing colonial masculinity. Boehmer describes Jim as a late imperial hero who has lost his ability to act. (cf. Boehmer 2005, 58–62) I have decided to focus on the less critically acclaimed *The "Narcissus"* as it brings into focus marginalised masculinity. For interpretations of colonial masculinity in *Lord Jim*, cf. Jayasena (2006); McCracken (1993); Mongia (1993).

127 There have also been several postcolonial rewritings of this tale, such as those of Ngugi wa Thiong'o (*A Grain of Wheat*, 1967) or V.S. Naipaul (*A Bend in the River*, 1979). However, as Said notes these often centre on a plot in which "the Black man journeys north into white territory" (*Culture and Imperialism* 30) and conversely seem to reproduce certain gendered assumptions of the tale. Only more recently, female postcolonial writers, such as Arundhati Roy, have also referenced this crucial text in their writing. For postcolonial perspectives and rewritings of *Heart of Darkness*, cf. Mongia (2005); Parry (2005).

men have come to terms with rather than marginalised masculinity that is at the centre in this "tale of the sea".

In terms of genre, Conrad's atypical adventure narratives are part of the modern crises of language[128] and writing and differ in many ways from the male crisis narratives of his contemporaries. Conrad becomes the narrator of modern failures not so much of a nostalgic look back at earlier nobler days. "[M]odernist narratives are about failure – the failure of traditional authority, inherited modes of representation, and the European subject – but they also derive their authority from the staging of this failure in the colonial space." (Gikandi 1996, 161) In this way, this failure – of both the classic hero as well as the language to describe this failure, the crisis of writing – is dependent on a self-aggrandising gesture of human universality that remains ultimately connected to the heroic failure of White men acquiring its strongest pathos staged against the backdrop of the colonies.

The Nigger [129] of the "Narcissus": Allegories of 'Black' Death and 'White' Camaraderie

The central problem everyone interpreting The "Narcissus" faces is how to read the title-giving character of James Wait. Rarely, did one find the representation of Black masculinity in such as central role in colonial fiction.[130] In a new foreword to the American edition entitled "To My Readers in

---

128 Gikandi sees "the modernism of Conrad's novel [as] an attempt to narrate the failure of […] hegemonic style" (Gikandi 1996, 173).

129 Obviously, a problem for the present-day critic is how to deal with the reproduction of such an offensive word that not only appears in the title of the text, but is repeated ubiquitously in the story. Conrad cannot be dismissed for simply being 'a child of his times' as can be gathered from the American editors' insistence to change the title to The Children of the Sea for the US edition as they feared for their sales. Another indication of the inappropriateness can be found within the narrative where the pejorative character of the word is underlined by Wait's disgust at being called by this title rather than by the, at the time more neutral, word 'negro'. Consequently, this offensiveness and the role of the narrator's constant repeating of this terminology will be a central aspect of this reading. Quoting these instances is done with an acute awareness of the violence every repetition of such an invocation entails, which means that I will use the short form The "Narcissus" as often as possible rather than the full title.

130 For a reading, which contrasts The "Narcissus" with Conrad's short story "An Outpost of Progress" that features another prominent Black male character, Henry Price, next to the two White male protagonists, cf. Schneider (2003).

America", Conrad comments on Wait's function in the narrative quite explicitly:

A negro in a British forecastle is a lonely being. He has no chums. Yet James Wait afraid of death and making Her his accomplice was an imposter of some character – mastering our compassion, scornful of our sentimentalism, triumphing over our suspicions. But in the book he is nothing; he is merely the centre of the ship's collective psychology and the pivot of the action. (NN 168)

As a consequence, there is hardly a reading that does not focus on Wait as a symbolic Black presence on the ship.[131] In accordance with Morrison's aforementioned notion of symbolical darkness that Black characters come to embody in fiction, Wait must be seen as an allegorical character. But although I read Wait as connected to allegories of blackness in contrast to White camaraderie on the ship, one also has to be careful not to equate Conrad's statement with the function of the character in the book: he is not "nothing" and his racial 'Otherness' is not coincidental. In the foreword, Conrad explains his attempt to pay tribute to the simple seafaring men and describes this book as a final farewell to his life as a sailor and his debut as a full-time writer. In this gesture of idealisation of the life of seafarers the race of the title-giving character is transcended as a literary device only, and Wait remains an allegorical dark presence on the ship. However, there is more behind the façade than the story at first seems to want to reveal. Benita Parry, for instance, points out the involvement in imperial trade of the ship that is seldom noted. (cf. Parry 1983, 69) The ship becomes the locus of a different society where the camaraderie of White men is still meaningful. Nonetheless, "London is the point from which an imperial narrative is recalled, or to which it returns" (Roberts 2000, 50), and in this way the connection to the colonial present is still granted. In the same vein, Wait's racial 'Otherness' is crucial for the construction of the crew as a homogeneous White collective (albeit from different national backgrounds) to which he poses the greatest risk. Michael North is quite right to call attention to the tendency to overlook this aspect and to simply speak of allegorical darkness with regard to *The "Narcissus"*. "For all the rivers of ink that have flowed over the tortuous racial politics of *Heart of Darkness*, it is hard to find a critique of *The Nigger of the 'Narcissus'* that takes

---

131 Cf. "Instead of women as foils [...] for plots involving white male characters, 'An Outpost of Progress' and *The Nigger of the 'Narcissus'* place black men in this strategic role." (Schneider 2003, 64)

serious the race of its title character." (North 1994, 37) In this reading, I will attempt to take Wait's racialisation seriously while also pointing to the need to allegorise his Blackness in the context of the story and Conrad's vision of aesthetic re-invention.

The *"Narcissus"* is generally not one of the well-received Conrad texts, and today many critics grapple with the conservative tone of the *novella*. This "tale of the sea" is characterised by a lack of plot compared to more classic adventure stories. There is no single individualised hero as well as no love interest – at least no female love interest, following the hetero-normative logic of the genre; in fact, during the voyage, there are no women present at all and only when the ship arrives in London, wives and sisters appear in tangential roles. Many critics remark how the crew functions as a collective that is opposed to, on the one hand, the character of James Wait and, on the other hand, the ship, which functions as the only feminine presence during the voyage.[132] The text can be read as an expression of the crisis of a genre connected to the decline of the heroic ideal of masculinity. Albert Guérard calls The *"Narcissus"* "a prose-poem carrying overtones of myth" (Guérard 1958, 100) and identifies 'grace' as the single most important term in the text. This endangered and embattled status of grace, a chivalrous code of seafaring masculinity is put to the test by the disruptive force of James Wait's intrusion.

In the beginning, the ship is to leave Bombay Harbour to return to England. All are onboard except one missing crew member. What follows is an introduction of the individual sailors, with Singleton as the most remarkable presence on board. "Old Singleton, the oldest able seaman in the ship, sat apart on the deck [...], stripped to the waist, tattooed like a cannibal chief all over his powerful chest and enormous biceps." (NN 2) Singleton embodies both the civilised and refined knowledge of his craft as the most experienced seaman but his tattoos – linking him explicitly to the 'savage cannibals' – also attest to the fact that he is aware of the fine line between 'civilised' and 'uncivilised'. Although the men to some extent represent a collective body, which has to stick together in the face of hardships such as the massive storm they are to encounter, they are also individualised as different people, stressed by the different names, national backgrounds and references to class, age and experience.

132 After the publication of this tale and the mostly unfavourable reception of the "lack of plot", one again finds more women characters and romance plots in Conrad's fiction.

Then James Wait is introduced, whose name at first tellingly is no more than a "smudge" on the list. In calling out his name "Wait" the word also functions as an appeal to wait for him before they leave. From the beginning, he is presented as an unsolvable mystery, an enigma. "The whites of his eyes and his teeth gleamed distinctly, but the face was indistinguishable. [...] The boy, amazed like the rest, raised the light to the man's face. It was black. A surprised hum – a faint hum that sounded like the suppressed mutter of the word 'Nigger' – ran along the deck and escaped out into the night." (NN 10) Conrad is well aware of the offensive word which is silently hummed by the men on deck, but it is also violently repeated time and again by the narrator as if this were the only proper name assigned to Wait. "It is a dehumanizing portrait, distancing him both from the white sailors and from Conrad's Victorian readers. Wait appears as a disruptive force intruding on a scene of ordered, fraternal domesticity." (Schneider 2003, 75) After the whisper of the denigrating appellation, the narration is continued using the word several times in a row: "The nigger seemed not to hear. [...] After a moment he said calmly: – My name is Wait – James Wait. [...] The nigger was calm, cool, towering, superb."[133] (NN 10) Wait's presence is simultaneously offensive and spectacular, and the men cannot take their eyes from what they perceive as his "mysterious" face: "He held his head up in the glare of the lamp – a head powerful and misshapen, with a tormented and flattened face – a face pathetic and brutal; the tragic, the mysterious, the repulsive mask of a nigger's soul." (NN 11) The continuous reference to Wait as the 'nigger' is only interrupted by Wait's question whether there is another Black man onboard: "Is your cook a coloured gentleman?" (NN 11) Here the narrative for the first time provides the outsider's point of view, and the more neutral phrase "coloured gentleman" is employed. The story is shaped by the often-noted inconsistency in point of view. The narration wavers between a third person and first person plural "they" and "we" rendering the narrator sometimes part of the crew and sometimes presenting events through the eyes of an omniscient observer only to change to a subjective male "I" who was part of the "brotherhood" onboard in the very end when he leaves the ship.

In his reading of the novel, Brian Richardson (2005) evaluates this not as a flaw in Conrad's writing but as a mark of artistic innovation. He

---

133 Evocatively, Conrad uses the same adjective "superb" to describe the 'wild' Black woman in *Heart of Darkness*, which links both male and female Blackness to an exoticised and eroticised spectacle. (cf. Messenger 2001, 72)

speaks of the establishment of an innovative "We narration" as a subversion of mimetic conventions and the establishment of a new powerful working-class collective onboard. And indeed, the men are often referred to as a single collective, which stands out despite the destitution they must endure and with which the narrator sympathises:

But in truth they had been men who knew toil, privation, violence, debauchery – but knew not fear, and had no desire of spite in their hearts. Men hard to manage, but easy to inspire; voiceless men – but men enough to scorn in their hearts the sentimental voices that bewailed the hardness of their fate. (NN 15)

Richardson expounds upon how the change to "we" marks a bond between the narrator and the crew.

[T]he term 'we' becomes the privileged perspective as the narration of solidarity between narrator and crew is affirmed. […] It is also a limited group, and does not usually extend to include the malcontent Donkin, the enigmatical Wait, or Singleton, who represents an earlier generation. (Richardson 2005, 217)

Strangely, however, Richardson focuses single-handedly on class (albeit pointing to the fact that men of different nationalities are included in this working-class collective body) but failing to address issues of gender – this is an all-male collective after all – and race completely. Consequently, is seems a bit odd that Wait's exclusion is solely motivated by his "enigmatic status".

Conrad clearly idealises a nostalgic image of the orderly sailor contented at sea, an ideal that both Singleton and Captain Allistoun come to embody more than anybody else onboard. Like the colonisers in foreign territories, these men have to keep up stern control and stick to their rituals, and we find the typical exaggerated references to hygiene as a means to uphold 'manly' discipline: "[Captian Allistoun's] hair was iron-grey, his face hard and of the colour of pump-leather. He shaved every morning of his life – at six – but once (being caught in a fierce hurricane eighty miles south-west of Mauritius) he had missed three consecutive days." (NN 19) Nonetheless, the class distinction, which Richardson mentions, is an important marker of difference. Seamen are not gentlemen, and onboard there is a short dispute on what marks the characteristics of a gentleman when one of the sailors maintains: "'It was […] bloomin' easy to be a gentleman when you had a clean job for life.'" (NN 20) These men have to work hard for their living and imperial trade for them is toil and labour rather than motivated by a colonial mission or zeal. As a consequence, this has to be seen as camaraderie of need rather than choice. In the logic of the story, Wait becomes a test for their male collective. The men never really know whether his illness is real or fake[134] or if he is really too ill to work properly, and therefore, they waver between sacrificially taking care of him – bringing him blankets and drinks – and the suspicion that he is simply a malicious imposter.

Characteristically for Conrad, lightness and darkness are used in contrasting ways, and Wait's skin colour becomes an important factor adding to this chiaroscuro effect: "In the blackness of the doorway a pair of eyes glimmered white, and big, and staring. Then James Wait's head protruding became visible […]. [T]he setting sun dipped sharply, as though fleeing before our nigger; a black mist emanated from him." (NN 21) His gaze on the White crew is described as "domineering and pained, like a sick tyrant overawing a crowd of abject but untrustworthy slaves" (NN 21). Wait becomes the "stalking death" and "obnoxious nigger" (NN 22) simultaneously. At this point in the story, there is the first mentioned shift in the narrative perspective. Suddenly, the narrator becomes part of the crew and the exclusion of Wait is marked explicitly. "We hesitated between pity and mistrust." (NN 22) Wait's illness turns the Manichean as well as the gendered logic on the *Narcissus* upside down and renders the White men into his slaves. Paradoxically, in their care for him, the crew is also feminised and addressed as a "blooming lot of old women" (NN 21), and the boatswain refers to the crew as a "crowd of softies" (NN 26). Lissa Schneider writes that "[i]n their fear of death, their self-identification as free white men becomes as unstable and uncertain as their sense of masculinity" (2003, 84). An ill crew member entails the risk of an epidemic endangering the collective onboard and consequently, Wait's connection to death causes silence and awe among the men. "[H]e had the secret of life, that confounded dying man, and he made himself master of every moment of our existence. […] Such was the infernal spell which that casual St Kitt's nigger had caused on our guileless manhood!" (NN 23) The colonial harmony is disrupted and the oncoming death of a Black man seems to rob the White men of their status as self-determined agents.

He fascinated us. He would never let doubt die. He overshadowed the ship. Invulnerable in his promise of speedy corruption he trampled on our self-respect; he

---

134 This indeterminacy is again projected to assumed racial characteristics: "You couldn't see that there was anything wrong with him: a nigger does not show." (NN 27)

demonstrated to us daily our want of moral courage; he tainted our lives. Had we been a miserable gang of wretched immortals, unhallowed alike by hope and fear, he could not have lorded it over us with a more pitiless assertion of his sublime privilege. (NN 29)

In light of this "weird servitude" (NN 26) they fail to perform their duties and Wait is removed from his post at the forecastle and put into a little cabin. In addition to the implications for the racialised hierarchy onboard, the gendered logic in the text remains ambivalent as well. At times, Wait functions as the feminised object of affection of the sailors and his racial 'Otherness' is erotically charged and, at other times, he seems to rob the men of their masculine authority by turning them into his feminised care-takers. On the whole, the allegorical Blackness of Wait functions as the backdrop of the crisis of the masculinity of the White sailors, whose cama-raderie and devotion to the ship is endangered by Wait's intrusion. I have already mentioned the implications of the name "Wait" who in many ways becomes the antagonist to the other (female) object of affection in the story, namely the ship *Narcissus*, which is, of course, another telling name. While Wait is in his cabin, the love for the ship by the sailors is languished throughout chapter three. Schneider notes the homoeroticism between Wait and the crew which is complicated by the erotic triangle consisting of the crew, the ship and Wait, in which Wait enables the men's quest for masculinity. (cf. Schneider 2003, 86) Similarly, Tim Middleton reads Wait as a closeted character connected to the continued reference to his secret and mysterious status. (cf. Middleton 2002, 145) Middleton speaks of a "troubling account of the tensions inherent in imperialist accounts of male identity in the late nineteenth century" (ibid., 135) and "the text's menacing queerness" (ibid., 136). Oddly, the question of Wait's racialisation is abso-lutely underdeveloped in Middleton's queer reading, and masculinity is again homogenised quite similarly to Richardson's cited focus on class.[135] The Sedgwickian analysis of homosexual panic is applied without contex-

---

135 Donna Packer-Kinlaw interprets the homoeroticism onboard as "a space for an entirely new type of masculinity" (Packer-Kinlaw 2006, 255) and the depiction of the ship as a reflection of the New Woman and Conrad's reaction to a new feminist spirit (again without any reference to the race of the title character). In contrast, I would strongly emphasise the racial encoding of masculinity onboard. The flexibility of hegemonic mas-culinity relies on an 'Othering' of both femininity and 'Other' masculinities such as queer and/or Black masculinities. This does not necessarily 'open a space' for new mas-culinities, quite the contrary, it can reinforce normative notions around masculinity in the first place.

tualising aspects of difference among men in this specific setting. According to Middleton, Conrad's *novella* reflects on male narcissism and enacts a menacing mimicry in the light of the discussions about the threat of the feminine, in the guile of the 'invert'/dandy and the New Woman. The homosocial gentleman is haunted by his *Doppelgänger*, the homosexual dandy. However, masculinity here again is only considered in its relationship to femininity, not in its interdependent relation to race. Is Wait's racialisation constitutive for this homoerotic attachment? Masculinity onboard is an elusive status that needs to be stabilised, and Wait's racial distinction is a welcome marker of difference which serves as a line of demarcation between 'self' and 'Other'. In this context, Wait's race becomes more than simply the allegorical Blackness that the White collective has to overcome. It is a specific Black masculinity in the colonial setting that disrupts the dichotomy of 'self' and 'Other' and, concurrently, functions as an eroticised spectacle. Class and race collide in conflicting ways in this male collective, all of whom try to establish their claim to masculinity. Consequently, when abused by Donkin as "a black-faced swine" Wait reproaches him for being "East-end trash" (NN 28) playing class against race in this 'contest' of masculinity. In another instance, Wait protests against his pejorative title this time referring to Belfast's subjugated status as both poor and Irish: "'You wouldn't call me nigger if I wasn't half dead, you Irish beggar!' boomed James Wait vigorously. – [...] You wouldn't be white if you were ever so well ... I will fight you.'" (NN 49)

The men's care for Wait is seen as a sign of their weakness and a dangerous feminisation of the crew who complain to their superior that Wait is not showing enough gratitude for their affection: "'Care for you!' exclaimed Mr. Baker angrily. 'Why should he care for you? Are you a lot of women passengers to be taken care of? We are here to take care of the ship – and some of you ain't up to that.'" (NN 49) The upcoming storm functions as the only real climax of this tale. Wait is fast asleep in his cabin and the storm initially re-establishes the male bonds and steers the men's attention away from Wait back to the 'right' female object of affection, the ship. During the storm, it is predominantly the heroic masculinity of Singleton, who never lets go of the steering wheel, which is celebrated. "Singleton lived untouched by human emotions." (NN 25) He combines White superiority with the 'manly' virtue of perseverance. The older sailor incorporates both civilised attributes and is also linked directly to savagery (by way of his mentioned tattoos, for example). He is described as a "learned and savage patriarch, the incarnation of barbarian wisdom" (NN 3). Singleton stands for a version of masculinity which has witnessed the 'savage' abyss but has successfully retained its superior civilised status and commitment to duty and his fellow sailors, and in this sense he can be read as a successful counterpart to Kurtz in *Heart of Darkness*. Similar to Kim, he is yet another version of the successful colonial hybrid.

After the storm the sailors suddenly realise the absence of Wait and fear for his life. Belfast yells: "'Jimmy, darlin', are ye aloive?'" (NN 40) once more falling back to their role as the caretakers of Wait. The Black man is alive and starts screaming because he is locked in his cabin which is dangerously close to the waterline: "The agony of his fear wrung our hearts so terribly that we longed to abandon him [...]." (NN 41) Again, the men focus on their "darling" Jimmy and once more perilous darkness sets on the scene as a "cloud driving across the sun would darken the doorway menacingly" (NN 41). The whole operation of his rescue is described emphasising Wait's insolence and uncooperativeness. The sailors risk their lives to save Wait – "that hateful burden" (NN 44) who shows no gratitude at all. By now, there is a love-hate relationship established between the crew and Wait, who detests and still cannot let go of him. There also exists the enormous suspicion that he fakes his illness what they perceive as his "unmanly lie" (NN 45) to which he, paradoxically, holds on "manfully – amazingly" (NN 45). It is a continued struggle for manliness between Wait and the crew.

The insolent Donkin, who remains the other disruptive force never becoming part of the collective of sailors, tries to take advantage of the tense mood onboard. He is presented as an unlikeable working-class agitator.[136] The simple sailors feel underpaid and underappreciated by their superiors, who get all the credit for mastering the crisis of the storm. Donkin, who unlike the others has never shown sympathy towards Wait, suggests they could all be "sick" for the rest of the journey, implying mutiny, which is not a success. Once more, the men master the temptation to put their individual plight over the cause of the group. Towards the end of the journey, the sailors speculate about Wait's possible death, and it remains unclear whether he is an imposter. His Blackness is clearly linked to death

---

136 Casarino calls Donkin the "modern political subject of the working class" (Casarino 2002, 239) who disrupts Conrad's world of male bonds which rests on a "mystique of labour and the homoerotic as well as homophobic mystique of the male body" (ibid., 241).

and he is seen as the 'dark' companion. Over again, Conrad weaves lightness and darkness inextricably to each other:

The lightning gleamed in his big sad eyes that seemed in a red flicker to burn themselves out in his black face, and then he would lie blinded and invisible in the midst of an intense darkness. [...] Life seemed an indestructible thing. It went on in darkness, in sunshine, in sleep; tireless, it hovered affectionately round the imposture of his ready death. It was bright, like the twisted flare or lightning, and more full of surprises than the dark night. It made him safe, and the calm of this overpowering darkness was as precious as its restless and dangerous night. (NN 64)

In this passage, both the lightness of sunshine and the darkness of the night are dangerous and connected to death. In the very end, Wait wants to return onboard and start working again in order to receive full pay. However, by now the captain does not believe him any more surmising that Wait was just pretending all along. To this allegation Wait responds angrily: "'He lies,' gasped Wait, 'he talked about black devils – he is a devil – a white devil – I am alright.'" (NN 73) Speaking of a "white devil", Wait tries to turn around the colour-coded connection of Whiteness with goodness/purity and Blackness with evilness/depravity. However, in the context of the story, there is little room for Wait to emerge as a full-fledged character; it is the White men, who have to go through these trials and tribulations, and it is the death of the Black character that enables their claim to subjectivity.

For the rest of the passage, the dying noises of Wait disturb the men in their daily chores. His death hangs in the air, and there is also an association with slavery which Singleton had still witnessed first hand: "'And a black fellow, too,' went on the old seaman, 'I have seen them die like flies.' He stopped, thoughtful, as if trying to recollect gruesome things, details of horrors, hecatombs of niggers." (NN 80) In this passage, Wait's allegorical Blackness and his connection to death is put into relation with the material effects of slavery and colonialism which has cost so many Black lives. Wait cannot let go of the illusion that he will survive the journey and his presence proves to be a test of the morale of the crew:

He was demoralising. Through him we were becoming highly humanised, tender, complex, excessively decadent: we understood the subtlety of his fear, sympathised with all his repulsions, shrinkings, evasions, delusions – as though we had been over-civilised, and rotten, and without any knowledge of the meaning of life. (NN 85)

Their concern for Wait is not interpreted as a sign of human compassion, on the contrary, it is read as dangerous (and implicitly 'effeminising') sign of "over-civilisation"; it endangers their masculinity which is reliant on a clear demarcation from the 'Other'. Accordingly, even in this care for Wait, Conrad's tale adheres to a colonial logic that cannot grant full subject status to the denigrated masculinity of James Wait, who ultimately remains the 'Other' of both the narrative voice and the crew.

The idea of bringing Wait home alive functions as a uniting bond: "We wanted to keep him alive till home – to the end of the voyage." (NN 87) It is especially the sailor Belfast, who cannot let go of this 'effeminacy' and consequently is also 'denigrated' to the status of femininity. He continues to take care of Wait: "He tended to him, talked to him, was as gentle as a woman, as tenderly gay as an old philanthropist, as sentimentally careful of his nigger as a model slave-owner." (NN 86) But as the quote demonstrates, this is an affection that sees the 'Other' as an eroticised property and cannot conceive of a common human bond. James Wait dies still on the ship: "[H]is death, like the death of an old belief, shook the foundations of our society. A common bond was gone; the strong effective and respectable bond of a sentimental lie." (NN 96) Their 'love' for him was nothing than a "sentimental lie" that the men have to learn to abandon. Even during his funeral at sea Wait's body will not fall over board 'like a man': "'He won't go' [...] 'Jimmy, be a man!' [...] 'Go, Jimmy! – Jimmy, go. Go!'" (NN 99) In death, too, Wait cannot achieve proper masculinity, and the men have to expunge this symbolic darkness and racial outsider amidst them.

In the end, the *Narcissus* enters the harbour in London where the only women in the story are present. Wait seems forgotten and only the 'effeminate' Belfast, who tellingly is not greeted by a woman, mourns him. Belfast remains a queer character and in a sense he takes on the role of Wait's 'widow': "'I thought I would take 'im ashore with me.' [...] [T]he bereaved Belfast went over the rail mourning and alone." (NN 103) Belfast, Wait's saviour during the storm, cannot detach himself from the memory and starts crying and his (for men improper) display of emotionality links him to the femininity that has become attached to Wait. In his mourning, Belfast approaches the – now first person narrator –, who appears as one of the men, who leave the ship to go for a round of drinks.

I disengaged myself gently. Belfast's crying fits generally ended in a fight with some one, and I wasn't anxious to stand the brunt of his inconsolable sorrow. Moreover, two bulky policemen stood near by, looking at us with a disapproving and incorruptible gaze. – 'So long!' I said, and went on my way. (NN 106)

In addition to the expulsion of the Black outsider Wait, Belfast's queer masculinity is also denigrated and the narrator quickly dissociates himself from this corrupted 'whiny' masculinity. In light of the furore around the Wilde trial, men increasingly came under public surveillance of the police, and male bonds had to be acquitted from any doubt of 'indecent' behaviour. After this final temptation is resisted, the narrator looks at the crew one last time from a distance; he has turned into a nameless part of the collective, who now however, as a result of their collective struggle, have 'earned' their individual claim to subjective masculinity, and the narrator celebrates a nostalgic farewell to this brotherhood of the sea: "A gone shipmate, like any other man, is gone forever; and I never met them again. [...] Good-bye, brothers! You were a good crowd." (NN 107)

The original preface, which was included as an "after-word" to the fifth instalment in the serialised version of the tale and was omitted from the first book editions of The "Narcissus" altogether, has by now generated almost more critical attention than the text itself. North (1994) calls Conrad's preface a preface to literary modernism in which Conrad's aesthetic vision is spelled out.[137] Conrad urges writers to develop a new language that can incorporate the effect of music or the plasticity of sculptures and in a sense overcomes the restrictions of the written word. "All art, therefore, appeals primarily to the senses, and the artistic aim when expressing itself in written words must also make its appeal through the senses." (NN 146) Famously Conrad continues to express his newfound credo as a writer: "My task which I am trying to achieve is, by the power of the written word, to make you hear, to make you feel – it is, before all, to make you *see*!" (NN 147, original emphasis) How is this artistic programme connected to the narrative itself and the prominent presence of a Black character on the ship? North speaks of a contradictory correlation:

The relationship that seems to exist between the aesthetic program of Conrad's preface and the subject of his novel is, therefore, one of blank contradiction. In fact, the opening scene of the novel seems to be an allegorical enactment of the defeat of reading, and therefore of writing, by difference. (North 1994, 39)

---

137 Jones links Conrad's preface to Wordsworth's Romantic vision in the Preface to the *Lyrical Ballads* (cf. Jones 1985, 23–43) and speaks of a "failing romanticism" (ibid., 36).

In this sense, the failure of language is also a failure to cope with difference. Christensen speaks of the importance to understand "Conrad's fascination with racialized bodies, and recognize their centrality to his inquiries into the problem of literary representation" (Christensen 2006, 30). But Christensen himself reduces the racialised body to a Lacanian *objet a*, "an empty form of desire [...] at the limit of the subject and the community" (ibid., 40). Similarly, Nigel Messenger reads Wait as a figure of abjection, with reference to Julia Kristeva, in light of the fears around degeneration at the *fin de siècle*. This allegorisation of Wait is the most common approach in interpretation. "Wait is identified as a seductive figure of threatening modernity, as well as atavistic regression, as he passively challenges the old-fashioned, self-sacrificial values of life before the mast." (Messenger 2001, 76) Following this logic, the enigma of James Wait's physical and allegorical Blackness connotes the White fear of failure and death onboard. It also fills the void of language which cannot express the struggle for subjectivity in appropriate words. But as I have argued, Wait's Blackness is not only allegorical but points to the specificity in a colonial setting that this tale, like much of Conrad's fiction, seeks to translate to a more abstract universal dilemma. "On the level of aesthetics, Wait seems to be something the ship and crew must be rid of so as to achieve any meaning." (North 1994, 40) This universality of male subjectivity in a colonial setting can only be established at the cost of the 'Other' who ambivalently is desired and rejected.[138] This ambivalent relationship between 'Otherness' and 'selfness' is a continuous process of negotiation and libidinal investment. As Conrad writes in the foreword, "[t]he Nigger, remains very precious" (NN 168) to him and many critics construe Wait as an expression of Conrad's own 'Otherness' as an émigré writer.[139] "Approaching English, as Conrad did, from the sea, was to approach it in the role of racial outcast." (North 1994, 51) But can the character of James Wait really be reduced to an expression of Conrad's own 'hybridity', as North suggests? This line of argument fails to notice the gesture of appropriation that goes along with such a literary agenda. In light of the modern crises of writing and the end of more simple tales of adventure, the appropriation of 'Otherness' becomes a catalyst of artistic renewal and a foil for the expression of crises of White mascu-

---

138 North speaks of "Conrad's simultaneous identification with and desire to escape from all that James Wait represents" (North 1994, 54).

139 Messenger speculates that in The *"Narcissus"*, "Conrad seeks to assert his new persona as a 'manly' British author" (Messenger 2001, 68).

linity. Bhabha explains how it is "not Self and Other but the otherness of the Self [that is] inscribed in the perverse palimpsest of colonial identity" (Bhabha 1994, 63). Conrad's tale in a sense 'absorbs' racial difference and employs Wait's Blackness as an allegorical plot device, which Conrad needs as a backdrop to establish his vision of White camaraderie as well as artistic programme of aesthetic innovation. In *The "Narcissus"*, James Wait is sacrificed so that social order can be restored onboard. However, Conrad's next major work does not restore order; on the contrary, it is often regarded as the archetypical text, focusing on White masculinity gone astray for good.

Heart of Darkness: White Men on the Verge of a Nervous Breakdown[140]

Conrad's famous *novella* or longer tale, *Heart of Darkness*, is undoubtedly one of the most influential English colonial narratives. Originally published as a three part series in *Blackwood's Magazine* in 1899, it was later included in *Youth: A Narrative; and Two Other Stories* in 1902. *Heart of Darkness* employs a doubly oblique narration: an anonymous character reports the story within the story told by the second narrator Marlow, a recurring character in Conrad's world. This renders it extremely difficult to identify whose perspective is central in the story and whose perspective is privileged in the text. Conrad often constructs complex narrative structures where the reader is confronted with multiple narrators within a single story. This unreliable narrative framework also reflects skepticism towards language and the ability to convey human experience in words.

In the beginning, this unidentified first narrator recounts meeting Marlow on the *Nellie,* a ship cruising down the river Thames in London. When darkness begins to fall, the narrator relates to the imperial past of the river: "What greatness had not floated on the ebb of that river into the mystery of an unknown earth! … The dreams of men, the seed of commonwealths, the germs of empires." (HD 105) In this gloomy atmosphere – and again darkness and light feature prominently – Marlow remarks: "And this also […] has been one of the dark places of the earth" (HD 105) continuing with a reference to the Roman conquest of Britain and how light was brought to the uncivilised banks of the very river Thames. "[D]arkness was here yesterday." (HD 106) Hence, right from the beginning, imperialism is identified as one of the oldest ills of mankind. For Marlow, all imperial

---

140 Cf. 53fn.61.

adventures culminate in violence, and he sardonically remarks: "The conquest of the earth, which mostly means the taking it away from those who have a different complexion or slightly flatter noses than ourselves, is not a pretty thing when you look into it too much." (HD 107) The boyhood dream of adventure that has influenced many men of the late nineteenth century seems to be an ideal of the past. Accordingly, Marlow continues to tell of his boyhood fantasies.

Now when I was a little chap I had a passion for maps. I would look for hours at South America, or Africa, or Australia, and lose myself in all the glories of exploration. At that time there were many blank spaces on the earth, and [...] I would put my finger on it and say, When I grow up I will go there. [...] [But it] had got filled since my boyhood with rivers and lakes and names. It had ceased to be a blank space of delightful mystery – a white patch for a boy to dream gloriously over. It had become a place of darkness. (HD 108)

Paradoxically, the adventurous spirit entails its own end. Too much exploration brings about the end of the "delightful mystery" that is connected to these so-called "blank spaces" of the earth. What follows is an account of Marlow's initial involvement in England's imperial trade. After a number of voyages in the Orient and India, Marlow decides to travel that "mighty big river" (HD 108) that always fascinated him. Conrad distinctly refrains from using the geographical name Congo River to give his tale a more universal appeal. This is an account of moral decline in the perverse age of imperialism rather than a reference to the moral corruption of one single man at a distinct geographical location. Before Marlow can start his search for Kurtz, however, he is inspected by a doctor: "'It would be,' he said, without taking notice of my irritation, 'interesting for science to watch the mental changes of individuals, on the spot, but ...'" (HD 112) And the doctor offers more good advice: "'Avoid irritation more than exposure to the sun. [...] In the tropics one must before everything keep calm.'" (HD 112) It is precisely this need to keep calm or, put differently, the fear of losing control that White masculinity is confronted with in the colonies. *Heart of Darkness* revolves around this possible abyss that supposedly lurks in the depth of the African continent. Conrad does not redeem his heroes by having them solve petty adventures on their quest of moral enlightenment. This familiar pattern of colonial fiction is alluded to and subverted by the fact that his heroes do in effect fail to pass the test and in the case of Kurtz ultimately lose control.[141]

Once Marlow's morbid journey has started, disorientation is soon to follow. On the steamer to the Company's Station he suffers from "isolation amongst all these men with whom I had no point of contact" (HD 114). Marlow cannot in any way relate to the men around him who seem quite alien and especially the Black men are belittled to mere corporality by him. At the sight of another boat, he comments:

It was paddled by black fellows. You could see from afar the white of their eyeballs glistening. They shouted, sang; their bodies streamed with perspiration, they had faces like grotesque masks – these chaps; but they had bone, muscle, a wild vitality, an intense energy of movement, that was as natural and true as the surf along their coast. (HD 114)

The White man is both fascinated and repelled by this assumed "wild vitality" of Black masculinity. As indicated before, typically for writing of the period, Blacks are reduced to their bodies and often directly linked with animals. Individuality – a burden and privilege at the same time – is reserved for White masculinity. From Marlow's point of view, Black people become an undifferentiated de-individualised mass of ants. "A lot of people, mostly black and naked, moved about like ants." (HD 116) These are the first impressions on his arrival at the Company's Station. There he also meets the Company's chief accountant – a White man whose appearance seems to clash with the overall morbidity of the place. The fact that he achieved to preserve his 'civilised clothes' (with the help of a Black woman servant) is his greatest accomplishment:

Yes, I respected his collars, his vast cuffs, his brushed hair. His appearance was certainly that of a hairdresser's dummy; but in the great demoralisation of the land he kept his appearance. That's backbone. His starched collars and got-up shirt-fronts were achievements of character. He had been out nearly three years; and, later on, I could not help asking him how he managed to sport such linen. (HD 119)

---

141 In her study, *Joseph Conrad and the Imperial Romance* (2000), Linda Dryden analyses how Conrad draws on the adventure tradition – of which Haggard and Kipling were chief representatives – in his early Malay tales and subverts many of the romance tropes. Although not at the centre of attention in her study, *Heart of Darkness* is also informed by these patterns. Andrea White, too, offers this connection in her *Joseph Conrad and the Adventure Tradition* (1993).

Unlike Quatermain's comic but fond depiction of Good's insistence on appropriate clothes, Marlow as a narrator shows a more ironic distance. But even though there is ridicule about this typically English over-investment in clothes, Marlow seems to be aware of the need to uphold appearances, to remain in control if you want to survive in the colonies. Frustrated about the slow progress of his journey and his being stuck in the chaos around him, he is mesmerised by the "big river". After some time, he notices the change the doctor predicted – like a self-fulfilling prophecy, Marlow "remembered the old doctor, – 'It would be interesting for science to watch the mental changes of individuals, on the spot.' I felt I was becoming scientifically interesting." (HD 122) The constant delay and endless waiting add to the nightmarish atmosphere of the story and is at odds with the plot-driven style of adventure fiction.

Finally, the journey down the river commences and Marlow feels rather claustrophobic on the ship always surrounded by the seemingly impenetrable jungle. The depiction of the colonial landscape is more typically related to the adventure tradition and is presented as mystical and hostile.[142] Marlow's quest is also linked to a prehistoric past of the surroundings. "Going up that river was like travelling back to the earliest beginnings of the world, when vegetation rioted on the earth and the big trees were kings." (HD 136) Characteristically, Conrad also refers to the theory of a temporal cleft – a by now familiar narrative pattern – which positions Africa as arrested in some prehistoric past that White civilisation has long ago overcome. This pattern is expressed in manifold ways: first of all, as a temporal aspect of the journey, going back in time, secondly, as a geographic journey travelling to the centre of the earth, and, thirdly, in terms of light and dark metaphors, as a journey into "the heart of darkness". Africa in more than one way is taken out of a political or historical context and delineated as the symbolic antechamber of hell, a place of depravity where every decent man is confronted with the 'savage within'.

Marlow's crew consists of twenty Black men, who are described as cannibals, as well as a number of White pilgrims. The so-called cannibals

---

142 However, there are also differences in the way that this is achieved. Boehmer identifies two strategies by which "colonial unreadability" is managed: either by a "practice of symbolic reproduction" whereby names and rhetorical structures from the home country are repeated (and this is closer to Haggard's strategy of coping with the foreign territory) or by a "strategy of displacement" whereby the description of foreign landscapes and people "admits defeat, submitting to the horror of the inarticulate" (Boehmer 2005, 90). This second strategy is obviously closer to Conrad's writing.

are appalling and fascinating at the same time. Around the mid of the century, there is quite an obsession with cannibalism which came to represent the "nadir of savagery" (Brantlinger 1988, 185) in British writing and which was popularised in sensationalist travelogues of the time. More than likely, many of these reported incidents of anthropophagy never took place and can be ascribed to the European fantasies about African 'barbarism' which found a huge audience at home. Marlow reflects about the cannibals' status as humans but comes to the conclusion that, despite their monstrosity, they are not devoid of humanity.

No, they were not inhuman. Well, you know, that was the worst of it – this suspicion of their not being inhuman. [...] They howled, and leaped, and spun, and made horrid faces; but what thrilled you was just the thought of their humanity – like yours – the thought of your remote kinship with this wild and passionate uproar. Ugly. Yes, it was ugly enough; but if you were man enough you would admit to yourself that there was in you just the faintest trace of a response to the terrible frankness of that noise, a dim suspicion of there being a meaning in it which you – you so remote from the night of first ages – could comprehend. And why not? The mind of man is capable of anything – because everything is in it, all the past as well as all the future. (HD 139)

As I have emphasised earlier, the idea of universal kinship between all human races introduced by Darwin causes insecurity in late Victorian thinking. The cannibals symbolise a stage of moral corruption that still lurks in every 'civilised' man. They remain some prehistoric symbolic incorporation of evil and not real characters. However, in contrast to Kurtz they also show restraint and do not give in to their 'primitive urges', which leads Raval to argue that: "The savage and the civilized are separated only by the cloak of time, and their apparent distance does not imply moral progress." (Raval 1986, 26)[143]

Nonetheless, the colonised again figure as a dark counter image to civilisation rather than characters in this narrative as the Nigerian author Chinua Achebe has forcefully criticised. In his 1975 controversial speech, "An Image of Africa: Racism in Conrad's *Heart of Darkness*", Achebe points out that Conrad has "set Africa up as a foil to Europe, as a place of nega-

---

143 Hence, Conrad's reception of Darwinian evolution is bleaker as he emphasises the ethical dilemma of altruism versus egoism implied in the notion of progress and seriously doubts that even 'civilised man' can ever let go of his darker qualities. For a more detailed discussion of the influence of Darwin's writing on Conrad, cf. A. Hunter (1983); O'Hanlon (1984).

tions at once remote and vaguely familiar, in comparison with which Europe's own state of spiritual grace will be manifest" (Achebe 1977, 2). Some controversy arose out of Achebe's claim that Conrad was a "bloody racist" which was then demoted in a later version of the essay to "a thoroughgoing racist" (ibid., 8). His attack has since then provoked many critics to respond with equally committed defences of Conrad.[144] One of the central concerns in this debate is the question whose politics is represented in passages denigrating Blacks: Conrad's or Marlow's. And indeed, Achebe, although aware of the problem, seeks to conflate the author with the narrator at times. Achebe justifies his stance with the overall ambiguity of the tale and argues that Conrad shields himself off against any clear positioning due to his use of the second narrator. Patrick Brantlinger in his important study on British literature and imperialism, *Rule of Darkness*, also names the ambiguity of the several literary voices in the narrative as one of the main reasons why it becomes extremely difficult to identify any obvious politics of the text. On top of that, the relationship between Marlow and Kurtz remains quizzical.

> The fault-line for all of the contradictions in the text lies between Conrad and both of his ambiguous characters (not to mention the anonymous primary narrator). Is Marlow Kurtz's antagonist, critic, and potentially redeemer? Or is he Kurtz's pale shadow and admirer, his double, finally one more idolator in a story full of fetishists and devil worship? (Brantlinger 1988, 264)

It is never entirely clear if Kurtz is to be despised, or, in some sense admired. Even though the outgrowth of imperialism is certainly criticised, Kurtz's evilness is also appealing. This multi-layeredness and ambiguity clearly mark one of the major differences between Conrad's impressionistic writing and Haggard's formulaic adventure tales and their plain allocation of good and evil or Kipling's saving reference to White racial superiority.

Nonetheless, it is not merely the question of whose opinion is represented here, and in so far Achebe weakens his own argument in some respect focusing on the personal politics of the author Conrad. His critique is much more convincing when he points to the structural problem of Kurtz as a representative of humanity's moral decline. In confronting the reader with the evils of colonialism and the failure of the White man, Conrad was praised as an ardent critic of imperialism. Cedric Watts (1983), in his defence of Conrad, emphasises that Conrad has to be read as a writer

---

144 For a discussion of the politics involved in these quarrels, cf. Mongia (2001).

of his times and not be judged by today's moral standards. This argument is brought up against the charge of Conrad's pejorative language describing Black characters. Therefore, let me clarify that I am not interested in the question of Conrad's personal principles, but in his writing as part of a discourse on White masculinity in crisis that perpetuates and stabilises what Said calls "imperial ideology".

[W]e must also try to grasp the hegemony of the imperial ideology, which by the end of the nineteenth century had become completely embedded in the affairs of cultures whose less regrettable features we still celebrate. (Said 1994, 12)

This "hegemony of the imperial ideology" rests comfortably on a very distinct image of White masculinity which to a certain degree still informs today's notions of race and gender in Britain. Accordingly, in the *novella*, it is the evils of the cruel Belgians that are criticised from a distinctly English perspective which focuses on the ideal of the manly gentleman:

Marlow comes through to us not only as witness of truth, but one holding those advanced and humane views appropriate to the English liberal tradition which required all Englishmen of decency to be deeply shocked by atrocities in Bulgaria or the Congo of King Leopold of the Belgians or wherever. (Achebe 1977, 7)

Conceding that *Heart of Darkness* does indeed at many points offer a critical perspective towards imperialism, one must, however, bear in mind Achebe's point that colonialism is in this tale only presented as a problem in so far as it challenges the moral integrity of an Englishman – not because it costs the lives of Africans.[145] He continues his critique aptly analysing that "white racism against Africa is such a normal way of thinking that its manifestations go completely unremarked" (ibid., 8). In Conrad's tale Africa serves as a

metaphysical battlefield devoid of all recognizable humanity, into which the wandering European enters at his peril. Can nobody see the preposterous and perverse arrogance in thus reducing Africa to the role of props for the break-up of one petty European mind? (ibid., 8)

Referring to this passage, Watts objects that Achebe ignores Kurtz's "representative significance" (Watts 1983, 197), by which Watts unintentionally

---

145 Said, too speaks of a polyvocal work and the "two visions" of Conrad. According to Said, Conrad, on the one hand, criticises imperialism but, on the other hand, fails to envisage an alternative and a "native subjectivity". (cf. "Two Visions in *Heart of Darkness*" in *Culture and Imperialism* (Said 1994, 19–31))

describes one of the chief privileges of hegemonic masculinity. Insisting on this representative significance of Kurtz, all of mankind is reduced to White masculinity, the failure of which is the one problem around which everything revolves once again. On top of that, Brantlinger illustrates that the moral corruption which the White men fall prey to is presented as their failure to uphold difference – Kurtz is degraded to this lower stage of civilisation that is ultimately connected to the racist perception of the 'dark continent'[146] as an earlier phase of mankind.

> Evil, in short, *is* African in Conrad's story; if it is also European, that is because some white men in the heart of darkness behave like Africans. Conrad's stress on cannibalism, his identification of African customs with violence, lust and madness, his metaphors of bestiality, death, and darkness, his suggestion that traveling in Africa is like traveling backward in time to primeval, infantile, but also hellish stages of existence – these features of the story are drawn from the repertoire of Victorian imperialism and racism that painted an entire continent dark. (Brantlinger 1988, 262, original emphasis)

To do justice to the complexities of the narrative, one has to comprehend that *Heart of Darkness* in this light can, indeed, paradoxically be described as "an anti-imperialist novel that is also racist" (ibid., 265).

In the course of the story, Marlow and his men are attacked by arrows from the banks of the river in their search for Kurtz. During this ambush, the Black Helmsman is killed, pierced by a spear. Marlow, more and more unsettled, fears the death of Kurtz, not knowing that these aggressors are part of Kurtz's disciples. In a fit following the attack, Marlow throws one shoe overboard. He seems to be on the verge of a nervous breakdown and becomes obsessed with Kurtz, who by now has become more than anything a fixation of Marlow: "I couldn't have felt more of lonely desolation somehow, had I been robbed of a belief or had missed my destiny in life." (HD 151) This fit, this losing of control, emasculates Marlow who, as the reader knows, confesses this story to his male listeners on board the *Nellie* in London. Hence, he is quick to continue how he got his grip back after this breakdown restoring his male integrity: "Now I think of it, it is amazing I did not shed tears. I am, on the whole, proud of my fortitude." (HD 152)

---

146 For more elaboration on the emergence of the concept, cf. Brantlinger's chapter "The Genealogy of the Myth of the 'Dark Continent'" in *Rule of Darkness* (Brantlinger 1988, 173–197); Frank (2006, 182–184).

After Marlow regains his manly composure, he finally meets Kurtz and what is disclosed is a sight of horror:

The wilderness had patted him [Kurtz] on the head [...]; it had taken him, loved him, embraced him, got into his veins, consumed his flesh, and sealed his soul to its own by the inconceivable ceremonies of some devilish initiation. (HD 153)

Hybridity is often embodied in the crime of 'miscegenation' and the 'mix-raced' offspring in the colonies. But hybridity can also be understood as a characteristic of White men who have been 'contaminated' by the jungle such as Kurtz or, as has been pointed out with reference to Kipling's Kim, due to the lack of proper English education.[147] In *Heart of Darkness*, the danger is located precisely at the point where Kurtz has lost his 'race superiority' and in his failure to uphold control, he embodies "no restraint" (HD 174).

He has become a hybrid of the colonies. In fact, the jungle has altered his body. In this passage, Conrad employs a highly sexualised language which suggests that Kurtz has been penetrated and feminised by the hostile environment. His White masculinity is out of order.[148] Contrasted with the orderly gentleman Sir Henry Curtis of Haggard's *King Solomon's Mines* or even the well-dressed accountant of the Central Station, this becomes particularly evident. The voyage on the steamer is a journey into the "heart of darkness" – a passage that leads to a gradual diminishing of the superiority of White masculinity, also in bodily terms. Kurtz becomes the epitome of Europe's moral failure with regard to the 'Scramble for Africa' and Marlow describes this as his "nerves went wrong" (HD 155). In this context, Mahood reads Kurtz as representing two faces of colonialism: as exploiter and degenerate. (cf. Mahood 1977, 19)

In giving Kurtz an English father and a French mother, Conrad alludes to the two most influential colonial powers of the time. "His mother was half-English, his father was half-French. All Europe contributed to the

---

147 Tom Henthorne (2008) identifies "intentional hybridity" (with reference to Bakhtin) as Conrad's chief literary strategy to succed as part of the English literary establishment and simultaneously "hide" his more radical cirtique of imperialism by introducing multiple narrators which can function as "trojan horses". In this explicietly not poststructuralist reading Henthorne postulates a somewhat problematic assumption about intentional subtext that is "hidden" in a text only to reveal the 'real' meaning of the author.

148 In terms of the quest for Kurtz, he is also positioned in the feminine role of the "enchanted princess in a fabulous castle" (HD 147) that the men come to rescue. (cf. Schneider 2003, 104)

making of Kurtz." (HD 154) Once again, Kurtz, rather than read as an individual character, must be understood in terms of his symbolic significance – he is the product of Europe's greed – which is emphasised throughout the tale.[149]

At the station, Marlow learns about the fact that Kurtz wrote a report for the "International Society for the Suppression of Savage Customs". Marlow is quite impressed by this seventeen-page document of noble words and benevolence which reflects the common attitude of the day. "He began with the argument that we whites, from the point of development we had arrived at, 'must necessarily appear to them [savages] in the nature of supernatural beings […]'." (HD 155) The manuscript, drawing on the idea of the civilising mission, however, is ended by a shocking postscript, evidently added much later and in a hardly legible handwriting that tells of Kurtz's devastation at the time of writing. It reads: "Exterminate all the brutes" (HD 155) and is a sign of the final moral degeneration of Kurtz. But it also points to a failure of language to convey the horrors of the human psyche, and this is connected to a crisis of storytelling that *Heart of Darkness* enacts.

The experience of *Heart of Darkness* does not necessarily invalidate notions of coherence and completeness, but it questions them, and questions the coherence and completeness which fiction traditionally has conveyed. […] Marlow's narrative […] recaptures his own experience of profound disorientation. (Raval 1986, 36)

Onboard Marlow interrupts his narrative at one point and muses about the shortcomings of language and narrative: "'No, it is impossible; it is impossible to convey the life-sensation of any given epoch of one's existence – that which makes its truth, its meaning – its subtle and penetrating essence. It is impossible. We live, as we dream – alone. …'" (HD 130) Here, the importance of the first narrator, who listens to Marlow, can be felt as this second narrative instance adds to the verbal distance and the impotency of language to convey the impenetrable 'dark secrets' of this tale. This narrator comments on Marlow's reflections: "I listened, I listened on the watch for the sentence, for the word, that would give me the clue to the faint uneasiness inspired by this narrative that seemed to shape itself without human lips in the heavy night-air of the river." (HD 130)

---

149 Parry writes: "Europe does not manifest itself as the vital force of progress proposed by imperialist propaganda, but as the parent of degenerate progeny, of sordid ambitions pursued by corrupt human agents." (Parry 1983, 36)

Conrad's story of disorientation becomes a chronicle of the failure of conventional storytelling in general and Marlow's failure to tell the truth in the end when faced by the Intended (Kurtz's fiancée) in particular, to which I will come back. This mode of speechlessness in light of male failure however is also idealised as a motor for innovative writing, or as Raval has phrased it, "the abyss is privileged and idealized, made into an oracle of modern art" (Raval 1986, 39).

More than in other colonial texts, the themes of loneliness and isolation are centred in *Heart of Darkness*. Conrad makes recurring references to the seclusion and solitude men face in the colonies. In contrast to most colonial adventure heroes, Marlow is a solitary protagonist who is not surrounded by a group of White comrades. In his article, "The Beast in the Congo", Donald Wilson (2000) – drawing on Sedgwick's discussion of Henry James's short story "The Beast in the Jungle" (in *Epistemology of the Closet*, 1990) and her analysis of male homosexual panic – develops a reading that focuses on a possible homosexual secret at the core of the tale. In Marlow's obsession with Kurtz, there is an almost feverish desire to get to know the mysterious man, to understand his secret – all tropes that can allude to a homosexual secret, as Wilson points out. On top of the infatuation with Kurtz, Marlow is also clearly mesmerised by the Black men surrounding him. The description of the vivid and muscular Black bodies is contrasted with the less energetic White males all through the text. On the one hand, marginalised men are reduced to corporality and, on the other hand, this very 'flaw' is highly envied and eroticised. When first meeting the Helmsman, Marlow mocks and adores him simultaneously. At first sight, the Helmsman was

[a]n athletic black belonging to some coast tribe, and educated by my poor predecessor [...]. He sported a pair of brass earrings, wore a blue cloth wrapper from the waste to the ankles, and thought all the world of himself. He was the most unstable kind of fool I had ever seen. (HD 148)

Now, as a result of the deadly blow during the attack, Marlow is faced with the dead body of the adored Helmsman still on deck and he is suddenly – and to his own surprise – quite grief-stricken.

I missed my late Helmsman awfully, – I missed him even while his body was still lying in the pilot-house. Perhaps you think it passing strange this regret for a savage who was no more account than a grain of sand in a black Sahara. Well, don't you see, he had done something, he had steered; for months I had him at my back – a help – an instrument. It was a kind of partnership. He steered for me – I had to look after him, I had to look after his deficiencies, and thus a subtle bond had been created of which I only became aware when it was suddenly broken. And the intimate profundity of that look he gave me when he received his hurt remains to this day in my memory – like a claim of distant kinship affirmed in a supreme moment. (HD 156)

The intention of this passage is at least two-fold. While admitting the kinship between Black and White, this kinship is immediately qualified as "distant"; there is a partnership between the two men, but it can never be a relationship of equals. In this light, the bond between the men is one of clear hierarchies. Referring to the same passage, Wilson calls attention to the fact that this description also entails the even greater threat of an interracial homoeroticism:

The idea of a racial connection with savages (the oppressed) represents, of course, the most obvious and significant 'horror' to the imperialist (the oppressor's) psyche; yet, as with other instances of indeterminacy in the text, this highly abstruse – and possibly homoerotic – 'supreme moment' represents an even greater threat to the male psyche. (Wilson 2000, n.p.)

In what Wilson describes as a moment of male panic, Marlow realises that he has to let go of the body of the deceased. Only in death is a physical touch between the men of different races possible. Consequently, it is abruptly terminated: "I hugged him from behind desperately. [...] Then without more ado I tipped him overboard." (HD 156) In this instance, Marlow reinstalls the boundary between 'self' and 'Other' which is endangered by a possible homoerotic link between the men.

What my reading so far has emphasised is that the story wavers between the restoration and the utmost failure of White masculinity, which is also connected to a narrator who often in a dream-like mode fails to find the right words. A containment of the crisis is no longer possible, and in this sense, Conrad's writing points to a new phase of the more clearly exposed crisis of masculinity. Accordingly, I agree with Bristow, who writes that: "The pre-eminence of masculinity (rather than just morality) persists at the coda of the story." (Bristow 1991, 164) It is, yet again, a story of a privileged male crisis. Marlow despairs and mourns over an ideal of heroic masculinity.

Heart of Darkness, no matter how unorthodox its narrative methods, bears a fundamental allegiance to the adventure story whose shallowness and propagandist aims it implicitly condemns. Marlow's narrative is, at base, a story by a heroic man about a heroic man told to men – all in a seafaring context. (ibid., 163)

Kurtz is the incorporation of this failure of heroic masculinity. But Kurtz is not only fallen himself: in the fashion of Mephistopheles he seeks to convert to evil. Facing Kurtz, Marlow has to pass the test, resist temptation and return to civilisation to which Kurtz can no longer go back.

After Marlow has retrieved Kurtz from the jungle, he is brought to the ship where he can only await his final destiny feverishly hallucinating. Everyone on the ship is in anticipation of his death. A few evenings later, Kurtz eventually dies, with the single most famous sentence of the *novella* on his lips: "The horror! The horror!" (HD 178) The crew is informed of his passing during dinner: "Suddenly the manager's boy put his insolent black head in the doorway, and said in a tone of scathing content – 'Mistah Kurtz – he dead'." (HD 178) This short remark remains one of the few instances in which a non-White character is given the opportunity to speak in a tale of White introspection. At the sight of the long-longed for and finally dead Kurtz, Marlow muses:

Kurtz – Kurtz – that means 'short' in German – don't it? Well, the name was as true as everything else in his life – and death. He looked at least seven feet long. His covering had fallen off, and his body emerged from it pitiful and appalling as from a winding-sheet. (HD 166)

Further, Marlow describes him as an "animated image of death carved out of old ivory" (HD 166). The linking of ivory with death is of great importance here. Conrad's numerous references to the symbolism of light and dark, his repeated use of the phrase "heart of darkness", result in an at times complicated system of white and black metaphors.[150] Occasionally, for example, by linking ivory with death and evilness, Conrad seems to subvert the colonial Manichean logic whereby everything white is good and pure and opposed to the vile darkness of Africa. But, he does not really go to the core of this constructed dichotomy. Rather, Conrad seems to suggest that everything good and pure has been infested, penetrated and hybridised by the darkness that is, and ultimately remains, associated with the darkness of the jungle and Africa.

On his return to the city, to White civilisation, Marlow is still haunted by the image of the dying Kurtz. He has inherited all his belongings including the picture of Kurtz's beautiful fiancée whom he is to meet. Dur-

---

150 Henthorne points out that the second narrator often describes the landscape in a greater variety of colours, and it is mainly Marlow who tends to see everything in black or white (cf. Henthorne 2008, 124).

ing the journey, Marlow had repeatedly raised doubts about women's fitness to face the ugly truth of the colonial endeavour, and it is his male duty
to protect the 'fair sex' from this vileness.

It's queer how out of touch with truth women are. They live in a world of their
own, and there had never been anything like it, and never can be. It is too beautiful
altogether, and if they were to set it up it would go to pieces before the first sunset
(HD 113).

The world of the colonies is a male homosocial surrounding and should
stay that way. "They – the women I mean – are out of it – should be out of
it. We must help them to stay in that beautiful world of their own, lest ours
get worse." (HD 153) This state of mind is likely to be at the root of Marlow's decision of not spoiling the Intended's illusion about Kurtz. "Marlow's motivation, like the notion of chivalry itself is tainted with suspect
attitudes since he evokes two contrasting but related images of women to
serve respectively as figures of Europe's casuistry and its delusions." (Parry
1983, 37)

By introducing the only two female characters in the last part of the
story, Conrad ultimately contrasts the 'wild' Black woman with the angelic
White English woman. In the jungle, the reader learns Kurtz has been
tempted by "a wild and gorgeous apparition of a woman" (HD 167). Her
appearance in this all-male surrounding is heavily eroticised – an allure that
Marlow is not immune to either. "She was savage and superb, wild-eyed
and magnificent." (HD 168) Following the stereotype of the hyper-sexual-
ised image of the Black woman, she symbolises sexual corruption.[151]
Clearly, Kurtz has given into this temptation.

Conversely and in accordance with the image of the 'angel in the
house', the Intended is described in the following terms as the exact opposite of the evil Black woman: "This fair hair, this pale visage, this pure
brow, seemed surrounded by an ashy halo from which the dark eyes
looked out at me." (HD 183) When the woman asks Marlow what Kurtz's
final words were, he lies and says that it was her name. Marlow states that
to tell the truth would have been "too dark – too dark altogether" (HD
186). The narrator clearly dissociates himself from femininity. In Marlow's

---

151 In an attempt to save Conrad from the underlying racism of this image, Ian Watt
    problematically describes the woman as "the most affirmative image in the narrative, the
    embodiment of the confident natural energy of the African wilderness" (Watt 1979, 138)
    thus, reiterating the same stereotype eighty years after Conrad.

mind, at least the female domain, the English home, must be protected from these unspeakable horrors he has witnessed and which will haunt him forever. The failure of men needs to be withheld from women, and in this sense Conrad's crisis of masculinity still holds on to ideals of a contained hegemonic crisis.[152]

Marianna Torgovnick has stressed the identification of the 'primitive' landscape with the female body and identifies a "yearning for and yet fear of boundary transgression, violence, and death – which may well be the text's real interests" (Torgovnick 1990, 156). However, in her psychoanalytical reading of the modern investment in the 'primitive', Torgovnick too often neatly parallels the 'primitive' and the feminine. This somewhat obscures the differences between how marginalised as well as hegemonic femininities and masculinities are conceptualised and, as has been noted, Conrad's tale heavily relies on these exaggerated differences between the wild Black woman and the White Intended; race and gender in this context are erotically charged and need to be understood as interdependent rather than parallel markers of difference.

As a result, I would also disagree with her claim that "masculine identity and the need to maintain 'masculinity' as something separate, apart, 'restrained', and in control are hidden motivators and hidden themes" (ibid., 158). It is not so much a secret of the 'male psyche' to dissociate itself from inherent fears of femininity. Rather, the threat of a boundary violation is blatantly spelled out and an explicit motor of the plot. This crisis of masculinity is not hidden, but quite the opposite; it has become a privileged narrative theme.

Back on the *Nellie* on the river Thames, the tranquil waterway leads "into the heart of an immense darkness" (HD 187). Until the end, there is no triumphant return to civilisation but rather the sombre feeling of utter failure.

---

152 Carola M. Kaplan (2005) argues that much criticism has too quickly equated Conrad's writing with a 'masculine' and misogynist viewpoint. She elaborates on how Conrad depicted more rounded and complete female characters, especially in *The Secret Agent* and *Under Western Eyes*, who did not embody stereotypical gender ideals of the time. My intention is not to automatically link the discourse of the crisis of masculinity with explicit misogyny. An author can present complex female characters (as is the case with most of the writers included in the postcolonial section) and *still* eschew in a re-privileging understanding of masculinity as a hegemonic reference point. However, in most of Conrad's fiction, male failure remains the single most important narrative reference point.

To recapitulate, in terms of style and its handling of colonialism, the narrative remains ambiguous. Conrad replicates tropes and patterns that have shaped adventure writing, such as the quest into the unknown, and transforms them. Nonetheless, Conrad still relies on a notion of heroic masculinity which Brantlinger terms "conservative and nihilistic":

Conrad's critique of empire is never strictly anti-imperialist. Instead, in terms that can be construed as both conservative and nihilistic, he mourns the loss of the true faith in modern times, the closing down of frontiers, the narrowing of the possibilities for adventure, the commercialization of the world and of art, the death of chivalry and honor. (Brantlinger 1988, 274)

Indeed, what Conrad constructs as a moral dilemma of humanity is in actuality the crisis of White Western masculinity generated by the atrocities committed by the very same men in the name of imperialism. Hence, this focus on moral failure, and ultimately, Marlow's capacity to re-emerge from the antechamber of hell also manifests the sublime state of White masculinity. Brantlinger further elaborates that Conrad constructs a sort of negative heroism that ultimately elevates White masculinity once more. He explains that "acts which are condemned as the vilest of crimes when committed in the supposedly civilized West can be linked to a heroism of the spirit and to Stygian authenticity when committed in Africa against Africans" (ibid., 270). The colonised become only the backdrop of the moral corruption and their suffering is written out of the story. White women, too, have to be kept out of this dirty business of colonialism lest their 'fair spirits' will be sullied as well. Even if shattered to pieces, Conrad's world remains ultimately a world of White men.

Conrad establishes a complex web of metaphors of lightness and darkness in his not always easily accessible prose which overflows with adjectives. In his oeuvre, both darkness and lightness can connote the challenges that modern 'Man' faces. Describing this ambivalent sense of failure, the end of heroism is an achievement of Conrad's writing that was in fact quite exceptional at the time. In *The "Narcissus"*, it is the fascination and appropriation of racial 'Otherness' which becomes the vehicle for Conrad to develop his own model of artistic and aesthetic innovation. The White men desire and have to repudiate both Black and queer masculinity in order to stabilise their own hegemonic masculinity. Although Conrad shows a world which has been tainted by imperialism, he also languishes the male bonds at sea and reinforces White camaraderie, a notion that *Heart of Darkness* questions much more radically.

In his evaluation of Conrad's writing, which focuses mainly on *Lord Jim*, Fredric Jameson describes Conrad's style as "unclassifiable, spilling out of high literature into light reading and romance" (Jameson 1994, 206). Located between nineteenth-century adventure tale and the aesthetics of twentieth-century literary modernism, *Heart of Darkness* marks an important shift in the writing of empire. Said argues that

Conrad dates imperialism, shows its contingency, records its illusions and tremendous violence and waste [...], he permits his later readers to imagine something other than an Africa carved up into dozens of European colonies, even if, for his own part, he had little notion of what that Africa might be. (Said 1994, 26)

Rather than conveying a realistic image of Africa, he transforms the River Congo into a symbolic underworld. The journey into the "heart of darkness" becomes a voyage into the abyss of man's depravity. Said places Conrad's writing explicitly in stark contrasts to the writing of Haggard and Kipling with their basis in

exhilaration and interest of adventure in the colonial world. [...] Conrad's tales and novels in one sense reproduce the aggressive contours of the high imperialist undertaking, but in another sense they are infected with the easily recognizable, ironic awareness of the post-realist modernist sensibility. (ibid., 187–188)

However, as has been noted, Said at times fails to note the investment in a certain idealisation of male crisis in this very modernist sensibility[153] that I have delineated in this chapter and which – more than in other modernist writers – is clearly evident in Conrad's texts. As Ricœur writes, the challenge to established notions of subjectivity also affects the way identity becomes narratable:

[T]o the degree the narrative approaches the annulment of the character in terms of identity-as-sameness, the novel loses its properly narrative qualities. To the loss of identity of the character corresponds a loss of the configuration of the narrative and in particular a crisis of its closure. (Ricœur 1991, 78)

Conrad's allegorical tales move away from generic adventure stories as well as more realistic character descriptions. Language becomes elusive and seems to fail to convey human experience accurately. "Conrad suggests

---

153 Of course, there exists a 'female modernism' with Virginia Woolf as one of the most prominent authors. Nonetheless, it is often writers such as James Joyce or T.S. Eliot who will be identified as the most rigorous modernist innovators of language – a gesture resonating with stereotypes of 'male genius'. (cf. Roberts 2000, 118–120) As has been argued, Conrad specifically rests his innovative potential on notions of male failure.

that both the artist and the imperialist explore worlds in which there are no external controls over their deepest drives." (McClure 1981, 90) Therefore, the modern crisis of writing can also be conceived as a crisis of narrative closure in Ricœur's terminology. It is this very crisis of writing that serves as a backdrop of male modernism and the reinvention of a new mode of writing – a mode that Conrad among others has established. Texts like *Heart of Darkness* and to a certain degree *The "Narcissus"* "reject the European episteme and turn this rejection into the motor that drives the modernist narrative" (Gikandi 1996, 48). In Conrad's writing, colonialism is delineated as a corrupt system doomed to failure. John McClure even speaks of "the birth of the new critical self-consciousness" (McClure 1981, 154).

But by the end of the nineteenth century, the redemptive myth behind the journey verged upon failure. [...] Indeed, the areas of heroic adventure are now turned inward, and the idea of a journey becomes a metaphor not simply for the rediscovery of a cultural order, but also, in its most radical extensions, for the metaphysical explorations of the mind. This is a crucial development not only in the fiction of adventure, but also in the English novel, because it thrusts the novel into experiences alien to its nineteenth-century social and literary conventions. From a strictly literary perspective, Conrad's problem is to find a language to talk about such experience. (Jones 1985, 22)

It is the classical hero who fails to complete his tasks, and it is the author who fails to convey the complexity of this experience in an adequate language. The horrors of colonialism are perceived as triggering a breakdown of meaningful communication that can only find expression in the uttering of "The horror! The horror!" Nonetheless, colonialism is first and foremost perverted because it has produced the failure of White men. Failing in this context remains a privileged position as it implies the idealised hero's fall and the establishment of a new male anti-hero. "A new writing of masculine hegemony is constructed in which masculinity is reaffirmed through its encounter with otherness as distinct 'essence.'" (McCracken 1993, 38) Conrad no longer tries to contain male crisis but is one of the first authors to expose these crises of his anti-heroes, and thereby, his texts foreshadow later postcolonial narratives of failure.

2. Postcolonial Masculinities: Hybrid Men, Fanatics and Anti-Heroes

This section is concerned with the way in which the narratives of masculinity in crisis have been altered by postcoloniality and by the way masculinity is conceptualised at the end of the twentieth century. As has been noted in the introduction, narratives of postcolonial masculinities in crisis often function more self-reflexively than in previous periods. By now, the hegemonic status of masculinity is clearly more strongly contested and the crises of men in fiction become more pronounced and exposed. In a certain sense, crises now appear volitional, and plural crises of masculinities become conceivable. In a globalised context, – characterised by postcolonial migration – perspectives have changed. The resistance to racial exclusion and the emergence of concepts such as Black and Asian Britishness as well as women's emancipation and the broader acceptance of non-heteronormative lifestyles influence how White heterosexual masculinity can be conceptualised and narrated.

In addition, British identity and Britishness are no longer self-evident concepts but signs that are re-interpreted in a number of texts and contexts. Gikandi explains that this process of redefining British identity has been seen as both a crisis and a turning point.

But if the disappearance of empire has left Great Britain with nothing more than nostalgia and the signs of postimperial atrophy – the decaying infrastructure, racism, and cultural hysteria – it has also generated questions about colonialism's surreptitious function in the forms of British identity. (Gikandi 1996, 21)

Both masculinity and national identity no longer seem to stand for fixed reference points – which they, in fact, never were but as which they are retrospectively imagined and which is a sign of conservative and nostalgic discourse. (cf. Gilroy 2005) By this time, the idea of crisis is linked to the narrative pattern of *guilt* and the need to readjust in a postcolonial context. This can include the bemoaning of lost privileges as well as attempts to renegotiate notions of masculinity.

In this section, I do not focus on (historical) re-writings of colonial narratives, but on postcolonial literature[154] and films which address the dilemma of male failure and readjustment in the aftermath of the British empire in a contemporary context. This encompasses the stories of hegemonic and marginalised masculinities. Interestingly, the texts that most clearly privilege the perspective of hegemonic men, such as Coetzee's self-reflexive anti-heroes, are located in the periphery of the former colonies

---

154 In the largely influential book *The Empire Writes Back*, Ashcroft, Griffiths and Tiffin introduce a very broad definition of this term. (cf. Ashcroft, Griffiths and Tiffin 2002, 2) While I opt for an understanding of postcolonial literature that includes writing in the West dealing with what Hall calls the "process of *diaspora-ization*" (Hall 1996c, 447) of cultures, I share some critics' unease with an all-encompassing definition of postcoloniality that includes major neo-imperial powers. It remains relevant to mark differences according to the situatedness of authors and literatures in various postcolonial settings. Especially the difference between settler and invaded colonies and the respective effects on contemporary societies need to be taken into consideration in this context. Although I agree with Roy Sommer (2001) that in the wake of *The Empire Writes Back* the genre of canonical rewritings and the focus on hybridity have become the most privileged modes in postcolonial literature and literary studies, I do not share his rejection of the term postcolonial literature for fictions dealing with second- or third-generation migrants in the West. For Sommer, these are to be considered "fictions of migration" and he differentiates between the "novel of migration", the "multicultural *Bildungsroman*", the "revisionist historical novel" and "transcultural hybrid novels". Sommer's argument for a differentiation between postcolonial literature and "fictions of migration" in my view assumes a too narrow understanding of both postcoloniality and hybridity (which he attaches too closely to the concept of colonial mimicry and the relationship between coloniser and colonised. Bhabha (1994), however, stresses that hybridity has to be seen not necessarily as a sign of postcolonial societies or a conscious subversive practice solely. Rather, in Bhabha's view, cultural formations of 'self' and 'Other' have always been hybrid processes). The history of migration and diasporas, especially in Britain, are inseparably linked to Britain's colonial past and have to be understood as part of a post- or neo-colonial continuum, which is why I employ the term 'postcolonial' for authors dealing with these processes both in former colonies and in Britain. In this sense, I regard literature by Black British authors as part of postcolonial literature even though terminologies as these always remain problematic and provisional. (cf. Boehmer 2005, 4; Stein 2004, xv) Consequently, as mentioned before, the locatedness of these authors is of importance, and it is relevant to read authors, such as Kureishi and Smith, as British postcolonial voices rather than as voices outside the centre. Another problem occurs with attaching the label postcolonial to writers in a hegemonic position in former colonies such as White writing in South Africa. Understood not as a simple "after" colonialism, but as dealing with the after-effects *and* ongoing processes of a heritage of imperialism and exploitation, 'postcolonial(ism)', in my opinion, remains a productive term – although one that (like other theoretical concepts) – needs to be constantly challenged and reassessed.

while the novels that focus more thoroughly on marginalised men, as the writing of Kureishi and Smith, in the metropolitan centre London.

In contrast to colonial fiction, marginalised masculinities now appear as more rounded characters: the question of how to find one's place in a racist society comes to the fore but also the possibility to acquire male privilege is introduced. These postcolonial stories are informed by the questions of what it means to be British or, whether there is – as Kureishi phrased it – "a new way of being British" (Kureishi 2002a, 55). The narrative pattern of an alleged '*in-betweenness*' or *hybridity* is distinctive of these postcolonial texts, and in contrast to the earlier hegemonic hybrid figures who are endangered by the colonial setting, it is now mainly the crisis of the racialised character in the metropolis that is negotiated.

Starting with the two most well-known novels by Hanif Kureishi, *The Buddha of Suburbia* and *The Black Album*, I will analyse Kureishi's fictions of hybrid masculinity. Kureishi's texts, on the one hand, include a polyphony (cf. Ranasinha 2002, 51) of different voices and challenge notions of clearly distinguishable 'hegemonic' and 'marginalised' masculinities. On the other hand, his novels also demonstrate what could be termed male flexibility. Contemporary British cinema is concerned with finding a visual vocabulary that is more representative of the changes in British society. As a clear departure from the heritage cinema of the early eighties, Fears' and Kureishi's *My Beautiful Laundrette* focuses on a derelict London and the social changes that Thatcher's government affected. The failure of clear binaries at challenges to gendered looking relations is at the heart of the Neil Jordan film *The Crying Game*. In the third chapter of this section, I examine Zadie Smith's *White Teeth*, one of the most successful English novels of the last few years. Centring on the two middle-age men, Archie Jones and Samad Iqbal, her story presents a version of "hysterical realism" (cf. Wood 2005) in which one clearly finds reference to male crises but also a certain farcical tone that focuses more strongly on plot than on character development. In a not strictly chronological order, I have chosen to situate J.M. Coetzee at the end of this section as I will try to highlight the parallels with Conrad, who had served as the bridge between the two parts on colonial and postcolonial literature. In the South African context and in light of the legacy of apartheid, questions of *guilt* are much more pronounced in Coetzee's writing than in any of the other texts in this section. Hegemony now becomes a burden that men have come to terms with. This will be analysed with reference to his novels *Waiting for the Barbarians* and *Disgrace*.

While hegemonic masculinity in the colonial period encompassed figurations such as *gentlemen* and *hunters* as well as the *hybrid 'Sahib'* and *failures*, one can speak of *hybrid men*, *fanatics* and *anti-heroes* in the postcolonial context. In these stories of manifold and exposed crises of masculinities, there is a sense of awareness that the recourse to a stable identity and the clear opposition of 'self' and 'Other' ultimately no longer holds true. Nonetheless, this multiplication of narratives of male crises and the renegotiation of the concept of masculinity in itself does not necessarily do away with the related privilege.

Hanif Kureishi: New Ways of Being British

Hanif Kureishi has been celebrated as one of the most promising writers of a "first generation of children of 'New Commonwealth' origins to be born in Britain" (Moore-Gilbert 2001, 13). The son of a Pakistani father and British mother no longer represents a 'writing back' from the colonies but a new distinctly British voice from the centre. Being a monoglot of English with nearly all his work set in London, Kureishi's writing stands in the tradition of the 'condition of England novel'. He seldom directly addresses the relationship of the former colonies and England as has been central to the texts of 'world writers' such as V.S. Naipaul or Salman Rushdie. Nonetheless, his work is immensely telling with regard to the construction of postcolonial masculinities. The lives of characters with a biracial heritage in Britain are at the centre of many of his stories and challenge what it means to be British today. Kureishi's celebratory angle at hybridity has been applauded and criticised alike and will be expounded upon in my reading of *The Buddha of Suburbia*. A versatile writer, Kureishi is at home in a number of genres. Having started out successfully in the fringe theatre scene of London, he collaborated with Stephen Frears on some of the most successful English films of the Thatcher era, one of which, namely, *My Beautiful Laundrette*, will be analysed in the following chapter on postcolonial films. Following his initial success at the theatre and as a writer for the big screen – resulting in an Academy-Award nomination for best original screenplay for *My Beautiful Laundrette* – today Kureishi works as a writer of novels, short stories and the occasional screenplay. The changing conceptions of masculinities have been at the heart of most of his texts, or, as he himself put it in an interview:

I guess I'm interested in men because I'm a bloke myself but also because I was very interested in the revolutions of my time: for gays, women, blacks and Asians – with people becoming aware of their positions. And white blokes got rather left out of that. But of course when everybody else's position changed so the white bloke's position changed as well. (Kureishi quoted in Yousaf 2002, 14)

As Kureishi colloquially phrases it, male hegemony and the conception of masculinity are not fixed and react to social changes.

The diaspora experience has been central to writers of his generation who often did not experience migration themselves but are the second or third generation living in Britain. In Hall's terms, this is essentially a hybrid experience.

The diaspora experience [...] is defined, not by essence or purity, but by the recognition of a necessary heterogeneity and diversity, by a conception of 'identity' which lives with and through, not despite, difference; by *hybridity*. (Hall 1996b, 119–120)

Hall also established an important critique of an understanding of diaspora that tends to glorify notions of past, heritage and roots. He criticises the idea of pure cultures or a "law of origin".

Cultural identities are the points of identification, the unstable points of identification or suture, which are made, within the discourses of history and culture. Not an essence but a *positioning*. Hence, there is always a politics of identity, a politics of position, which has no absolute guarantee in an unproblematic, transcendental 'law of origin'. (ibid., 113)

Following Hall's momentous critique, critics such as Gayatri Gopinath in her study *Impossible Desires* (2005) help to establish a queer understanding of diaspora which seeks to disrupt naturalised notions of both the categories heterosexuality and the nation. Her definition of queer diaspora is as follows:

The category of 'queer' [...] works to name this alternative rendering of diaspora and to dislodge diaspora from its adherence and loyalty to nationalist ideologies that are fully aligned with the interests of transnational capitalism. Suturing 'queer' to 'diaspora' thus recuperates those desires, practices, and subjectivities that are rendered impossible and unimaginable within conventional diasporic and nationalist imaginaries. (Gopinath 2005, 10–11)

Kureishi's writing as a novelist and for the cinema can be seen as a predecessor for such a queer understanding of diaspora, which is hinted at, but never quite realised. His writing is, on the one hand, informed by such a queering of both diaspora and Englishness, while on the other hand, there is also a tendency to re-centre his male heroes who seek success and approval. It is these ambivalences that I want to trace in this chapter starting with his first novel of 1990, *The Buddha of Suburbia*, and then turning to his second book, *The Black Album*.

In his latest stories, Kureishi has shifted his attention from the margin to the centre (albeit both in a Western context), which is an interesting move for a writer who has been constantly marked as an 'ethnic writer'. As a consequence, many critics have noted a change of focus from ethnicity to masculinity in his more recent writing, such as *The Body* or *Intimacy*. This statement is problematic in so far as it negates the masculinity of his 'ethnic' characters and the ethnicity of his White male protagonists in later fictions. I argue that crisis narratives of masculinities have also played an important role in his earlier fictions (cf. Ranasinha 2009, 298) which will be the focus of the following readings.

The Buddha of Suburbia: "A funny kind of Englishman"[155]

Set in seventies Britain, *The Buddha of Suburbia* is a rather classical coming-of-age story featuring the seventeen-year-old Karim Amir who introduces himself to the reader on the first page.

My name is Karim Amir, and I am an Englishman born and bred, almost. I am often considered to be a funny kind of Englishman, a new breed as it were, having emerged from two old histories. (BS 3)

Karim, who has an English mother, Margaret, and an Indian father, Haroon, has to learn how to deal with his so-called position 'between cultures'. In terms of style, Kureishi follows a realist pattern and does not experiment too much with language or genre conventions. This auto-diegetic narrative is split into two parts, "In the Suburbs" and "In the City", and follows Karim's movement from the first to the latter.

The adolescent Karim is highly influenced by his father, Haroon, who is the title-giving "Buddha of Suburbia". Anglicised by his wife's English family, he is immediately addressed as "Harry" rather than by his real name Haroon. Now, he in some sense relives his youth and grows up once more alongside his son. Working as a yoga instructor after quitting his regular job, Haroon can finally capitalise on his status as racialised 'Other'. As "a renegade Muslim masquerading as a Buddhist" (BS 16), he sells spiritual enlightenment to the eager White middle classes of the suburbs. Moore-Gilbert identifies this as a reversal of the "evangelising project" in the colonies. "Instead of Indian natives compliantly absorbing the religious wisdom of the West, the native British seek deliverance from their ersatz immigrant *guru*." (Moore-Gilbert 2001, 123)

Growing up in the South London suburbs, Karim has to grapple with the falling apart of his parents' marriage, his sexual awakening and, in more general terms, figuring out what he wants to do with his life. During these

---

155 An earlier shorter German version that focuses on "intersectional queer readings" has been published as Haschemi Yekani (2008).

everyday struggles, he is constantly made aware that because of his Indian origins, he is not in a position of privileged masculinity.

Contrasting Karim with the main female protagonist Jamila, whose story features as a subplot of the novel, I hope to demonstrate how the novel privileges Karim's perspective while allowing for interjections from manifold side characters who express opinions different from Karim's. Sangeeta Ray calls this "the cacophony generated by the multiplicity of heterogeneous positions" (Ray 1998, 234). This polyphony, I argue, figures as a queer potential of the novel.

In the beginning, Jamila, the daughter of Haroon's friend Anwar, lives with her parents, Anwar and Jeeta, above their store. Jamila and Karim begin a sporadic sexual relationship, but this never entails a serious commitment on either side. Jamila is also identified as more mature and advanced indicated by her interest in politics, and through her influence Karim becomes familiar with the writings of Simone de Beauvoir, Angela Davis, Malcolm X, James Baldwin and Kate Millett. In this context, the writings of politicised African Americans offer the two teenagers a way to express their racial 'Otherness' in a language that is not available to them in seventies England: "Yeah, sometimes we were French, Jammie and I, and other times we went black American. The thing was, we were supposed to be English, but to the English we were always wogs and nigs and Pakis and the rest of it." (BS 53) This quote underlines the apparent incompatibility of non-Whiteness with the concept of Englishness. A challenge to this ethnicised version of British national identity is a recurring narrative pattern of Kureishi's writing and has been theorised by Hall in his much-quoted essay on "New Ethnicities". Hall explains that "ethnicity, in the form of a culturally constructed sense of Englishness and a particularly closed, exclusive and regressive form of English national identity, is one of the core characteristics of English racism today" (Hall 1996c, 446). This dilemma of not being accepted as a 'proper English lad' is part of Karim's adolescent quandaries and thus, fuels his quest for acknowledgement.

Whereas Karim, for most of the novel, experiences racism as a personal drawback, Jamila engages actively in anti-racist politics. Thomas comments that "[i]t is a woman who seeks political solutions and the men who are looking for love" (Thomas 2005, 78). Racism for Karim, for instance, means that he faces the dangers of the racist White father of his White girlfriend, Helen. In comparison to the woman Jamila, Karim can more easily pursue his personal happiness. In contrast to Karim, Jamila's parents are both of Indian descent, and she also faces more resistance from her family. Similar to Haroon, Jamila's father, Anwar, is discontented with his situation in England which the men of the first generation experience quite differently than their children. Puzzled about the sudden changes in his father's and his friend's behaviour, Karim muses over the reasons:

Perhaps it was the immigrant condition living itself out through them. For years they were both happy to live like Englishmen. [...] Now, as they aged and seemed settled here, Anwar and Dad appeared to be returning internally to India, or at least to be resisting the English here. (BS 64)

However, neither of the two men actually express the wish to return to that "rotten place" (BS 64), India. Instead they feel a growing sense of 'unbelonging' that Kureishi terms the "immigrant condition" (BS 64).

As a way to resist this 'unbelonging', Anwar suddenly rediscovers his faith and insists on an arranged marriage for his rebellious daughter. Comparable to Haroon's Buddhism, this is an adopted state of mind rather than a deeply felt conviction or belief.[156]

It was certainly bizarre, Uncle Anwar behaving like a Muslim. I'd never known him believe in anything before, so it was an amazing novelty to find him literally staking his life on the principle of absolute patriarchal authority. (BS 64)

When Jamila rejects his plans for her, Anwar begins a hunger strike in order to manipulate Jamila to ultimately bend to his will. In this way, Anwar's hunger strike 'perverts' the anti-colonial resistance of Gandhi to turn it into an oppressive mechanism used against the Asian woman. Kureishi's gender politics have been at the centre of some controversial debates.[157] His focus on masculinity, some argue, has led him to perpetuate a marginalisation of the 'Asian woman' in his writings. It seems, indeed, as if Kureishi is actively trying to get rid of the "burden of representation"[158] of

---

156 In the context of different marginalised masculinities, Buddhist masculinity is obviously perceived as more tolerant and less threatening than Muslim masculinity, which is always implicitly linked to fundamentalism.

157 Most prominently this controversy focused on the film *Sammy and Rosie Get Laid* (1987) for which Kureishi wrote the script. One can contrast bell hooks' reading (1990), which accuses Kureishi of a "stylish nihilism" with that of Gayatri Spivak (1989), which applauds the film's openness to multiple voices and montage as examples of the two separate ends in the spectrum of the debate.

158 The phrase was coined by Kobena Mercer. He explains: "When artists are positioned on the margins of the institutional spaces of cultural production, they are burdened with the

always being read as an 'Asian' or 'ethnic' writer who has to portray 'his community' in a favourable light. As a consequence, Mark Stein proposes the term "postethnic literature" with regard to Kureishi's writing. Stein employs this term as explicitly not denoting a transcending of ethnicity but rather a "writing that shows an awareness of the expectations that so-called ethnic writing faces" (Stein 2004, 112). Given his controversial gender politics, his inclusion of explicit sex scenes, queer characters and dislikeable Thatcherites among his Asian British characters, Kureishi cannot be said to sugar-coat his image of 'the community'.

After yielding to Anwar's wishes, Jamila meets her husband to be, Changez. Changez still very much represents the uncritical, clumsy, "mimic Englishman" – which by now may have itself become a stereotype of the newly immigrated Indian. Coming from an Indian upper-class background, Changez adopts an air of superiority over the other uneducated immigrants trapped in their menial work. In contrast to Karim, who was born in England, he is perplexed by being racially abused on the streets. Kureishi succeeds in painting a multi-dimensional image of the intersections of class and race in the English context. While Karim, a member of the second generation, aspires for upward mobility, immigrants with an upper-class background, such as Changez or Jeeta, are confronted with downward mobility, suddenly losing the status of privilege they enjoyed in their countries of origin. Changez is mocked for his adoration of what he calls 'the classics' of English literature, namely P.G. Wodehouse and Sir Arthur Conan Doyle. Kureishi often employs these literary cross-references to characterise his protagonists. Changez' reading preferences are contrasted with Jamila's politicised preference for African American literature, and also with Karim's (adolescent) 'male' references to *Tropic of Cancer* (Henry Miller) and *On the Road* (Jack Kerouac). His dislike of his mother's habit of watching soap operas and his predilection for high literature also mark him as slightly arrogant in this respect. (cf. Moore-Gilbert 2001, 118)

Despite the criticism Kureishi has received for depicting an arranged marriage, and although they are hardly ever the sole narrative centre of attention, his female characters are more complex than simple misogynist stereotypes. Jamila is not to be confounded with a silent victim. She pursues her sexual freedom and continues to sleep with Karim after she has married Changez, with whom she refuses to have sex. When Changez tries

---

impossible task of speaking as 'representatives', in that they are widely expected to 'speak for' the marginalized communities from which they come." (Mercer 1994, 235)

to assert his authority over her, he fails, and it is Changez who adapts to the ways of his wife rather than vice versa. Changez fails in asserting 'traditional masculinity'. In addition, his disability also marks his status as marginalised; his injured left arm further distances him from the ideal of hegemonic masculinity. Nonetheless, although Karim is at first ashamed of being seen with Changez, "in case the lads saw he was a Paki and imagined I was one too" (BS 98), a friendship between the two develops. Kureishi manages to avoid a one-dimensional image of his characters and endows them with room to evolve. Through his failure to assert himself as the patriarchal head of his marriage, Changez is actually freed to explore different aspects of masculinity. In his pursuit to have an affair with the Japanese sex worker Shinko, Changez enjoys sexual experimentation. Consequently, what began as a stereotypical story of an arranged marriage seemingly ends in queer emancipation. In the end, Changez and Jamila live together as a patchwork family in a commune where Jamila gave birth to a baby (she had with another man) and lives in a lesbian relationship.

It is no coincidence that Kureishi focuses on the seventies in his debut novel, which was published in 1990.[159] Kureishi is interested in how different models of masculinity, femininity and family relations became imaginable at that time. Both Karim and Jamila are sexually open-minded and have multiple partners of both sexes. In this sense, *The Buddha* is also a nostalgic look back at the era of the so-called sexual revolution which was dramatically different than what teenagers of the AIDS era were currently experiencing. Connected to the popular culture of glam and glitter rock in the early seventies, androgyny – prominently popularised by David Bowie (who attended the same school as Kureishi) – is glorified, and bisexuality is presented as the norm rather than a deviation. Set before Thatcher's conservative backlash of the eighties, Kureishi is well aware that many of these progressive changes in gender and sexual norms would be short-lived. The search for alternative lifestyles, communal living and sexual experimentation was strongly delimited by the new emphasis on 'traditional' family values under Thatcher. But Kureishi's nostalgic image is already tainted by

---

159 Susanne Reichl points out incongruities in references to popular culture and other historical events in the novel which would suggest that the plot in effect spans from ca. 1970–1979, which seems an unrealistically long period, and she interprets this as Kureishi's disregard for the "narrow confines of history" (Reichl 2007, 150).

the pressure to 'sell-out' which dominates the end of the novel.[160] In this sense, the novel also emphasises the constantly changing concepts such as gender, sexuality and nation, which do not follow a linear progressive logic. Quite the contrary: the novel ends at a time when possibilities seem to lessen.

Ambivalence is linked to many aspects of Karim's identity. He is not only ethnically ambivalent; it is also his sexuality that is marked as queer. In this context, Gopinath's understanding of a queer diaspora proves helpful. While Bhabha's concept of hybridity functions as a destabilising factor concerning the construction of nationality, gender and heteronormativity tend to be overlooked. But hybridity can also be linked to sexuality. In Kureishi's works, the desire of the diasporic characters is not confined by a nationalist logic of 'purity' of the family or community. There are various and changing sexual couplings in the novel: Karim and Jamila, Karim and Charlie, Karim and Eleanor, Karim, Eleanor, the director Pyke and his wife Marlene. Out of all couples it is the heterosexual marriage within the same ethnic community between Jamila and Changez which remains un-consummated in this novel full of sexual activity. Instead, there are the couples Changez and Shinko, as well as Jamila and Simon (the father of her daughter) and Jamila and her lesbian lover, Joanna.

A repeated pattern in Kureishi's work is the (not unproblematic) desire for the racial 'Other'. In the beginning, Karim describes his own sexual preferences as follows:

It was unusual, I knew, the way I wanted to sleep with boys as well as girls. I liked strong bodies and the back of boys' necks. I liked being handled by men, their fists pulling me; and I liked objects – the ends of brushes, pens, fingers – up my arse. But I liked cunts and breasts, all of women's softness, long and smooth legs and the way women dressed. (BS 55)

Karim is quite untroubled by his sexual inclinations. For him, it seems perfectly 'natural' to explore both genders sexually. In contrast to a coming-out story, however, Karim never feels the urge to reveal his sexuality or to claim a gay or bisexual identity. There is no narrative reference to the closet in this novel. Sexual experimentation is simply part of the rebellious seventies atmosphere. From the start, he is enchanted by Charlie, the son

---

160 Claus-Ulrich Viol traces how more recent fictions stress the "liberating power of the period's social and intellectual climate" (Viol 2005, 153) despite the fact that the seventies in Britain were also often conceived as a time of social crisis and economic depression.

of his father's girlfriend Eva, who is adored in explicitly erotic terms and with whom he has sexual contact. After their first meeting, Karim describes Charlie's beauty in a comically exaggerated declaration typical of the novel's humorous tone.

> He was a boy upon whom nature had breathed such beauty – his nose was so straight, his cheeks so hollow, his lips such rosebuds – that people were afraid to approach him, and he was often alone. Men and boys got erections just being in the same room as him; for others the same effect was had by being in the same country. Women sighed in his presence, and teachers bristled. (BS 9)

Charlie, working on his career as a rebel rock star, embodies hegemonic White masculinity. His looks – a straight nose, hollow cheeks and rosebud lips – ensure he will not experience racial discrimination. For that reason, Karim does not only desire Charlie, he also envies his position in society: "My love for him was unusual as love goes. [...] It was that I preferred him to me and wanted to be him." (BS 15) While the novel at first glance seems unquestioning in its celebration of sexual liberation and fluid sexualities, Kureishi is not unaware of the power relations at work in sexual hierarchies. Sleeping with men might seem perfectly alright to Karim, but his father is not pleased when he catches Karim and Charlie making out. The later revelation that Karim (also) sleeps with women is a great reassurance to Haroon.

> This was a relief to my father, I knew, who was so terrified that I might turn gay that he could never bring himself to mention the matter. In his Muslim mind it was bad enough being a woman; being a man and denying your male sex was perverse and self-destructive, as well as everything else. (BS 174)

In this sense, Kureishi has his male characters explore queer sexuality but a heterosexual stabilising element is often reintroduced.[161] Kureishi employs a similar construction concerning Shahid's gender identity in his later novel *The Black Album*. Here, as will be expounded upon in my following reading of the novel, the protagonist flirts with femininity but still tries to claim a macho heterosexual masculinity.

In general, this space to experiment is literally connected to the depiction of London which Kureishi has once described as "his playground"

---

161 *My Beautiful Laundrette* marks an exception here, as the protagonists Omar and Johnny are clearly conceived as gay men and consequently, Omar ignores Tania's advances.

(MacCabe and Kureishi 1999, 37).[162] In London, Karim enjoys the new exciting city life.[163] Suddenly, he does not feel singled out because "there were thousands of black people everywhere, so I wouldn't feel exposed" (BS 121). Karim drops out of school and tries to launch his career as an actor but soon learns that he has to compromise his principles in order to succeed. With the help of upwardly-mobile Eva, he meets Shadwell, an amateur director, who will cast him for one of his productions and who is immediately enamoured by Karim's 'exoticness':

He said, 'What a breed of people two hundred years of imperialism has given birth to. If the pioneers from the East India Company could see you. What puzzlement there'd be. Everyone looks at you, I'm sure, and thinks: an Indian boy, how exotic, how interesting, what stories of aunties and elephants we'll now hear from him. And you're from Orpington. [...] The immigrant is the new Everyman of the twentieth century. Yes?' [...] 'She [Eva] is trying to protect you from your destiny, which is to be a half-caste in England. That must be complicated for you to accept – belonging nowhere, wanted nowhere. Racism. Do you find it difficult? Please tell me.' (BS 141)

In these situations, Karim often finds himself misunderstood as an 'exotic' "half-caste" when in reality, he feels like an average 'English bloke'. He has never been to India, speaks no other language than English and his cultural role models come from British popular culture. Consequently, he is dismayed when, of all roles, he is cast as Mowgli in Shadwell's semi-professional production of Kipling's *Jungle Book* – one of the most stereotypical colonial texts. "'In fact, you are Mowgli. You're dark-skinned, you're small and wiry, and you'll be sweet but wholesome in the costume. Not too pornographic, I hope'." (BS 143) Karim is supposed to wear a brown loin cloth and brown make-up so that he "resembled a turd in a bikini-bottom" (BS 146). His own 'Indianness' is not authentic enough; he has to wear his alleged race as a mask made of brown make-up. He is also asked to fake an Indian accent, though he at first refuses, hoping for support from the politically active actors:

---

162 For the importance of London as a setting in Kureishi's fiction, cf. Ball (1996); McLeod (2004); Sandhu (2000).

163 However, Susan Brook (2005) also traces the importance of the suburb as a setting of the novel and argues that the clear dichotomy of the city as liberated and the suburb as the haven of conservative ideals does not hold true. James Procter reads Kureishi's focus on the (White English) suburb as an attempt to "provincialise Englishness" (Procter 2003, 126).

In the evenings we talked of inequality, imperialism, white supremacy and whether sexual experimentation was merely bourgeois indulgence or a contribution to the dissolution of established society. (BS 148)

But this seems to have been mere theoretical talk, as they do not support him. Karim quickly abandons his political convictions for the advantages of being lead actor. He is, on the one hand, quite aware of the racism that he is confronted with, while on the other hand, he is willing to capitalise on his presumed exoticised status as long as it works to his own advantage. In this way, Karim becomes the individualistic hero seeking a personal rise in the city, with London the corrupt backdrop of this tale of adolescence. In some ways, Kureishi succeeds in transforming or hybridising the genre of the *Bildungsroman* by focusing on the son of an immigrant as a new Dickensian hero. Nonetheless, with the strong emphasis on personal success he does not do away with many of the presuppositions of the genre.[164]

After they saw *The Jungle Book*, Haroon and Jamila are shocked by Karim's performance. Haroon comments:

'That bloody fucker Mr Kipling pretending to whity he knew something about India! And an awful performance by my boy looking like a Black and White Minstrel!' (BS 157)

Jamila's judgement is similarly harsh:

'So innocent and young, showing off your pretty body, so thin and perfectly formed. But no doubt about it, the play is totally neo-fascist –' […] 'And the accent – my God, how could you do it? I expect you're ashamed, aren't you?' (BS 157)

Although Karim does indeed feel ashamed, *The Jungle Book* is also the vehicle of his career when he is hired by Pyke, a famous director. This causes dismay among the older and more professional actors in the company:

---

164 For a discussion of a possible hybridisation of genre in the context of Black British or postcolonial literature and *The Buddha*, cf. Stein (2004) who speaks of "novels of transformation" (focusing on the formation of its protagonists and on the transformation of British society) or Sommer (2001) who labels it a "multicultural *Bildungsroman*". Moore-Gilbert is more hesitant as to whether Kureishi's style is to be considered innovative/hybrid. There is rarely any recourse to the postcolonial situation outside of Britain and Kureishi's writing is almost always set in Britain. Since the novel is written in Standard English (there is hardly any usage of other languages/dialects), follows a realist mode, and adheres to genre conventions rather clearly, one could argue that Kureishi appropriates rather than subverts or hybridises the genre. (cf. Moore-Gilbert 2001, 29)

Boyd [...] said, as he took off his trousers and shook his penis at me, 'If I weren't white and middle class I'd have been in Pyke's show now. Obviously mere talent gets you nowhere these days. Only the disadvantaged are going to succeed in seventies' England.' (BS 165)

In a reversal of what one would expect, here Karim's marginalised masculinity works to his advantage and to the disadvantage of the hegemonic White men. The assumed crisis of 'in-betweenness' or unbelonging becomes an asset. Suddenly, the success of the White middle-class man does not seem to be the norm and Whiteness is associated with an alleged disadvantage. However, Karim's accomplishment is a compromise. The fact that he is favoured over his White colleague is a sign of positive racism rather than a reversal in the power relations which still influence the way he is treated.

While the father-son relationship is prominent in *The Buddha* and other Kureishi texts, Karim's relationship to his mother is also revealing. When he meets her after a theatre production where he plays a character based on Changez, she comments:

'You've never been to India. You'd get diarrhoea the minute you stepped off that plane, I know you would.' 'Why don't you say it a bit louder,' I said. 'Aren't I part Indian?' 'What about me?' Mum said 'Who gave birth to you? You're an Englishman, I'm glad to say.' 'I don't care,' I said 'I'm an actor. It's a job.' 'Don't say that,' she said. 'Be what you are.' (BS 232)

Karim's mother realises that he is capitalising on his Indian heritage and she feels left out. She sees Karim as English and with very little connection to his 'Indian origins'. From the beginning, Margaret feels that everybody is drawn to her husband and notes disparagingly that she is "only English" (BS 5). Here again it is as if White Englishness has lost its appeal and other ethnicities seem more exciting, and that is also why the White middle class feels so drawn to Haroon's Buddhism and Karim is happy to emphasise his 'Indianness' when it suits him. Karim's mother is identified with limitations, and Karim has a difficult time maintaining a good relationship with her: "I was reluctant to kiss my mother, afraid that somehow her weakness and unhappiness would infect me." (BS 104)

As a new member of the London avant-garde theatre scene, Karim is invited to Pyke's house and the discomfort during Karim's sexual encounter with Pyke and his wife is comically narrated:

England's most interesting and radical theatre director was inserting his cock between my speaking lips. I could appreciate the privilege, but I didn't like it much: it seemed an imposition. He could have asked politely. So I gave his dick a South London swipe – not viciously, nor enough to have my part in the play reduced – but enough to give him a jolt. (BS 203)

Despite the humour of the scene, Karim is very well aware that his part in the play depends on his sexual availability to the White director and his wife, with the latter being depicted as lusting after the young 'exotic' boy. Interracial sexual relationships are generally of great interest to Kureishi. In a reversal of the taboo theme of White men's relationships with Black women in the colonies, Kureishi's postcolonial writing features the recurring pattern of marginalised men and their relationships with White women (and also with White men as will be seen in *My Beautiful Laundrette*). This pattern of marginalised men sleeping with White women – often from the upper classes – is repeated in a number of Kureishi's texts: Karim dates Helen and then the actress Eleanor in *The Buddha of Suburbia*, Sammy and Rosie in the film *Sammy and Rosie Get Laid*, Shahid and Deedee Osgood in *The Black Album* (to be explored in the following chapter). Thomas argues that Kureishi portrays these relationships between White women and non-White men as "a way of gaining acceptance, a revenge against racism, and an attempt to transcend both" (Thomas 2005, 80). For her, this means in the context of *The Buddha of Suburbia* that "Karim's love for Charlie stems from his feeling of 'racial' inferiority, [while] his love for Eleanor is tied up with class envy." (ibid., 79) 'Conquering' the White woman can be read as a way to revenge the humiliation of racism while also indicating upward class mobility. Race, gender, class and sexuality clash and intertwine in conflicting ways, while the narrative resists sinking to what is often pejoratively referred to as 'postmodern playfulness', or the notion of 'anything goes'. Again, Karim experiences both male privilege as well as ethnicised marginalisation. He is singled-out and exoticised.

Being 'Black' is usually a perception that is inflicted on Karim rather than claimed by him, which becomes evident in his remark about the new theatre company where he works: "Two of us [were] officially 'black' (though truly I was more beige than anything)." (BS 167) Karim's status is repeatedly characterised as an 'in-betweenness'. Kureishi contrasts Karim's opportunism to the insistence on identity of Black actress, Tracey, who criticises his willingness to 'sell out'. Like Jamila, Tracey is not of mixed heritage, and as a Black woman, she feels the need to protect herself from White exploitation. Some critics, such as Berthold Schoene, have been quick to identify Tracey's insistence on her Black identity as lack of progression, whereas Karim has supposedly already transcended racial confines. Schoene reads Tracey as having failed "to imagine the possibility of cultural black/white hybridity or the emancipation of individual identity from perceptions of allegedly innate ethnic propensities and characteristics" (Schoene 1998, 123). He continues to claim that Kureishi promotes a view which entitles everybody to "their own singular cultural ethnicity" (ibid., 123). In my opinion, however, Schoene mixes up the naïveté of the character with the author's intentions. In fact, the female characters, such as Jamila and Tracey, seem to be important voices of dissent in the novel. It is not clear that Karim will be successful in his attempt to sell his hybridity. For instance, Kureishi includes the story of Eleanor's ex-boyfriend's suicide. Gene was a talented actor of Caribbean descent who could not cope with always playing the villains rather than being able to perform important roles in Shakespeare or Ibsen productions for the fact of his skin colour.[165] Therefore, although Karim remains a likeable character, the reader is also invited to question many of his decisions.

In this way, I would caution against an over-emphasis on Kureishi's role as a "herald of hybridity" (cf. Schoene 1998). Within the narrative, all characters adopt multiple identities along the intersections of race, class and sexuality. Haroon takes on Buddhism, Charlie performs working-class Englishness, Eva signifies upward class mobility and Jamila turns an arranged marriage into an alternative lifestyle. This performativity and fluidity of identifications has been emphasised by many critics. Nonetheless, although Kureishi plays with the stereotype of a 'feminised oriental masculinity'[166], he does not radically contest male privilege. The central crisis in this novel remains male privilege. Although the genre of the *Bildungsroman* is disturbed by a multiplicity of queer and ethnically diverse voices, there seems to be a re-centring of the (male) individual hero associated with the genre that Kureishi cannot quite do away with. While it is important to stress that Kureishi is quite successful at conveying the notion that Black *and* White Englishness are constructed and performative, I would argue that this assumed playfulness has also led to a somewhat premature cele-

---

165 P. Childs, Weber and Williams call Gene the "most powerful catalyst in the construction of Karim's identity" (P. Childs, Weber and Williams 2006, 241).

166 Moore-Gilbert notes that: "Haroon and Allie are at times disorientingly feminised and Changez actually develops breasts after the birth of Jamila's child. Conversely, his wife is strongly 'masculinised'; not only does her adolescent moustache put Karim's in the shade, but she beats her husband." (Moore-Gilbert 2001, 113)

bration of an all-encompassing hybridity.[167] The protagonist Karim is often portrayed as the archetypical hybrid Englishman, who appears "to inhabit an ethnicity-free no-man's land between the polar opposites of Englishness and Indianness" (Schoene 1998, 117). This alleged liberty associated with his ethnicity does in fact conceal the racial bias and ignores the power relations and struggles which Karim faces throughout the story. In this novel, as in present-day England, who can reinvent himself or herself and what kind of identity can be claimed by whom is still clearly predetermined by racialised and gendered as well as classed power relations. Charlie Hero can very well become a working class punk "selling Englishness" (BS 247)[168], but Karim cannot become 'un-Indian'.

As an exoticised 'Other', his Indianness can at times be to his benefit, but this does not conceal the racism (and limited options for an actor) with which he is confronted. Englishness – and I would add masculinity – remains a hegemonic and embattled privilege. Hall has discussed how the privilege of the unmarked position is still steadfastly connected to Whiteness.

We are beginning to think about how to represent a non-coercive and a more diverse conception of ethnicity, to set against the embattled, hegemonic conception of 'Englishness' which, under Thatcherism, stabilizes so much of the dominant political and cultural discourses, and which, because it is hegemonic, does not represent itself as an ethnicity at all. (Hall 1996c, 447)

But, unlike Schoene who claims that "Karim is free continuously to reinvent his identity which – due to the 'creamy' colour of his skin, his nomadic lifestyle and bisexual inclinations – remains ultimately unintelligible within the framework he inhabits" (Schoene 1998, 119), I argue that like everyone else Karim has to adopt an ascribed ethnicity in order to remain intelligible. Schoene brushes over the several instances of racial violence and restrictions that Karim and other characters face. Although Kureishi's humorous tone may not add to a state of alarm, he, nonetheless, does not represent a naïve version of an "ethnicity-free no-man's land". Moreover,

---

167 Thomas likewise cautions: "Despite its emphasis on transformation and multiple identities, the novel does not entirely dispense with the notion of an 'authentic self'." (Thomas 2005, 67)

168 In New York, Karim notes how Charlie's white teeth give away his middle class origins and how he is profiting from an anger that in reality is not his own. In America, he adopts a fake Cockney accent. Karim is disenchanted and observes laconically: "He was selling Englishness, and getting a lot of money for it." (BS 247)

Hall also emphasises with reference to his concept of "new ethnicities" that the racial binary is not likely to be easily or playfully overcome. Promoting a more diverse understanding of the term 'Black' in the British context Hall calls for a counter-hegemonic discourse of ethnicities.

> Racism, of course, operates by constructing impassable symbolic boundaries between racially constituted categories, and its typically binary system of representation constantly marks and attempts to fix and naturalize the difference between belongingness and otherness. [...] Consequently, the discourse of anti-racism had often been founded on a strategy of reversal and inversion, turning the 'Manichean aesthetic' of colonial discourse upside down. However, as Fanon constantly reminded us, the epistemic violence is both outside and inside [...]. [And leads to an] internalization of the self-as-other. Just as masculinity always constructs femininity as double – simultaneously Madonna and Whore – so racism constructs the black subject: noble savage and violent avenger. And in the doubling, fear and desire double for one another and play across the structures of otherness, complicating its politics. (Hall 1996c, 445)

Hall challenges and complicates notions of Englishness. Likewise, Kureishi's writing promotes a broadening understanding of Englishness. In his more explicitly autobiographical and political essay "The Rainbow Sign", he concludes:

> It is the British, the white British, who have to learn that being British isn't what it was. Now it is a more complex thing, involving new elements. So there must be a fresh way of seeing Britain and the choices it faces: and a new way of being British after all this time. Much thought, discussion and self-examination must go into seeing the necessity for this, what this 'new way of being British' involves and how difficult it might be to attain. (Kureishi 2002a, 55)

Both Hall and Kureishi are well aware of limitations in this project. These 'mixes and permeations' still operate along axes of dominant and marginalised ethnicities. Whereas English culture today is clearly in constant flux, this still is framed within a logic of acculturation: Britain includes the marginalised into the mainstream, not vice versa. In the end, Karim, as the star of a soap opera, is the commodified product of inclusion. To emphasise these relations of dominance does not imply a simplistic or linear understanding of power relations from the top to the bottom. As has been noted several times, it is these multiple axes of stratification of gender, sexuality and ethnicity that collide in conflicting ways which produce a complex web that does not result in an easy binary of subversive versus opportunistic.

After his visit to New York City and upon his return to England, Karim is joined by his family to celebrate his new job, and the novel ends with Karim's supposedly grown-up voice at the eve of the elections of 1979: "I could think about the past and what I'd been through as I'd struggled to locate myself and learn what the heart is. Perhaps in the future I would live more deeply." (BS 283–284) This optimistic note is not unequivocal. His younger brother, Allie, embodies a 'new generation' of children of immigrants. He is tired of taking on the status of the oppressed; for him the Thatcherite emphasis on work ethics is a positive value to embrace. In the end, Allie lectures his older brother for his old-fashioned leftist ideals:

'We all hate whining lefties, don't we? [...] And I hate people who go on all the time about being black, and how persecuted they were at school [...]. Let me say that we come from privilege. We can't pretend we're some kind of shitted-on oppressed people. Let's just make the best of ourselves.' (BS 267–268)

But many readers in the nineties were well aware that this idea of 'making the best of it' would prove a big disappointment in the near future. In the years to come, the pressure to 'sell out' would only increase and so *The Buddha* remains a reminder of nostalgic images of a time of experimentation, sexual liberation, life in communes, and the fringe theatre that is no more.

Following the immense popularity of *The Buddha of Suburbia*, Kureishi offers a bleaker version of 'multicultural' London in his next novel, *The Black Album*. Here he focuses on an ethnicised masculinity that cannot so easily adjust itself to the mainstream and reacts with extremism. Tellingly in *The Black Album*, there is a cross-reference to Karim Amir, who has become a phoney celebrity whose picture appears in *Hello!* magazine.

The Black Album: Hybrid Crisis

As has become apparent in the previous part, Kureishi's protagonists struggle with an identity between resistance and acculturation. On the one hand, they can be described as longing for what Connell has termed the "patriarchal dividend" (Connell 1995, 79), i.e. their share in male privilege and, on the other hand, they have to come to terms with their marginalised status as migrants/children of migrants. In *The Black Album*, it is male youths from a Muslim background and the role of fundamentalism in the early nineties that Kureishi explores.[169] His second novel was much less well-received and lacks both the comic tone and lightness of his earlier work.[170]

Although influenced by British popular culture, the protagonists of *The Black Album* turn to extremism and an idealised Muslim heritage. These young men actually have not had the experience of migration; they were born and raised in Britain. I want to describe this ambivalence – to borrow Bhabha's terminology – as a *hybrid crisis* of masculinity. In contrast to *The Buddha*, the sense of unbelonging is much more negatively connoted in *The Black Album* and a sense of (male) crisis much more pronounced. Instead of depicting successful hybrid men, Kureishi now turns to fanatics.

The novel's protagonist, Shahid Hasan, can be described as the archetypical male youth in crisis. In the beginning, Shahid is enchanted by the singer Prince whose LP The Black Album is used as the title for the novel and was itself a reference to the so-called White Album by The Beatles, as has been often noted. The masculinity of the pop star, who is of mixed racial origin and incorporates both a 'machismo masculinity' and 'feminine traits' in his stage persona, serves as a figure of identification for Shahid. In the course of the action, Shahid is torn between his youthful married English Professor Deedee Osgood with whom he starts a passionate affair and a group of young Muslims he meets when initially moving to his college dormitory in Kilburn, London where he has newly arrived from Kent. Meeting so many people of Asian descent is a new experience for the adolescent, and Shahid embarrassingly recounts how his self-hatred made him want to share the 'privilege' of being a racist when he was younger: "'My mind was invaded by killing-nigger fantasies.' [...] I wouldn't touch brown flesh, except with a branding iron. I hated all foreign bastards." (BA 11)

Meeting self-proclaimed young Muslim men initially works as a positive identificatory foil for Shahid as he longs to be part of the group. However, London as the hubbub of popular culture and drugs also catches the young man's interest. It is an exciting time for him, and it reflects an ongoing ambivalence of delving deep into a lifestyle including drugs, raves and sex as opposed to a politically aware choice of living as a Muslim man in a

---

169 For a focus on the crises of British Muslim masculinities in contemporary British cinema, cf. Haschemi Yekani (2007a).

170 For an overview of the critical reception of Kureishi's writing, cf. Buchanan (2007, 147–164).

Britain that has become increasingly hostile towards its immigrants and their children.

It is explicitly the younger generation in this novel that feels drawn to Islam, many of whom have not had a Muslim upbringing or do not come from strictly religious families. The generation of Shahid's friends back home in Kent is characterised in the following terms: "Their parents had come to England to make an affluent and stable life in a country not run by tyrants. Once this was done, their remaining ambition rested with their sons, particularly the eldest." (BA 53) However, many sons feel that they cannot or do not want to cope with these expectations. Shahid does not want to take over the travel agency of his deceased father in Kent; he longs to be a writer, and therefore – as has been widely mentioned – the novel can also be read as a *Künstlerroman*. Still trying to find his voice as an aspiring artist, Shahid remembers how he first used to write as a teenager in his parents' house. He had written a text and included a scene where boys from his class yelled: "Paki, Paki, Paki, Out, Out, Out!" (BA 72) When his mother found the piece she destroyed it angrily:

> More than anything she hated any talk of race or racism. Probably she had suffered some abuse and contempt. But her father had been a doctor; everyone – politicians, generals, journalists, police chiefs – came to their house in Karachi. The idea that anyone might treat her with disrespect was insupportable. Even when Shahid vomited and defecated with fear before going to school, or when he returned with cuts, bruises and his bag slashed with knives, she behaved as if so appalling an insult couldn't exist. (BA 73)

The experience of blunt racism bewilders the generation of the parents – especially those who had come from middle or upper middle class backgrounds in their countries of origin. Shahid does not feel connected either to the British present or his Pakistani origin. Initially in the novel, his restlessness is described in terms that emphasise his need for belonging and a fixed identity:

> Shahid was afraid that his ignorance would place him in no man's land. These days everyone was insisting on their identity, coming out as a man, woman, gay, black, Jew – brandishing on whichever features they would claim, as if without a tag they wouldn't be human. Shahid, too, wanted to belong to his people. (BA 92)

Shahid longs for spirituality in his life which is why he feels drawn to the Muslim brotherhood. Confronted with the decadent spending habits of his brother Chili and his sister-in-law Zulma – both of whom endorse an entrepreneurial lifestyle and approve of Thatcher's conservative politics –

Shahid is more questioning politically. The modest and politicised way of life of the young Muslims attracts his interest, and he ventures into a mosque, which is a new experience for him. In the mosque, Shahid tries to pray, but he "frequently fell into anxiety about his lack of faith" (BA 96). Shahid wants to feel as religious as his friends:

The problem was, when he was with his friends their story compelled him. But when he walked out, like someone leaving a cinema, he found the world to be more subtle and inexplicable. He knew, too, that stories were made up by men and women. (BA 133)

In passages like these, Kureishi stresses that the consciousness of an artist, someone who believes in the power of stories and story-telling, is hard to reconcile with strict religious dogmas. Consequently, Shahid is equally inspired by Deedee's classes in college she teaches about African American writing and popular culture, which offer a new vocabulary to express his identity as a Black British subject. However, Shahid struggles with Deedee's, at times, patronising behaviour towards her Black students, and there are allusions that she frequently sleeps with 'exotic' young Black men she meets in college. During the rather explicit sex scenes in the novel, Deedee is often portrayed as the knowledgeable elder woman (with Oedipal/maternal overtones to their relationship) who is fond of her lover's 'exoticness', and at one point, she remarks to Shahid how she loves "that café-au-lait skin" (BA 210). While politically aware, the White feminist Deedee remains fundamentally disconnected from the experience of racism – a fact with which Shahid has come to terms.

When he is with the Muslim brothers, Shahid feels part of a community of Asian Britons but lacks the opportunity to express his ideals of artistic and sexual freedom. With Deedee, he explores the exciting aspects of London's nightlife, sex and drugs, but he also feels alienated in almost exclusive White venues. Deedee was "taking him to places where there were only White people. 'The White Room's very, well, you know, white.'" (BA 66) And later even at Deedee's house "[p]eople came and went, but he was the only person with dark skin. That would be the fact in most places he went with Deedee." (BA 122) The relationship between Black men and White women remains complicated in all of Kureishi's fiction, and similarly to the liaison of Karim and Eleanor in *The Buddha*, Shahid longs for the acceptance and possible upward (class) mobility that this relationship promises. This becomes evident when the angry White working-class drug dealer Strapper attacks Shahid for his double standards: "'You just wanna be white and forget your own.' [...] 'You and your bro just wanna shag the white bitches.'" (BA 263) Shahid is aware of Deedee's fetishising attitude towards him, but he is also quite willing to invest in this relationship which equips him both with sexual and cultural knowledge.

Deedee is anxious that Shahid might get involved with the wrong people, and she tries to warn him by telling him that his idol, Chad from the brotherhood, only recently discovered Islam. Chad used to be called Trevor Buss. Deedee explains: "'He was adopted by a white couple. The mother was racist, talked about Pakis all the time and how they had to fit in.'" (BA 106) She tells him how Chad changed his name to "Muhammad Shahabuddin Ali-Shah" and "tried to learn Urdu as a teenager but felt he fitted in neither cultures." Sardonically Deedee remarks that "'Trevor Buss's soul got lost in translation.'" (BA 107–108). However, Shahid still is not convinced and wants to find out for himself, and he keeps arguing with Deedee throughout the novel: "'The thing is, Deedee, clever white people like you are too cynical. You see through everything and rip everything to shreds but you never take any action.'" (BA 110)

The triangle of Shahid being torn between Riaz (the leader of the brotherhood) and Deedee is a constitutive element of the novel, and the scenes are carefully paralleled, such as the visit to a rave with Deedee and the mentioned visit to the mosque with Riaz and his followers. Both Kaleta (1998) and Stein (2004) note the parallels between how Shahid is first dressed up and feminised by his lover Deedee and later in the story when Riaz dresses Shahid in a traditional garment.

Shahid's search for identity is explicitly addressed as a male crisis. He feels the pressure to conform to a certain type of masculinity in relation to his elder brother and his deceased father: "Chili's relentless passion had always been for clothes, girls, cars, girls and the money that bought them. When the brothers were young he made it clear that he found Shahid's bookishness effeminate." (BA 41) Chili's toughness is often contrasted with Shahid's undecidedness, and "Kureishi's juxtaposition of Shahid with such hyper-masculine figures makes Shahid seem especially effeminate" (Buchanan 2007, 20). In this context, the figure of the male artist/author seems to be especially prone to charges of 'effeminateness', which somehow lacks the attributes of 'proper masculinity'. Consequently, it is also the struggle for an inclusion of 'feminine' creativity into this 'masculine' *Künstler*-ideal without having to forsake heterosexual privilege which is a prominent theme in the novel.

During one of the sex scenes, Deedee wants Shahid to wear make-up, and they play Madonna's song "Vogue". Shahid is trying to overcome the 'burden' of a rigid understanding of masculinity and explore a more feminine gender expression.

She hummed and fussed over him, reddening his lips, darkening his eyelashes, applying blusher, pushing a pencil under his eye. [...] It troubled him; he felt he were losing himself. What was she seeing? She knew what she wanted; he let her take over; it was a relief. For now she refused him a mirror, but he liked the feel of his new female face. He could be demure, flirtatious, teasing, a star; a burden went, a certain responsibility had been removed. He didn't have to take the lead. (BA 117)

This scene of "gender trouble" involves a reversing of the economy of the gaze, and Shahid becomes the object of his female lover's gaze. This manoeuvre poses a great risk for him. As a man of Asian descent, he has a harder time 'claiming' masculinity as the Orientalist stereotype links Asian masculinity rather paradoxically with both a lack, as effeminacy, and a surplus, in the shape of 'perverse' sexuality, such as 'sodomy'.[171] Shahid feels relieved from the pressures to match a normative version of masculine sexuality and perceives this exploration of femininity as liberating.

Nonetheless, there is also a problematic inclusion/absorption of femininity and queerness into a privileged model of a potent and flexible heterosexual masculinity at work here, and it is especially the ideal of *Künstler*-masculinity that is susceptible to this kind of inclusion, I would argue. In contrast to Karim in *The Buddha*, Shahid never doubts his straightness, and the whole book centres very much on his erotic fantasies involving Deedee.

In terms of genre, *The Black Album* is unusual for a coming-of-age story in its sexual explicitness and use of elements of pornography. This issue of pornography is addressed explicitly in the novel. Deedee poses naked for Shahid and "without losing her soul she was turning herself into pornography" (BA 119). Kureishi links pop to pornography, Shaheed to Prince and Deedee to Madonna: she "represents herself as pure representation" (Degabriele 1999, paragraph 15) Again, the dichotomy of a sex-positive West versus an uptight and chauvinistic Islam is presented rather rigidly by Ku-

---

171 Puar has explored this paradox in her provocative reading of the Abu Ghraib torture scandal and speaks of the production of a queer Muslim terrorist body. (cf. Puar 2007, 79–113)

reishi.[172] Shahid is supposed to edit the manuscript of Riaz's religious writings but instead finds he is "making adjustments here and there" (BA 180). In fact, he is merging his own erotic fantasies with Riaz's pious text, which causes a great uproar among the brothers who doubt his support at this point. Maria Degabriele (1999) highlights the importance for Kureishi to link pornography with humour which is seen as one of the greatest provocations by the fundamentalists, and in the novel, he writes: "Like pornography, religion couldn't admit the comic." (BA 150)

Kureishi is interested in the correlation of religion, pornography and comedy.[173] But the idea to present the serious issue of fundamentalism in a comic manner does not prove entirely successful, and the novel often, somewhat didactically, discusses freedom of speech using the Salman-Rushdie-affair and book burning as examples in the story. It seems clear from the outset of the novel that "Kureishi sees aspects of Islam as incompatible with liberalism" (Thomas 2005, 105). Kureishi highlights the assumed absurdity of blind faith by including a satirical episode in which an eggplant is worshipped by the community because supposedly "God had inscribed holy words into the mossy flesh" (BA 171). Shahid also has an ongoing dispute with Riaz whether the writing of stories is to be considered the fabrication of lies or necessary for human reflection. In the wake of the Rushdie affair, it is no longer an Orientalised exotic masculinity (as in *The Buddha*) that is portrayed at the margins, but rather, religion becomes the decisive factor of difference. Riaz wants Shahid to call him a Muslim, not a Paki. "'No more Paki. Me a Muslim. We don't apologize for ourselves neither.'" (BA 128)

---

172 For instance, the only woman in the group the reader gets to know, Tahira, cannot be compared to the outspoken Jamila of *The Buddha* and stereotypically accepts the men's orders, wears a hijab and is quite content with her subordinated role in the group (although at one point she asks the men not to wear tight trousers as a concession for the female members of the group). The Muslim men cannot accept 'excessive' female sexuality, which Deedee represents, and to add to the impression of their 'backwardness' Hat mentions casually that homosexuals should be beheaded. (cf. BA 199) Again, Kureishi does not explore these statements but rather presents them as necessary and pre-given character traits of 'male Muslim fundamentalists'.

173 Michael Ross emphasises Kureishi's indebtedness to Rushdie and calls "erotic joking" (Ross 2006, 230) characteristic of Kureishi's style. Ross traces Kureishi's use of grotesque elements and laughter back to Bakhtin and his understanding of the ambivalent role of humour as both demeaning and liberating. (cf. ibid., 232) Kureishi's "joking, even when aimed at the racially othered, raises more wide-ranging issues, partly because it is self-interrogating" (ibid., 234).

At one point, Chad, another member of the group, mentions the "fat-wah" approvingly, and the central conflict around the burning of "the book", which refers to Salman Rushdie's *Satanic Verses* (although the title is never given explicitly, it is mentioned that Shahid admired the author of *Midnight's Children* (cf. BA 169)), is introduced. "'That book been around too long without action. He insulted us all – the prophet, the prophet's wives, his whole family. It's sacrilege, and blasphemy. Punishment is death. That man going down the chute." (BA 169) At the climax of the novel, the group try to stage a book burning at the university. Deedee calls the police, and the situation escalates.

The crisis of masculinity often centres on a conflict between masculinity and femininity, but there is also an increasing conflict among masculinities. For the most part, it is the middle-aged White woman Deedee who is the antagonist to Riaz and the other young Muslim men, but also, it is the estranged husband of Deedee, Dr Andrew Brownlow, who plays a central role. Interestingly, the crisis of hegemonic masculinity although not absent from the story no longer takes centre stage, and tellingly Brownlow has to fight with a stutter – White masculinity has lost its unchallenged ability to claim universality/language. Andrew Brownlow represents boring middle-aged, middle-class White masculinity which has somehow failed to make the right adjustments and as a consequence, it is stuck with an idealised retrospective view on the sixties and seventies. Brownlow represents the "Left's inability to articulate anything of relevance to young Britons" (Buchanan 2007, 21). The new political demands of the younger generation of migrants are fascinating to him, but in his inability to really understand their situation, he becomes an easy target for them: "He comes to this college to help us, the underprivileged niggers and wogs an' margin people. He's not a bad guy – for a Marxist-Communist." (BA 32) They can recruit him for their cause, and he supports their ambitions to stage the book burning which reminds him of his more radical days, despite his qualms with their political agenda.

Andrew is the clichéd liberal who has to deal with his emancipated wife and her constant affairs while trying to stick up for the 'under-privileged', ending up making the wrong decisions. This leaves him drunk and bitter, and ultimately, he decides to leave his wife. "Those women, they'll make you run around like a servant, before stripping you of your money, your pride, every-fucking-thing, as if it were your fault they were put down."

(BA 238) In this typical expression of male bemoaning of lost privilege, feminism becomes the scapegoat for his male disorientation and crisis.

As a consequence of the book burning fiasco, Shahid has to make a final decision between his desire for Deedee and his commitment to the brotherhood. By now, he has realised that he cannot be part of a venture that does not tolerate artistic expression, a belief that has become central to him. He tries to distance himself from the group, and in the end, he joins Deedee to flee for a weekend outside of London and plans to stay with her "until it stops being fun" (BA 276) after having made his decision to live as an independent artist rather than regress into fundamentalism. One of the young men from the brotherhood is badly injured in a failed attempt to set fire to a bookstore, implying to the reader that harming freedom of speech is a self-destructive venture in the end.

As has been mentioned in the introduction, the early nineties seem to have witnessed a certain flexibility of identity expressions, and masculinity functions no longer as a monolithic marker of difference. In many respects, Kureishi has his characters explore a possible transgression of limits of gender and race. Shahid wants to be a macho-man who can nevertheless incorporate feminine traits. But in the novel's logic, this also never really endangers his status as a heterosexual man. On the contrary, it renders him even more attractive to women. Shahid yearns to belong to a Muslim community without having to forsake the 'perverted' pleasures of the West, such as sex, drugs and music. It is a constant struggle with extreme and irreconcilable opposites.

The aforementioned "burden of representation"[174] also shaped the reception of Kureishi's second novel.[175] This time Kureishi was attacked for playing into the hands of White prejudice by portraying male Muslim youths as fanatics (and indeed, the motives of these young men remain rather vague throughout the novel).[176] Ruvani Ranasinha speaks of "Muslimophobia" in this context and explains: "In reinforcing stereotypes of devout Muslims as fundamentalists that are already inscribed in the media, his work offers little prospect of any kind of constructive dialogue between

---

174 Cf. 162fn.158.

175 Donald Weber (1997) sees a connection between Kureishi's inclination to shock 'his community' and the provocative writing of Jewish American writers such as Philip Roth.

176 Of course, it is important to deal with (Muslim) fundamentalism; my point of critique is that it turns out to be almost the only representation of male migrants so much so that it gradually becomes the only legible code – even more so after the 9/11 and 7/7 attacks.

polarized communities or indeed within Muslim communities." (Ranasinha 2002, 82)

Nonetheless, while part of Kureishi's writing remains somewhat naïve or rather stereotypical in his depiction of Muslim masculinities, he is also one of the first authors to give voice to a generation of young Muslim men who experience, what I have tentatively called, a *hybrid crisis*. Similar to *The Buddha*, discussions of hybridity are prominent when it comes to interpreting these lines of conflict. But again, it needs to be stressed that hybridity is not to be equated with the playful adoption or mixture of different identities.

These Muslim men in Kureishi's novels are the stereotypical cosmopolitan hybrid men that Bhabha talks about when he characterises the "postcolonial site" (as which London surely can be read). Trying to characterise the contradiction of the postcolonial condition Bhabha calls for an "enunciative 'present'" that

would provide a political space to articulate and negotiate such culturally hybrid social identities. Questions of cultural difference would not be dismissed – with a barely concealed racism – as atavistic 'tribal' instincts that afflict Irish Catholics in Belfast or 'Muslim fundamentalists' in Bradford. It is precisely such unresolved, transitional moments within the disjunctive present of modernity that are then projected into a time of historical retroversion or an inassimilable place outside history. (Bhabha 1994, 359)

Consequently, these "hybrid identities" do not exist outside of British society. They are no longer the 'Others', but are an integral part of the "present of modernity" and, as Bhabha explains, the constant vocabulary of atavistic or premodern tendencies, which is employed when referring to so-called 'Muslim fundamentalists', fails to recognise that these are indeed signs of postcoloniality – of the here and now. Bhabha calls for "a postcolonial, critical discourse that contests modernity through the establishment of other historical sites, other forms of enunciation" (ibid., 365). However, with its stern faith in Western freedom of speech and the right of artistic expression, Kureishi's novel in a certain sense fails to offer such a radical contestation of modernity.[177] Yet, I would also argue that it is the constant failure to produce such a new discourse that shapes not only Kureishi's writing but also many aspects of contemporary Britain. Kureishi

---

177 Sheila Ghose links this failure to the genre of the *Bildungsroman* and its "liberal humanist idea of subjectivity" (Ghose 2007, 128) which Kureishi reproduces.

tries to show this irreconcilability and ultimately is stuck in the status quo. The failure to depict a more complex and nuanced image of 'fanatic Muslims' is therefore also a mark of the current discourse on (violent/terrorist) 'Muslim men in crisis' of which *The Black Album* is but one example.

While hegemonic masculinity in the shape of Brownlow has lost its ability to speak, to represent the norm, marginalised men violently demand their right to voice their own narratives of male crisis. But for many marginalised men, this crisis of masculinity is a hybridised crisis. They are marked as the 'outsiders within' in terms of their ethnicity and their constant failure to stabilise masculinity. Their hybrid crisis is, in fact, one that more generally disrupts notions of a monolithic understanding of the discourse of the crisis of masculinity.

Shahid seems to realise that a simplistic version of masculinity (or identity for that matter) that must choose between Muslim and Western cannot be the solution to his problem. In the very end, he distances himself from his initial urge to belong to a fixed place and instead praises instability and fluidity. He has come to understand that:

He had to find some sense in his recent experiences; he wanted to know and understand. How could anyone confine themselves to one system or creed? [...] There was no fixed self; surely our several selves melted and mutated daily? There had to be innumerable ways of being in the world. (BA 274)

Shahid's hybrid crisis includes his struggle with his marginalised position in terms of his ethnicity, but he is also re-centred in terms of gender and sexuality. He flirts with queerness with regard to his expression of gender and sexuality without really ever endangering his status as a heterosexual man. He also flirts with fanaticism but again, never seriously questions the 'universal' right of the artist.

Nonetheless, Kureishi's focus on the hybrid crises of marginalised young Muslim men destabilises the often assumed coherence of the concept of masculinity and consequently, of the narrative pattern of masculinity (in its singular form) in crisis. But, it also has re-centring tendencies, which seem inherent to the notion of the crisis of masculinity – even a hybrid crisis. This diversification of different crises does not do away with the hierarchisation among masculinities, nor their hegemonic position with regard to femininities, but it does have a disruptive potential.

As Kureishi's writing shows, male hegemony is not stable and reacts to social changes. Kureishi is an author of the exposed crisis of a new generation of Asian British men. For him, the renegotiation of masculinity is often interlinked with the ethnicised attributions and a flirt with queer masculinity. There is a privileging of a flexible understanding of masculinity that can also entail a re-centring of masculinity. Even in Kureishi's re-writing of genre conventions, he adheres to certain ideals of coming-of-age stories and the male artist from a distinctly male and Western perspective. This narrative strategy connects his texts to the discursive construction of masculinity in crisis. Kureishi queers Englishness by depicting same-sex and straight interracial desire at the centre of his work. Nonetheless, masculinity remains his key frame of reference which often marginalises female characters like Jamila in terms of their space in the narrative. But there is also an astonishing polyphony of both male and female, Black and White characters that is new to British writing and which has undoubtedly influenced later writers such as Zadie Smith. Kureishi's ambivalences and multi-faceted voices enable him to depict very different racialised and sexualised characters in their strengths and weaknesses. He enables a retrospective queer glance at the diaspora that was not very common at the beginning of the nineties. The polyphony in an autodiegetic narrative such as *The Buddha of Suburbia* is quite unusual, and despite male re-centring, it allows for a queer potential shining through. In *The Buddha of Suburbia*, this potential is clearly connected to a time before Thatcher, and this underlines that a queer diaspora is significantly shaped by discourses on family, the nation and heterosexuality which are flexible and always changing and need to be constantly challenged.

In *The Black Album* however, Kureishi is less willing to explore reasons for the new rise in Muslim fundamentalism in young men from an Asian background in Britain of the early nineties. Although he is successful at locating these developments as results of a hostile and racist climate, Kureishi never seriously challenges a West versus Islam binary that caters to a number of clichés. Despite the fact that this story is told by a hetero-diegetic narrator, the focus is limited to Shahid's view as a focalizer[178] and centres on his sexual experimentation and aspirations as a male artist. In this sense, there is clearly a more traditional narrative of male crisis that involves the re-centring of masculinity.

---

178 I employ the term focalization as suggested by Genette (1980). For a critical discussion of the concepts of narrative voice and focalization, cf. Fludernik (2001).

Postcolonial Films: Queering the Imperial Gaze?

In a number of British films form the mid-eighties to the early nineties, the intersections of gender, sexuality and race were the centre of attention. Directors Stephen Frears and Neil Jordan began to engage with the changing image of British masculinities. In contrast to the colonial spectacle of the 'self', that I addressed in the chapter on colonial photography, I want to examine two movies that have been hailed for the 'spectacular' new and postcolonial imagery of Britain. I want to analyse the extent to which the two films *My Beautiful Laundrette* and *The Crying Game* are part of male crisis narratives and in how far they offer a disturbance of heteronormative visual codes. Stephen Frears and Hanif Kureishi collaborated on film projects that were more directly engaged with contemporary England at a time when the so-called Raj Revival[179] films reproduced an un-critical and nostalgic image of England's colonial past. Rather than offering a nostalgic glance back at the Raj, both films analysed in this chapter provide multi-layered and conflicting images of Britain in the eighties and nineties. The themes of nationality and masculinity feature prominently in both movies, somewhat paradoxically focusing on male crises as well as challenging clear binaries.

While *My Beautiful Laundrette* established a rough look at urban London in the eighties and provided viewers with one of the first (positive) images of an interracial gay couple, *The Crying Game* became famous for its blending of a story of political conflict with the visual destabilisation of the gender binary. In how far both movies (re)negotiate and are part of the exposed crisis of masculinity will be the central concern in the following readings.

My Beautiful Laundrette: Coming-out 'In-Between'

After his time at the fringe theatre, Kureishi felt that theatre was essentially an elitist institution which seldom reached minority audiences. Consequently, film as a more popular medium appealed to him. (cf. Kaleta 1998, 39–42) Before launching his career as a novelist, Kureishi collaborated with

---

179 For a discussion of the Kureishi/Frears films against the backdrop of the Raj Revival cinema, cf. Moore-Gilbert (2001, 67–106). For a more general discussion of the Raj Revival and its connection to a specific conception of White femininity, cf. Dyer, "'There's Nothing I can do! Nothing!'" in *White* (1997, 184–206).

director Stephen Frears to write his first screenplay in 1985. Stephen Frears had his breakthrough as a film director comparatively late in life. He started at the Royal Court theatre and then worked for television for years (mainly the BBC and ITV). His collaboration with Hanif Kureishi on *My Beautiful Laundrette* (1985) and *Sammy and Rosie Get Laid* (1987), but also his acclaimed *Prick Up Your Ears* (1987) (which was written by Alan Bennett), paved the way for an international career that has to date culminated in his latest great success, *The Queen* (2006). From the start, he was interested in project work and liked to collaborate closely with authors and actors rather than see himself as an *auteur* director, demanding full artistic control of his films. Other successful productions include *Dangerous Liaisons* (1988), *The Grifters* (1990) and *Mrs Henderson Presents* (2005). Although Frears has been nominated twice for an Academy Award, he has never received the prize himself but is famous for having directed several actors and actresses to win the trophy.

In the early eighties, the experience of non-White Britons was rarely found in visual representations either on TV or in the cinema. Rather, British film in general was informed by its focus on costume drama and the imaginary ethnic monolithicity of the country side. The past seemed to have had more appeal than the contemporary unsettling 'state of the nation'. English heritage cinema continuously ran the risk of playing down Britain's colonial legacy or, worse, glorifying its imperialist past.[180] In this climate, Kureishi and Frears hit a raw nerve with their focus on the roughness of urban, contemporary London, inhabited by a host of ethnically diverse people. Nonetheless, *My Beautiful Laundrette* does not depict unequivocally 'happy multiculturalism'. White and non-White characters are represented as equally likeable and flawed. Consequently, Hall famously comments,

My Beautiful Laundrette is one of the most riveting and important films [...] [because of] its refusal to represent the black experience in Britain as monolithic, self-contained, sexually stabilized and always 'right-on.'" (Hall 1996c, 449)

Shot for only 600,000 pounds and financed by Channel 4, which was established in 1982, it was astonishing that this movie shot on 16mm film

---

180 Only more recently, films such as Patricia Rozema's *Mansfield Park* (1999), Gurinder Chadha's *Bride and Prejudice* (2004) and Mira Nair's *Vanity Fair* (2004) have quite successfully presented postcolonial versions of classical heritage cinema based on novels by Jane Austen and William Thackeray.

would reach such a large audience and garner critical acclaim. *My Beautiful Laundrette*'s low-budget aesthetic is rough, a style that Thomas describes as a "blend of gritty documentary realism, wit, and flamboyant fantasy" (Thomas 2005, 28). Nevertheless, the film profits from a great cast of actors, many of whom Kureishi had worked with before at the fringe theatre or established enduring working relationships afterwards.

There is a sense of urgency in the way Kureishi and Frears connect to changing conceptions of masculinity and race relations, both significantly influenced by the massive changes Thatcher's government had inspired. In *My Beautiful Laundrette*, White unemployed male adolescents clash with a new class of immigrant entrepreneurs. These 'masculinities in crisis' are embodied in the odd couple of Omar (Gordon Warnecke) and Johnny (Daniel Day-Lewis), the protagonists of *Laundrette*.

In the beginning of the movie, unemployed Omar, the son of a British mother and Pakistani father, is sent to his uncle Nasser (Saeed Jaffrey) to work for his successful business. Although his father Hussein (Roshan Seth), called Papa, insists this is a temporary position until he can take up college, Omar seems to flourish within the entrepreneurial spirit of the eighties. The smug and corrupt businessman Salim (Derrick Branche) introduces Omar to his new job: "[Y]ou'll be able to afford a descent shirt and you'll be with your own people. Not in a dole queue. Mrs Thatcher will be pleased with me." (MBL 15) Omar is quickly promoted from car washer to accountant and given an unsuccessful laundrette by his uncle in order to prove himself. In a comment that seems to comically reflect the image of the overdressed English gentleman in the colonies, reminiscent of Rider Haggard's fiction that I addressed earlier, Nasser explains the many opportunities available to make money by taking advantage of the English obsession with clean clothes. "Take my advice. There is money in muck. What is it the gora[181] Englishman always needs? Clean Clothes!" (MBL 23)

A recurring narrative pattern in Kureishi's oeuvre is his recourse to hybridity as a potential disruption of racial binaries. As in *The Buddha of Suburbia*, interracial couples of different generations (and sexual orientations) are among the protagonists. Most notably, the budding relationship between Omar and Johnny is of interest here. The attraction between the two men is immediately apparent, visually represented through their longing glances at each other. The audience learns through dialogue that the former school

---

181 Gora means 'White person' or 'fair-faced'.

friends lost contact due to Johnny's involvement with nationalist/racist politics, while it is also revealed that he continues to associate with the nationalist White youth group that terrorises the neighbourhood.

The decision to depict the desire for the racial 'Other' between these two characters was a novel and risky undertaking. (cf. Gopinath 2005, 1; Ranasinha 2009, 299) In response to the flim, there was some discomfort and critique voiced by members of the Asian community, who felt that showing gay Asians and corrupt businessmen was doing harm to the image of British Asians who were underrepresented in the visual media. But as Hall's earlier quote suggests, these 'politics of representation' were not really of great interest to Kureishi or Frears, who had not intended to present "right-on" positive images of Asian British people or, to speak for a community.

Interestingly, similar to Jordan, who focuses on a transgender character as a means to visualise a transnational conflict, Kureishi seems drawn to homosexuality as an image of reconciliation. Both men are marginalised: Omar by his ethnic background and Johnny by his class background. But instead of playing off different crisis narratives against each other, the film presents the queer desire between these two men. Kureishi has commented on this allegorical use of homosexuality as a visualisation of conflicting conceptions of racialised English masculinity. "The boys are really the two sides of me: a Pakistani boy and an English boy, because I'm half Pakistani and half English. I got the two parts of myself together ... kissing." (Kureishi quoted in Moore-Gilbert 2001, 14) The homosexuality of the characters is not really at the centre of the plot and is portrayed in a matter-of-fact way that was unusual in 1985. Consequently, while one can criticise his application of homosexuality as merely allegorical, it is also quite subversive to have a story featuring an interracial homosexual couple without resorting to painful coming-out narratives or focusing on clashes within the family. The audience sees the men kissing in close-up, and Moore-Gilbert speculates that this is very likely the first interracial gay kiss in British film targeted at a larger audience. (cf. Moore-Gilbert 2001, 87) Instead of problematising homosexuality, the film yields to a pleasurable visual depiction of the two men's desire for each other.

Kureishi's and Frears' interest in 'doubling' and 'couples' becomes a visual strategy of the film. At the ceremonial opening of the laundrette, the spectator is confronted with a layering of couples. Omar and Johnny are in the back making out, while his uncle and his British mistress Rachel

(Shirley Anne Field) arrive through the front. As they cannot find the boys upon first glance, Nasser and Rachel enjoy the music, waltzing along. The atmosphere in the laundrette can be described as mildly surrealist with the "mysterious bubbling sounds (the movie's theme music)" (Buchanan 2007, 125) playing in the background for most of the time. In the next shot, the camera directs the spectators towards the young gay couple juxtaposed with the second image, through a mirror in the back room, of the older heterosexual couple dancing.

Plate 9: Film still: Stephen Frears, My Beautiful Laundrette, Film/DVD-ROM, 97:00, 1985, 54:56

Both interracial couples are marked as illegitimate in multiple ways: the younger for being homosexual and the elder for being extra-marital and in this way "drawing together into one textual moment multiple mergers of race, class, sexuality, and generation" (Hammond 2007, 234).

The film succeeds in presenting pleasurable relationships that do not seem to conform to the 'norm'. In all of Kureishi's writing, there is a strong emphasis on the need for new models of belonging – to create new versions of the nuclear family. The film illustrates this need, which seems especially relevant in light of the eighties emphasis on traditional family values and its glorification of marriage as monogamous, heterosexual and patriarchal as well as racially unambiguous. But the new enterprise culture also seems to offer new opportunities to the aspiring and often Thatcherite Asian British middle class. In a sense, the laundrette is marked somewhat paradoxically both as a vulgar and materialistic space (cf. Hammond 2007, 235) and also as a space of erotic pleasure that does not conform to the norm.

Again, the image of the 'oppressed Asian woman' is at the centre of a debate that sees Kureishi reproducing the misogynist stereotype. The central female character in *My Beautiful Laundrette*, Tania (Rita Wolf), in many respects seems like an earlier and less developed version of Jamila from *The Buddha of Suburbia*. Growing up in a financially well-off Asian family, she feels trapped by her family's traditional understanding of gender. Tania is not allowed to participate in her father's business and is only able to marry in order to change her situation. In hopes of escaping, she tries to convince Omar to marry her. Tania is visually marked as rebellious, for example, by wearing Western clothes, such as jeans in contrast to the other women who dress in traditional Indian attire. As a strong visual clue in one scene, Tania bears her breasts from behind a window to Omar, while he talks to her father and the other men in the 'master's chamber'.

Plate 10: Film still: Stephen Frears, My Beautiful Laundrette, Film/DVD-ROM, 97:00, 1985, 15:29

What is in question during this scene is whether Tania and her act are for the benefit of the dominant White male gaze or to be understood as an assertion of her own independent sexuality. In the visual logic of the shot, Tania is sexualised as her body is exposed without granting her any real sexual autonomy within the narrative. She is interested in Omar. At least, she sees him as her ticket to leave the constraints of the family, even though Omar is not sexually attracted to her. Tania is less politicised than Jamila and only craves independence from her family. It seems as if Tania lacks the kind of sexual freedom and political wit that characterises the character of Jamila and Tania's story is pushed to the side in favour of the boys' love story. In the end, Tania's image is literally erased from the screen. When her father is looking for her from a window, she is shown standing at the tracks of a railway station, a train passes, and she magically disappears. With that, the character exits the film, and her story takes place out of frame.

Nonetheless, Tania is not a silent victim. During a scene of confrontation between Tania and her father's girlfriend, the film depicts the two women as caught up in complicated hierarchies of age, race and class. The young and somewhat liberated Tania feels that being the mistress of a man ultimately degrades a woman. This is easy to say from her position of being financially secured. She attacks Rachel arguing, "I don't like women who live off men. [...] That's a pretty disgusting parasitical thing, isn't it?" To which Rachel replies: "But tell me, who do you live off? And you must understand, we are of different generations, and different classes. Everything is waiting for you. The only thing that has ever waited for me is your father." (MBL 46) While women of Tania's generation might have the luxury to adopt a liberated point of view, it proves much harder for the older Rachel, who is of the same working-class background as Johnny. Even though she wears fancy clothes now, Rachel recognises Johnny, whose mother she knew well. While Tania seeks to be 'freed' from the subjugation of her father, Rachel's relationship with him grants her new class mobility and financial security.

As a general theme, *My Beautiful Laundrette* addresses the question of whether to pursue personal happiness or a more politicised form of protest, or, to put it differently, assimilation versus resistance. The film depicts who can assimilate to England and the new Thatcherite logic of mobility – and at what costs. Nasser is the embodiment of someone who has assimilated, and he has put his qualms aside to fully embrace 'the system'. In some ways, he regards his success as retaliation of the colonised against the coloniser. Starting off as the "mimic Englishman", Nasser has become the entrepreneur immigrant who knows how to take advantage of England. He explains his philosophy to Omar in the following terms:

In this damn country which we hate and love, you can get anything you want. It's all spread out and available. That's why I believe in England. You just have to know how to squeeze the tits of the system. (MBL 17)

He is not a patriotic businessman but only embraces the system as long as it is to his advantage, and tellingly, the English system is feminised, linking sexual and economic exploitation in a reversal of the stereotypical feminisation of the colonies.

In what ultimately also figures as a coming-of-age narrative, Omar is confronted with two male role models. There is, on the one hand, his father, a leftist socialist and journalist in Pakistan who has now become an unemployed alcoholic, while, on the other hand, his rich and influential uncle who resides as the patriarch over a number of businesses, a large family and an English mistress. Omar is happy to embrace his uncle's philosophy while he ignores his father's pleas to not forget his education. Although Hussein initially wants him to start working for his brother, he also warns him: "Don't get too involved with that crook. You've got to study. We are under siege by the white man. For us education is power." (MBL 18) Hussein still dreams of anti-colonial resistance, a feeling his son cannot share. At his uncle's house, Omar is scolded by relatives for being an English monolingual who is not even able to speak 'his own language'. Omar knows too little of 'his past'. This is emphasised in his encounter with Salim's White Anglo-Indian wife, Cherry (Souad Farres), who has spent every summer in Pakistan and knows more about life in Karachi, which she calls her home, than does Omar. Disapprovingly she calls Omar an "in-between" (MBL 20). This cultural 'in-betweenness', similar to his homosexuality, never really troubles Omar. He seems unworried and content with his position that everyone else is quite eager to problematise.[182]

---

182 While the film does not present Omar's sexual orientation as 'a problem' that he has to come to terms with (as would be typical for a coming-out narrative), Omar's father is constantly worried about his son's possible queerness. Omar, in contrast to Karim, is not at all sexually interested in girls, which is an ongoing concern for Papa, who asks his brother Nasser to find a girl for his son: "Try and fix him up with a nice girl. I'm not sure if his penis is in full working order." (MBL 12) Characteristically, Kureishi can de-

However, Omar and Johnny are both confronted with a set of challenges, most notably the economic hardships and unemployment that have changed both men's lives to some extent and which were seen as an unsettling force in men's lives at the time. In this sense, the figure of the unemployed White male is a reference to the discourse of White masculinity in crisis that fostered anti-migrant and anti-feminist resentments in eighties Britain. Consequently, the question of Johnny's involvement with racism is a central theme in the film. In some ways, Papa functions as a father figure to Johnny as well as to Omar. Tellingly, White English fathers are for the most part absent, calling to mind the father of Charlie Hero who does not appear in *The Buddha of Suburbia*. Middle-aged White men or hegemonic masculinity is not the focus of Kureishi's earlier writing; only his later short stories have their qualms at the centre. In addition to his concern for Omar's possible homosexuality, Hussein fears that his son too quickly and uncritically adopts what he perceives as the typical English ways. With reference to the racist agitation in eighties England and Johnny's part in this, he warns his son: "He went too far. They hate us in England. And all you do is kiss their arses and think of yourself as a little Britisher!" (MBL 25) As his relationship with Johnny develops, Omar confronts his lover about his involvement in the racist marches. "It was bricks and bottles and Union Jacks. It was immigrants out. It was kill us. People we knew. And it was you. He saw your face marching. You saw his face watching you." (MBL 43) Kureishi is quick to link the White youths' involvement with right wing politics as a direct development of an unsettled White working class. These young men (in crisis) face mass unemployment and are confronted with changing conceptions of race in Britain, changing gender relations and changing sexual hierarchies. This suggestion remains problematic. At this juncture, Kureishi and Frears run the risk of joining a dangerous rhetoric of the White fascist as a victim. As I have stressed repeatedly, the discourse of masculinity in crisis is often based on reiterating conservative ideas about a need for a restoration of masculinity. Narratives about men shape the ways masculinity and its ongoing hegemony is (re)produced. Yet, this does not mean that we are not in need of complicated and conflicting stories of what it can mean to perform masculinity at different times and places.

---

pict homophobia but also racism in a humorous tone. This allows him not to sound overly didactic while still being able to address these important issues.

In the film, Johnny is quickly rehabilitated and seems to regret his past actions. However, this is presented less as an informed political decision. The conflict is broken down to the personal level. The reconciliation is not a matter of words but is represented in the physical contact between the protagonists hugging and kissing each other. All Johnny can say in this matter attests to this speechlessness: "Nothing I can say to make it up to you. There's only things I can do to show you that I am … with you." (MBL 44) This visual focus on the physicality between the men becomes especially explicit in a close-up of Johnny licking his lover's neck in front of his disapproving former friends.

Plate 11: Film still: Stephen Frears, My Beautiful Laundrette, Film/DVD-ROM, 97:00, 1985, 45:22

The body language here takes over, and it is the pleasurable depiction of the two men's bodies that is to brush away the discomfort the viewer might have with identifying with an ex-skinhead. From another perspective, their relationship turns the hierarchies between what is marked as the colonialist situation upside down[183]: Johnny becomes Omar's 'servant', and Omar cannot help but enjoy his newfound authority:

---

183 Moore-Gilbert reads the couple as a reversal of the relationship of Fielding and Aziz in E.M. Forster's *A Passage to India* where the racialised Indian is clearly in a subservient position to the virile Englishman. (cf. Moore-Gilbert 2001, 73)

I want big money. I'm not gonna be beat down by this country. When we were at school, you and your lot kicked me all round the place. And what are you doing now? Washing my floor. That's how I like it. Now get to work. Get to work I said. Or you're fired. (MBL 51)

Johnny's new job evokes scorn, and he is confronted by his past when one of the thugs from his former gang comes in. "Why are you working for them? For these people? You were with us once. For England." And the bully continues: "I am angry. I don't like to see one of our men grovelling to Pakis. They came here to work for us. That's why we brought them over. OK?" (MBL 38) Having grown up in the image of England's great colonial past, these White men cannot cope with a loss of privilege. The sight of Omar instructing Johnny proves unbearable to them and sparks violence. The accused Johnny can only justify himself with his tiredness of being unemployed. He desperately wants to work. And, indeed, he is quite willing to compromise his principles as a consequence. The film begins with Johnny being evicted. In the course of the story, it becomes his job to evict other squatters from Nasser's property. Obviously, uncomfortable with this position, he confronts Nasser about convicting a fellow Pakistani tenant. "Aren't you giving ammunition to your enemies doing this kind of … unscrewing? To people who say Pakis just come here to hustle other people's lives and jobs and houses." (MBL 41) But Nasser does not feel his identity obliges him to have compassion for other Pakistanis or Black people and responds: "But we're professional businessmen. Not professional Pakistanis. There's no race question in the enterprise culture." (MBL 41) As the traditional image of the privileged White man crumbles so does the image of the Pakistani who ardently cares for his fellow countrymen when they come under attack. In reference to Thatcher's politics, the only thing that seems to matter in *My Beautiful Laundrette* is how to run a successful business.

However, although Frears works in a realist mode a majority of the time, many of the characters' decisions are not very convincing in terms of psychological motivation.[184] As I mentioned, the relationship between Omar and Johnny is not really motivated and functions as an image of the healing of a conflict rather than as a realistic depiction of a gay relationship. The pleasure can be found on the visual rather than on the narrative level. Despite theses shortcomings, Kureishi and Frears also succeeded in sub-

---

184 Moore-Gilbert also criticises improbabilities at the level of plot. (cf. Moore-Gilbert 2001, 99)

verting the typical bemoaning of lost male privilege that is typical of the discourse of masculinity in crisis. Johnny, the embodiment of White British masculinity, is quite willing to become the erotic object of his lover's and the viewer's gaze rather than the moaning subject, and in this sense, the film subverts the rhetoric of a new crisis of masculinity, often unemployed working class masculinity.

But there are other inconsistencies in the logic of the narrative. Although strongly critical of Thatcherite gender and sexual politics, the movie remains quite ambivalent in its representation of Omar's and Johnny's rise as successful businessmen. Their willingness to engage in the entrepreneurial spirit of the eighties seems to clash with Johnny's past as a squatter and the disgust they both seem to feel at the sight of Salim's corruptness. Moore-Gilbert summarises that "if Salim is represented unsympathetically as a caricature Thatcherite for whom [...] other people are 'shit', it is troubling that Omar and Johnny so readily become his accomplices" (Moore-Gilbert 2001, 103).

Kureishi and Frears seem at a loss to really address the dilemma of being caught up between political conviction and personal success. This is most evident in the depiction of the brothers, Hussein and Nasser, who represent another important couple in the movie: the ardent leftist idealist versus the corrupt assimilated businessman. At one point, Salim inquires about Omar's father, who having been an important intellectual in Pakistan has become a tragic failure in England. "How's your Papa? So many books written and read. Politicians sought him out. Bhutto was his close friend. But we're nothing in England without money." (MBL 48) England has broken his spirit. He has become an alcoholic whose wife committed suicide, and now dreams of returning 'home'. Nasser, in contrast, has assimilated and found his home in England. For him, there is no option of going 'home' due to the growing interference of religion with business in Pakistan. He prefers living and making money in England. (cf. MBL 66) In many ways, making money has become his new religion. Both options, the nostalgic longing for a past that is no more, and, the overhasty, enthusiastic embrace of a new future seem to be flawed solutions.

The film ends with the reconciliatory image of Omar and Johnny lovingly teasing and washing each other, stripped to the waist sprinkling water over their naked torsos.

Plate 12: Film still: Stephen Frears, My Beautiful Laundrette, Film/DVD-ROM, 97:00, 1985, 90:55

Is it this generation of younger men who are to leave behind the colonial legacy and reconcile the 'old' with the 'new' versions of Britishness? The film does not offer any smug answers to these pressing questions, but succeeds in depicting a wonderful range of British characters that were so blatantly missing from visual representations at the time. It also introduces a new visual spectacle of a queer interracial couple on the big screen – an image that disrupts the unitary logic of masculinity in crisis and opts for a reconciliation of different British masculinities. The depiction of interracial couples is still not widespread in cultural representations. In this context, Moore-Gilbert sees Kureishi's and Frears' focus on the gay couple as a subversive move. "If miscegenation is a threat to mono-cultural models of British identity, gay relationships across the racial barrier are a yet more 'perverse' and subversive proposition." (Moore-Gilbert 2001, 87)[185] The depiction of such a queer couple then can indeed be read as an intervention into traditional understandings of masculinity and economies of the

---

185 Interestingly, this slightly contradicts Dyer's statement that in the colonies, interracial homoerotic relations were far more permissive than interracial heterosexual relations, which due to possible offspring, were regarded as the greater boundary violation. (cf. Dyer 1997, 20–35)

gaze. However, similar to other writings by Kureishi, this focus on masculinities unfortunately still goes hand in hand with a marginalisation of non-White and White femininities, and to a certain extent, his writings reproduce the privilege of crisis. Agency in this film is granted to men, not to the ethnicised woman. Nevertheless, the film succeeds in queering a monolithic understanding of masculinity that is more radical than in Kureishi's later accounts of flexible male heterosexuality as seen in *The Black Album*.

The Crying Game: Male Femininity as a Spectacle[186]

Whereas Frears and Kureishi were inspired by the anarchic tradition of fringe theatre in their approach to movies, the Irishman Jordan can more classically be described as an *auteur* film maker, demanding full artistic control over his project and having written the Academy-Award-winning screenplay for *The Crying Game* himself. Additionally, he has also directed several adapted screenplays. Jordan initially had the idea for *The Soldier's Wife*, which was the first working title for the film, in 1982, and it took him more than ten years to finish the script and to arrange for the film's financing. The film's budget of 2.3 million pounds came from a number of international sources, and due to the 'risky' content of the script, no US-American money was invested. Channel 4 provided the lacking funds that allowed the production to finish. (cf. Giles 1997) When *The Crying Game* was released in 1992, it became immensely successful, especially with American critics and audiences, and earned six Academy Award nominations as well as record-breaking figures at the US box office. This was mainly due to Miramax's (the American distributor) smart marketing strategy that was built around 'the big secret' of the movie. Ironically, the film flopped in Britain and became a big success, especially for an art house production, around the world.

Beginning his career as a fiction writer, Jordan turned to writing and filmmaking with his first feature film *Angel* in 1981. Other films include *The Company of Wolves* (1984), adapted from a story by Angela Carter, *Mona Lisa* (1986), *Interview with the Vampire* (1994), based on the bestseller by Anne Rice, *Michael Collins* (1996), *The Butcher Boy* (1997), based on the novel by

---

186 Part of this reading has been published in an earlier German version as Haschemi Yekani (2007b) which contrasts *The Crying Game* with the German-Turkish movie *Lola and Bilidikid* (1999).

Pat McCabe, *Breakfast on Pluto* (2005), also based on a novel by McCabe, and more recently *The Brave One* (2007). Jordan likes to play with genre conventions and gaze structures of classical Hollywood cinema. That is why before focusing in greater detail on *The Crying Game*, I want to briefly explain some theoretical assumptions on how transgender femininity[187] affects gaze theories and conventions of classical narrative cinema that rely on the notion of the 'woman' as spectacle on the screen.

Woman displayed as sexual object is the *leitmotif* of erotic spectacle [...]. The presence of woman is an indispensable element of spectacle in narrative film. (Mulvey 1997, 442)

While classical film theories presuppose a binary structure of the gaze which juxtaposes the 'masculine' position of looking with the 'feminine' position of being looked at (which Mulvey calls "to-be-looked-at-ness" (ibid., 442)), I want to focus on the implications that arise when this femininity is not performed by women. How is this destabilisation of binary gender norms in the shape of male femininity connected to the more classical male crisis narratives and to the genre conventions of the *film noir* in *The Crying Game*, and how does this affect the visual economy of the film?

Visual pleasure is structured by the reproduction of images of bodies and looking relations. This influences which bodies are perceived as desirable and how this desire is structured. Psychoanalytical film theory, still one of the most dominant strains of film theory, can be characterised as heteronormative in two respects: it assumes a binary conception of gender and a clear dichotomy of heterosexual and homosexual. The more prominent depiction of transgender characters in the nineties challenges these assumptions. In this context, the desire *for* and *of* transgender characters in

---

187 When talking about transgender femininity here I assume a continuum of transgender characters with a female gender identity. This encloses the representation of 'biological males' who perform femininity as drag queens (often as part of gay subculture and the camp humour associated with it) as well as in everyday-life passing male femininities (hormonally assisted or not) and transwomen (surgically treated or not) who understand themselves to be women (as opposed to performing femininity on a stage) within the narratives. Let me emphasise that it is not my intention to pigeonhole characters in fixed identity categories. Within the filmic narrative, there is often no explicit reference or self-description along these lines and even in the nineties one repeatedly finds the cliché of the (spectacular) tragic trans character. Accordingly, Britta Madeleine Woitschig is quite right to criticise the lack of depiction of transmen and trans masculinities as well as the recurring stereotypical depiction of trans femininities as "divas", the "angel in the house" or the "willing whore". (cf. Woitschig 2002)

film needs to be addressed.[188] In addition, psychoanalytically inflected film theory often does not pay enough attention to the intricate relations of racialisation and gender and how this is reflected in the filmic gaze.[189]

Halberstam finds fault in the way psychoanalytical gaze theory cannot deal adequately with queer looking relations. The position of the spectator, which is always conceived as either male or female, should – following a queer critique – be able to allow for more diverse modes of identification and desire.[190] Halberstam stipulates

the ability to multiply the gendered positions afforded by the gaze and to provide a more historically specific analysis of spectatorship. A less psychoanalytically in-flected theory of spectatorship is far less sure of the gender of the gaze. Indeed, recent discussions of gay and lesbian cinema assume that the gaze is 'queer' or at least multidimensional. It is important, I think, to find queer relations to cinematic pleasure that are not circumvented by the constrictive language of fetishism, sco-pophilia, castration, and Oedipalization. (Halberstam 1998, 179)

Despite the increasing lesbian/feminist and queer critique (cf. Evans and Gamman 1995; de Lauretis 1987; P. White 1999) of this clear allocation of the man as active spectator and the woman as the eroticised object of this gaze, the conception of woman as spectacle is still discursively powerful and continues to have an effect on the depiction of trans femininities. According to this notion, "cinema builds the way she [the woman] is to be looked at into the spectacle itself" (Mulvey 1997, 447). In classical Holly-wood cinema then, the image of the woman needs not necessarily to serve any narrative purpose; her image in itself conveys pleasure. She is the spectacle, or as Silverman writes, she is "obliged to bear the burden of

---

188 Of course, it is somewhat problematic to speak of a character's desire in a film as the desire is only produced in the montage of images afterwards. But clearly a film can be cut in a way that privileges the gaze of one character on another character, and in this sense the character who is the object of that gaze seldom is realised as an autonomous desiring subject and reduced to an eroticised spectacle.

189 For critical approaches that address these shortcomings, cf. Dyer (1997); Gaines (1988).

190 Silverman, in an attempt to provide a psychoanalytical framework that can account for individual agency, distinguishes the gaze, which is connected to the apparatus of the camera, from the look, which evokes the eye/individual spectator whose look bears the capacity to 'see things differently'. In this sense, although the gaze is ideologically charged and part of conventional looking relations there is, of course, no predetermined way of seeing and Silverman proposes to speak of a "productive look" (Silverman 1996, 164). However, I specifically speak of the gaze here as I am interested in the more con-ventional codes of femininity that are reproduced in *The Crying Game* rather than a re-sistant viewer.

specularity so that the look of her male counterpart can be aligned with the camera" (Silverman 1996, 140). The problem then is how to label the desire, one indispensable element of cinematic pleasure, connected to the body and the performance of the transwoman since the desire for her all too often is violently translated as an unambiguous desire for the (heterosexual) woman or the gay man.

Male femininity is usually associated with gay male subculture and to a lesser extent with lesbian subculture, which overlooks the fact that the desire *for* and *of* female transgenders needs to be understood as multidimensional, which is to say, that it can be gay, lesbian, straight or bisexual.[191] It seems useful in the context of film analysis to ask whether there exists a distinct cinematic desire of and for trans femininity. Let me propose the preliminary term *transdesire* to connote this desire. I am aware that this term might fall prey to fetishising transgenders in their assumed 'Otherness'. Therefore, to propose a term like this offers advantages and disadvantages. With regard to reading practices of films, it is important to disrupt the clear binary allocation of desire and the gaze to ask what transgender means in this context. Transdesire is meant to advert to an independent desiring and desirable subject, who within bigendered norms cannot, or only in limited terms, be represented. In this respect, the designation is a claim for a space for marginalised desire. However, in the context of transsexuality, it is significant not to ignore the demands for an unequivocal female or male gender identity. This is to say that many transsexuals do not understand themselves as living 'between the sexes' and are very willing to accept the term heterosexual, bisexual, gay or lesbian as a description of their desire. Drawing a line between transgender and transsexual[192] is especially difficult with regard to characters in a film. While acknowledging MtFs clearly as women who can have a heterosexual or lesbian desire, there are also trans people whose desire and the desire for

---

191 These thoughts pertaining to desire are not meant to suggest that desire is not always multi-dimensional also for non-trans characters. A gay man on the screen can, obviously, also serve as the object of a heterosexual or other desire. With regard to trans characters however, there is often an extra effort on the level of plot to make these gender ambiguous characters unequivocally readable with reference to their sexuality.

192 For an overview of the "border wars" between butches and transmen, cf. Franzen (2002); Halberstam, "Transgender Butch: Butch/FTM Border Wars and the Masculine Continuum" in *Female Masculinity* (1998, 141–173). This is not intended to render invisible the many and productive alliances between butches and transmen.

whom can only very unsatisfyingly be described as either heterosexual or homosexual.

Claudia Breger poses one of the central questions regarding this dilemma: "When and in how far is 'male femininity' masculinity?" (Breger 2001, 123, my translation). Drawing on Halberstam's conceptualisation of female masculinity, but not as a simple analogy, it would be productive to offer greater space to an analysis of male femininity apart from drag and camp. Not every expression of male femininity is equitable with transvestism or transsexuality. It is important then to emphasise that transgender does not consist of drag, but everyday-lived subject positions. (cf. ibid., 124) This becomes apparent also in narrative cinema which has departed from the classical cross-dressing narrative, often as part of comedy plots, such as in *Tootsie* (1982) or *Mrs Doubtfire* (1993), since the nineties. Nonetheless, movies still conceptualise female transgender characters as especially prone to drama and tragic ends. Against this background, Breger speaks of "a performance of femininity of male-to-female transsexuals marked by a seemingly insurmountable theatricality" (ibid., my translation). While the performance of masculinity supposedly involves less theatricality, Halberstam speaks of "downplayed masculinity" (Halberstam 1998, 239), the representation of femininity is always linked to the spectacular and, hence, artificial[193] which renders it especially attractive for filmic representation. In addition, any form of 'in-betweenness', the undetermined or hybrid offers a certain attraction and is often associated with the spectacular. It is by no means accidental that many transgender characters are also hybridised along the lines of race as will be expounded upon with regard to the character Dil in *The Crying Game*.

It is important to emphasise the reciprocity of male femininity with the conceptualisation of hegemonic male masculinity. Normative gender roles are also performative and by no means fixed. The appearance and visibility of transgender characters on the big screen influence the way gender is understood for 'biological unequivocal' bodies as well. Bearing these thoughts in mind, I want to turn to *The Crying Game*, a film that addresses the way "gender trouble" and postcoloniality coincide yet is still quite dependant on privileged White male crisis narratives.

---

193 This follows a misogynistic logic which comprehends masculinity as 'real' and as a result sacrosanct.

Fergus: "You're something else, Dil, you know that?"
Dil: "Never said a truer word." (CG 45)

In the much-talked about film *The Crying Game* by Neil Jordan, the story of the renegade IRA-member Fergus (Stephen Rea) is depicted. Initially, he and his girlfriend Jude (Miranda Richardson), both White Irish, work together for the IRA. As a female decoy, Jude seduces the Black British soldier Jody (Forest Whitaker), who subsequently is held hostage. Fergus becomes his guard and after long and intense talks, he is unable to kill Jody when the order comes. Nonetheless, Jody is killed in his attempt to escape, but not before he convinces Fergus to promise to take care of his girlfriend, Dil (Jaye Davidson), who is in London.

Plate 13: Film still: Neil Jordan, The Crying Game, Film/DVD-ROM, 107:00, 1992, 15:43

The narrative clearly falls into two separate strands and the second part of the movie centres on the slowly developing relationship of Fergus, now an IRA-dropout living incognito as the supposedly Scottish Jimmy in London, and Dil, a Black British hairdresser. The big 'secret' around which the film revolves is the fact that Dil's femininity is performed by a biologically male body and culminates in Jimmy's nausea at the sight of her penis.[194] Jimmy/Fergus is haunted by his past in the shape of Jude, who wants to force him to commit a political assassination for the IRA. Now, it is Dil who can come to his rescue. In conclusion, it is Fergus who goes to prison for Dil's murdering of Jude.

---

194 For a discussion of the visual taboo of male nudity in *The Crying Game* and other movies, cf. Lehman (2007).

The multilayered and politically complex plot of the film is broken down to be represented in the form of different relationships and constellations of desire. Within the plot, two erotic triangles emerge, which can be read as either hetero- or homosexual according to the gender assignment of Dil. The homosexual triangle includes Fergus – Jody – Dil while the straight one is Fergus – Jude – Dil, whereby both options remain valid in the final coupling, Fergus – Dil.[195] However, due to the repeated disgust that Fergus voices at the sight of Dil's biologically male body, it seems safe to say that his desire for the transwoman is a heterosexual one. After Fergus has learned of her 'secret'[196], he only kisses her hesitantly and denies any further sexual contact: "Can't pretend that much. Should have stayed a girl." (CG 48) In contrast to the visual pleasure of the gay couple in *My Beautiful Laundrette*, Jordan shies away from depicting intimacy between the two protagonists after the revelation. As far as Dil's desire can be judged, she clearly identifies as female, speaking of herself as "girl" and "young thing" wearing female attire and passing in every-day life as a woman, who looks for gallant male lovers who can protect her. Only Jody seems to have been fully aware of her pre-op trans-body and had no problem with it. In the context of labelling Fergus a heterosexual man, only the dream sequences, which show a highly illuminated Jody, work as moments of disruption.[197] During fellatio and after learning about Dil's male sex, Fergus is revisited by Jody, and there is a cut from Fergus's face to a picture of Jody in Dil's flat which dissolves into another sequence of Jody, brightly lit wearing his white cricket uniform throwing a ball.

---

195 Gender ambiguity is inscribed in the names of almost all protagonists (Jude, Jody and Dil); only Fergus/Jimmy is rather unequivocally considered a man's name.

196 The term 'secret' remains problematic as Dil assumed that Fergus was aware of her transgender identity. Consequently, one should maybe rather speak of Fergus's ignorance than of Dil's secret.

197 The desire for Jody is clearly something that Fergus cannot or fights to acknowledge. As has been widely noted, Fergus's homosexual panic is most evident when he is to hold Jody's penis to help him urinate while his hands are bound (cf. McGee 1997, 126) and Jody tries to calm him by assuring him that it is "only a piece of meat" (CG 13). This is, of course, a remark that foreshadows the revelation of Dil's penis.

Plate 14: Film still: Neil Jordan, The Crying Game, Film/DVD-ROM, 107:00, 1992, 55:26

But this image must not be a threat to Fergus's heterosexuality. Within the triangle, there is a passing on of the woman (Dil) from one man (Jody) to another (Fergus).[198] Dil becomes desirable only because Jody desired her, and Fergus feels guilt-ridden and thinks he needs to protect her. The problem is not the legitimate homoerotic desire for Jody as it is projected onto the *woman*, Dil. This economy of authorised homosociality between men is, however, fundamentally disrupted when it becomes apparent that Dil might actually be a *man* herself. In this way, Fergus's position as a heterosexual man would be challenged and his desire might, against his better judgement, actually be homosexual or queer. In contrast to my reading of the triangle as either heterosexual or homosexual, Pramaggiore stresses Jody's possible bisexual identity but also acknowledges that this potential disruption is absent form the narrative which clearly privileges Fergus's view.

Jody and Jude are violently eliminated from the ever-shifting romantic triangle, the former in a tragically inevitable 'accident' of colonial military might, the latter in an equally inevitable confrontation with Dil that the film constructs as anything but tragic. (Pramaggiore 1996, 285–286)

While it initially seems that the movie offers multiple and shifting identities along the lines of gender, race and sexuality, White male heterosexuality remains the privileged site here and clearly re-centres a more traditional

---

198 Sedgwick explains – with recourse to René Girard and Gayle Rubin – that "in any erotic rivalry, the bond that links the two rivals is as intense and potent as the bond that links either of the rivals to the beloved" (Sedgwick 1985, 21).

crisis narrative of hegemonic masculinity.[199] Kristin Handler writes, *"The Crying Game* unself-consciously essentializes sexual and racial difference to fix the identities of Jody, Jude and Dil, in order to free Fergus to be all he can be." (Handler 1994, 32)

This centring of heterosexuality is also connected to the way *The Crying Game* was marketed. Subcultural knowledge about gender ambiguity was not presupposed, quite the contrary. The film speculates that an audience will not have a lead on Fergus when it comes to reading Dil's sex, and therefore, hopes for a most spectacular revealing of the body of the transgender character for the film's climax. As Halberstam notes, "more knowing audiences" (Halberstam 2005, 80) are ignored, and the protagonist Fergus remains the person through whose eyes the story is told and with whom the viewers share the spectacle of Dil. Moreover, Andrew Moor argues that "Jordan's liberal fascination [...] with transgressive sexuality, and with race, has a touristic flavour" (Moor 2006, 157). The viewer is clearly invited to share Fergus's crisis as is most obvious in the scene after the 'revelation'.

Plate 15: Film still: Neil Jordan, The Crying Game, Film/DVD-ROM, 107:00, 1992, 61:48

---

199 Of course, this does not mean that there can be no queer or pleasurable viewing of the flim. "The spectator is neither the repository nor the origin of desire; rather, as subject, he or she is constituted as a function of desire, or rather of desires. [...] [B]ut identificatory desire is not completely free either." (McGee 1997, 130–131) In this reading, I am interested in identifying the re-inscriptions of hegemonic masculinity in this at first sight 'subversive'/queer movie.

Criticised by many, *The Crying Game* is a political conflict narrated via an eroticised story[200], in which racialised male femininity works as a spectacle of hybridity and becomes the backdrop of the White man's crisis.[201] Nevertheless, postcolonial relations are more complicated with reference to the Northern Ireland conflict. Fergus is a White man, but he is also a militant IRA-member fighting what he perceives as colonial occupation. Jody, marginalised by his status as a Black man both in England and Ireland, takes up just "a job" (CG 12), which paradoxically puts him in the position of the coloniser in relation to the Irish Fergus. "Jody stands for the British colonial presence in Ireland, but neither his national nor sexual identity is capable of being recuperated by traditional definitions of race, citizenship, or monosexual orientation." (Pramaggiore 1996, 285) The presence of the Black British Jody is also a reversal of the stereotypical colonial situation, which turns the Black man into the potential coloniser. Nonetheless, Jody also faces racism in Ireland and remarks that Northern Ireland is the "only place in the world they call you nigger to your face" (CG 12). Jordan here is playing with the intersections of race and masculinity in postcolonial Britain and connects those to the crisis narrative of his central character, Fergus. In this sense, Fergus is also not performing unambiguous hegemonic masculinity, and Jordan links Black British and Irish masculinity here as both affected by British imperialism. Both men also bond over their working-class roots in their talks. Despite the obvious differences between Jody and Fergus, Jordan implies a strong commonality between the two. This becomes evident when Fergus, similar to the racial slurs that Jody faces, is repeatedly insulted by being called "Paddy" once he is in London. London, however, serves as the place where he can possibly overcome the demands of Jude, who represents Irish nationalism in its fanatical shape, to be rid of his terrorist Irishness. In this context, hege-

---

200 In Neil Jordan's more recent film, *Breakfast on Pluto* the focus is again on transnationality embodied by the spectacular transwoman/transvestite Patrick/Patricia "Kitten" Braden (Cilian Murphy). In its allegorical use of transgender to connote a transnational conflict *Breakfast on Pluto* shows strong parallels with *The Crying Game*.

201 Carl Dahlman claims that the crisis narrative of Fergus ends in his "liberation from biologically determined gender categories [...] [and that] Fergus is able to gain his desired liberation from the seemingly natural geopolitical categories of the conflict" (Dahlman 2002, 137). This reading however, fails to note the privilege that is connected to the White man's crisis. The non-White queer characters, whose subjectivities are marginalised in the narrative, serve as a backdrop in this learning process that re-centres Fergus's crisis.

monic Whiteness 'trumps' nationality because although Jody is, in fact, British, he cannot be rid of his marker of Blackness when he is stationed in Northern Ireland; whereas, Fergus can cope with his failure as an Irish 'national liberator' and 'pass' as Scottish Jimmy, or at least assume a new non-terrorist Irish identity, in London.

However, despite the almost fairy tale happy ending, things become slightly more complicated as masculinity and femininity seem even less stable in this framework than hitherto discussed. The character Dil, a Black transwoman (with a penis), is marked as 'Other' on more than one level and is rendered into an 'exotic' spectacle.

> Ultimately, the transgender character Dil never controls the gaze, and serves as a racialized fetish figure who diverts the viewer's attention from the highly charged political conflict between England and Ireland. (Halberstam 2005, 81)

Dil remains – also in her class position as a hairdresser as not exactly financially well-off – marked as the 'Other' whose desire is located outside of the film. It is Fergus's desire and his quest for redemption that is at the centre of attention. He desires Dil in order to come clean over Jody's death and his possible suppressed homoerotic/homosexual feelings for Jody. In contrast to Dil's gender identity, Fergus's masculinity is anything but spectacular. Quite to the contrary, Stephen Rea's performance stresses the 'ordinariness' of this character, and Fergus is portrayed as just a 'regular bloke' both in his looks and manners. Although his national identity is less stable, and he switches from Irish to Scottish, his hegemonic Whiteness is obviously normalised in contrast to Dil's exotic Blackness or 'in-betweenness'. In a sense, this doubling of racial and gender ambivalence works as a means to enhance the spectacular value of Dil's performance.[202]

Rosemary Hennessy discusses how the movie, despite the prominent presence of a transgender character, remains caught up in a "heterosexual imaginary":

> Through the continued proddings of the heterosexual imaginary, both Fergus's homoeroticism and Dil's transvestism find a secure place within the heterosexual matrix.[203] (Hennessy 2000, 151)

---

202 Lola Young (2007), however, stresses that many of the reviews of the film initially only focused on the spectacular gender performance and systematically de-thematised both Dil's and Jody's racialisation.

203 However, the term 'transvestism' used by Hennesy (2000) and others to describe Dil is more than problematic. Mark Simpson similarly reads Dil as a gay man/transvestite and

Halberstam identifies this "heterosexual imaginary" also in the way the nightclub, the Metro, which becomes a central location of the film, is portrayed through the point of view of Fergus. At first, it seems as if a mixed crowd of straight people frequent the place, but later in the story, the Metro is clearly marked as a subcultural space where homosexual couples and people in drag are present. Tellingly, these become visible only after Fergus has realised Dil's 'true' identity, and as a result, the imagery of the film changes according to Fergus's perspective. "Dil is always seen from Fergus' point of view, but rarely in a straightforward way: Fergus follows Dil voyeuristically, glimpsing her through blinds, veils and mirrors, courting her with a series of looks." (Giles 1997, 55) The universality of the White straight male gaze is firmly rooted in the logic of the film, and Fergus's crisis to a large degree depends on his inability to recognise 'wrong' femininity. Despite this re-centring of the male gaze in *The Crying Game*, the destabilisation of gendered binaries is not completely deferred but rendered slightly out of focus. The privileged crisis here is Fergus's.[204]

In accordance with Hennessy's and Halberstam's critique, one can summarise that the movie needs the spectacular transwoman, but it is not interested in a portrayal of a transdesire as I have tried to explain. Femi-

---

sums up the politics of the film: "Real femininity is exterminated, real homosexuality is kept at bay, blackness is not engaged with but merely appropriated, and transvestism – something that *might* represent an identification with femininity – is used to do away with the feminine altogether." (Simpson 1994, 175) Moor (2006), too, argues that many critics have robbed Dil of the possibility to be read as a feminine/campy gay man and by addressing him as "she" rob him of his gay/queer masculinity. However, Moor also supposes a very clear binary between gay femininity and transsexual femininity. By calling Dil a transgender character or transwoman I wish to highlight the instability of such labels. In this understanding, transgender would also include the performative appropriation of femininity by certain gay men or masculinity by lesbian/butch women. The "she" does not signify some 'gender truth' but refers to Dil's adoption of a female gender identity that the film also depicts as her habitual gender expression. The conception of Dil as *really* a gay man or transvestite is not altogether convincing as she seems more attracted to heterosexual men than to gay men (all her lovers, Jody, Dave and Fergus, are presented in their looks and habitus as 'ordinary straight' rather than 'stereotypical gay' men). Dil is not only a drag queen or someone who dresses up as a woman occasionally. She lives as a woman in her every-day life in addition to performing as a drag queen at the night club.

204 When Fergus spots Dil for the first time in the Metro there is a triangulation of gazes as Dil asks the bar tender Col (Jim Broadbent) if she is right that Fergus is watching her. In this sense, she returns Fergus's gaze. However, she is not looking at Fergus as an erotic object, rather she spots him looking at her; she is aware of her own feminine position of being looked at in this relation.

ninity becomes instrumental in mirroring the conflict of the male protagonist, which is also due to genre conventions of the *film noir* that influence
Jordan. Early in the movie, Jody as a sort of motto for the whole film
warns Fergus that "women are trouble" (CG 18).

Read against this foil as a 'neo-*film noir*' *Crying Game* depicts the identity crisis of a
man that circles around the discovery and mastery of women, whereby the *good girl*
supports the male hero in his attempt to shield himself off from the *bad girl*, the
threatening woman. (Warth 1999, 129, my translation)

In the case of *The Crying Game*, Dil is the 'good girl', while the 'biological
female', Jude is conceptualised as the 'bad girl'.

*Plate 16: Film still: Neil Jordan, The Crying Game, Film/DVD-ROM, 107:00,
1992, 74:32*

Jude embodies the image of the 'phallic' woman bearing a gun in almost
every sequence in which she features, sporting her cool new and darker
haircut as her *femme fatale* look, which is also used prominently for the
movie poster. In contrast, Dil holds the gun very reluctantly when shooting
Jude in the final confrontation. In her critique of the portrayal of a not
very emancipated or feminist femininity, Warth is surely right. However,
when she continues in her argument that in this constellation, in which
female femininity is warded off and destroyed by "a femininity adopted by
men" (ibid., 129, my translation), and herein she identifies an especially
sexist motive, she opens her theory up to the same transphobic stereotypes
which equate transwomen repeatedly with transvestites and in the worst

case, with sexist men who rob 'real' women of their femininity.[205] Film analysis of this kind perpetuates its binary assumptions and falls short of recognising trans femininity that does not necessarily adhere to this logic.

When Fergus tries to turn Dil into a man as a measure of protection from his IRA comrades, this gives him also the opportunity to revisit his homoerotic attachment to Jody, whose fetishised cricket uniform Dil is now wearing, and which Simpson labels a "*Vertigo*-like necrophile obsession" (Simpson 1994, 173). In addition to wearing 'male clothes', the cutting of Dil's hair is a central scene in this transformation.

Plate 17: Film still: Neil Jordan, The Crying Game, Film/DVD-ROM, 107:00, 1992, 82:54

The visual prominence of the scissors is interesting here, and in a classical psychoanalytical reading of the film, they can probably be seen as alluding to the castration threat. At this point, rather paradoxically something is 'cut off' in order to produce masculinity, which Dil, however, never performs convincingly. Although Dil supposedly has something too much (a penis), her gender identity is clearly feminine and performing masculinity can be assumed to be the more 'artificial' gender expression for Dil, who in the end can grow back her hair to adopt her 'true' feminine gender.

Apart from the fact that the 'good girl' of the movie is embodied by a transwoman, Jordan attempts little to re-think the foundations of gender clichés in the relationship of Dil and Fergus. Fergus can finally rehabilitate his sense of lost heroic masculinity by 'doing time' for the (non-phallic)

---

205 Let me add that this logic also does not take into account the fact that some 'real' women prefer to live a masculine gender identity.

woman he saved – a typical gesture of masculinity which is marked by the willingness of the hero to sacrifice himself for someone else. As the song "Stand by Your Man"[206] plays in the background, Dil and Fergus appear as the happy old couple who go about their routines. When Dil visits Fergus in prison and affectionately calls him "Hon'," he replies: "Don't call me that." Dil responds "sorry, love" (CG 69). Fergus recounts the story of the scorpion and the frog that Jody had told him and which thereby establishes the closing narrative frame between the first and second half of the film. This fable explains his self-sacrificial (male) behaviour towards Dil as rooted in his 'nature'. The film fails to actually portray a (sexual) relationship between Dil and the supposedly 'normal' heterosexual man Fergus and postpones the happy ending to a fictional 'after the plot'.[207] Visually the viewer is deprived of the gratification of consuming the relationship – or in a transphobic logic, she or he is spared this sight.

Let me return briefly to my initial thoughts on whether transdesire is a useful concept for film analysis. Underlying this idea is not the intention of further labelling and narrowing definitions of desire. On the contrary, it was introduced as a temporary tool that in the best case should facilitate talking about queer constellations of desire in narrative cinema without having to reiterate the homo/hetero binary yet again. As long as the desire of and for femininity and masculinity is not described in more complex ways than classical film theory has done for a long time, the question of transdesire needs to be continually addressed. In this context, the hopefully ever greater presence of more complex trans characters needs to be acknowledged and the binary description of filmic desire more radically queered.

---

206 On the level of the soundtrack however, Jordan is more willing to engage in 'audio gender trouble'. There is a mixture of male and female performers singing the same songs and tellingly, there is a certain irony when Lyle Lovett voices the final "Stand by Your Man" (which was first performed by Tammy Wynette). The title song "The Crying Game" is performed three times by different artists in the film: first, Dil listens to the original version by Dave Berry, then lip-synchs the version sung by Kate Robbins and during the final credits the audience hears Boy George's adaptation (produced by Neil Tennant and Chris Lowe of the Pet Shop Boys) of the song which is now marked by a rather gender-ambiguous singing voice. (cf. Moor 2006, 159)

207 Pramaggiore sees a subversive move in this "deferral of sexual consummation" and a resistance to the "'happily ever after' formula" (Pramaggiore 1996, 286). In contrast, as I pointed out, I read this deferral as a (transphobic) blinding out of the visual (sexual) desire of the transgender character.

British cinema in the mid-eighties and early nineties presented a fresh look on how race, gender, nationality and sexuality collide in postcolonial Britain. Both films discussed in this chapter engage in the visual re-coding of the stereotypical imperial gaze that glorified White masculinity and objectified the 'Other's' body.

Kureishi and Frears queer British masculinity by centring the visual pleasure of the film *My Beautiful Laundrette* on the interracial homosexual couple Omar and Johnny. The odd couple works as a reconciliatory image with Johnny representing the new 'underprivileged' White male working class who suffer from mass unemployment and Omar as an example of the more class-mobile immigrant communities. The film brings together these two British masculinities and in this move risks to instrumentalise homosexuality as simply an allegorical 'healing' image. However, by portraying the queer desire between the two men, seen in their glances and physical contact, matter-of-factly, the film also introduces a queer visual spectacle that disrupts some of the presumptions of classical narrative cinema. Kureishi and Frears clearly attempted to present a rough urban and postcolonial look that coincided with the nostalgic 'postcolonial' colonial films labelled Raj Revival cinema. Nonetheless, their strong focus on queer masculinities simultaneously produces a visual blank: Tania's erasure from the screen reiterates the lack of visual representation of femininity and reproduces the male privilege of being at the centre of the narrative.

Somewhat paradoxically, *The Crying Game*, which is one of the first feature films to present a transwoman in a central role, relies on a strong recourse to the male privilege of crisis as well. The sexual desire of the transwoman Dil does not occupy much of this film's story – a lack that is common in other movies as well.[208] In the end, the possibility of less restrictive gender norms is diverted to the future. Nonetheless, when transgender characters are portrayed on the big screen, they do pose a challenge to gender norms even though they are still all too often depicted as tragic figures. A complex figuration, including the colonial relations between Ireland and England, the performativity of gender and its intersections with race and nationality are the backdrop of *The Crying Game*. However, it is, unfortunately, still very much a hegemonic White male look

---

208 The highly acclaimed movie *Transamerica* (2005) also only very hesitantly alludes to a relationship between the transsexual protagonist Bree (Felicity Huffman) and the Native American Calvin (Graham Greene). In *Better Than Chocolate* (1999) for a change there is a (very chaste) lesbian happy ending for the transwoman Judy (Peter Outerbridge).

on these events that Jordan presents, which is also mirrored in his conservative film language locked in a heterosexist gaze structure lingering on the spectacle of the transwoman as a new ingredient for the old formula of the *film noir*.

Zadie Smith: Hysterical Realism and Happy Multiculturalism?

Zadie Smith is currently one of the most highly acclaimed postcolonial writers in English and has often been described as an aspiring young talent. The extreme success of her debut novel *White Teeth* in 2000, which sold more than one million copies, led many critics to comment on the well-orchestrated marketing campaign surrounding the publication of this book whose success sometimes is interpreted as a sign of commodified cultural marginality.[209] Similarly to Kureishi, Smith's own 'mixed' ethnic background is often mentioned in reviews and stereotypically – and in contrast to most reviews on books by male authors – one also often finds comments on her 'exotic' good looks. By now, Smith has published two more novels, *The Autograph Man* in 2002 and *On Beauty* in 2005 both of which have received slightly less attention and praise than their predecessor.

In contrast to Kureishi, who focuses most prominently on male protagonists and thereby risks to marginalise female characters in his writing, and other postcolonial authors, such as Monica Ali, who seem to foreground 'women's stories', Zadie Smith favours family histories in which both male and female characters are equally at the centre of attention. Nonetheless, especially *White Teeth* satirises the crises of men from different ethnic backgrounds and thereby ironically addresses many of the fears of the 'new millennium' among which the 'decline' of traditional hegemonic masculinity features prominently. This makes her book a relevant comment on the prevalent discourse on the crisis of masculinity that has become inseparable from the notion of a crisis of national identity in general, and 'Englishness' in particular. This emphasis on national identity is often the sole or primary focus in discussions of the book. In the following, I will attempt to show how Smith's comic text self-consciously takes up prominent issues of postcolonial discourse, for instance hybridity, but also the problem of fundamentalism(s), and interweaves them with a rather ironic version of the narratives of the crises of two different generations of men in post-World War II Britain.

---

209 For a critique of the successful marketing of cultural difference and hybridity, cf. Huggan (2001); Jakubiak (2008); Thomas (2006).

White Teeth: Back to the Future

White Teeth features an obtrusive, almost Dickensian heterodiegetic narrator who constantly comments on the lives of the characters who are mildly ridiculed in their follies and mishaps. At times, they appear as more rounded individuals, and at other times, as rather flat caricatures, which is a balancing act in this farcical *tour de force* that seems to privilege plot over character. The plot of *White Teeth* begins in 1975 and spans the lives of three different generations to the eve of New Year in 1992 and ends with a flash forward to the possible future in 1999. Smith self-reflexively inter-weaves three family histories, that of the British-Jamaican Joneses, the Bangladeshi(-British) Iqbals and the supposedly "more English than the English" (WT 328) Chalfens, who are in fact of Polish-Jewish and English-Catholic descent, with such historical events as the assassination of Indira Gandhi in 1984 or the fall of the Berlin Wall in 1989. There are also many analepses, for instance to Bulgaria in World War II and as far back as to the 1857 'Indian Mutiny' in colonial Bengal as well as the 1907 earthquake in Jamaica. Nonetheless, London in the years 1975 to 1992 remains the central setting of the text, particularly the neighbourhood of Willesden in the North of London, a place that is known for its inhabitants from vari-ous ethnic and religious backgrounds. But Willesden is neither as notorious as Brixton, nor as cosmopolitan as Soho, both of which feature much more prominently in other postcolonial fictions of London. Rather, it is a fairly 'un-metropolitan' area of town which makes it the perfect backdrop of Smith's version of "everyday hybridity" (cf. Moss 2003).[210]

While most critical work on Smith's writing so far focuses on postcolo-niality, hybridity and multiculturalism rather generally – questions that the text inevitably provokes –, I want to ask in how far Smith needs to fashion the crisis of English national identity in the wake of postcoloniality also as a crisis of masculinity. More specifically, I am interested in the construction and contrasting of the various male crises, as Smith clearly presents a plu-rality of masculinities in contemporary Britain.

In *White Teeth*, the reader can laugh at almost everybody's crisis. Despite the manifold female characters, male middle-aged men feature prominently in this tale of three families. Walters even states that "Smith's female char-

---

210 Christine Sizemore argues with reference to Paul Gilroy that Willesden figures as a site of "demotic" and local cosmopolitanism which renders *White Teeth* into a postcolonial city novel which "is centered not in the middle of the city, but on its edge" (Sizemore 2005, 78).

acters lack development because they are overshadowed by white male protagonists" (Walters 2008, 125). In the story, the three families are not equally present. While the Joneses and Iqbals take up more narrative space, the Chalfens occupy a more marginal role, and the portrayal of them has been commented on as provoking the least amount of empathy. (cf. Squires 2002, 36) Consequently, it is mainly Archie Jones and Samad Iqbal, as well as his sons, the twins Magid and Millat, who are at the centre of attention and to a lesser degree Marcus Chalfen and his eldest son Joshua. The only main female protagonist is Irie Jones, who has been described as the centre of the reader's sympathy by Sigrun Meinig. (cf. Meinig 2004, 248) Despite this focus on male characters it is, of course, the interaction with their wives and daughters that shapes the crises of these men.[211] In this sense, there is a strong particularisation of masculinity in general and White British masculinity specifically in this "polyvocal novel" (Cuder-Domínguez 2004, 183).

The one 'true' English bloke, Archie Jones, seems to be characterised first and foremost by his lack of specific characteristics. He is extremely indecisive and throws a coin whenever life-changing decisions have to be made. This belief in chance is contrasted with the Muslim Samad's stern belief in fate. The friendship of Archie and Samad goes back to World-War-II Bulgaria where they were stationed as young soldiers. The narrator comments on the unlikely couple: It is "the kind of friendship an English-man makes on holiday, that he can make only on holiday. A friendship that crosses class and colour, a friendship that takes as its basis physical prox-imity and survives because the Englishman assumes the physical proximity will not continue." (WT 96) But despite these doubts, the friendship sur-vives, and the two are reunited in London where both marry younger wives in the seventies.

Alfred Archibald Jones is depicted as an English everyman who finds himself in unlikely situations, and it is primarily mediocrity that character-ises him. After an unsuccessful marriage of almost thirty years to an Italian woman, whom he supposedly drove mad, and who tellingly, is named Ophelia, Archie finds himself lost in the streets of London in the early morning of New Year 1975. This is the starting point of the plot: Archie

---

211 This focus is also supported by the structure of the novel itself, which is divided into four main sections entitled "Archie 1974, 1945", "Samad 1984, 1857", "Irie 1990, 1907" and "Magid, Millat and Marcus 1992, 1999", all of which are subdivided into several subchapters.

attempts suicide but is saved by the Halal butcher Mo Hussein-Ishmael on whose property he had parked his car to try to suffocate himself. This humorous episode of a failed suicide attempt is linked to Archie's ordinariness by the narrator.

No matter what anyone says, suicide takes a lot of guts. It's for heroes and martyrs, truly vainglorious men. Archie was none of these. He was a man whose significance in the Greater Scheme of Things could be figured along familiar rations:
Pebble: Beach.
Raindrop: Ocean.
Needle: Haystack. (WT 11)

But rootlessness, a central concern of the novel, is only initially a problem for Archie (cf. Walters 2005, 320), and he quickly decides to start his life anew. At "The End of the World Party", he meets Clara Bowden, a young woman of Jamaican descent with whom he instantly falls in love. The forty-seven-year-old Archie and the nineteen-year-old Clara marry only six weeks later. Despite their age difference and difference in background, Clara seems to be attracted paradoxically by Archie's very ordinariness.

Clara understood that Archibald Jones was no romantic hero. [...] No white knight, then, this Archibald Jones. No aims, no hopes, no ambitions. A man whose greatest pleasure were English breakfasts and DIY. A dull man. An *old* man. And yet ... good. He was a *good* man. (WT 48, original emphasis)

In this novel, in which everybody seems to be obsessed with their roots or family history, Archie, who is originally from Brighton, does not really seem to care all that much. "I'm a Jones, you see. 'Slike a 'Smith'. We're nobody ... My father used to say: 'We're the chaff, boy, we're the chaff.' Not that I've ever been much bothered, mind. Proud all the same, you know. Good honest English stock.'" (WT 99) This remark, which can also be read as a self-reflexive humorous comment on the author's own name, Smith, demonstrates that "good honest English stock" has not become a sign of Archie's privilege or superiority, rather, it connotes his mediocrity. Archie is not concerned with notions of 'purity'. He marries Clara without realising that this might be considered 'inappropriate' by some. When he brings her along to one of the office parties, his co-workers are quite bedazzled, and Smith succeeds in wittily exposing their prejudice.

'Oh' Archie, you *are* funny, said Maureen sadly, for she had always fancied Archie a bit but never more than a *bit* because of this strange way he had about him, always talking to Pakistanis and Caribbeans like he didn't even notice and now he'd gone and married one and hadn't even thought it worth mentioning what colour she was until the office dinner when she turned up black as anything and Maureen almost choked on her prawn cocktail. (WT 69)

Smith constantly ridicules the conservative discourse of national or racial purity.

In addition to the challenges to the concept of 'Englishness', the assumed crisis of masculinity is often related to the changes in gender relations in the wake of women's liberation and the decline of the nuclear patriarchal family in the seventies. Archie, however, again is rather unaffected by this male angst. When Clara is pregnant with Irie, Archie naturally assumes that her genes will be dominant.

'And I arks the doctor what it will look like, half black, an half white an' all dat bizness. And 'im say anything could happen. Dere's even a chance it might be blue-eyed! Kyan you imagine dat?' Archie couldn't imagine that. He couldn't imagine any piece of him slugging out in the gene pool with a piece of Clara and *winning.* (WT 67)

Archie is quite happy to lose this 'battle of the sexes' and never challenges his wife's right to be the 'head of the family'. He is content to live a life that many would see as a sign of national decay and a sign of male weakness. Archie adapts to his role in a matrilineal Black British family, whose story can be traced back to Hortense Bowden, Clara's mother, and her grandmother Ambrosia Bowden. Although Hortense strictly opposes their marriage because she feels that 'bi-racial' marriages are doomed to failure, 'racial purity' in this family is questioned from the start. Already in colonial Jamaica, this 'Black' family had a White ancestor, Captain Charley 'Whitey' Durham, who had forced himself on Irie's great-grandmother, Ambrosia. As throughout the book, Smith seems to suggest that colonial and postcolonial histories are intertwined in a matter that affects personal family histories as well as historiography and renders dubious any notion of purity.

While Archie is to accept change and chance, his friend Samad Miah Iqbal is troubled by his holding on to notions of patriarchy and purity in his family. Smith contrasts the matrilineal Bowdens (and logically, Irie's child will be a girl as well) with the patrilineal family of the Iqbals. Initially, Samad faces a number of drawbacks in the army, which he originally perceived as a way to become 'included in the empire' and be accepted as an equal British citizen. On his third day in the army, he is shot and ends up with an injury of one hand – and this loss of ability can be seen as another factor destabilising his sense of secure masculinity. He is transferred to another division of "the rejects of war" (WT 89) where he meets Archie and where he constantly has to explain why somebody of his origin is fighting in the British army.[212] Samad refuses to be called by the short form "Sam" or "Sammy", which could be wrongly interpreted as a short for "Samuel" and undermine his Muslim identity. (cf. WT 112) Consequently, Samad "takes the Anglicization of his name as a verbal assault on his identity" (Mirze 2008, 191). This sense of not being understood or appreciated for who you are is a permanent feeling of Samad's. After his service in the British military and some time in Bangladesh, Samad is presented at the beginning of the novel as a middle-aged man, who, like his friend Archie, seeks a fresh start as well.

Newly married to his twenty-year-old bride, Alsana Begum, he immigrates to England in 1973, and their twins are born around the same time as Irie Jones. In England, again, Samad constantly feels undervalued. His job as a waiter is hardly his ideal notion of a career, and he daydreams about wearing a placard that explains his educated background. (cf. WT 58) Samad also continuously has to repeat that he is not from India or Pakistan, but from Bangladesh, whose existence is an unknown fact to many of the addressed. (cf. WT 133) This assumed ignorance even stretches forth into his very family where he routinely blames his wife that she neglects her Bengali culture for the "Hindi brain popcorn" (WT 236). Samad continually worries about his family's reputation and his sons' proper Bengali upbringing because he fears they will be corrupted by the West.

Samad can trace his family history back to his great-grandfather Mangal Pande in the so-called 'Sepoy Rebellion' or 'Indian Mutiny'. While the word 'Pandy' has come to connote a proverbial coward (cf. WT 251), Samad dreams of rehabilitating Pande as the true hero he perceives him to be.

Tied to this humiliating representation of Samad's forefather as a coward is his dismay at the failure of his illustrious genealogy to manifest itself in his own life.

---

212 When his son Magid much later tries to explain to the perplexed old man J.P Hamilton that his father served in World War II for the British army, Smith, mockingly, exposes Hamilton's ignorance: "'I'm afraid you must be mistaken,' said Mr Hamilton, genteel as ever. 'There were certainly no wogs as I remember – though you're probably not allowed to say that these days are you? But no … no Pakistanis … what would we have fed them? No, no,' he grumbled, assessing the question as if he were being given the opportunity to rewrite history here and now." (WT 172)

Indeed, the more uncertain Samad grows of his genealogical roots, the more fearful he becomes about his own failure and dissolution. [...] [H]is failure to live up to his ancestor's heroic legacy leaves him feeling like a bastard whose mixed English and Bengali cultural identity has destroyed his masculinity. (A. Dawson 2007, 158)

Ashley Dawson convincingly links Samad's fear of cultural alienation with his pronounced male (mid-life) crisis. This crisis is tied to his fantasies of successful patrilineal decent in his family which he projects both to the future of his sons and to the past given his obsession with his forefather Mangal Pande. In 1989, Samad to his great joy can finally convince the owner of Archie's and Samad's regular meeting spot, the pub O'Connell's[213], Abdul-Mickey, to hang a portrait of Pande. Brought up as a colonial subject, Samad now seeks a stable cultural postcolonial identity as a Bengali living in Britain. His qualms are those of the stereotypical "mimic man", who tries to have his failure compensated by his sons' success; he "yearns for the East and blames the West" (Cuder-Domínguez 2004, 184).

This yearning for stability is also expressed in his adherence to religion. But Samad practices a very convenient version of Islam. His bigotry is exposed in the novel as religion seems to be more a matter of negotiation than an unshaken foundation to him. Samad constantly tries to make 'deals' with God. First, it is the sin of masturbation that he tries to circumvent by inventing his own justification, "To the pure all things are pure" (WT 137) and later changes his motto to "Can't say fairer than that" (WT 139) to swap masturbation for the sin of drinking alcohol. Despite his bad conscience, he cannot part with any of his weaknesses, and he indulges in a new wave of sexual impurity as he is almost caught having an affair with the music teacher of his sons, Poppy Burt-Jones, who naïvely is enamoured in her own Orientalist fantasies of Samad.

Generally, Samad is not really doing well in his relationships with women. He likes to imagine himself a successful patriarch, but in a role reversal of stereotypical violence in a Muslim relationship, it is his wife who keeps the upper hand in their grotesque physical fights, scenes that Smith presents in a manner reminiscent of wrestling or slapstick comedy. (cf. WT 200) Given his lack of patriarchal assertiveness, Samad decides to send his first-born and academically more successful twin Magid abroad to Bangladesh where he is supposed to receive a 'proper' Bengali education.

---

213 O'Connell's is a central setting in the novel and the stereotypical "hybrid business" (WT 246) which despite its Middle Eastern owner, holds on to the Irish name.

After Alsana finds out about the kidnapping, a mission that only Archie knew about, she offers passive resistance by refusing to answer any question of Samad's with "yes" or "no" resorting to "maybes" and thereby indulges in an exquisite revenge (cf. WT 213–214) that nearly drives Samad insane.

During their lifetime, Archie and Samad, who in contrast to their younger wives belong to a generation that still experienced World War II, are confronted with a range of changes in gender relations and the ethnic makeup in post-war/postcolonial Britain. These developments directly affect their families. But while Archie is able to adapt to the changes in British society much more easily, Samad holds on to an old-fashioned and out-dated model of patriarchy which he can only enforce by tricking his wife. In the course of the novel, Alsana and Clara, both of whom find many decisions of their older husbands quizzical, are somewhat out of focus, and it is the stories of the younger generation and their interaction with the Chalfens that shape the events of the second half of the book. *White Teeth* portrays different kinds of fundamentalism(s), a problem that seems to affect mostly, but not exclusively, the younger generation of men.

When Magid and Millat are reunited, Samad to his great dismay has to realise that his attempts to tamper with fate have utterly failed: "The one I send home comes out a pukka Englishman, white suited, silly wig lawyer. The one I keep here is fully paid-up green bow-tie wearing fundamentalist terrorist." (WT 407) Millat becomes absorbed in a Muslim fundamentalist group while Magid has become a disciple of Marcus Chalfen and "Chalfenism" (cf. WT 314), the belief in Western science and rationality, which is delineated as equally fundamentalist.[214] Whilst Millat has become almost too dangerously hybrid, Magid fails to construct a hyphenated British identity and imitates mainstream Englishness, which he associates with rationality and class privilege. (cf. Mirze 2008, 194–195)

In her depiction of second- and third-generation migrants, Smith does not focus on hybridity or the 'in-betweenness' of individuals between *two* cultures, rather she illustrates a diverse urban mix-and-match approach to

---

214 Hortense Bowden, a member of the Jehovah's Witnesses, and her constant waiting for the end of the world exemplifies another kind of fundamentalism and Joshua Chalfen, in an attempt to rebel against his scientist father, joins the radical animal rights group FATE. In the final showdown and in their protest against FutureMouse©, the different fundamentalist groups are united in the end.

ethnicity that is also reflected in the polyphony of the different languages
of the characters:

> The combination of Archie Jones's working-class, Cockney accent, Samad's Asian
> English and Clara's Creolized Caribbean represent socio-linguistic deviations from
> Standard English as the centripetal forces of language undermining any notion of a
> homoglossic centre to the nation's language and culture. (Bentley 2007, 496–497)

Especially the language of the younger generation is characterised as a
funky mixture of 'ethnic dialects' and popular culture jargon. (cf. Walters
2005, 317–319) Millat and his friends, for instance, are described as an
entirely "new breed", "Raggastanis":

> Raggastanis spoke a strange mix of Jamaican patois, Bengali, Gujarati and English.
> Their ethos […] was equally a hybrid thing: Allah featured, but more as a collective
> brother than a supreme being, a hard-as-fuck geezer who would fight in their
> corner if necessary; Kung Fu and the works of Bruce Lee were also central to the
> philosophy; added to this was a smattering of Black Power […]. (WT 231)

Smith light-heartedly shows that it is precisely Millat's involvement in
Western popular culture and his love for the image of the gangster of
Hollywood Mafia films which render him so susceptible to Muslim fundamentalism. (cf. WT 446) Like all other forms of fundamentalism in the
novel, it is a caricature rather than psychological insight that Smith is presenting. Hilariously, the Islamic fundamentalist group KEVIN, Keepers of
the Eternal and Victorious Islamic Nation suffer from an "acronym problem" (WT 295). Thomas (2006) stresses that the influence of both Salman
Rushdie, and more importantly Hanif Kureishi, on Smith's writing has
gone strangely under-researched so far, and critics are more willing to
compare Smith's writing to Dickens. As in *The Black Album*, there is a reference to the book burning of the *Satanic Verses*. Millat, who has neither
read the book nor knows the author, still claims to know "all about that
shit" (WT 233) and enthusiastically joins his friends for the book burning
in Bradford. When Alsana catches his face on TV, she in turn burns all of
Millat's 'secular' belongings, such as posters, music tapes and the like, all of
which are signs of Western consumer culture that he now supposedly abhors. (cf. WT 237) A typical London teenager, Millat is not a firm believer,
but is enamoured with the rebellious pose. Thomas (2006) attests that after
9/11 and 7/7, Smith's more optimistic and comic depiction of fundamentalism loses relevance while Kureishi's earlier, bleaker version, which he
developed in *The Black Album* and "My Son the Fanatic", again gains mo-

mentum. While it is true that this rather optimistic version of fundamentalism as a funny episode seems less plausible after recent terrorist attacks in Western cities, Smith is still able to identify an important contradiction. In Britain, "such militant religious youth groups thrive partly by virtue of the very cultural values they denounce" (Head 2003, 113). In contrast to Kureishi's rather didactic approach, which also does not offer any real psychological insights into the terrorists' motives, Smith uses comedy and even farce as her weapons of choice against the short-sightedness of fundamentalisms of various kinds. Again, it is not only Millat who becomes absorbed into fundamentalism, Hortense, Marcus and Magid as well as Joshua are all drawn into their very own fundamentalisms. Archie and Irie seem to be the only characters that are not affected by fundamentalisms in a strict sense: Archie believes in chance while Irie is a stern atheist.

As has been mentioned, the trigger for Samad's decision to send one of his sons abroad was his fear of the corruption of the second generation, who he feels has lost touch with their 'original' culture. He laments, "[t]hey won't go to mosque, they don't pray, they speak strangely, they dress strangely, they eat all kinds of rubbish, they have intercourse with God knows who. No respect for tradition. People call it assimilation when it is nothing but corruption. Corruption!" (WT 190) Comments like this point to the central theme of the whole novel, namely, the question of the current state of cultural identity in Britain and the debates on multiculturalism.

Whereas Samad is obsessed with securing his cultural roots for himself and for his children, Archie wishes that "people should just live together, you know, in peace or harmony or something" (WT 190). While Archie – in his simple-heartedness – can let go of hegemonic conceptions of purity, Samad from a marginalised perspective fears for his cultural heritage. Conversely, for the children's generation it seems as if "concepts of 'migrancy' and 'exile' have become too distant to carry their former freight of disabling rootlessness" (Head 2003, 107–108). Their turn to radicalism does not rest on a desire for a pure 'original' culture or home but is rooted in their social marginalisation in their actual home country, Britain. Nonetheless, Irie especially initially feels frustrated with her 'mixed' cultural background and tries to change her 'Jamaican' looks by unsuccessfully attempting to straighten her hair. She feels like a "stranger in a stranger land" (WT 266). Yet, Irie is also the one character who actively tries to get rid of a longing for a stable ethnic or cultural identity. These issues are connected to the themes of race, genetic engineering and eugenics in the novel.[215] Her family history consists only of "rumour, folk-tale and myth" (WT 338), a fact that is illustrated in the novel in a picture of a mock family tree. (cf. WT 338) The children, rather than perceiving themselves as either British or Bengali or Jamaican, are clearly London teenagers who grow up in an ethnically diverse neighbourhood where children interact and form their distinctive mix of various cultural codes.

When Irie, Magid and Millat meet Joyce Chalfen for the first time, the children keep answering "Whitechapel" as Joyce tries to find out where they are from "*originally*" (WT 319). Smith constantly mocks the insistence on a real origin that has become only an imaginary reference point in what she calls "the century of strangers":

This has been the century of strangers, brown, yellow and white. This has been the century of the great immigrant experiment. It is only this late in the day that you can walk into a playground and find Isaac Leung by the fish pond, Danny Rahman in the football cage, Quang O'Rourke bouncing a basketball, and Irie Jones humming a tune. Children with first and last names on a direct collision course. Names that secrete within them mass exodus, cramped boats, cold arrivals, medical checks. (WT 326)

Rather dismissively, Wood terms this a "Rushdie-like lecture" (Wood 2005, 189) which risks being too naïvely positive about the possibilities of living harmoniously together.[216] Nonetheless, *White Teeth* does not only focus on the 'exoticness' of these new hybrid identities, the purity of the White English is denounced as well. Irie becomes more and more fascinated with and envious of the Chalfens and their claim to one 'true' ethnicity that they can trace in an elaborate family tree, in contrast to her mentioned mock family tree.

---

215 In her insightful article, "Genetics, Biotechnology, and the Future of 'Race' in Zadie Smith's *White Teeth*", A. Dawson (2007) comments on the way *White Teeth* offers a critique of race in science by linking the stories of the Nazi eugenic research of Dr Perret with Marcus Chalfen's project of genetic engineering, FutureMouse©.

216 Like *The Buddha of Suburbia*, which was turned into a television series in 1993, *White Teeth* was successfully filmed for TV in 2002. In an interview given on this occasion, Zadie Smith herself compares scenes likes these to a Benetton ad, which she claims still to a large degree respond to the realities in neighbourhoods like Willesden. She does not feel that this has changed much after 9/11. Interview available at:
<http://www.pbs.org/wgbh/masterpiece/teeth/ei_smith_int.html>
(accessed 18 September 2008).

She wanted their Englishness. Their Chalfishness. The *purity* of it. It didn't occur to her that the Chalfens were, after a fashion, immigrants, too (third generation, by way of Germany and Poland, née Chalfenowsky), or that they might be as needy of her as she was of them. (WT 328)

Of course, it is somewhat problematic to assume that everybody is an immigrant, if you only go back far enough in their family histories, given the undoubted privileges of the Chalfens' normally unquestioned White middle-class Englishness that sets them apart from the other two families. Although their (secular) Jewishness to a certain degree marginalises them from mainstream British society as well, they still represent the successful middle-class family in the novel that is enamoured with the 'exoticness' of their neighbours, which Joyce calls the stimulating influence of "brown strangers" (WT 326). In a sense, White Englishness has become 'dull' to her, and Joyce longs for the children's 'Otherness' to be incorporated into her own family.

Smith quite successfully debunks Englishness as an imaginary construct that first and foremost serves nationalist and conservative ideas, and while her book is funny in tone, racism in not absent. Quite the contrary, the strangely backward ways of racists become the punchline for many jokes in *White Teeth*. (cf. Knopp 2009) Smith clearly ridicules racism as a strange thing of the past, mentioning "Rivers of blood[217] silly-billy nonsense" (WT 62–63), or the so-called "Cricket Test" of Norman Tebbit. (cf. WT 123) Also, the children's acquaintance with the racist old man J.P. Hamilton[218] (cf. WT 168–174) illustrates the backwardness of racist thinking in the novel. But, as has been mentioned, more liberal characters, such as Poppy Burt-Jones and Mrs Chalfen, are also slightly ridiculed in their failed attempts to be inclusive of 'Other' cultures because they fetishise them.

Nonetheless, questions of cultural identity and purity are not only the concern of mainstream society, but affect the migrant communities as well. Smith contrasts English fears of 'swamping', as Margaret Thatcher termed it, by cultural aliens and the threat of 'miscegenation' with the immigrants' fear of dissolution and "disappearance" (WT 327), which in *White Teeth*

---

217 This, of course, refers to Enoch Powell's (a rightwing Conservative Member of Parliament) infamous "rivers of blood" speech (20 April 1968), in which he sparked racist fears of an 'overflow' of migrants 'infiltrating' the British nation.

218 Kris Knauer interprets Hamilton as a satirical reference to the Conradian worldview and his depiction of the Congo. (cf. Knauer 2008, 181–182)

most prominently Alsana and Samad express, and who both consequently try to protect the 'Bengali-ness' of their children.

But despite their efforts, their sons have become part of a generation that is characterised as utterly hybrid. Nevertheless, it is important to stress that hybridity in *White Teeth* is no longer dramatised as a clash of cultures or an extraordinary syncretic mixture of cultures. Whereas Kureishi to a certain degree still eroticises hybridity and his 'in-between' heroes are often singled out as one of a kind, Smith attempts a "'normalisation' of hybridity" (Moss 2003, 12). In the historical flashbacks, Smith illustrates that mixture has always been part of British history. She depicts an ordinary and unspectacular form of cultural blending. "Smith creates a new Black/British text, a story that includes the experiences of characters from diverse ethnic backgrounds, whose racial differences actually account for the commonality of their shared experiences and their Britishness." (Walters 2005, 321) In this sense, Britishness can become a denominator that is inclusive of variety rather than based on an exclusive sense of national identity.[219] Although the often-cited phrase of a "happy multicultural land" (WT 465), which Smith employs in the novel, is undoubtedly an ironic label, and Thompson calls it "clearly oxymoronic" (Thompson 2005, 137), Smith's version of hybridity has been criticised for being too naïvely optimistic. This vision of hybridity is first and foremost a description of what Britain's future is supposed to look like rather than a realistic depiction of race or gender relations in Britain to date. This optimism can also be linked to the motto of the text. Despite its historical outset and reference to past events, the motto of the novel is connected to the future.

The line, "What is past is prologue", quoted as an "Inscription in Washington museum" can be found on a statue called 'Future' and, of course, refers to the line in Shakespeare's *The Tempest* (Act 2, scene 1). Smith focuses on a perfect future despite an imperfect past, or, as is repeatedly stated in the novel, "past-tense, future-perfect" (WT 18). *White Teeth* seems to suggest that the future of multicultural society rests on leaving behind the colonial past. However, the focus on roots and origins remains somewhat ambivalent. On the one hand, the text seems to suggest that immigrants cannot control their fates or the loss of their identities:

219 Nonetheless, Raphael Dalleo emphasises that while there is a normalisation of cultural hybridity, Smith remains skeptical of the concept of biological hybridity because of its roots in essentialist discourses on race, and this is illustrated with reference to Future-Mouse©. (cf. Dalleo 2008, 99)

"Because this is the other thing about immigrants (fugees, émigrés, travellers): they cannot escape their history anymore than you yourself can loose your shadow." (WT 466) They are haunted by their shadows and the historical past. But, on the other hand, there is also a positive outlook on a future generation that can live without the historical baggage of roots. Despite a longing for roots, the novel seems to emphasise more strongly the insight that national identity has been and always will be a phantasmatic construct: "Do you think anybody is English? Really English? It's a fairytale!" (WT 236) After Irie sleeps with both Iqbal twins in an interval of only thirty minutes, *White Teeth* ends with a 'fatherless' daughter, because neither of the twins can be identified as the child's father since they share identical genetic material. In the final flash forward to the future, the narrator comments on how Irie in the end falls in love with Joshua Chalfen – "for you can only avoid your fate for so long" (WT 541). Ultimately, the family histories are completely intertwined, and at the end of the genealogy, the readers find a girl of English-Jamaican-Bengali descent coming from a line of families that when their religious practices are combined, include Jehovah's Witnesses, Muslims, secular Jews and atheists. The choice to end this family epic with a girl who "feels free as Pinocchio, a puppet clipped of paternal strings" (WT 541) also comments on gender relations. In the end, male colonial genealogy is replaced by a female fatherless genealogy. While the men seem more prone to get caught up in fundamentalisms of various kinds and cannot let go of the past nor their expectations, the women of the younger generation are more free to reinvent themselves: "In a vision, Irie has seen a time, a time not far from now, when roots won't matter any more because they can't because they mustn't because they're too long and they're too tortuous and they're just buried too damn deep. She looks forward to it." (WT 527) This vision of the future implies that despite the historical baggage, a more harmonious living together is possible. Archie's motto in life, that chance ultimately wins over fate, seems to hold true. On the very last page, FutureMouse©, the genetically pre-programmed experiment of Marcus Chalfen, escapes through an air vent and Archie hopefully thinks, "*Go on my son.*" (WT 542) Despite the fact that the life of the mouse is supposedly genetically predicted, it can escape into an unforeseeable future in the end. Given Archie's outlook on life, it is only fitting that FutureMouse© has become his son eventually.

Helga Ramsey-Kurz argues that Smith in her comic approach identifies "chaos as an inevitable but not necessarily deleterious corollary of cultural diversification" (Ramsey-Kurz 2005, 84). This diversification is also a feature of the makeup of the text itself. Sommer, for instance, stresses multiple perspectives and montage (cf. Sommer 2001, 186), and one finds linear and non-linear narration, dialogue and narrative commentary as well as graphics included in the text. (cf. Squires 2002, 55–56) In its inclusion of manifold unbelievable co-incidences, such as the simultaneous breaking of the twins' noses in continents apart, and the strange plot twists, the reappearance of Dr Sick in the end, for instance, are quite far-fetched to fit the label of a 'realistic' novel. The narrator self-reflexively addresses these unlikely events: "Ah, but you are not convinced by coincidence? You want fact fact fact?" (WT 220) In comments like these, "[t]he assumption of the reader's disbelief […] foregrounds the fictionality of the work" (Squires 2002, 63). In this sense, Smith's writing clearly fits the label postmodern, and because of her excessive use of metafictional strategies, some reviewers have occasionally even employed the term "post-postmodern".[220] The chaotic ending, especially, has provoked some scorn among critics, and the narrator again comments on the unsatisfactory solution of a hasty wrap-up and "endgames" (WT 540) at the grand finale. There are fast cuts that bring together all the different narrative threads, and this technique is explicitly compared to another medium, TV. The narrator mentions "focus groups" like "young professional women aged eighteen to thirty-two" (WT 541) as a possible target audience who influence this inevitable outcome of the story.

James Wood convincingly terms this narrative strategy "hysterical realism"[221]: "This is not magical realism but what might be called hysterical realism. Storytelling has become a kind of grammar in these novels […]. The conventions of realism are not abolished but, on the contrary, exhausted, overworked." (Wood 2005, 179) Wood links this excess of storytelling and a foregrounding of plot to a failure to provide psychologically

---

220 Paproth, however, argues that Smith's fiction does not question conventional writing modes, and he calls her style "uncomplicated" and "traditional" and relates it both to modernist and postmodernist traditions. (cf. Paproth 2008, 14) While this is true to a certain extent, Paproth fails to take into consideration the continuous metafictional comments of the narrator and the incorporation of techniques which are associated with other media, such as TV. In this context, Wood's term "hysterical realism" seems a more appropriate label than to call Smith's writing modernist.

221 Wood (2005) also names Salman Rushdie's *The Ground Beneath Her Feet* (1999), Thomas Pynchon's *Mason & Dixon* (1997) as well as Don DeLillo's *Underworld* (1997) as examples of this genre.

rounded characters. "Smith's principal characters move in and out of human depth. Sometimes they seem to provoke her sympathy, at other times they are only externally comic." (ibid., 182) Furthermore, and despite his generally complaisant review of *White Teeth*, Wood criticises that there is no character development and that the novel lacks moral seriousness. (cf. Wood 2005, 187, 193; Squires 2002, 66–67) The question is what happens to the narratives of masculinities in crisis once "moral seriousness" is abandoned?

In contrast to earlier crisis narratives, Smith's depiction of men of different generations and their qualms with their place in postcolonial British society remain superficially comic. Contrary to her farcical approach, Kureishi, for instance, follows a more moderate comic tone. He does not really subvert the genre of the *Bildungsroman* or realism, but tries to focus on marginalised masculinities, and thereby sheds a light on a generation of men who, despite their marginalised status, have arrived at the centre of British society. Similarly, the two films, *My Beautiful Laundrette* and *The Crying Game*, that I have discussed, incorporate a diverse cast of characters but both in their specific ways tend to eroticise and single out hybrid identities. The featured hybrid characters, like Omar in *My Beautiful Laundrette*, or Dil in *The Crying Game*, are often even overtly marked as 'extra-hybrid' by adding queerness, in terms of sexual orientation in the former and gender identity in the latter, to a display of 'ethnic ambivalence'. In Smith's microcosm, hybridity has lost its spectacularity and has become a feature that is characteristic of all expressions of Britishness.

Smith, by interweaving three different family histories, presents a postmodern plurality of crises – that have become more 'normalised' than in her predecessors' texts. In a sense, she sabotages the privileged discourse of the crisis of masculinity as the sole moral focus by particularising the hegemonic centre. In her novel, it is the two characters Archie and Irie who can let go of the 'baggage of roots' and a belief in racial purity, and as a consequence, they can look forward to an optimistic future. Nonetheless, the recourse to male crises is also central to her plot. In direct comparison of the two main male characters, Archie and Samad, Samad's ideal of being the head of a culturally monolithic family is the cause for laughter and ridicule. In contrast, Archie, the pre-destined White middle-aged man in crisis, is actually quite successful in adapting to the changes that are often perceived to be the cause for the bemoaning of a crisis of masculinity.

While other authors who are discussed in this book, most prominently Conrad and later Coetzee, react to a renewed interest in 'male crises' by indulging in a self-reflexive focus on failure, Smith attempts to depict a positive re-negotiation of hegemonic masculinity. However, in light of the more recent terrorist attacks that have also sparked the recourse to more conservative notions of a 'clash of cultures', it remains to be seen whether her positive outlook can be more than a funny farcical interlude, or whether it will survive to have a more long-lasting legacy.

J.M. Coetzee: Postmodern Despair

As the Nobel Prize winner of 2003, J.M. Coetzee is the most critically acclaimed author within the postcolonial literature section. His work has drawn a lot of critical attention, and there exist a number of monographs as well as special issues of journals, which deal exclusively with his work. Coetzee is a studied linguist as well as mathematician and has worked as a computer programmer in Britain for some time as well as in the USA. At the University of Texas, Austin he completed his PhD thesis on Samuel Beckett to finally return to South Africa where he taught as Professor of Literature at Cape Town University. Since 2002, Coetzee has lived in Australia.

I am aware that there is a certain imbalance in attaching the label 'postcolonial' to a writer based in South Africa (cf. Head 1997, 17–19; Kossew 1996, 7–15; Marais 1996) as well as to artists working from the 'first world' metropolis like all the other writers and directors in this section. However, Coetzee connects the story of male crisis with issues of postcoloniality unlike few other authors. It is his explicit self-reflexive hegemonic viewpoint in a former colonised territory rather than the marginalised voices in the centre, as in the writing of Kureishi and Smith, that can be analysed in his writings. The postcolonial narrative pattern of guilt features prominently and he has been characterised as a "first-world novelist writing out of a South African context" (Huggan and S. Watson 1996, 1).

It is first and foremost the role of the intellectual and his or her responsibility in a totalitarian regime, such as South Africa's apartheid system, that has been at the centre of attention in responses to his works. As Coetzee's writing stylistically is associated with postmodernism, the question of language and whether literature can be seen as an ethical instrument have also been prominent themes. Although Coetzee comes from a White Afrikaner background, he has written all his fiction in English. While both Afrikaans and English are part of a colonial legacy in South Africa, the use of English is often seen as a more neutral choice, as it is considered a unifying language. (cf. Gallagher 1991, 37–41; Head 1997, 17; Kossew 1996, 12–13; van Schalkwyk 2006, 10) However, Coetzee's writing can also be read as a comment on how no language can 'really' convey the horrors of human existence. As the protagonist, David Lurie, in *Disgrace* muses, "English is an unfit medium for the truth of South Africa" (D 117). It is this crisis of language that Coetzee paradoxically enacts in the written word. Both

Waiting for the Barbarians and *Disgrace* are novels about the crisis of masculinity and the failure to write or convey experiences linguistically, as will be expounded upon.

In my analysis of these two selected texts, I focus on the construction of failing White masculinity and the relation to the current postcolonial context. However, Coetzee has also experimented with (White) female narrative voices as well as more marginalised masculinities.[222] Thus, Coetzee clearly has centred on plural narrative voices, and I explicitly place his writing in the context of re-negotiating hegemonic masculinities. While admittedly, he is aware of White male hegemony and is very critical of it, his writing also has re-privileging tendencies.[223] This becomes evident in the narrative voice of his novels *Waiting for the Barbarians* and *Disgrace*. By focusing exclusively on the construction of his White male protagonists and their function as main focalizers in the text, I wish to stress the more difficult qualities of his work.

The Swedish academy of the Nobel Foundation writes: "It is in exploring weakness and defeat that Coetzee captures the divine spark in man. [...] His protagonists are overwhelmed by the urge to sink but paradoxically derive strength from being stripped of all external dignity."[224] This

---

222 His historical metafiction *Foe* (1986), for instance, is a postcolonial re-writing of Daniel Defoe's *Robinson Crusoe* (1719). In this text, there are a number of interesting narrative voices, next to Robinson Crusoe. There is a female narrator, Susan Barton, as well as the fictional author Foe present in the text. Tellingly, Friday is mute and it is this muteness of the subaltern position that is a central theme of the novel. Parry criticises that in staging the inability to achieve a voice in the symbolic order, Coetzee paradoxically re-enacts a silencing of these marginalised voices despite his better intentions. (cf. Parry 1996, 46) She focuses on the 'coloured' character Michael K in *Life & Times of Michael K* (1983) and the Black slave Friday in *Foe* as well as female narrators Magda in *In the Heart of the Country* (1977), Elizabeth Curren in *Age of Iron* (1990) and Susan Barton in *Foe*. For a discussion of these female narrative voices, cf. Wright (2008). More recently, Coetzee also employed the fictional novelist Elizabeth Costello as a sort of female alter ego, and she appears in the series of fictional talks *Elizabeth Costello* (2003) and reappears in the novel *Slow Man* (2005).

223 In his collection of essays, *White Writing* (1988), Coetzee critically examines White South African settler writing. Hence, despite the claim that his writing is often celebrated as 'universal', Coetzee himself is aware of the dangers of re-enforcing White privilege through claims of universality. Nonetheless, his writing, paradoxically at times falls behind this critical insight, as I will argue in this chapter.

224 Cf. the website of the Nobel Foundation:
<http://nobelprize.org/nobel_prizes/literature/laureates/2003/press.html>
(accessed 14 March 2008).

celebration of failure has resonance with earlier aggrandising narratives of the sublime failure of masculinity that can also be found in Conrad's texts. The Swedish academy emphasises the importance to read these crises of men as universally valid, which has become one of the most recurring *topoi* in the praise of a literary text. Granted that the academy mentions that Coetzee also represents various marginalised voices, literature is regarded as achieving its greatest value when it supposedly speaks to all of 'man'. This homogenising gesture brushes over particularities, and once more, there is a tendency or danger to re-centre hegemonic masculinity. Nonetheless, Coetzee's writing is more critical of notions of universality than the statement by the academy might suggest, and I doubt that his intentions are in fact to "capture the divine spark in man". Indeed, it is this notion of the crisis of the universality of White masculinity that characterises his writing.

Emerging from this debate is a sense of quandary, of crisis. This crisis is seen, in part, as the result of intellectual stalemate: of a paralysing process by which white South African writers (and/or critics) are obliged to reconfirm their own displacement. This process is seen, in turn, as part of a European modernist inheritance. (Huggan and S. Watson 1996, 8)

Despite Coetzee's problematisation of White hegemony and universality, his postmodern anti-heroes – in the lingering on their failure – ironically again become the placeholders for the human condition, and in this sense, truly remain inscribed in a modernist European framework. Read in this way, Coetzee's novels become paradoxically 'universal' stories about the problem of White universality. Ultimately, it seems as if Coetzee wavers between universality and trying to establish a 'new' particularised White male identity.

Waiting for the Barbarians: Allegories of the Failure of 'Self' and 'Other'

Dating back from 1980, *Waiting for the Barbarians* is the oldest text included in this section on postcolonial literature. Written at a time when most formerly colonised countries had gained independence while the Republic of South Africa was still under the aegis of the apartheid system, this novel reflects the burden of the colonial legacy unlike the later more optimistic metropolitan fictions of Kureishi or Smith. Postcolonial discourse is already in place while South Africa witnesses atrocities of racism and police brutality against dissenting voices. Coetzee's third novel is a balancing act that, in its highly allegorical mode, manages to evoke both this concrete political context and more abstract issues, such as the crisis of representation. In this narrative of male failure, gender and sexuality as well as the question of dissent and violence under an oppressive regime are themes addressed. Both the plot and the characters of the novel remain rather elusive compared to more realistic modes of fiction.

In the novel, no concrete place or time is ever specified.[225] There is an unnamed autodiegetic narrator, the magistrate, working in a remote border town in an unspecified Empire, who recounts the events of roughly a year in six sections. Rather than presenting psychologically rounded characters, the allegorical mode is continued all through the text. The magistrate is an 'everyman' in crisis, and only military titles and the names of his antagonists, Colonel Joll and Warrant Officer Mandel, are provided. In this present-tense narration, the mentioning of the changing seasons remains the only manifest reference point. The title of the novel, *Waiting for the Barbarians*, is an allusion to the poem of the same name from 1904 by the Greek poet Constantin Cavafy.[226] In the poem, as in the novel, the aspect of waiting is emphasised.[227] The barbarians remain a fantasy construct rather than a real threat to the Empire. In this way, they become a means of constructing the 'self' through the 'Other'. Time and again, this process includes physical violence.

To address the theme of torture, albeit in a historically unspecified manner, only three years after the violent death of the anti-apartheid activist Stephen Bantu Biko in police custody in 1977 obviously recalls the current South African political context of the time (cf. Kehinde 2006) and can also be seen as a strategy to circumvent possible censorship. With the appearance of Colonel Joll at the border town, violence and torture arrive at the peaceful 'outpost of civilisation' and prisoners are maltreated. The magistrate is angry with himself for not intervening, and as a result of his lack of involvement, two prisoners die, which, for the first time, shakes his assumptions of his civilised superiority: "Throughout a trying period he

---

225 Cf. "Intentionally the setting is no-time, no-space, a quality which underscores the allegorical nature of the novel." (Penner 1989, 76)

226 For a reading that stresses the intertextual connections between the poem and the novel, cf. Boletsi (2007).

227 As has been widely noted, the title of the novel also evokes the title of Samuel Beckett's play *Waiting for Godot*, which together with Franz Kafka's story "In the Penal Colony" is seen as an important literary influence on the novel.

[Colonell Joll, E.H.Y.] and I have managed to behave towards each other like civilized people. All my life I have believed in civilized behaviour; on this occasion, however, I cannot deny it, the memory leaves me sick with myself." (WB 25) Like Kurtz, Colonel Joll epitomises the 'dark side' of Empire that the magistrate has to face. The question is whether there can be an innocent collaborator of Empire as the magistrate wishes to see himself initially.[228] "I did not mean to get embroiled in this. I am a country magistrate, a responsible official in the service of Empire, serving out my days on this lazy frontier, waiting to retire." (WB 8) This false sense of peace is utterly disrupted, and the magistrate's ethical sense of self put to the test: "As a humane and just man, he knows Joll has passed into the realm of the forbidden and unclean, into 'the horror,' as Conrad termed it." (Penner 1989, 80) Again, these inconvenient questions of collaboration also pertain to a class of White intellectuals to which Coetzee himself belongs who might not necessarily agree with apartheid policies, but, as part of the privileged White minority, remain beneficiaries of the system nonetheless. After the first wave of tortures, one barbarian woman stays behind, her feet have been smashed and her eyes partially blinded by the torturers. The magistrate takes care of her and ritually engages in the demure gesture of washing her feet. It is this relationship between the magistrate and the unnamed woman that furthers the magistrate's introspection.

More and more, he comes to question the construction of the barbarians as the 'Others' of the Empire. He knows, for instance, that selling alcohol to the barbarians and making them drunk confirms "the settlers' litany of prejudice: that barbarians are lazy, immoral, filthy, stupid. Where civilization entailed the corruption of barbarian virtues and the creation of a dependant people, I decided, I was opposed to civilization [...] (I say this who now keep a barbarian girl for my bed!)" (WB 41) On the one hand, the magistrate is quite aware of the demonisation and production of the racial stereotypes surrounding the barbarians, on the other hand, he is also benefiting from the system by taking advantage of the dependence of the barbarian woman. While he would like to consider himself exterior to the cruelty of the system, he is utterly enmeshed in it. He is part of the military, he writes maps and reads "the classics" (WB 41). Hence, the magistrate

---

228 While Michael Valdez Moses describes the magistrate as an "inverted version of Conrad's Kurtz" (Moses 1993, 119), I agree with Shaffer that it makes more sense to link the magistrate to the figure of Marlow (cf. Shaffer 2006, 239, fn. 32) and conversely, Colonel Joll to Kurtz.

remains part of the very system that is suddenly suspect to him, and as the parenthetical self-reflexive comment in the quote underlines, he is quite conscious of these inconsistencies. Anxiously he proclaims: "I must assert my distance from Colonel Joll! I will not suffer for his crimes! (WB 48) Nonetheless, "[h]is desperate resolve, [to assert his distance from Colonel Joll, E.H.Y.] is a familiar attempt to conjure up a difference where he is starting to admit there may be a kinship" (Kerr 2000, 26). It is this realisation of kinship that initiates a crisis for the magistrate. Being confronted with the scarred body of the girl, he can no longer clearly draw a line between his alleged innocence and Colonel Joll's guilt. "The distance between myself and her torturers, I realize, is negligible; I shudder." (WB 29) Before I will focus more specifically on the relationship between the magistrate and the girl, I want to address the question of torture and the aporia of resistance in the novel.

After he has accompanied the girl back to her relatives, the magistrate himself is suddenly in the line of fire and taken into custody on the grounds of "treasonously consorting with the enemy" (WB 85). What at first can be seen as redemption from his position as collaborator, entails the risk of his physical harm. "I have set myself in opposition, the bond is broken, I am a free man. Who would not smile? But what a dangerous joy! It should not be so easy to attain salvation." (WB 85) Coetzee self-reflexively addresses the danger of a glorification of dissent or subversion as easily available choices under an oppressive regime. He also negates the religiously connoted language of deliverance. The magistrate admits that "[i]n my opposition is nothing heroic – let me not for an instant forget that" (WB 86). At first, the magistrate is only incarcerated: "No one beats me, no one starves me. How can I regard myself as a victim of persecution when my sufferings are so petty? Yet they are all the more degrading for their pettiness." (WB 93) In the novel, both psychological and physical violence features prominently. After a period of relative calm, the magistrate suffers from physical torture by Warrant Officer Mandel and his men. The magistrate tries to assert his distance from the system, but it is also impossible for him to access the position of the 'Other' or to indulge in fantasies of a glorified or religiously motivated opposition. Rather, he is caught up in a Kafkaesque machinery of which he still remains a part, which becomes evident when he is re-established as magistrate after the period of incarceration and life as a vagabond. It is this impossibility of radical dissent that Coetzee concentrates on by including the conflicting thoughts of the magistrate on this matter.

After he finds himself in the new situation of being the tortured rather than the torturer, he initially holds on to his importance as one dissenting individual when he claims for himself that "in this farthest outpost of the Empire of light there existed one man who in his heart was not a barbarian" (WB 114). But this desire, based on a simplified binary opposition of good and evil, is constantly questioned and even mocked by Colonel Joll, who sardonically remarks to the magistrate, "'You seem to want to make a name for yourself as the One Just Man, the man who is prepared to sacrifice his freedom to his principles'" (WB 124). While the magistrate originally adheres to his suffering as meaningful – as a sign of his manly resistance – he soon lets go of this illusion. "There is no consoling grandeur in any of this." (WB 128) Torture is seen as a means to erase intellect; it annihilates language. "In my suffering there is nothing ennobling. [...] They were interested only in demonstrating to me what it meant to live in a body, as a body, a body which can entertain notions of justice only as long as it is whole and well." (WB 126)

In representing violence in fiction, there is always the danger of reproducing or even glorifying that violence by detailing gruesome particulars. Rosemary Jolly calls attention to the fact that Coetzee's novel should be read as an "attempt to depict violence without inviting sensationalism" (Jolly 1996, 110). By explaining the effects of bodily harm linguistically, Coetzee's text is also a metatext about the shortcomings of language to put the body and its suffering into words.

For the narrative of *Barbarians* is structured so as to (per)form a caveat both to itself and to other fictions that attempt to represent the act of torture. This caveat consists of the suggestion, made by the metanarrative of the text, that the assumptions underlying the hermeneutic of inquisition – a hermeneutic that is taken to its extreme in torture – may well be adopted by the fiction itself in its attempt to investigate, to interrogate, the acts of torture it describes. (ibid., 123)

In other words, in the worst case the violence is perpetuated in the language of the text rather than simply represented. Coetzee's novel is not so much a text that recreates torture; it is a text that questions the ability of language to denote torture in all its physical brutality. "Thinking of him [Mandel, E.H.Y.], I have said the words *torture ... torturer* to myself but they are strange words, and the more I repeat them the more strange they grow, till they lie like stones on my tongue." (WB 129) The word 'torture' cannot adequately convey the somatic effects. Like the image of stones on the tongue, they render impossible the speech act.

In its representation of masculinity, there is a stark contrast to typical tales of male sublime suffering – a notion that the text adamantly rejects. In a violent scene of a mock execution that the magistrate has to endure, he is humiliated by being dressed in a woman's garment. He is stripped of military manliness and ridiculed. However, the magistrate more and more accepts the role of the social outcast. He describes himself and his ragged looks as that of an "old clown" (WB 136). In this way, Coetzee's protagonist can be linked to the literary tradition of the figure of the fool who in his adopted state of insanity often has more insight into the truth than other characters. The magistrate's earlier role of opposing the regime is now marked as outdated: "What, after all, do I stand for besides an archaic code of gentlemanly behaviour toward captured foes." (WB 118) This ideal of gentlemanly opposition in the name of civilisation is itself circumspect, and he accepts his participation in the system – and his similarity to the despised Colonel Joll. "I was the lie that Empire tells itself when times are easy, he the truth that Empire tells when harsh winds blow. Two sides of Imperial rule, no more, no less." (WB 148–149)

Not only the relationship between pain and language, but also the linguistic production of the opposition of 'self' and 'Other' is a prominent theme in the text. The distinction between the Empire and the barbarians is first and foremost marked as a linguistic barrier, as Boletsi emphasises with reference to the etymology of the word 'barbarian':

[T]he ancient Greek word *barbarian* [βάρβαρος] is supposed to imitate the incomprehensible mumblings of the language of foreign peoples, sounding like 'bar-bar' (or, as we would say today, 'bla bla'). As such, it has a double implication: on a first level, it signifies a lack of understanding on the part of the other, since the language of the other is perceived as meaningless sounds. At the same time, it suggests an unwillingness to understand the other's language and thus to make the encounter with the other a communicative occasion. (Boletsi 2007, 68)

But the text does not only focus on the (deliberate) lack of understanding, rather, it stages how representation in language actually creates the 'Other'. This binary is not simply dissolvable by goodwill, but constitutive of male European hegemony, as has been pointed out in my introduction more generally and as Sam Durrant explains with reference to Coetzee's writing specifically:

The figure of the native, the black man or the Jew produces a crisis in European consciousness precisely because their existence as humans had to be denied in order for the European to retain a sense of his own subjectivity. Insofar as this denial founds the European subject, it constitutes the *prehistory* of the European subject. This denial is not simple forgetting that occurred at a particular point in history [...] but a *foreclosure* of the very possibility of the other's humanity [...]. (Durrant 2004, 5, original emphasis)

To admit to one's own guilt of torturing 'equal' human beings is to endanger one's status as human – to avoid this dilemma a distance is inserted and the tortured subject is created as less than human. It is this performative production of 'Otherness', which has been constitutive of colonial texts and which this postcolonial novel, self-reflexively re-enacts. When, for instance, a group of men, who are supposed to be barbarians, are captured and publicly punished, the word "ENEMY" (WB 115) is written on their backs. It is the act of writing which renders the men enemies and which also sanctions their corporal maltreatment. There are only stories and rumours about barbarian unrest and the text self-consciously marks these as stereotypes and hearsay rather than as facts.

There is no woman living along the frontier who has not dreamed of a dark barbarian hand coming from under the bed to grip her ankle, no man who has not frightened himself with visions of the barbarians carousing in his home, breaking the plates, setting fire to the curtains, raping his daughters. (WB 9)

The perception of oneself as the civilised 'self' here crucially relies on a distance to the uncivilised acts of the barbarians. The setting of a border town marks a specific liminal space in which this distinction is always on the verge of collapse, and it is this ambivalence – as Bhabha emphasises – that threatens the binary of coloniser and colonised. The ultimate horror vision of the rape of a civilised woman by a "dark barbarian" is evoked. In *Waiting for the Barbarians*, race in a sense becomes completely abstracted or allegorised into the distinction of civilised versus barbarian, and there are hardly any references to racialised physical features as the motivation for these distinctions. In this way, 'civilised' and 'barbarian' become abstract Manichean markers rather than signifiers of a biologically founded concept of race. In contrast, the rape in Coetzee's later novel *Disgrace* is clearly more grounded in the every-day political discourse of post-apartheid South Africa and its racialised politics, as will be explained in the following reading. When in *Waiting for the Barbarians* a girl in the village is raped, "[h]er friends claim a barbarian did it. They saw him running away into the reeds. They

recognized him as a barbarian by his ugliness." (WB 134) It is the stereotype uttered as a speech act that precedes and in this way creates the
'Other' and not vice versa. In the novel, it is never quite clear if the barbarians exist at all, and when a group of soldiers follow them into the desert, the barbarians seem like a mirage that constantly moves further away
once the soldiers get closer. (cf. Shaffer 2006, 130–132) The artificial border between 'self' and 'Other' is questioned both on the more general level
of the Empire versus the barbarians and on the personal level of the magistrate versus Colonel Joll.

However, there is another opposing couple that features prominently in
the novel. The barbarian girl as the 'Other' becomes a sexualised object of
knowledge that the magistrate tries to decode. Coetzee here points to the
interdependent correlation between sexuality, language and power. The
relationship between the old man and the young maimed woman is presented in all its ambivalence. The magistrate is not quite sure what it is that
draws him to the girl, and the sexual act is at first not consummated. It is
the continued deferral that the text lavishly performs. Time and again, the
magistrate spends hours washing and oiling the disfigured feet of the girl
exploring her body. He wavers between "wanting and not wanting her"
(WB 35). Her body is turned into a script which becomes his obsession:
"[U]ntil the marks on the girl's body are deciphered and understood I cannot let go of her." (WB 33) The woman reluctantly tells him about the
torture, but it is only the script of her body, her scars that can really 'tell'
the whole story of her abuse. He wonders, "is it she I want or the traces of
a history her body bears?" (WB 70)

'Difference' is evident on many levels in this unequal relationship. The
age difference, for instance, is repeatedly emphasised as well as how her
impairments render her more reliant on the magistrate. The girl is the
daughter of one of the first torture victims. As a result, the magistrate, who
feels partially responsible for his death, considers himself 'her new father',
which has an incestuous undertone, given their physical intimacy and later
sexual act. But this gesture of patriarchal appropriation is problematised as
a remnant of the past. "But I came too late, after she had ceased to believe
in fathers." (WB 88) The crisis of colonial hegemony is here clearly connected to a crisis of (middle-aged) masculinity and male authority.

In the text, sexuality, reading and writing are metaphorically joined together. The magistrate, a reader of the classics and writer of history, fights
both with sexual impotence and his impotence as a writer which seem to

have become interchangeable. "[I]n the middle of the sexual act I felt myself losing my way like a storyteller losing the thread of his story." (WB 48) In this passage, writing is connected to the 'man's' appropriation of the 'woman', which can also be read as a comment on the gendered assumptions underlying the creation of art, which virtually render impossible female authorship in this androcentric logic. "It seems appropriate that a man who does not know what to do with the woman in his bed should not know what to write." (WB 63)

As has been noted, in *Waiting for the Barbarians*, Coetzee creates several opposing couples. In more abstract terms, he questions the boundary between 'self' and 'Other' by exhibiting the performative construction of the barbarians. A second binary that is challenged is that of culprit and perpetrator in the pair of the magistrate and Colonell Joll. "Paradoxically, the magistrate's unity with the barbarians also allows him to perceive his complicity in the acts of the Empire." (Gallagher 1991, 130) While the text attests to the failure or the collapse of the boundary of the 'self' and the 'Other', which is created in language, it is nonetheless striking that the stereotypical and sexualised opposition of the 'civilised' man and the exoticised female body remains intact for the most part. Whereas the magistrate can admit to proximity between himself and Joll, the fetishised body of the 'Other' woman remains unknowable to him.

The magistrate has no access to the girl and her feelings. "I think: 'she could have spent those long empty evenings teaching me her tongue! Too late now.'" (WB 78) Here language is represented as an unbridgeable gap between the 'self' and 'Other' and not as a linguistic construct that can be debunked – as is the case in the opposition of the magistrate and Colonel Joll. "She is a sleeping dictionary in a script he cannot read." (Kerr 2000, 25) Again, the text self-consciously addresses the fact that the girl as a character in the novel does not have a voice of her own, but is only present through the magistrate's point of view. Coetzee does not paternalistically 'give voice' to the subaltern but focuses on the creation of 'Otherness' from a hegemonic point of view.

This is the last time to look on her clearly face to face, to scrutinize the motions of my heart, to try to understand who she really is: hereafter, I know, I will begin to re-form her out of my repertoire or memories according to my questionable desires. (WB 79)

In a report used to bring charges against him, the reader gets the first view on their relationship from an outside perspective in this otherwise strictly autodiegetic narrative, which highlights his "questionable desire" – as he self-consciously admits. In the report it says: "He was besotted with her, but she did not care for him." (WB 91) This attests to the fact that the girl merely exists as a fantasy to him and might, in fact, be completely indifferent to the magistrate's failed attempts of empathy. By means of this narrative strategy, "the reader is invited to identify with the narrator's inability to identify with the other" (Durrant 2004, 27). Coetzee, on the one hand tries to unmask this very position of privilege that is based on a limit to understand the 'Other', but, on the other hand, in the act of articulating this stereotype, he ultimately reiterates it. Thereby Coetzee narratively re-centres the very position of the hegemonic man exploring a racialised woman who can stereotypically only be read as a body. The girl is not really a character; she becomes an allegory of the sexualised 'Other' as an indecipherable object of knowledge of the 'self'.

This failure to read the girl is also linked to the other project of deciphering of the magistrate. As a hobby archaeologist, he tries to interpret pieces of wood with an unknown barbarian script on them which he found in the ruins surrounding the town: "In the long evenings I spent poring over my collection I isolated over four hundred different characters in the script, perhaps as many as four hundred fifty. I have no idea what they stand for." (WB 121) The magistrate has to admit that "he is as ignorant of the language of the past (the barbarians') as he is of the language of the future (the New Empire's)" (Kossew 1996, 94). In this way, the text addresses the problem of writing and mediating history, which recalls Hayden White's (1976) argument that there exist strong parallels between the discourse of fiction and historiography.

In the end, the army has left, and the magistrate is again in his former post and the people of the town are left waiting in vain for an enemy, who might have been an invention from the very start. Quite unwanted, his sexual urge, in the form of uncontrollable erections returns. Writing and (male) sexuality are again correlated: his impotence is 'cured' and the magistrate can resume writing although this now returned sexual potency is considered an unwanted burden by him. It coincides with the task of writing a history to which he only reluctantly commits himself.

[T]o write such a history no one would seem to be better fitted than our last magistrate. […] But […] what I find myself beginning to write is not the annals of an Imperial outpost or an account of how the people of that outpost spent their last year composing their souls as they waited for the barbarians. […] I wanted to live outside history. I wanted to live outside the history that Empire imposes on its subjects, even its lost subjects. [...] Of all the people in this town I am the one least fitted to write a memorial. (WB 168–169)

Instead of producing a factual history of the events, he writes a lyrical plea that ends in the sentence: "This was paradise on earth." (WB 169)[229] The magistrate accepts his failure as a writer of factual fictions and ultimately finds consolation in the lyrical mode. More and more he loses himself in his dreams, which recur all through the narrative, and the last sentence attests to this disorientation. "I leave it feeling stupid, like a man who lost his way long ago but presses on along a road that may lead nowhere." (WB 170)

The novel deliberately does not produce psychological insight. There is not only the mentioned lack of insight into the feelings of the 'Other' but also the representation of the 'self' remains blurry and the magistrate a rather vague character – despite the fact that it is his point of view taken in the narrative. In this sense, the novel is also a text about the failure to give a voice to the 'self'.

Waiting for the Barbarians tells its story in the present tense, and leaves its hero surviving into an unwritten future, where transgression will have to find a new meaning, since you cannot step across a boundary if the boundary is no longer there. (Kerr 2000, 27)

The magistrate has accepted the role of the 'fool' and remains an unreliable narrator whose authoritative capacity is challenged in the end. In a gesture that is characteristic of postmodern writing, Coetzee includes in his writing a metatext about writing, reading and the creation of meaning – or, to be more precise, the failure to create stable meaning. Durrant terms this a "crisis of knowledge" (Durrant 2004, 44) that the text enacts.

The unknown letters of the barbarians function as a self-reflexive allegory in an allegorical text.

They form an allegory. They can be read in many orders. Further, each single slip can be read in many ways. Together they can be read as a domestic journal, or they can be read as a plan of war, or they can be turned on their sides and read as a history of the last years of the Empire – the old Empire I mean. (WB 122)

---

229 Moses reads this as a recourse to the Romantic and pre-capitalistic utopia of idleness – a utopia which, according to Moses, Coetzee links to African traditions. But this utopia cannot be represented in language; the language of the barbarians remains the language of the body. (cf. Moses 1993, 125–127)

Here, Coetzee evokes the trope of allegory which is, of course, characteristic of his own text. "The in-built irony and 'rewriting' of traditional allegory that the text imposes is therefore an essential part of the function of the post-coloniality of the text." (Kossew 1996, 87) This refusal to provide fixed meanings is at the heart of the critical debate on *Waiting for the Barbarians*. Teresa Dovey (1996) is the most prominent advocate of Coetzee's allegorical mode. She stresses that Coetzee's writing subverts liberal discourse and points out the crisis of interpretation, what Head calls "the use of allegory against itself" (Head 1997, 24). Importantly, as has been briefly mentioned, Dovey also emphasises that the allegorical mode can function as a means to avoid censorship, which was still in effect in South Africa at the time and which Coetzee successfully circumvented. In addition, allegory functions as a means to question the category race, which is completely substituted by the opposition of 'civilised' and 'barbarian' in the novel. In this way, Coetzee deconstructs biological oppositions and highlights the role of language in the construction of meaning.

Coetzee's novels [...] [are] double-sided allegories: on the one hand, they constitute allegories of prior modes of discourse, wittingly inhabiting them in order to deconstruct them and divest them of their authority [...]; on the other hand, they are self-reflexive allegories which refer to their status as speech acts engaged in a process of subject-constitution. (Dovey 1996, 140)

Dovey refutes critical voices that call Coetzee's postmodern strategies depoliticising and criticises their privileging of political over literary discourse. However, she assumes a somewhat problematic 'pure' literary criticism as opposed to those political critiques of ideologies. Even in a strictly literary analysis of allegories, the implications of gender and race in these allegorical frameworks need to be taken seriously and an unsettling aspect of "ambivalent mimesis" (Kehinde 2006, 67), to which Coetzee subscribes, remains.

From this more critical perspective, JanMohamed identifies a problematic 'universalising' gesture in Coetzee's allegorical mode of writing which evokes the 'irresolvable human condition' rather than a specific historical and geo-political setting – in which race cannot be deferred to the realm of a linguistic signifier.

Coetzee's *Waiting for the Barbarians*, a deliberate allegory, epitomizes the dehistoricizing, desocializing tendency of colonialist fiction. [...] The novel does justice to the themes of a liberal complicity with fascism, his [the magistrate's, E.H.Y.] sense of guilt, and, most important, the function of Manichean polarity within the empire; it shows without hesitation that the empire projects its own barbarism onto the Other beyond its borders. Although the novel is obviously generated by white South Africa's racial paranoia and the guilt of its liberals, *Waiting for the Barbarians*, unlike Conrad's *Heart of Darkness*, refuses to acknowledge its historical sources or to make any allusions to the specific barbarism of the apartheid regime. The novel thus implies that we are all somehow equally guilty and that fascism is endemic to all societies. (JanMohamed 1985, 73)

While I agree with many of JanMohamed's objections, I see stronger parallels between Conrad and Coetzee here. Both Conrad and Coetzee tend towards allegories, and this is not in itself apolitical. However, similar to Conrad's allegories of 'Black' death and 'White' camaraderie in *The "Narcissus"*, the character of the girl, like James Wait, inhabits the position of the irresolvable 'dark' mystery to the White man. Both writers re-centre hegemonic failure that is then often interpreted as a sign of the dilemma of the human condition. It is this universalising moment which renders the historical references obscure. In an attempt to counter these criticisms, Attwell however, reads the non-specific milieu not as a form of ethical universalism but a strategic refusal of specificity. "[I]t is intrinsic to the critique of Empire in the novel that a barbarian subject-position remains unrepresented." (Attwell 1993, 82) Similarly, Michael Marais argues that Coetzee's use of metafictional strategies is a deliberate act of a "politicisation of interpretation" (Marais 1996, 80), for example, by 'forcing' the reader to adopt the view of the perpetrator rather than develop empathy with the victim, which is prevalent in more realist modes of fiction. Nonetheless, creating a position of paralysed privilege, which prevents Coetzee from creating a speaking position on behalf of the 'Other', has the effect that his novels tend to enact a waiting for the end of apartheid and consequently "hover undecidedly between activity and passivity" (Durrant 2004, 19).

In this way, there is, I argue, an unsettling resemblance to Conrad's tales of male failure which provide an exclusive focus on the psychology of the coloniser. Even though Coetzee addresses this dilemma much more self-reflexively in his writing than Conrad, he ultimately cannot really let go of a mode of writing that he implicitly criticises. "J. M. Coetzee is struggling, albeit behind an extraordinary control and stylistic elegance, to combine his Western, modernist literary culture with an African historical reality which is hardly welcoming to it." (S. Watson 1996, 34) Parry sums up this paradox which characterises almost all of Coetzee's fictions:

A failure to project alterities might signify Coetzee's refusal to exercise the author-ity of his dominant culture to represent other, subjugated cultures, and might be construed as registering his understanding that agency is not something that is his to give or withhold through representation. Yet […] European textual power [is] reinscribed in the formal syntax required of Literature, [and] eventually survives the attempted subversion of its dominion. (Parry 1996, 40)

Failure, both in Conrad's modernist writing and Coetzee's self-reflexive postmodern appropriation time and again, functions as a motor for artistic innovation and male authorship. The crisis of language and masculinity as well as the failure to represent both the 'Other', and in a sense the 'self', is intertwined in this self-reflexive allegorical narrative web, in which the crisis of the hegemonic White man is re-privileged. There is no representa-tion of the 'Other' subject position in *Waiting for the Barbarians* – similar to his later novel *Disgrace*. However, in *Waiting for the Barbarians*, this failure to represent 'barbarian' subjectivity coincides with a strong focus on the alle-gorical, fetishised body of the female 'Other'. While the text, on the one hand, self-consciously addresses this fetishisation of the 'barbarian' female body by the magistrate, it, on the other hand, is always in danger of repro-ducing this very fetishisation in the narrative passages that describe the body of the woman. In this way, the narrative recreates a problematic tex-tual desire for and lingering on 'Otherness'.

Disgrace: Male Author-ity in an Age of Disgrace?

J.M. Coetzee's first novel, which was published in post-apartheid South Africa, the so-called 'new' South Africa, generated a heated debate. In South Africa, the reception was much more hostile than the international reactions to the Booker Prize winner of 1999. The novel *Disgrace* centres on the violence White South Africans have experienced from the hands of Black South Africans after the end of the apartheid regime. The first half of the novel recounts the sexual mores of the fifty-two-year-old White male protagonist David Lurie: twice divorced, father of a grown daughter, professor of communications at the fictional Cape Technical University specialised on Romanticism (Byron and Wordsworth) who has only little enthusiasm left for his job – a job that has marginalised the role of litera-ture for the pragmatic focus on 'communications'. This is the (stereotypi-cal) story of a male mid-life crisis as the very first sentence of the novel referring to his short-lived arrangement with the sex worker, Soraya, underlines: "For a man of his age, fifty-two, divorced, he has, to his mind, solved the problem of sex rather well."[230] (D 1) This statement will be, of course, proven completely wrong in the course of events. It is Lurie's sexuality and his inability to abstain from the charms of one of his young students, Melanie Isaacs, which will trigger his downfall.

The novel's focus on a history of violence in South Africa implies complicated gendered, racialised and sexualised politics that the text self-consciously addresses. To begin with, Melanie's racial background is never explicit in the novel; nevertheless, many critics argue that she can, and indeed should be, read as Black, or, in the terminology of apartheid race classifications, as 'coloured' (mixed race).[231] Hence, under apartheid their relationship would not only be a taboo but in fact a crime. Poyner (2000), like others, legitimises this interpretation with Lurie's musings about her name, "Meláni: the dark one" (D 18) and a remark of Melanie's enraged boyfriend who demands of Lurie "to stay with his own kind" (D 194). None of these statements necessarily need to be interpreted this way, and especially the latter assertion can also refer to the class background of Lurie, but it does not seem implausible especially given the role reversal of racialised violence in the attack on Lucy in the second half of the novel. However, in much of Coetzee's writing the specific physical 'racial markers' are intentionally not explicated and remain rather vague, and by means of this narrative strategy of rendering race uncertain (Arndt (2009) speaks of race-evasiveness), Coetzee lets the readers assume the race of some of the characters. David Attwell argues, "*Disgrace* contains and sublimates race, by drawing it into larger patterns of historical and ethical interpretation" (Attwell 2002, 336). In this sense, race needs to be produced in the act of reading rather than being stated merely as a 'fact'. But Coetzee also does not try to construct a strictly 'race neutral' novel by not making any reference to race or racial markers. Especially in the second part of the novel, the problematic of a racialised conflict is foregrounded and characters more clearly described as White and Black South Africans. Therefore, the novel clearly differs from the more allegorical *Waiting for the Barbarians*.

---

230 Katherine Stanton (2006) points out that South Africa has become an important setting of sex trafficking of women of various racial and regional backgrounds and emphasises Lurie's involvement in these dubious affairs.

231 The contributors in the special issue of *Interventions* (2002) on Coetzee univocally voice the assumption that both Soraya and Melanie should be read as 'coloured' and Attridge, too, states that the portrayal of the Isaacs family supports such a reading. (cf. Attridge 2004, 173)

Disgrace is a text of many narrative gaps on other levels as well. In the first half of the story, the question of sexual violence is deliberately held in limbo. From the actual descriptions it is never entirely clear whether one should assume that Lurie has raped Melanie, and critics are divided over this question.[232] In the novel, the scene is described in the following terms: "She does not resist. [...] Not rape, not quite that, but undesired never-theless, undesired to the core. As though she had decided to go slack, die within herself for the duration." (D 25) Lurie is aware that the non-con-sensual sexual act is going to become a problem for him and his career. He knows immediately that it was a "mistake, a huge mistake" (D 25). The sober descriptions of the narrator respond to Lurie's decision not to de-fend or excuse his actions; he chooses to face the consequences of his behaviour. Lurie's deeds are not ameliorated and "these interactions, par-ticularly with women, seem readily open to reader critique" (Meffan and Worthington 2001, 139).

The decisive factor for the ambivalence of this and other scenes in the novel is the focalization of the novel. Lurie is, in Genette's terminology, the focal character. The extradiegetic-heterodiegetic narrator is reliant on the internal focalization of Lurie. His gaze affects and limits what the reader learns. All through the text, it is Lurie's incapability to understand other characters that characterises the dense and, at times, cold language of the novel. The narrator conveys Lurie's reflections on certain groups of words, such as the difference between "*burned* and *burnt*" (D 71) that he initially explains to his students. The same pair of words is repeated at different instances in the novel: a second time when he examines his wounds after the attack: "Everything is tender, everything is burned. Burned, burnt" (D 97), and a third time when he tries to explain his pas-sion for Melanie: "Burned – burnt – burnt up." (D 166) (cf. Holland 2002, 402) Coetzee's use of free indirect speech in these and other passages has the effect that the boundary between the narrator and Lurie the focal char-acter becomes blurry. (cf. McDonald 2002, 326) The style and choice of words of the novel are influenced by the professor's thoughts. There are numerous literary references as well as foreign language terms in French and Italian interspersed in the narrative, and there are also Lurie's thoughts on etymology, which shape the intellectual discourse of the novel.

---

232 One finds "rape" but also "assault" and similar terminologies applied to this scene in the secondary literature.

Michael Holland argues that the reader of the novel is implicitly gendered male – a 'man of the book', like Lurie. However, this equation of the gender of the focal character with the gender of the implied reader is somewhat problematic. In privileging Lurie's perspective, Coetzee highlights the self-centred male crisis of the protagonist which does not necessarily need to be equivalent with the perspective of the reader. Both then, the male perspective and also the stylised language of the novel, are prone to cause discomfort in its readers – disregarding their gender. As Holland writes, "the novel suspends the reader awkwardly between aesthetic pleasure and moral unease" (Holland 2002, 398). Coetzee depicts David Lurie's White male middle-aged crisis as highly problematic and exposes his shortcomings, which paradoxically makes it hard for the reader to empathise with him although he is the chief focalizer. It is this self-reflexive language of Lurie, which puts two crises centre stage: the crisis of masculinity and the crisis of language.

In stark contrast to the exposed eloquence of intellectual discourse are the descriptions of the instances of violence in the novel. By refusing to put into words the sexualised violence, the novel attests to the failure of language. The act of rape in "its enormity swallows words; it is an instance of the sublime of terror" (Pechey 2002, 381). This is part of a critique of the power of language that the novel enacts on many levels. At the university committee of inquiry into sexual harassment, Lurie adamantly refuses to perpetuate the ritualised rhetoric of remorse and guilt that might have saved his job. He stubbornly explains, "[w]ell, I make no confession. I put forward a plea, as is my right. Guilty as charged. That is my plea. That is as far as I am willing to go" (D 51) and later he adds, "[r]epentance belongs to another world, to another universe of discourse" (D 58). Coetzee seems to suggest that ritualised formulas cannot adequately convey guilt. The inclusion of this inquiry can clearly be linked to the 1995 Truth and Reconciliation Commission, which were public hearings, intended to come to terms with the past atrocities of the racist regime of apartheid. This must be seen as a deliberate subtext by Coetzee and has been commented on by many critics.[233]

---

233 For readings that focus specifically on this aspect, cf. Easton 2006; Jolly 2006; Poyner 2000. As has been mentioned, *Disgrace* itself was also part of some public controversy in South Africa. The African National Congress referred to the novel in its submission to the Human Rights Commission's Inquiry into Racism in the Media on 5 April 2000. (cf. Attwell 2002)

The novel also shows how women repeatedly become the victims in these male-dominated conflicts, and it is Lurie's failure to see his own violent entanglement in these stories of hegemonic White crisis that characterises the second part of the story. After the dishonourable end of his career, Lurie leaves Cape Town to visit his daughter, who lives in the rural area of the Eastern Cape in a place with the evocative name Salem.[234] When he arrives at the farm, Lurie is to work for Petrus, Lucy's Black neighbour and co-proprietor of the land.[235] "'Give Petrus a hand. I like that. I like the historical piquancy.'" (D 77) Again, the racialised connotations of this relationship are immediately foregrounded. The White male focal point of view is continued, and David Lurie's shortcomings in understanding the 'Other', be it Petrus or his lesbian daughter, are integrated into the narration in the second part. His daughter's homosexuality, for instance, remains a quizzical cliché to Lurie.

But what does he know about what women do together? Maybe women do not need to make beds creak. [...] Perhaps they sleep together merely as children do, cuddling, touching, giggling, reliving girlhood – sisters more than lovers. [...] Sapphic love: an excuse for putting on weight. (D 86)

In passages like these, the author exhibits the ignorance of his central character and although the reader is invited to share David Lurie's thoughts, the novel does not necessarily invite an endorsement of his views.

During the atrocious attack on Lucy and her father, Lurie tries to defend his daughter but fails miserably in his attempt. He is locked behind a door, and suffers from burn bruises when the attackers try to set him on fire. Again, one has to emphasise that "the scene is presented, disturbingly, through Lurie as focalizer" (Graham 2002, 13). Hence, although there is no description of the event, it is clear that Lucy has been raped. In this way, the central crisis of the daughter becomes the traumatic event for the broken father and anti-hero in this story, which is the only viewpoint to which

---

234 Kai Easton explains that there is in fact a real Salem in this region and provides references to the situatedness of the novel in a number of local debates. However, she also acknowledges that Coetzee will very likely have chosen this name for its biblical and literary allusions to Nathanial Hawthorne's *The Scarlet Letter* (1850) and Arthur Miller's *The Crucible* (1953). (cf. Easton 2006, 192)

235 The setting on a rural farm also connects *Disgrace* to the genre of the Afrikaans *plaasroman*. Van Coller argues that *Disgrace* can be read as a parody of this genre. (cf. Van Coller 2006, 19–25)

the reader has access. It is a narrative gap in the novel – it remains beyond the capacity of language.

Afterwards, Lurie is excruciatingly aware of his failure to protect his daughter which he also connects to his role as an intellectual whose skills in such a situation of life and death have little value.

He speaks Italian, he speaks French, but Italian and French will not save him here in darkest Africa. He is helpless, an Aunt Sally, a figure from a cartoon, a mission-ary […] waiting with clasped hands and upcast eyes while the savages jaw away in their own lingo preparatory to plunging him into their boiling cauldron. Mission work: what has it left behind, that huge enterprise of upliftment? Nothing that he can see. (D 95)

The inclusion of this rape in a novel set in post-apartheid South Africa is, of course, an incredible provocation. How can Coetzee describe White victimhood in a racist context? In the quoted section, Lurie himself seems to be aware of this dilemma by evoking the imagery of a racist cartoon and the stereotypical formulation of the "darkest Africa". In this way, "the novel invites suspicion of racism, especially in its portrayal of black-on-white rape" (Attwell 2002, 332). Accordingly, McDonald emphasises the self-reflexivity of this passage and the deliberate display of 'white fear': "By giving privileged space to the idea of the white as victim, and by using the colonial nightmare *topos* – the violation of white women – it can also be seen to play up to 'white fears'." (McDonald 2002, 326) Lucy's rape then is not merely an attack on an individual but entrenched in a history of South African violence. This reference is commented on by the characters of the novel as well.

After the crime, Lucy steadfastly refuses to push charges on the grounds of rape and acts against her father's wishes. Lurie cannot empa-thise with or understand his daughter. Immediately after the rape, David Lurie poses the almost sarcastic question whether the rape of a lesbian is worse than the rape of a virgin (cf. D 105), and he also wonders whether this attack was not only a 'Black attack' against a 'White woman' but also whether it is a sexualised assault of heterosexual violence against a lesbian woman. These thoughts are an unsettling comment on how 'different' rapes are constructed. Nonetheless, the history of rape in South Africa, which currently still has horribly high rape statistics (cf. Farred 2002a, 353), is linked to a history of sexualised and racialised violence. Lucy sees it as her burden not to repeat the charge of rape against Black men. "'You tell what happened to you, I tell what happened to me,' she repeats" (D 99) and, as her point of view is absent from the novel, the reader never really learns what happened to her. Lucy only repeats her conviction not to speak: "'The reason is that, as far as I am concerned, what happened to me is a purely private matter. In another time, in another place it might be held to be a public matter. But in this place, at this time, it is not. […] This place being South Africa.'" (D 112) Here, in stark contrast to earlier writings, Coetzee clearly sets his story in a specified time and place and evokes a concrete geopolitical setting, which renders *Disgrace* less abstract or allegorical than *Waiting for the Barbarians*, for example. The character Lucy is aware that to claim a position of White victimhood in post-apartheid South Africa becomes an almost impossible subject position.[236] By telling the story of a Black-on-White rape in the novel, the author Coetzee, on the one hand, breaks this taboo, but, on the other hand, self-reflexively addresses the problematic aspects of representing such a crime by blanking out Lucy's perspective and by having her persistently refuse the position of the victim.

Only in one instance in a dialogue between father and daughter, Lucy's perspective seems to come to the fore: "'It was so personal. […] It was done with such personal hatred. That was what stunned me more than anything. The rest was … expected. But why did they hate me so? I had never set eyes on them.'" (D 156) To this Lurie replies: "'It was history speaking through them. […] A history of wrong. Think of it that way, if it helps. It may have seemed personal, but it wasn't. It came down from the ancestors.'" (D 156) As father and daughter have to realise, colonial and personal history become inseparable at this historical junction. The novel interrogates the capacity of language to represent human suffering, and it also questions the emotional capacity of humans to empathise with other people's suffering.

There is a link between the two instances of sexualised violence in the novel. The molestation/rape of the possibly 'coloured' Melanie by the White man David is mirrored in the rape of the White woman Lucy by the three Black men. Ariella Azoulay (2002) argues that to establish a connec-

---

236 Susan Arndt argues that both characters consider their Whiteness as being in crisis: She links David Lurie's crisis to his lost sense of autonomy and Lucy Lurie's crisis to guilt. (cf. Arndt 2009, 186) Given the mentioned focalization, I find it hard to parallel the crises of Whiteness of father and daughter as it is quite clearly David's perspective which becomes the privileged crisis here. Arndt herself emphasises that David's "race-evasion" is the self-reflexive focus of the novel.

tion between the two women is the task of the reader; a task at which, according to her, Lurie himself fails. However, I would question whether Lurie really fails to understand the link between the two events.[237] Initially after the crime, he reflects on the limits of his capacity to show compassion: "[H]e does understand; if he concentrates, if he loses himself, be there, be the men, inhabit them, fill them with the ghost of himself. The question is, does he have it in him to be the woman?" (D 160) In this instance, Lurie seems to be aware that he may, in fact, also be part of the male aggression against women. What he cannot come to terms with – at least initially – is to accept disgrace as a state of living as his daughter does.

On the level of the novel again, Coetzee by centring on the male crisis of David Lurie also "does not have it in him" to represent Lucy – to fill this gap remains the task of the reader. Consequently, it is primarily the dispute over how to interpret the character of Lucy that has shaped the critical debate on the novel to date. In the end, Lucy is pregnant with the child of one of the rapists and agrees to give up the land and accepts Petrus's protection by becoming her 'third wife'. Lurie, as most likely the majority of readers, is struggling to understand this decision. "'This is not how we do things.' *We*: he is on the point of saying, *We Westerners*." (D 202) Here again Coetzee immediately includes a self-critical problematisation of Western universality.

It is no longer unquestioned how things are supposed to work or how things are done. New relations need to be negotiated. Lucy's construction of a 'new family' – based on an incredible act of violence – is not a 'natural' family according to racialised or sexualised notions of 'normality', but it is a union of allegiance. The mixed-race child, begotten in hostility, will be, in Lucy's words, "a child of this earth" (D 216). While in this constellation, Black men finally are conceded the dubious 'privilege' to assert control over White women, White patriarchy is delineated as a phenomenon of the past. This is epitomised in the figure of the neighbour Ettinger who will not leave his estate without a gun. He cannot accept the fact that with the abolition of apartheid he has forfeited White privilege. (cf. D 100) There is no future for men like Ettinger and tellingly, he is left without a family in this country. His wife is dead and his children have gone back to Germany to the place of Ettinger's origin. The figure of the 'White father' is no

---

237 Nonetheless, Azoulay is absolutely right when she emphasises the difference in tone between the two scenes: "The first story is presented as an almost administrative matter, the second as a traumatic event." (Azoulay 2002, 35)

longer needed. This is a painful realisation that David Lurie, too, has come to terms with. After her decision to stay on the land, David tried to persuade Lucy of the opposite in a letter: "I plead with you, listen to me. 'Your father.'" (D 160) Lucy replies with a written note in which she explains, "'I cannot be a child forever. You cannot be a father forever. I know you mean well, but you are not the guide I need, not at this time. 'Yours, Lucy.'" (D 161) In this statement and by signing with her name rather than 'Your daughter' as an equivalent to David's signature 'Your father', she severs the bonds that are thought to be natural and effectively disowns David as her father – a position that is, indeed, usually considered to be life-long. Neither heterosexuality, nor White supremacy, is the foundation of this 'new family' that has its roots not in love but in aggression.

Nonetheless, as critics have remarked, the violated and pregnant body of a (lesbian) woman as a symbol of reconciliation in a male-dominated conflict remains a problematic image. (cf. Horrell 2002, 2008) Others, such as Marais, read Lucy's decision not as a sign of victimhood but as a conscious political choice to disidentify with White privilege.

Lucy Lurie's passivity may be seen as a refusal to remain in the oppositional position relative to the rapists that she is forced to occupy at the time of the rape. […] [S]he resists a form of resistance that would require of her to remain a term in an opposition which violates her difference. […] Through her passivity, she refuses to perpetuate the cycle of domination and counter-domination out of which colonial history erects itself. (Marais 2001, 37)

The conflict in much of postcolonial fictional and critical writing on who is given voice is central to understanding Coetzee's texts. Coetzee centres on the failure of White men and deliberately refuses to give voice to the 'Other'. Spivak argues that Coetzee's narrative strategy provokes an active counter reading:

When Lucy is resolutely denied focalization, the reader is provoked, for he or she does not want to share in Lurie-the-chief-focalizer's inability to 'read' Lucy as patient and agent. No reader is content with acting out the failure of reading. This is the rhetorical signal to the active reader, to counterfocalize. […] This provocation into counterfocalization is the 'political' in political fiction – the transformation of a tendency into a crisis. (Spivak 2002, 22)

If one agrees with Spivak, then it is the political gesture of the writer to attest to the limits of the written word.

In the arrangement of counterfocalization within the validating institution of the novel in English, the second half of *Disgrace* makes the subaltern speak, but does not presume to give 'voice,' either to Petrus or Lucy. This is not the novel's failure, but rather a politically fastidious awareness of the limits of its power. (ibid., 24)

However, Spivak, somewhat optimistically evokes a very politically conscious and aware reader here.[238] While it is true that Coetzee does not fall prey to the paternalistic gesture of simply giving voice to the 'Others' of humanism, which critics such as Canepari-Labib (2005) view as one of his greatest achievements[239], I maintain that it is problematic to construct the story of male crisis against the 'unrepresentable' backdrop of the rape of a woman. "Lucy's rape is overdetermined – not merely by South African politics but by the novel itself. This is a significant weakness, and it returns us to Coetzee's limitations, which are the limitations of allegory." (Wood 2005, 256)

The character Lucy, in a remark that self-reflexively comments on her marginalised role in this novel of male crisis, says to her father, "'You behave as if everything I do is part of the story of your life. You are the main character, I am a minor character who doesn't make an appearance until halfway through. Well, contrary to what you think, people are not divided into major and minor.'" (D 198) The 'humanness' of Lucy is emphasised in this comment; she is not only a minor character. Nevertheless, in the microcosm of the novel, this humanness, like the humanness of the Black characters, remains inaccessible and unrepresentable.

Post-apartheid South Africa is characterised as a situation of disgrace, and the conflict between 'self' and 'Other' is not simply solvable by liberal goodwill. Human solidarity is questioned, and it is animals, most prominently dogs (cf. DeKoven 2009), which play an important role all through the novel but most significantly in the end. Lurie helps Bev Shaw, a White neighbour with whom he has an affair, to put to sleep stray and sick dogs.

---

238 Obviously, like all fiction, *Disgrace* is neither *per se* subversive nor reactionary. Rather these connotations are created in the construction of meaning and different reading practices. In Sedgwick's terminology, Spivak's reading can be seen as a "reparative reading" assuming an active counterfocalization, while my reading – with its emphasis on re-centring tendencies in the representation of masculinity in crisis – must adopt, again in Sedgwick's terms, a more "paranoid" perspective. (cf. Sedgwick 1997)

239 Cf. "Coetzee's protagonists do not follow the successful life of visibility, and by either consciously refusing to communicate, or by simply being unable to establish a real contact with those surrounding them, they somehow refuse to be subjugated by the language of 'civilization'." (Canepari-Labib 2005, 278)

There is a crematory and provocatively the German word, *Lösung*, which, of course, evokes the Holocaust, is employed to describe this procedure.[240]

Initially, it was Petrus's job to take care of the dogs, and by assuming this position, Petrus and David figure as the second Black and White pairing in the novel next to Melanie and Lucy. David accepts the role of the "dog-man": he lets go of the notion of the divine spark of humans and starts to take care of mere animality. Kay Sulk argues that it is Coetzee's innovative accomplishment to describe transgressive experiences without the reference to catharsis: "While Lurie in his earlier deeds and reflections thought he could ultimately rely on a socially qualified life, he must in his state of 'disgrace' base his entire ethical actions, the associations with his environment in relation to this speechless, unqualified life." (Sulk 2005, 188, my translation)

Finally, he can see why Lucy wants to accept a state of disgrace as a foundation to begin anew. When he first struggled to understand her decision to stay on the farm, she explained that to let go of privilege might actually entail the possibility of a fresh start – a start that includes the debasement of humans to the state of animals – biological survival rather than divine humanity is evoked:

'Yes, I agree, it's humiliating. But perhaps that is a good point to start again from. Perhaps that is what I must learn to accept. To start at ground level. With nothing. Not with nothing but. With nothing. No cards, no weapons, no property, no rights, no dignity.'
'Like a dog.'
'Yes, like a dog.' (D 205)

The novel ends on a Sunday when Lurie is putting dogs to sleep at the shelter. He kills a dog that he has grown fond of without resistance, and Bev Shaw asks him, "'Are you giving him up?' 'Yes, I am giving him up.'" (D 220) This ending can be read as an attempt of a new beginning for David Lurie as well, a readjustment albeit a very bleak one. He has finally put aside his own need for company and prioritises the animal's suffering. "Coetzee has furnished *Disgrace* with the structure of an anti-*Bildungsroman*,

---

240 This analogy remains highly problematic and unsettling as it relates Lurie's position to that of Nazi mass murderers. What does it mean then in this context when Lurie gives up his favourite dog as the precondition for his new start? Ultimately, it remains unclear to me whether Coetzee wishes to compare the White South African guilt after apartheid with that of German guilt after World War II.

a novel which involves the forfeiture rather than consolidation of the protagonist's sense of self." (Marais 2006, 79)

With *Disgrace* Coetzee also seems to offer a rather bleak and resigning commentary on the role of literature. South African literature is often seen as an important tool to convey social awareness and political responsibility.[241] However, of course, literature can not only be treated as a mimetic tool of social reality.[242] Coetzee questions an optimistic liberal tradition that sees the main requirement of literature to mirror social realities and affect political change. (cf. Meffan and Worthington 2001) As Spivak explained, Coetzee is more skeptical of the powers of literary discourse, and in a typically postmodern manner, includes these reflections on language in his writing.

Coetzee describes the incapacity of language to resolve problems. The postcolonial context, in which the hegemonic role of White masculinity has been challenged, functions as the backdrop of this failure. In contrast to the often voiced charge against Coetzee, it is not my argument that postmodern writing practices are *per se* apolitical. My critique is aimed at Coetzee's recourse to the narrative pattern of male failure, which, even as part of a political intervention, remains complicit in a discourse that re-centres hegemonic masculinity. The same problem relates to Coetzee's style. In his act of writing stylised texts, part of an allusive web of references to other 'great' works of literature, about the failure of language and Western universalism, a certain unease must remain and his mentioned indebtedness to the European modern tradition is obvious – granted that his writing also advances a reflection of exactly these aspects.

Africa becomes yet again the stereotypical setting of White failure and herein one can see the postmodern reference to Conrad. Coetzee is aware of the problematic 'White position' in South Africa.[243] Similar to Conrad,

---

241 Much of the dispute between Nadine Gordimer and J.M. Coetzee as well as the critical debate focusing on the difference between the two writers centres on this problem. This binary of Gordimer as part of the realist/political tradition as opposed to Coetzee's postmodern/apolitical approach, however, tends to postulate a rather limited notion of political writing. (cf. Attwell 1993)

242 Attridge, somewhat problematically, argues that "the only responsible way to engage with *Disgrace* is as a literary work, not as historical reportage, political prescription, or allegorical scheme" (Attridge 2002, 319). This is at least in so far puzzling as it attests very strict boundaries between different kinds of discourse.

243 For an overview of the debate on representation and realism and the role of the author in the South African context and Coetzee's contentious position in these debates, cf. Attwell (1993, 9–34); Head (1997, 8–14); Kossew (1996, 16–28); Parker (1996); Poyner

who fashions failure as a motor for aesthetic modern innovation, Coetzee employs self-reflexive White male failure as the basis of postmodern writing. This also becomes evident in the metatext of the novel. The fictional character Lurie is the author of a text within a text – again, a very typical postmodern metatextual strategy. Lurie is working on a chamber Opera about the Romantic and scandalous poet Byron called *Byron in Italy*.[244]

In the course of the story, the idealised Romantic masculinity of Byron is debunked as a proper theme of representation, and increasingly, Lurie focuses on the women in Byron's life. Due to the recent traumatic events in his own life, the Romantic notion of 'wild' and ecstatic sexuality is suddenly linked to rape in Lurie's mind. "He thinks of Byron. Among the legions of countesses and kitchenmaids Byron pushed himself into there were no doubt those who called it rape. [...] From where he stands, from where Lucy stands, Byron looks very old-fashioned indeed." (D 160) In this way, this novel about failing masculinity also includes as a metatext the failure to write a text (about failing masculinity). Lurie wants to centre on the role of the woman, Byron's mistress Teresa Guccioli. But instead of focusing on the young sensual woman, he attempts to write a part for the middle-aged widow Teresa he imagines. But he cannot find the proper words for her either. "Can he find it in his heart to love this plain, ordinary woman? Can he love her enough to write a music for her? If he cannot, what is left for him?" (D 182) Lurie still does not have it in him "to be the woman". He has found the rather 'un-opera-like' instrument of a (toy) banjo which he uses to compose. "He is in the opera neither as Teresa nor as Byron nor even as some blending of the two: he is held in the music itself, in the flat tiny slap of the banjo strings [...]. So this is art, he thinks, and this is how it does work! How strange! How fascinating!" (D 184–185) Lurie learns to privilege the non-linguistic, the music rather than the language in a way that, one could argue, Coetzee conversely privileges aesthetics in his writings over context. Lurie has to give up his dream of being a successful subject-author. Of his opera only the pathetic sounds of a banjo remain: "*Plink-plunk* squawks the banjo in the desolate yard in Af-

---

(2009, 1–13). Again, I am less interested in the personal role of the individual author but rather in the discourse on and the literary representation of White masculinity in crisis in English postcolonial literature.

244 Easton (2007) describes the interrelations between Byron's scandalous life and the history of the region of the Eastern Cape. Sheils (2003) compares Lurie both to Byron himself and the figure of Lucifer from Byron's poem "Lara".

rica." (D 214) Again, the setting of Africa as the place of the 'Other' is highlighted. Writing an opera in Italian with recourse to the 'great' European tradition suddenly appears an absurd enterprise. "It would have been nice to be returned triumphant to society as the author of an eccentric little chamber opera. But that will not be." (D 214) On this metatextual level, ambivalence remains: Lurie cannot finish his opera but the author, Coetzee, by focusing on Lurie's failure can complete his 'master piece'. Is the narrative pattern of failure the precondition for this novel, or, is the novel written despite its recourse to failure? Is Lurie's failure particular or universal, and does his gesture in the end point towards an abnegation of Western supremacy?

These are not easily resolvable questions and ultimately, there remains an irresolvable ambivalence in Coetzee's response to these fundamental challenges to 'Western' writing. Nonetheless, this recourse to failure implies a certain inevitability of things that might be read as a sign of a privileged 'White' perspective. Dyer analyses the role of women in so-called "end-of-empire fictions" where they often act as figures of paralysis rather than indicate the need for political change. He writes, "[w]omen take the blame, and provide the spectacle of moral suffering, for the loss of empire. For this they are rewarded with a possibility that already matches their condition of narrative existence: nothing." (Dyer 1997, 206) Interestingly, a similar role is assumed by White masculinity in Coetzee's postcolonial *Disgrace*. Lurie is shaped by his incapacity to act in this state of disgrace, and it is this standstill that he has to accept. He becomes "a man overmastered by a power that exceeds and disrupts the rationalizations of his age" (Attridge 2004, 190). As a narrative of White guilt, *Disgrace* might also be read to sublimate 'White' capacity to stand in, to live "like a dog", as a result of all the harm that has been caused in the name of colonialism and apartheid. However, at its worse this focus on, or even indulgence in, moral suffering might abnegate the political implications and paradoxically re-centre Whiteness and masculinity.

Boehmer also highlights these re-centring tendencies in this narrative of male crisis, especially by contrasting the characters, David and Lucy Lurie.

Lurie abjects selfhood and achieves a kind of unselfconscious redemption; Lucy has abnegation forced on her and has herself committed no wrong. Coetzee would want to see her embodiment as signifying a certain power, yet it is a power traduced by its fixity, its entrenchedness. She must make herself ready for more of such violation. For her any sympathy for the other must mean to live in inevitable disgrace. For Lurie, by contrast, sympathy involves a limited yet still *willing* identification with another's suffering. Lurie in this sense remains a subject, even if a self-substituting one; Lucy's self-substitution involves becoming reconciled to the position of conventional object. (Boehmer 2006, 145)

Coetzee does not represent a hero; his protagonist is debased and accepts this position in the end. He paradoxically becomes a successful anti-hero. Meffan and Worthington speak of Coetzee's "refusal in *Disgrace* to do more than suggest the need to ask new questions of the self" (Meffan and Worthington 2001, 146).

Although almost twenty years separate the two novels and despite the important differences in content, style and context, *Waiting for the Barbarians* and *Disgrace*, show striking similarities in the way the crisis of a man is constructed against the foil of a woman whose perspective is marginalised in the narrative. Under apartheid, it is torture and the ethical response from a position of privilege that is the focus of Coetzee's writing. While the novel attests to the linguistic creation of 'Otherness' and the magistrate comes to admit his own involvement in a system that has become suspect to him, the barbarian girl remains the undecipherable mystery to him. Granted that Coetzee does not paternalistically bestow a voice to the subaltern, the text still somewhat problematically re-enacts what it attempts to criticise, namely the construction of the 'exoticness' and unknowability of the body of the 'Other'. *Waiting for the Barbarians* self-consciously marks the position of privilege, but it lingers in a paralysed and stylised state of exalting 'meaninglessness' in the end. *Disgrace*, in contrast, via its focalization presents narrative blanks when it comes to the depiction of the 'Other' and in this sense, I would argue, is somewhat more successful in presenting a critique of the 'self' from a hegemonic point of view. The text strictly focuses on the male anti-hero and his acceptance of his fall from grace. In this way, Coetzee partakes in what could be called a spectacle of the failing 'self', as a slight alteration of the chapter title on colonial photography. What remains is a wavering between particularisation and re-centring of hegemonic masculinity that shapes Coetzee's texts, especially in their privileging of the hegemonic male perspective. In his insistence on White male crisis, albeit a consciously exposed male crisis, Coetzee does not ultimately let go of the privileged discourse of masculinity in crisis.

Conclusion: Towards a Particularisation of the Crisis of Masculinity – En/Countering Post-9/11 Crisis Narratives of Uncertainty

The crises of masculinity have never been monolithic, neither in colonial nor in postcolonial sources. While representation challenges, it also changes conceptions of different masculinities. Consequently, this book should be understood as an attempt to disrupt the narrations of an untroubled history of *the* discourse of the crisis of masculinity – with both terms in their singular form.

When one is confronted with the colonial accounts that celebrate hegemonic masculinity, there is initially a strong urge of simply demonising these sources as conservative, racist and misogynist, and I am not saying that some of the narratives do not have this impetus. Nonetheless, one should also take seriously the contradictions and ambivalences that these texts yield, and it is telling that many of these works still find a wide audience today. As I tried to explain, hegemony and marginality are interrelated and exist in an asymmetrical but unstable balance. The assumed crisis of masculinity implies ruptures and fissures, and therefore, can also allow for a (re)negotiation of obsolete conceptualisations of masculinity. Nevertheless – and this has been emphasised throughout this book – the danger of a conservative re-centring of masculinity appears to be inherent in the prevalent discourse of crisis, which turns the very reference to crisis into a privileged framework time and again. It is the normative and privileged structural position of hegemonic masculinity that causes this continued recourse to crisis which seldom affects more marginalised expressions of identity. The very idea of crisis implies that one is in a position of privilege – that there is something to lose. By joining the chorus that calls for a restoration and stabilisation of ideals of masculinity the moment they are perceived to be in danger, some fiction, paradoxically, helps to uphold the fictitious stability of hegemonic masculinity.

The focal point of this study have been English colonial and postcolonial narratives, which are part of the ubiquitous reference to a crisis of masculinity in response to the challenges of modernity at the *fin de siècle* and again resulting from the destabilisation of postmodern identity formations and postcolonial migration towards the end of the twentieth century. This negotiation of crisis takes place in various genres and media, including more traditional canonical sources as well as popular culture. My aim was to illustrate how the different narratives and visual strategies that are employed help to create what I call contained crises for the colonial period and exposed crises with reference to the postcolonial sources. The recurring burgeoning of the discourse of masculinity in crisis also highlights the heterogeneity in this discursive field. With regard to the succession of the different readings, the build-up from Haggard's colonial romances to Conrad's modernist narratives attests to the increasing complexity with which the crisis of masculinity is addressed in colonial fiction, and Conrad can be considered the link between the colonial and postcolonial crisis narratives. Nonetheless, this sequence should not be prematurely read as a linear progression. The recurrence of crises narratives indicates that masculinity is conceived of as challenged in various periods and in this sense, both more conservative and more progressive conceptions of masculinity can recur without adhering to a teleology of 'emancipation'. In Kureishi's writing, for instance, the 'backlash' under Thatcher in the eighties figures as a subtext, which implies that he assumes earlier conceptions of masculinity in the sixties and seventies to have been more open and progressive. Not strictly in chronological order, the section on postcolonial sources has first addressed the British postcolonial rewritings of masculinity in crisis and at the end of this section J.M. Coetzee functions as a tie to the earlier colonial crisis narratives. By explicitly linking his postmodern version of the male anti-hero to Conrad's colonial failures, the book, in a sense has come full circle.

The narratability of masculinity, the way that masculinity can be conceptualised in fiction and visual media, relies on genre conventions, but also on shifting historical and cultural conceptions of masculinity that produce both continuities and discontinuities – a dynamic that becomes evident when one compares colonial and postcolonial sources. There is, for example, continuity in the way the coming-of-age story provides both Kipling and Kureishi with the framework to narrate the quest for male identity, albeit very different masculinities. Kipling envisions the hegemonic hybrid boy in the colonies while Kureishi gives voice to the young marginalised hybrid man in the postcolonial metropolis. While both authors do not radically alter the formula of the *Bildungsroman*, there are significant differences in their conception of establishing male identity. Kim has to come to terms with his 'Sahib' status and accept that he is not a 'native' in order to be successful while Karim has to learn how to benefit from his status as racialised 'Other' in the mainstream. In addition to genre conventions, there are also parallels in the way focalization affects storytelling and the privileging of male crises. Both Conrad and Coetzee provide male introspection on failure. But despite this parallel, there is also considerable difference in the degree of self-reflexivity they share. While in Conrad the nostalgic impetus of containment is not entirely absent, Coetzee's writing is highly self-reflexive of the textual re-privileging effects that he seeks to expose. Finally, the analysis of gaze structures in photography and film demonstrates that staging conventions and visual pleasure are closely connected to conceptions of subjectivity. Whose perspective is privileged in a shot and who is turned into a fetishised object of the gaze? While the photography in *The Illustrated London News* attempts to establish the 'manly pose' that would ensure subject status, *My Beautiful Laundrette* turns the interracial queer couple into the focal point of more plural conceptions of masculinity that undermine the 'imperial gaze'. In *The Crying Game*, in turn, it is again racialised 'Otherness' which serves as a backdrop of a more conventional (male) crisis narrative.

Accordingly, masculinity in both colonial and postcolonial sources is contested ground, and the mentioned narrative strategies and genres cater to different degrees of the re-centring of masculinity. Very generally then, one can attest that while there are, in fact, parallels in the construction of male crises in the colonial and postcolonial period, the reference to containment in colonial sources and the more self-reflexive exposure of crisis remains a valid distinguishing feature.

It is important to further the renunciation of a continued uncritical reference to the discourse of the crisis of masculinity by severing the link of masculinity, crisis and universality even more radically. As the variety of readings in the previous chapters demonstrates, there are a whole range of cross-connections between colonial and postcolonial conceptions of masculinity. To return to the photograph by Tillim on the cover, one might want to push the artefacts of White male hegemony off the pedestal (or even urinate at the remnants, as the boy in the picture), but one cannot simply render the ruins of the ideals of heroic masculinity out of focus. Despite calls for a more diversified understanding of masculinity, it is still continuously naturalised as stable and uniform. This idealised notion of masculinity informs the symbolic gender order to date, which tends to privilege male crises and scandalise 'masculinity in decline' in ways that attest to the privilege of the hegemonic position. In these closing remarks, I want to briefly address the writing of terror after 9/11 which can be interpreted as yet another wave of crisis narratives that shape contemporary writing. Once more, these texts seem to re-connect universality and the crisis of masculinity in ways that can be interpreted as re-privileging.

The terrorist attacks of September 11th 2001 have shaken the Western self-image and figure as a caesura in the way that the hegemonic 'self' can be narrated. A new period of postcolonial writing, which we can only begin to assess as novels and other works of art are being produced in response to these events, has emerged. In postcolonial writing and theory the binary opposition of the 'West versus the rest' has been challenged time and again and is closely linked to the concept of hybridity. In 2003, Tobias Wachinger writes in his book *Posing In-between. Postcolonial Englishness and the Commodification of Hybridity* that Zadie Smith has to be considered one of the last authors of the celebration of hybridity or 'in-betweenness' and is very skeptical of the future significance of the concept of hybridity in both postcolonial literature and theory. With regard to Kureishi's turning away from hybridity in his more recent writing, Wachinger asserts:

"It remains to be seen if this radical stepping out of the framework of the 'space-in-between' will prove the model for other writers as well who may be exasperated with the clichéd terms and programmatic writing that have dominated postcolonial discourse throughout the last decade of the 20th century" (Wachinger 2003, 204).

He postulates a farewell to the debate on hybridity, which, he claims, has dominated postcolonial writing for too long. In contrast to this argument and in alignment with critics such as Mita Banerjee and the authors of the *Wasafiri* special issue on *Postcolonial Writing and Terror* from July 2007, I draw a different conclusion regarding the current importance of the concept of hybridity. Instead of a farewell to the concept, one has to speak of a renaissance of hybridity as a crisis of postcolonial studies in light of the terror of 9/11. Banerjee calls 9/11 the "ground zero of the very paradigm of postcolonial studies" (Banerjee 2007, 309). Both Kureishi in *The Black Album* and Smith in *White Teeth* address the issue of the hybrid terrorist in the Western metropolis already before 9/11 – as was explained with reference to the figuration of the *fanatics* – but it is still a somewhat light and comic tone that characterises these narratives.[245] This conception of everyday hybridity does in fact seem to belong to the past, and in this sense, Wachinger is right to a certain degree after all. While hybridity for a long time was connected to an almost playful destabilisation of binary attributions of cultural difference, it is now increasingly linked to a threat scenario that could endanger the West's hegemony for good, and the reflection of this vulnerability now takes centre stage.

The suicide bomber becomes a fascinating object of knowledge narratable as the figure of the *sleeper terrorist*, who in these texts often requires a secondary White focalizer. John Updike's novel *Terrorist* is an example for this kind of writing.[246] (cf. Banerjee 2008) At the same time, there seems to be a withdrawal of postcolonial authors, such as Kureishi or Rushdie, to Whiteness. One now blatantly encounters the "paradox between the fact of lived hybridity and the logic of religious fundamentalism. How can hybridity and fundamentalism be united in the same person" (Banerjee 2007, 309), Banerjee asks insightfully. She looks at recent novels by Rushdie (*Fury*) and Kureishi (*Gabriel's Gift*) and calls them a rebellion against the parameters of the postcolonial and a problematic desire for Whiteness, which she considers a conservative turn in the writings of both authors. (cf. ibid., 321)

In the age of the so-called "War on Terror" the new threat of hybridity is addressed by a whole range of novels which were published after 9/11, many in the year 2005. Robert Eaglestone describes this incision as "the end of one age (of happily mixed chutneys) and the start of another (of

---

245 Sara Upstone (2010) highlights the role of popular literature in creating the archetype of the Muslim terrorist in British fiction before and after 9/11. Although I am sympathetic to her line of argument that describes how this caters to a new form of Orientalism, I find her discussion of the literary sources that include Kureishi (*The Black Album*), Smith (*White Teeth*), McEwan (*Saturday*) as well as Monica Ali (*Brick Lane*) and Nadeem Aslam (*Maps for Lost Lovers*) somewhat truncated as it joins these very different texts under the rubric of "popular fiction" and fails to provide adequate emphasis on the manifold differences in tone, style and genre which, I would argue, produce more diverse points of view than she suggests.

246 In contrast, Mohsin Hamid's *The Reluctant Fundamentalist* (2007) attempts to present the perspective of the well-educated Muslim migrant in the Western metropolis who 'returns home' due to the hostile climate after 9/11. Again, we see new narratives of migration that complicate hybridity (rather than have it disappear) in a globalised perspective. Xenophobia becomes the trigger for narratives of migration that might include a renunciation of, rather than desire for, the West and in this process, paradoxically, the 'assumed fundamentalism' can trigger real fundamentalism(s).

fury and terror)" (Eaglestone 2007, 19). He demonstrates this with reference to Rushdie's *Shalimar the Clown*, Jonathan Safran Foer's *Extremely Loud and Incredibly Close* and the short story "The Last Days of Muhammad Atta" by Martin Amis. It is interesting that many of these writers, with the exception of Rushdie, have not been closely linked with postcolonial literature.[247] Another text that features prominently in this debate is Ian McEwan's 2005 novel *Saturday* on which I want to focus in some more detail in the following.

The book portrays the incidents of a single Saturday in the life of neurosurgeon Henry Perowne. The day is characterised by an all-encompassing fear of the next terrorist attack, which shapes the life of this picture-book White middle-aged Englishman from the upper-middle class. Accordingly, this day of numerous threats ends with the following thoughts of Perowne:

> [A] time will come when they [he and his wife Rosalind, E.H.Y.] find they no longer have the strength for the square, the junkies and the traffic din and dust. Perhaps a bomb in the cause of jihad will drive them out with all the other faint-hearts into the suburbs, or deeper into the country, or to the chateau – their Saturday will become a Sunday. [...] London, his small part of it, lies wide open, impossible to defend, waiting for its bomb, like a hundred other cities. [...] At the end of this day, this particular evening, he's timid, vulnerable, he keeps drawing his dressing gown more tightly around him. (SA 276–277)

In McEwan's novel, as elsewhere, the cultural change as well as the fear of a terrorist attack in the heart of London becomes tangible as the crisis of a White man and the British middle class which pulls out from urban spaces, wrapped in their own fears.[248] Despite a heterodiegetic narrator, the privileging of Perowne's crisis is once more connected to the strict focalization through the protagonist, Henry Perowne, happily married and father of two successful grown-up children. What is more interesting in McEwan's case, however, is that Islamic terrorism and the figure of the hybrid terrorist become a red herring in this narrative. The assumed plane crash in London at the beginning of the plot is simply a burning engine of a Rus-

---

247 Brandon Kempner (2009) also emphasises the conservative literary nostalgia that especially British and Irish authors, such as Seamus Heaney, Chris Cleave and Martin Amis, reproduce after 9/11.

248 Magali Cornier Michael (2009) parallels Perowne's withdrawal to the private sphere to Virginia Woolf's *Mrs Dalloway* and argues that men now take on the position of refuge in light of their sense of loss of power that has increased after 9/11.

sian cargo plane safely returned to Heathrow. The novel, published before
the 7/7 attacks on the London tube, was considered almost prophetic with
its concentration on of the fears of an attack in the London city centre.
The War on Terror becomes the backdrop of this crisis narrative set on
Saturday, 15th of February 2003 – the day of the anti-war march in London, the largest demonstration in the history of the city. As has been mentioned, despite these references, terror in the story is not connected to
Muslim fundamentalists at all. Follwoing a car accident with the thug Baxter, Perowne is attacked by him. His White working-class antagonist is
branded by a neuronal defect and embodies the terror that is to disrupt the
harmonious family idyll. Immediately Baxter is characterised as strikingly
unattractive – he, for instance, radiates a "general simian air" (SA 88). The
learned eye of the neurosurgeon instantly identifies Baxter's tremors as a
sign of Huntington's disease and starts an embarrassing conversation about
his illness in front of Baxter's mates. From now on, everything in Baxter's
life appears as pure determinism.

Here is biological determinism in its purest form. […] [T]he first small alterations
of character, tremors in the hands and face, emotional disturbance, including –
most notably – sudden, uncontrollable alterations of mood, jerky dance-like
movements, […] total loss of muscular control, rigidity sometimes, nightmarish
hallucinations and a meaningless end. (SA 93–94)

The distracting conversation gives Perowne the opportunity to escape. But
in the evening – there is to be a family dinner in celebration of the first
published collection of poems by the daughter Daisy – Baxter, armed with
a knife, and a friend enter the family mansion to take revenge for the humiliation. During the attack, Baxter forces Daisy to undress very likely with
the intention of raping her. But since this discloses her pregnancy – a fact
unknown to the rest of the family – Baxter lets go of her. Instead, he
forces her to read one of her poems. Daisy's grandfather – a renowned
poet – gives her a hidden clue to recite Matthew Arnold's "Dover Beach"
instead. It is the recitation of this poem which calms the agitated Baxter
and induces a mood swing. Finally, Perowne and his son, Theo, can over-
power the intruder. He falls from the stairs and it is Perowne himself who
is called to his rescue. After a successful brain surgery, Baxter can only
await his fate of bodily decline. Given Baxter's situation, Perowne decides
not to press charges. At this point the text makes explicit the obvious differences between the two men:

He, Henry Perowne, possesses so much – the work, money, status, the home, above all, the family – [...] and he has done nothing, given nothing to Baxter who has so little that is not wrecked by his defective gene, and who is soon to have even less. (SA 228)

Science and poetry become two conflicting answers to an 'Other', which once more is all body, no intellect, pathological and inexplicable within a narrative that situates crisis in the Western 'self' and seems to follow the discursive rules, which re-centre both Whiteness and masculinity and which I have described as the privilege of crisis. McEwan re-centres the White middle-class family, whose lineage will continue with Daisy's child at the end of the plot. Hence, while the novel reflects the threats of Islamic terrorism and is set in contemporary urban London, *Saturday* remains, due to the condensed temporal focus on a single day and the attention on Perowne's inner thoughts, clearly restricted in its perspective. As Elizabeth Kowaleski Wallace writes, "McEwan's novel continually glances at a multi-cultural and cosmopolitan society with which it resists engagement" (Wallace 2007, 467). The reflection of Perowne's unbroken desire for his wife, with the two sex scenes at the beginning and end contouring the novel, as well as the almost epical depiction of the squash game with an American colleague re-centre the heterosexual male perspective in addition to the described cultural homogeneity. Nevertheless, a certain degree of skepticism seems well-advised in relation to this kind of interpretation of the novel. In McEwan's text there are also fissures in this "seemingly rigid masculinism" (Hillard 2008, 186), as Molly Clark Hillard has explained. In the exposure of the crisis of its protagonist and the interaction with other characters – such as the disputes with his daughter over the importance of poetry and the Iraq War – Perowne's views are interrogated and can be challenged by readers. (cf. Wells 2006, 126) As has been argued in the previous chapters, re-privileging and ambivalences often coincide, which is connected to the degree of self-reflexivity in the postmodern sources. Nonetheless, the 'Other' remains strangely absent in the narratives after 9/11 and this absence is less reflected than in Coetzee's writing with its radical challenging of Western universality. After 9/11, we seem to witness a certain backlash and the crisis of the 'Other' becomes merely an en-thrallment that can be narrated as a crisis of the 'self'. Many of the above-mentioned novels refer back to a recourse on naturalised 'Otherness' – as the pathology of Baxter in *Saturday*. Eaglestone reads this literature as "in-teresting failures [...] to illuminate the limits in western responses to the 'age of fury' [...]: terror is simply evil (Foer), an illness (McEwan) or stems from universally comprehensible personal motives (Rushdie). [...] This movement itself is characteristic of western thinking, in its attempt to bring all 'otherness' inside its own hegemonic discourse." (Eaglestone 2007, 21)

In this way, these texts, which question their own hegemonic viewpoint only implicitly, aesthetically and politically lag behind the degree of self-reflexivity of an author such as Coetzee. The postcolonial hybrid again becomes a cipher for naturalised deviance and the critique of Robert Young regarding Bhabha's cultural concept of the "third space" gains momentum in light of these developments, which tend to re-situate hybridity away from the sphere of the cultural back to biology.

As with Conrad, who in a depoliticising gesture turned male White failure into the starting point of modernist narratives of colonialism, these postmodern narratives of the 'new' threat of terror rely on the failure of the Western 'self'. Hybridity is no longer the answer to the 'problem' of multicultural societies as in Kureishi's optimistic writing or in Smith's utopian comedy, in this time of renewed uncertainty, it becomes a threat and catalyst for new male crisis narratives.

The claim that the crisis of masculinity is a privileged discourse is not an apodictic statement but rather structurally tied to male hegemony. By pointing to two different periods of time in this book and by offering an outlook on the narratives of uncertainty after 9/11, it has become obvious that the so-called crisis of masculinity is a recurring and privileged discourse that is often organised around a conservative and restorative understanding of masculinity. Nevertheless, male hegemony is also not a simple, dominant discourse that cultural artefacts reproduce. Narrative patterns create textual effects which produce inconsistencies and ambivalences in this process. These texts can provide their readers pleasure by situating them in a position of identification with the male point of view, or they can create unease by self-reflexively highlighting this position.

Both the *fin de siècle* and the last turn of the century produced a discourse that saw masculinity endangered – by feminist claims but also the question of national identity and the influence of colonisation as well as decolonisation and migration, respectively. I have deliberately emphasised the aspects that pertain to a stabilising of the hegemony of masculinity, because despite the ongoing claims that masculinity is becoming marginalised, it is hegemonic masculinity that is often defined as the valid model for literary crisis and subject formations. What does it mean, for instance, when in 2008, the Nobel Prize in literature is awarded to Jean-Marie Gustave Le Clézio as an "author of new departures, poetic adventure and sensual ecstasy, explorer of a humanity beyond and below the reigning civilization"[249]. To be clear, it is not my intention to argue that, in fact, Le Clézio affirms this claim in his writing. It is this reference to supposedly self-evident concepts such as 'humanity' and 'civilisation' that cause unease. What does the committee imagine when they speak of "below the reigning civilization"? Is this Conrad's journey into the past, into the "Heart of Darkness", that is resurfacing once more and that makes it so hard to conceptualise simultaneity of difference instead of a notion of civilisatory progression of 'before' and 'after' or, in this case, 'below' and 'above'?

For the analysis of cultural artefacts, it is important to let go of the repeated discursive strategies that install this crisis of masculinity as a privileged framework. More significantly, it is mandatory to understand the privileging tendencies of this discourse. This means that in masculinity studies, it is crucial to continue to describe and analyse interdependent identities in ways that allow for a more pronounced focus on the differences within masculinities – understood as an interdependent identity formation. Masculinity – like all gender expressions – is always changing (and does not 'belong' to men exclusively). Different masculinities emerge at the interfaces of race, sexuality, nationality, age, ability and religion, and especially (but not only) within the British context, there is a need to understand masculinity as entangled and as part of colonial and postcolonial histories. Of course, it is valuable that people continue to tell and read stories of men and masculinities. But what is needed is a farewell to the scandalising gesture that is attached to any perceived threat towards male norms. 'Crisis' should be understood as an opportunity and a starting point to conceive of more enabling and inclusive models of masculinity rather than evoke the spectre of masculinity in decline, which still haunts current debates on topics as diverse as fatherhood, unemployment and violence in masculinity studies. As Segal (1997) and others have pointed out, changing conceptions of masculinity will not only be for the 'benefit' of those who have inhabited the position of 'Otherness' in relation to the figuration of hegemonic masculinity but also men themselves might, in fact, – if I dare

---

249 Cf. the website of the Nobel Foundation:
    <http://nobelprize.org/nobel_prizes/literature/laureates/2008/press.html>
    (accessed 23 October 2008).

use that word – be liberated from these obsolete notions of oppressive masculinity.

Stories of male crises are particular and do not unquestioningly represent human universality. The term 'universality' can only gain relevance again in a context that accepts particularity as a defining feature of the universal. I am not suggesting that 'universality' and 'humanity' are terms that are readily self-evident or even disposable, or, that the problem of hegemony would be 'solved' if everybody could simply let go of these 'outdated' conceptions. Rather, more research in light of postcolonial, feminist and queer interventions is needed to reassess what the universal in all its possibility would entail. What would a model of universality look like that actually takes the meaning of the word seriously? Frequently, the term 'universal' is used to describe that which is in fact particular. This interrogation of the concept of universality not only pertains to the analysis of narratives of male crises or cultural criticism; the question of the universal will affect more thoroughly how to think of the 'human' in future. Consequently, Butler stresses the importance of keeping open the notion of the 'human' to a continued re-articulation because all too often

the very notion of the 'human' is presupposed; it is defined in advance, and in terms that are distinctively western, very often American, and therefore parochial. The paradox emerges that the 'human' at issue in human rights is already known, already defined, and yet it is supposed to be the ground for a set of rights and obligations that are international. (Butler 2004, 222)

It is this contestation of universality that shapes the debates on human rights at the moment, but it also relates to the disputes on what the 'humanist ideal' of cultural expression stands for. Cultural artefacts can indeed change what it means to be human, and greatly needed are more texts that are 'universally' relevant by fostering the critical reassessment of universality.

Abbreviations

List of Illustrations

11. Film still: Stephen Frears, *My Beautiful Laundrette*, Film/DVD-ROM, 97:00, 1985, 45:22

12. Film still: Stephen Frears, *My Beautiful Laundrette*, Film/DVD-ROM, 97:00, 1985, 90:55

13. Film still: Neil Jordan, *The Crying Game*, Film/DVD-ROM, 107:00, 1992, 15:43

14. Film still: Neil Jordan, *The Crying Game*, Film/DVD-ROM, 107:00, 1992, 55:26

15. Film still: Neil Jordan, *The Crying Game*, Film/DVD-ROM, 107:00, 1992, 61:48

16. Film still: Neil Jordan, *The Crying Game*, Film/DVD-ROM, 107:00, 1992, 74:32

17. Film still: Neil Jordan, *The Crying Game*, Film/DVD-ROM, 107:00, 1992, 82:54

Bibliography

Primary Sources

Amis, Martin (2006). "The Last Days of Muhammad Atta." *The New Yorker*, April 24, 152.

Coetzee, J.M. (1992). *Doubling the Point. Essays and Interviews*. Ed. David Attwell. Cambridge: Harvard University Press.

— (1998). *Age of Iron*. 1990. New York: Penguin.

— (2000a). *Disgrace*. 1999. London: Vintage.

— (2000b). *Waiting for the Barbarians*. 1980. London: Vintage.

— (2003). *Elizabeth Costello. Eight Lessons*. London: Vintage.

— (2004a). *In the Heart of the Country*. 1977. London: Vintage.

— (2004b). *Life & Times of Michael K*. 1983. London: Vintage.

— (2006). *Slow Man*. 2005. New York: Penguin.

— (2007). *Foe*. 1986. London: Penguin.

Conrad, Joseph (1979). *The Nigger of the "Narcissus"*. 1897. Ed. Robert Kimbrough. New York: Norton.

— (1994). *Lord Jim*. 1900. London: Penguin.

— (2002). *Heart of Darkness and Other Tales*. 1899. Ed. Cedric Thomas Watts, Oxford World's Classics. Oxford: Oxford University Press.

Foer, Jonathan Safran (2006). *Extremely Loud & Incredibly Close*. 2005. London: Penguin.

Forster, E.M. (2000). *A Passage to India*. 1924. Ed. Oliver Stallybrass. London: Penguin.

Haggard, Henry Rider (1989). *King Solomon's Mines*. 1885. Ed. Dennis Butts. Oxford: Oxford University Press.

— (1991). *She*. 1886. Ed. Daniel Karlin. Oxford: Oxford University Press.

— (1995). *Allan Quatermain*. 1887. Ed. Dennis Butts. Oxford: Oxford University Press.

Hamid, Mohsin (2008). *The Reluctant Fundamentalist*. 2007. London: Penguin.

Jordan, Neil (1993). *The Crying Game. An Original Screenplay*. London: Vintage.

Kipling, Rudyard (1987). *Kim*. 1901. Ed. Edward W. Said. London: Penguin.

— (2000). *The Jungle Books*. 1894/1895. Ed. Daniel Karlin. London: Penguin.

— (2001). *Selected Stories*. 1987. Ed. Andrew Rutherford. Harmondsworth: Penguin.

— (2006). *The Complete Verse*. London: Cathie.

Kureishi, Hanif (1999). *The Buddha of Suburbia*. 1990. London: Faber and Faber.

— (2000a). *The Black Album*. 1995. London: Faber and Faber.

— (2000b). *My Beautiful Laundrette*. 1986. London: Faber and Faber.

— (2001). *Intimacy and Midnight All Day: A Novel and Stories*. 1998. New York: Simon and Schuster.

— (2002a). *Dreaming and Scheming. Reflections on Writing and Politics*. London: Faber and Faber.

— (2002b). *Gabriel's Gift*. 2001. London: Faber and Faber.

— (2003). *The Body and Seven Stories*. 2002. London: Faber and Faber.

Le Clézio, Jean-Marie Gustave (2005). *L'Africain*. Paris: Mercure de France.

McEwan, Ian (2006). *Saturday*. 2005. London: Vintage.

Rushdie, Salman (2002). *Fury. A Novel*. 2001. London: Vintage.

— (2006). *Shalimar the Clown. A Novel*. 2005. New York: Random House.

Smith, Zadie (2000). *White Teeth*. London: Penguin.

— (2003). *The Autograph Man*. 2002. London: Penguin.

— (2005). *On Beauty*. London: Hamish Hamilton.

Updike, John (2007). *Terrorist*. 2006. New York: Ballantine Books.

Films

My Beautiful Laundrette (1985). Dir. Frears, Stephen. Screenplay by Hanif Kureishi. Perf. Gordon Warnecke, Daniel Day-Lewis and Roshan Seth. Channel 4 Films/Working Title Films.

The Crying Game (1992). Dir. Jordan, Neil. Screenplay by Neil Jordan. Perf. Stephen Rea, Miranda Richardson, Forest Whitaker and Jaye Davidson. British Screen Productions/Palace.

Sammy and Rosie Get Laid (1987). Dir. Frears, Stephen. Screenplay by Hanif Kureishi. Perf. Ayub Khan-Din, Frances Barber, Shashi Kapoor and Roland Gift. Channel 4 Films/Working Title Films.

Secondary Sources

"History of Race in Science." Eds. Michelle Murphy, Jon Soske and Brian Beaton. History Department, University of Toronto.
<http://www.racesci.org> (accessed 18 September 2006).

The Bible (1998). Authorized King James Version with Apocrypha. Oxford: Oxford University Press.

Aaron, Michele (2004). "The New Queer Spectator." In Michele Aaron (ed.), *New Queer Cinema. A Critical Reader.* New Brunswick: Rutgers University Press, 187–200.

Achebe, Chinua (1977). "An Image of Africa: Racism in Conrad's *Heart of Darkness.*" In *Hopes and Impediments. Selected Essays 1965–1987.* Oxford: Heinemann, 1–13.

Ahmad, Aijaz (1995). "The Politics of Literary Postcoloniality." *Race & Class* 36.3, 1–20.

Aldama, Frederick Luis (2003). *Postethnic Narrative Criticism. Magicorealism in Oscar "Zeta" Acosta, Ana Castillo, Julie Dash, Hanif Kureishi, and Salman Rushdie.* Austin: University of Texas Press.

Appiah, Kwame Anthony (1991). "Is the Post- in Postmodernism the Post- in Postcolonial?" *Critical Inquiry* 17.2, 336–57.

Armstrong, Nancy (2005). "The Polygenetic Imagination." In *How Novels Think. The Limits of British Individualism from 1719–1900.* New York: Columbia University Press, 105–35.

Arndt, Susan (2009). "Whiteness as a Category of Literary Analysis: Racializing Markers and Race-Evasiveness in J. M. Coetzee's *Disgrace.*" In Michael Meyer (ed.), *Word & Image in Colonial and Postcolonial Literatures and Cultures.* Amsterdam: Rodopi, 167–89.

Arondekar, Anjali (2002). "Linerging Pleasures, Perverted Texts: Colonial Desire in Kipling's Anglo-India." In Philip Holden and Richard J. Ruppel (eds.), *Imperial Desire. Dissident Sexualities and Colonial Literature.* Minneapolis: University of Minnesota Press, 65–89.

Ashcroft, Bill, Gareth Griffiths and Helen Tiffin (2002). *The Empire Writes Back. Theory and Practice in Post-Colonial Literatures.* 2nd ed. London: Routledge.

Attridge, Derek (2002). "J.M. Coetzee's *Disgrace*: Introduction." *Interventions* 4.3, 315–20.

— (2004). "Age of Bronze, State of Grace." In *J.M. Coetzee and the Ethics of Reading. Literature in the Event.* Chicago: University of Chicago Press, 162–91.

— (2006). "Against Allegory, *Waiting for the Barbarians, Life & Times of Michael K,* and the Question of Literary Reading." In Jane Poyner (ed.), *J.M. Coetzee and the Idea of the Public Intellectual.* Athens: Ohio University Press, 63–82.

Attwell, David (1993). *J.M. Coetzee. South Africa and the Politics of Writing.* Berkeley: University of California Press.

— (2002). "Race in *Disgrace.*" *Interventions* 4.3, 331–41.

Azoulay, Ariella (2002). "An Alien Woman/A Permitted Woman: on J.M. Coetzee's *Disgrace.*" *Scrutiny2: Issues in English Studies in Southern Africa* 7.2, 33–41.

Bakhtin, Mikhail Mikhailovich (1994). *The Dialogic Imagination. Four Essays.* 1981. Ed. Michael Holquist. Trans. Caryl Emerson and Michael Holquist. 9th ed. Austin: University of Texas Press.

Ball, John Clement (1996). "The Semi-Detached Metropolis: Hanif Kureishi's London." *Ariel* 27.4, 7–27.

— (2004). "London Centre: The Familial Urban World of Recent 'Black British' Writing." *Imagining London. Postcolonial Fiction and the Transnational Metropolis.* Toronto: University of Toronto Press, 222–45.

Banerjee, Mita (2007). "Postethnicity and Postcommunism in Hanif Kureishi's *Gabriel's Gift* and Salman Rushdie's *Fury*." In Joel Kuortti and Jopi Nyman (eds.), *Reconstructing Hybridity. Post-Colonial Studies in Transition.* Amsterdam: Rodopi, 309–24.

— (2008). "'Whiteness of a Different Color'? Racial Profiling in John Updike's *Terrorist*." *Neohelicon* XXXV.2, 13–28.

Barber, Susan Torrey (2006). "Insurmountable Difficulties and Moments of Ecstasy: Crossing Class, Ethnic and Sexual Barriers in the Films of Stephen Frears." In Lester D. Friedman (ed.), *Fires Were Started. British Cinema and Thatcherism.* 2nd ed. London: Wallflower, 209–22.

Barnard, Rita (2002). "Coetzee's Country Ways." *Interventions* 4.3, 384–94.

Barthes, Roland (1994). *Camera Lucida. Reflections on Photography.* Ed. Richard Howard. 15th ed. New York: Hill and Wang.

Bate, David (1993). "Photography and the Colonial Vision." *Third Text* 7.22, 81–91.

Beer, Gillian (1983). *Darwin's Plots. Evolutionary Narrative in Darwin, George Eliot and Nineteenth-Century Fiction.* London: Routledge.

Behdad, Ali (1994). "Colonial Narrative and Its Discontents." *Victorian Literature and Culture* 22, 233–48.

Bennett, Tony (1988). "The Exhibitionary Complex." *New Formations* 4, 73–102.

Bentley, Nick (2007). "Re-writing Englishness. Imagining the Nation in Julian Barnes's *England, England* and Zadie Smith's *White Teeth*." *Textual Practice* 21.3, 483–504.

Berger, Maurice, Brian Wallis and Simon Watson (eds.) (1996). *Constructing Masculinity.* New York: Routledge.

Bernal, Martin (1987). *Black Athena. The Afroasiatic Roots of Classical Civilization.* Vol. 1. The Fabrication of Ancient Greece 1785–1985. New Brunswick: Rutgers University Press.

Bethlehem, Louise (2002). "Pliant/Compliant; Grace/*Disgrace*; Plaint/Complaint." *Scrutiny2: Issues in English Studies in Southern Africa* 7.2, 20–24.

Bhabha, Homi K. (ed.) (1990). *Nation and Narration.* London: Routledge.

— (1994). *The Location of Culture.* London: Routledge.

— (1995). "Cultural Diversity and Cultural Differences." In Bill Ashcroft, Gareth Griffiths and Helen Tiffin (eds.), *The Postcolonial Studies Reader.* London: Taylor & Francis, 206–09.

Boehmer, Elleke (2002). "Not Saying Sorry, Not Speaking Pain: Gender Implications in *Disgrace*." *Interventions* 4.3, 342–51.

— (2005). *Colonial and Postcolonial Literature. Migrant Metaphors.* 2nd ed. Oxford: Oxford University Press.

— (2006). "Sorry, Sorrier, Sorriest. The Gendering of Contrition in J.M. Coetzee's *Disgrace.*" In Jane Poyner (ed.), *J.M. Coetzee and the Idea of the Public Intellectual.* Athens: Ohio University Press, 135–47.

— (2007). "Postcolonial Writing and Terror." *Wasafiri* 22.2, 4–7.

Böhner, Ines Karin (1996). *My Beautiful Laundrette und Sammy and Rosie Get Laid. Filmische Reflexion von Identitätsprozessen.* Frankfurt am Main: Lang.

Boletsi, Maria (2007). "Barbaric Encounters: Rethinking Barbarism in C.P. Cavafy's and J.M. Coetzee's *Waiting for the Barbarians.*" *Comparative Literature Studies* 44.1–2, 67–95.

Booker, M. Keith (1997). *Colonial Power, Colonial Texts. India in the Modern British Novel.* Ann Arbor: University of Michigan Press.

Bordo, Susan (1993). *Unbearable Weight. Feminism, Western Culture, and the Body.* Berkeley: University of California Press.

— (1999). *The Male Body. A New Look at Men in Public and in Private.* New York: Farrar, Straus and Giroux.

Bourdieu, Pierre (2001). *Masculine Domination.* Trans. Richard Nice. Cambridge: Polity Press.

Bowler, Peter J. (1992). *The Eclipse of Darwinism. Anti-Darwinian Evolution Theories in the Decades Around 1900.* Baltimore: Johns Hopkins University Press.

Brah, Avtar and Annie E. Coombes (eds.) (2000). *Hybridity and Its Discontents. Politics, Science, Culture.* London: Routledge.

Braidt, Andrea B. (1999). "Geschlechterkonstruktion im Film: Kritische Anmerkungen zum angloamerikanischen Blickparadigma." In Sieglinde Klettenhammer and Elfriede Pöder (eds.), *Das Geschlecht, das sich (un)eins ist? Frauenforschung und Geschlechtergeschichte in den Kulturwissenschaften.* Innsbruck: Studienverlag, 163–73.

Brantlinger, Patrick (1988). *Rule of Darkness. British Literature and Imperialism, 1830–1914.* Ithaca: Cornell University Press.

Braun, Christina von (2001). "Technische Bilder: Photographie." In *Versuch über den Schwindel. Religion, Schrift, Bild, Geschlecht.* Zürich: Pendo, 220–26.

Breger, Claudia (2001). "Queering Macho-Identities? Roman- und Filmanalysen aus der Perspektive angloamerikanischer Männlichkeitsforschung." In Annette Jael Lehmann (ed.), *Un/Sichtbarkeiten der Differenz. Beiträge zur Genderdebatte in den Künsten.* Tübingen: Stauffenburg, 119–43.

— (2005). "Orientalische Landschaften – imperialistische Praktiken des Selbst. Askese und Verausgabung in der europäischen Literatur um 1900." In Irmela Marei Krüger-Fürhoff and Tanja Nusser (eds.), *Askese. Geschlecht und Geschichte der Selbstdisziplinierung.* Bielefeld: Aisthesis, 71–91.

Bristow, Joseph (1991). *Empire Boys. Adventures in a Man's World.* London: Unwin Hyman.

Bronfen, Elisabeth, Benjamin Marius and Therese Steffen (eds.) (1997). *Hybride Kulturen. Beiträge zur anglo-amerikanischen Multikulturalismusdebatte.* Trans. Anne Emmert and Josef Raab. Tübingen: Stauffenburg.

Brook, Susan (2005). "Hedgemony? Suburban Space in *The Buddha of Suburbia.*" In Nick Bentley (ed.), *British Fiction of the 1990s.* Oxon: Routledge, 209–25.

Brown, Judith M. and William Roger Louis (eds.) (1999). *The Twentieth Century. The Oxford History of the British Empire.* Oxford: Oxford University Press.

Brown, Richard (2008). "Politics, the Domestic and the Uncanny Effects of the Everyday in Ian McEwan's *Saturday.*" *Critical Survey* 20.1, 80–93.

Brown, Wendy (1987). "The Impossiblility of Women's Studies." *Differences* 9.3, 79–101.

Bruffee, Kenneth A. (1983). *Elegiac Romance. Cultural Change and Loss of the Hero in Modern Fiction.* Ithaca: Cornell University Press.

Buchanan, Bradley (2007). *Hanif Kureishi.* Basingstoke: Palgrave Macmillan.

Butler, Judith (1993). *Bodies That Matter. On the Discursive Limits of "Sex".* New York: Routledge.

— (1997). *Excitable Speech. A Politics of the Performative.* New York: Routledge.

— (1999). *Gender Trouble. Feminism and the Subversion of Identity.* 10th anniversary ed. New York: Routledge.

— (2004). *Undoing Gender.* New York: Routledge.

Butler, Judith, Ernesto Laclau and Slavoj Žižek (eds.) (2000). *Contingency, Hegemony, Universality. Contemporary Dialogues on the Left.* London: Verso.

Campbell-Hall, Devon (2009). "Renegotiating the Asian-British Domestic Community in Recent Fiction." *Journal of Postcolonial Writing* 45.2, 171–79.

Canepari-Labib, Michela (2005). *Old Myths – Modern Empires. Power, Language, and Identity in J.M. Coetzee's Work.* Oxford: Lang.

Casarino, Cesare (2002). *Modernity at Sea. Melville, Marx, Conrad in Crisis.* Minneapolis: University of Minnesota Press.

Castro Varela, María do Mar and Nikita Dhawan (2005). *Postkoloniale Theorie. Eine kritische Einführung.* Bielefeld: transcript.

Cawelti, John G. (1976). *Adventure, Mystery, and Romance. Formula Stories as Art and Popular Culture.* Chicago: University of Chicago Press.

Childs, Elaine (2006). "Insular Utopias and Religious Neuroses. Hybridity Anxiety in Zadie Smith's *White Teeth.*" *Proteus* 23.1, 7–12.

Childs, Peter (2000). *Modernism.* London: Routledge.

— (2007). *Modernism and the Post-Colonial. Literature and Empire 1885–1930.* London: Continuum.

Childs, Peter, Jean Jacques Weber and Patrick Williams (2006). *Post-Colonial Theory and Literatures. African, Caribbean and South Asian.* Trier: WVT.

Christensen, Tim (2006). "Racial Fantasy in Joseph Conrad's *Nigger of the 'Narcissus'.*" *Ariel* 37.1, 27–43.

Christian, Barbara (1988). "The Race for Theory." *Feminist Studies* 14.1, 67–79.

Clifford, James (1988). "On Ethnographic Self-Fashioning: Conrad and Malinowski." In *The Predicament of Culture. Twentieth-Century Ethnography, Literature, and Art.* Cambridge: Harvard University Press, 92–113.

Cohen, Cathy J. (2005). "Punks, Bulldaggers, and Welfare Queens: The Radical Potential of Queer Politics?" In E. Patrick Johnson and Mae G. Henderson (eds.), *Black Queer Studies. A Critical Anthology.* Durham: Duke University Press, 21–51.

Cohen, Morton (1960). *Rider Haggard. His Life and Works.* London: Hutchinson.

— (ed.) (1965). *Rudyard Kipling to Rider Haggard. The Record of a Friendship.* London: Hutchinson.

Collins, Patricia Hill (1999). "Moving beyond Gender. Intersectionality and Scientific Knowledge." In Myra Marx Ferree, Judith Lorber and Beth B. Hess (eds.), *Revisioning Gender.* Thousand Oaks: Sage, 261–84.

Collits, Terry (2005). *Postcolonial Conrad. Paradoxes of Empire.* London: Routledge.

Combahee River Collective (1981). "A Black Feminist Statement." In Cherríe Moraga and Gloria Anzaldúa (eds.), *This Bridge Called My Back. Writings by Radical Women of Color.* New York: Kitchen Table: Women of Color Press, 210–18.

Connell, R.W. (1995). *Masculinities.* Cambridge: Polity Press.

Connell, R.W. and James W. Messerschmidt (2005). "Hegemonic Masculinity: Rethinking the Concept." *Gender & Society* 19.6, 829–59.

Coombes, Annie E. (1994). "The Recalcitrant Object. Culture Contact and the Question of Hybridity." In Francis Barker, Peter Hulme and Margaret Iversen (eds.), *Colonial Discourse/Postcolonial Theory.* Manchester: Manchester University Press, 89–114.

Crenshaw, Kimberlé Williams (1997). "Mapping the Margins. Intersectionality and Identity Politics. Learning from Violence Against Women of Color." In Mary Lyndon Shanley and Uma Narayan (eds.), *Reconstructing Political Theory. Feminist Perspectives.* London: Pennsylvania State University Press, 178–93.

Cruz-Malave, Arnaldo and Martin F. Manalansan VI (eds.) (2002). *Queer Globalizations. Citizenship and the Afterlife of Colonialism.* New York: New York University Press.

Cuder-Domínguez, Pilar (2004). "Ethnic Cartographies of London in Bernadine Evaristo and Zadie Smith." *European Journal of English Studies* 8.2, 173–88.

Dahlman, Carl (2002). "Masculinity in Conflict: Geopolitics and Performativity in *The Crying Game.*" In Tim Cresswell and Deborah Dixon (eds.), *Engaging Film. Geographies of Mobility and Identity.* Lanham: Rowman & Littlefield, 123–39.

Dalleo, Raphael (2008). "Colonization in Reverse: *White Teeth* as Caribbean Novel." In Tracey L. Walters (ed.), *Zadie Smith. Critical Essays.* New York: Lang, 91–104.

Daly, Nicholas (1999). *Modernism, Romance and the Fin de Siècle. Popular Fiction and British Culture, 1880–1914.* Cambridge: Cambridge University Press.

Darwin, Charles (1985). *The Origin of Species by Means of Natural Selection or the Preservation of Favoured Races in the Struggle for Life.* 1859. Ed. John W. Burrow. London: Penguin.

—   (2004). *The Descent of Man, and Selection in Relation to Sex.* 1871. Eds. James Moore and Adrian Desmond. London: Penguin.

Dawson, Ashley (2007). "Genetics, Biotechnology, and the Future of 'Race' in Zadie Smith's *White Teeth.*" In *Mongrel Nation. Diasporic Culture and the Making of Postcolonial Britain.* Ann Arbor: University of Michigan Press, 149–73.

Dawson, Graham (1994). *Soldier Heroes. British Adventure, Empire and the Imagining of Masculinities.* London: Routledge.

De Lange, Attie and Gail Fincham (eds.) (2002). *Conrad in Africa. New Essays on "Heart of Darkness".* Boulder: Social Science Monographs.

De Lauretis, Teresa (1987). *Technologies of Gender. Essays on Theory, Film, and Fiction.* Bloomington: Indiana University Press.

Degabriele, Maria (1999). "Prince of Darkness Meets Priestess of Porn: Sexual and Political Identities in Hanif Kureishi's *The Black Album.*" *Intersections. Gender, History & Culture in the Asian Context* 2, <http://wwwsshe.murdoch.edu.au/intersections/issue2/Kureishi.html> (accessed 20 August 2006).

DeKoven, Marianne (2009). "Going to the Dogs in *Disgrace.*" *ELH* 76.4, 847–75.

Dietze, Gabriele (2001). "Race Class Gender. Differenzen und Interdependenzen am amerikanischen Beispiel." *Die Philosophin* 23, 30–49.

—   (2006). "‚I had a Farm in Africa…'. Karen Blixen und Kolonialität." Paper presented at *Ringvorlesung: 120 Jahre Karen Blixen – Kulturwissenschaftliche Perspektive auf eine dänische Ikone.* Humboldt-Universität zu Berlin, Germany, December 5.

—   (2011). *Weiße Frauen in Bewegung. Genealogien und Konkurrenzen von Race- und Genderpolitiken.* Bielefeld: transcript (in press).

Dietze, Gabriele, Elahe Haschemi Yekani and Beatrice Michaelis (2007). "‚Checks and Balances.' Zum Verhältnis von Intersektionalität und Queer Theory." In Katharina Walgenbach, et al. *Gender als interdependente Kategorie. Neue Perspektiven auf Intersektionalität, Diversität und Heterogenität.* Opladen: Budrich, 107–39.

Dinges, Martin (ed.) (2005). *Männer – Macht – Körper. Hegemoniale Männlichkeiten vom Mittelalter bis heute.* Frankfurt am Main: Campus.

Dixon, Robert (1995). *Writing the Colonial Adventure. Race, Gender and Nation in Anglo-Australian Popular Fiction, 1875–1914.* Cambridge: Cambridge University Press.

Doane, Mary Ann (1991). *Femmes Fatales. Feminism, Film Theory, Psychoanalysis.* London: Routledge.

Dovey, Teresa (1988). *The Novels of J.M. Coetzee. Lacanian Allegories.* Craighall: Ad. Donker.

—   (1996). "*Waiting for the Barbarians*: Allegory of Allegories." In Graham Huggan and Stephen Watson (eds.), *Critical Perspectives on J.M. Coetzee.* Basingstoke: Macmillan, 138–51.

Dryden, Linda (2000). *Joseph Conrad and the Imperial Romance.* Basingstoke: Macmillan.

Du Gay, Paul and Stuart Hall (eds.) (1996). *Questions of Cultural Identity.* London: Sage.

Durrant, Sam (2004). "Speechless Before Apartheid: J.M. Coetzee's Inconsolable Works of Mourning." In *Postcolonial Narrative and the Work of Mourning. J.M. Coetzee, Wilson Harris, and Toni Morrison*. Albany: State University of New York Press, 23–51.

Dyer, Richard (1997). *White*. London: Routledge.

Eaglestone, Robert (2007). "'The Age of Reason is Over ... an Age of Fury was Dawning': Contemporary Anglo-American Fiction and Terror." *Wasafiri* 22.2, 19–22.

Eagleton, Terry (1995). *Criticism and Ideology. A Study in Marxist Literary Theory*. 1978 9th ed. London: Verso.

Easton, Kai (2006). "J.M. Coetzee's *Disgrace*: Reading Race/Reading Scandal." In Jago Morrison (ed.), *Scandalous Fictions. The Twentieth-Century Novel in the Public Sphere*. Basingstoke: Palgrave Macmillan, 187–205.

— (2007). "Coetzee's *Disgrace*: Byron in Italy and the Eastern Cape c. 1820." *The Journal of Commonwealth Literature* 42.3, 113–30.

Eckstein, Barbara (1989). "The Body, the Word, and the State: J.M. Coetzee's *Waiting for the Barbarians*." *Novel* 22.2, 175–98.

Edwards, Elizabeth (1992). "Introduction." In Elizabeth Edwards (ed.), *Anthropology and Photography, 1860–1920*. New Haven: Yale University Press in Association with the Royal Anthropological Institute, 3–17.

Elkins, James (1997). *The Object Stares Back. On the Nature of Seeing*. San Diego: Harcourt Brace.

Ellis, Juniper (1995). "Writing Race: Education and Ethnography in Kipling's *Kim*." *Centennial Review* 39.2, 315–29.

Erhart, Walter (2001). *Familienmänner. Über den literarischen Ursprung moderner Männlichkeit*. Munich: Fink.

— (2005). "Das zweite Geschlecht: ‚Männlichkeit', interdisziplinär." *Internationales Archiv für Sozialgeschichte der deutschen Literatur* 30.2, 156–232.

Etherington, Norman (1984). *Rider Haggard*. Boston: Twayne.

— (ed.) (2005). *Missions and Empire*. Oxford: Oxford University Press.

Evans, Caroline and Loraine Gamman (1995). "The Gaze Revisited, or Reviewing Queer Viewing." In Paul Burston and Colin Richardson (eds.), *A Queer Romance. Lesbians, Gay Men and Popular Culture*. New York: Routledge, 13–56.

Falconer, John (2001). *India: Pioneering Photographers, 1850–1900*. London: The British Library and The Howard and Jane Ricketts Collection.

Fanon, Frantz (1967). *Black Skin, White Masks*. Trans. Charles Lam Markmann. New York: Grove Press.

Farred, Grant (2002a). "The Mundanacity of Violence. Living In A State Of Disgrace." *Interventions* 4.3, 352–62.

— (2002b). "Back to the Borderlines: Thinking Race *Disgrace*fully." *Scrutiny2: Issues in English Studies in Southern Africa* 7.2, 16–19.

Fausto-Sterling, Anne (1995). "Gender, Race, and Nation. The Comparative Anatomy of 'Hottentot' Women in Europe: 1815–1817." In Jennifer Terry and

Jacqueline Urla (eds.), *Deviant Bodies. Critical Perspectives on Difference in Science and Popular Culture*. Bloomington: Indiana University Press, 19–48.

— (2000). *Sexing the Body. Gender Politics and the Construction of Sexuality*. New York: Basic Books.

Ferguson, Roderick A. (2004). *Aberrations in Black. Toward a Queer of Color Critique*. Minneapolis: University of Minnesota Press.

— (2005). "Racing Homonormativity. Citizenship, Sociology and Gay Identity." In E. Patrick Johnson and Mae Henderson (eds.), *Black Queer Studies. A Critical Anthology*. Durham: Duke University Press, 52–67.

Ferris, Ina (1994). "Thackeray and the Ideology of the Gentleman." In John Richetti (ed.), *The Columbia History of the British Novel*. New York: Columbia University Press, 407–28.

Finney, Brian (2006). "Hanif Kureishi: *The Buddha of Suburbia* (1990)." In *English Fiction since 1984. Narrating a Nation*. Basingstoke: Palgrave Macmillan, 124–38.

Fludernik, Monika (1998). "The Constitution of Hybridity: Postcolonial Interventions." In Monika Fludernik (ed.), *Hybridity and Postcolonialism. Twentieth Century Indian Literature*. Tübingen: Stauffenburg, 19–53.

— (2000). "Beyond Structuralism in Narratology: Recent Developments and New Horizons in Narrative Theory." *Anglistik* 11.1, 83–96.

— (2001). "New Wine in Old Bottles? Voice, Focalization, and New Writing." *New Literary History* 32.3, 619–38.

Förschler, Silke (2005). "Die orientalische Frau aus der hellen Kammer. Zur kolonialen Postkarte." In Graduiertenkolleg Identität und Differenz (ed.), *Ethnizität und Geschlecht. (Post-)koloniale Verhandlungen in Geschichte, Kunst und Medien*. Cologne: Böhlau, 77–94.

Forster, Edgar J. (1998). *Unmännliche Männlichkeit: Melancholie, „Geschlecht", Verausgabung*. Vienna: Böhlau.

Foucault, Michel (1980). "The History of Sexuality. Interview with Lucette Finas." In Colin Gordon (ed.), *Power/Knowledge. Selected Interviews and Other Writings 1972–1977*. New York: Pantheon Books, 183–93.

— (1991). "Faire vivre et laisser mourir: la naissance du racisme." *Les Temps Modernes* 46.535, 37–61.

— (1994). *Überwachen und Strafen. Die Geburt des Gefängnisses*. 1975. Frankfurt am Main: Suhrkamp.

— (1998). *The Will to Knowledge*. The History of Sexuality. Vol. 1. 1976. Trans. Robert Hurley. London: Penguin.

— (2002). *Archaeology of Knowledge*. 1972 (French: 1969). Trans. A.M. Sheridan Smith. London: Routledge.

Frank, Michael C. (2006). *Kulturelle Einflussangst. Inszenierungen der Grenze in der Reiseliteratur des 19. Jahrhunderts*. Bielefeld: transcript.

Frankenberg, Ruth and Lata Mani (1996). "Crosscurrents, Crosstalk: Race, 'Postcoloniality' and the Politics of Location." In Padmini Mongia (ed.), *Contemporary Postcolonial Theory. A Reader*. London: Arnold, 347–64.

Franzen, Jannik (2002). "Grenzgänge: Judith ‚Jack' Halberstam und C. Jacob Hale. Weibliche Maskulinität, Transmänner und die Frage nach Bündnissen." In polymorph (ed.), *(K)ein Geschlecht oder viele? Transgender in politischer Perspektive*. Berlin: Querverlag, 69–91.

Fraser, Robert (1998). *Victorian Quest Romance. Stevenson, Haggard, Kipling, and Conan Doyle*. Plymouth: Northcote House.

Friedman, Lester and Scott Stewart (1994). "Keeping His Own Voice. An Interview with Stephen Frears." In Wheeler W. Dixon (ed.), *Re-Viewing British Cinema, 1900–1992. Essays and Interviews*. Albany: State University of New York Press, 221–40.

Frye, Northrop (1973). *Anatomy of Criticism. Four Essays*. 3rd ed. Princeton: Princeton University Press.

Gaines, Jane (1988). "White Privilege and Looking Relations. Race and Gender in Feminist Film Theory." *Screen* 29.4, 12–29.

Gallagher, Susan VanZanten (1991). *A Story of South Africa. J.M. Coetzee's Fiction in Context*. Cambridge: Harvard University Press.

Gallix, François (ed.) (1997). *The Buddha of Suburbia. Hanif Kureishi*. C.A.P.E.S. Agrégation Anglais. Paris: Ellipses.

Genette, Gérard (1980). *Narrative Discourse. An Essay in Method*. Ithaca: Cornell University Press.

George, Rosemary Marangoly (1996). "The Great English Tradition: Joseph Conrad Writes Home." In *The Politics of Home. Postcolonial Relocations and Twentieth-Century Fiction*. Cambridge: Cambridge University Press, 65–99.

Gestrich, Constanze (2008). *Die Macht der dunklen Kammern. Die Faszination des Fremden im frühen dänischen Kino*. Berlin: Nordeuropa-Institut der Humboldt-Universität zu Berlin.

Ghose, Sheila (2007). "Brit Bomber: The Fundamentalist Trope in Hanif Kureishi's *The Black Album* and 'My Son the Fanatic'." In Graham MacPhee and Prem Poddar (eds.), *Empire and After. Englishness in Postcolonial Perspective*. New York: Berghahn, 121–38.

Gikandi, Simon (1996). *Maps of Englishness. Writing Identity in the Culture of Colonialism*. New York: Columbia University Press.

Gilbert, Sandra M. and Susan Gubar (1989). "*Heart of Darkness*: The Agon of the Femme Fatale; Home Rule: The Colonies of the New Woman." In *No Man's Land. The Place of the Woman Writer in the Twentieth Century*. Vol. II. Sexchanges. New Haven: Yale University Press, 3–82.

Giles, Jane (1997). *The Crying Game*. London: British Film Institute.

Gillet, Robert (2003). "Learning to Look Askance. Explaining Queer Through Film." *Moderna Språk* XCVII.2, 147–65.

Gilmore, David D. (1990). *Manhood in the Making. Cultural Concepts of Masculinity*. New Haven: Yale University Press.

Gilroy, Paul (1987). *There Ain't No Black in the Union Jack. The Cultural Politics of Race and Nation*. London: Hutchinson.

— (1993). *The Black Atlantic. Modernity and Double Consciousness.* Cambridge: Harvard University Press.

— (1999). "A London sumting dis ..." *Critical Quarterly* 41.3, 57–69.

— (2005). *Postcolonial Melancholia.* New York: Columbia University Press.

Glawion, Sven, Elahe Haschemi Yekani and Jana Husmann-Kastein (eds.) (2007). *Erlöser. Figurationen männlicher Hegemonie.* Bielefeld: transcript.

Goddard, Kevin and John Read (1990). *J.M. Coetzee. A Bibliography.* Grahamstown: National English Literary Museum.

Goldberg, David Theo (ed.) (1990). *Anatomy of Racism.* Minneapolis: University of Minnesota Press.

Gopinath, Gayatri (2005). *Impossible Desires. Queer Diasporas and South Asian Public Cultures.* Durham: Duke University Press.

Gould, Stephen Jay (1996). *The Mismeasure of Man.* Rev. and expanded ed. New York: Norton.

Graham, Lucy (2002). "'Yes, I am giving him up': Sacrificial Responsibility and Likeness with Dogs in J.M.Coetzee's Recent Fiction." *Scrutiny2: Issues in English Studies in Southern Africa* 7.2, 4–15.

Gramsci, Antonio (2005). *Selections from the Prison Notebooks of Antonio Gramsci.* 1971. Eds. Quintin Hoare and Geoffrey Nowell Smith. Trans. Quintin Hoare and Geoffrey Nowell Smith. New York: International Publishers.

Green, Martin (1980). *Dreams of Adventure, Deeds of Empire.* London: Routledge & Kegan Paul.

Grist, Leighton (2003). "'It's Only a Piece of Meat': Gender Ambiguity, Sexuality, and Politics in *The Crying Game* and *M. Butterfly.*" *Cinema Journal* 42.4, 3–28.

Grosz, Elizabeth (1994). *Volatile Bodies. Toward a Corporeal Feminism.* Bloomington: Indiana University Press.

— (1999). "Darwin and Feminism. Preliminary Investigations for a Possible Alliance." *Australian Feminist Studies* 14.29, 31–45.

Guérard, Albert Joseph (1958). *Conrad the Novelist.* Cambridge: Harvard University Press.

Gymnich, Marion (1996). "Von *Greater Britain* zu *Little England*: Konstruktion und Dekonstruktion imperialistischer Denkweisen in Rudyard Kiplings *Kim*, E.M. Forsters *A Passage to India* und Joseph Conrads *Heart of Darkness.*" In Ansgar Nünning and Vera Nünning (eds.), *Intercultural Studies. Fictions of Empire.* Heidelberg: Winter, 149–66.

Ha, Kien Nghi (2005). *Hype um Hybridität. Kultureller Differenzkonsum und postmoderne Verwertungstechniken im Spätkapitalismus.* Bielefeld: transcript.

Hagiioannu, Andrew (2003). *The Man Who Would Be Kipling. The Colonial Fiction and the Frontiers of Exile.* Basingstoke: Palgrave Macmillan.

Halberstam, Judith (1998). *Female Masculinity.* Durham: Duke University Press.

— (2005). *In a Queer Time and Place. Transgender Bodies, Subcultural Lives.* New York: New York University Press.

Hall, Stuart (1996a). "Gramsci's Relevance for the Study of Race and Ethnicity." In David Morley and Kuan-Hsing Chen (eds.), *Stuart Hall. Critical Dialogues in Cultural Studies.* London: Routledge, 411–40.

— (1996b). "Cultural Identity and Diaspora." In Padmini Mongia (ed.), *Contemporary Post-Colonial Theory. A Reader.* London: Arnold, 110–22.

— (1996c). "New Ethnicities." In David Morley and Kuan-Hsing Chen (eds.), *Stuart Hall. Critical Dialogues in Cultural Studies.* London: Routledge, 441–49.

— (1997a). "The Spectacle of the 'Other'." In Stuart Hall (ed.), *Representation. Cultural Representations and Signifying Practices.* London: Sage, 223–90.

— (1997b). "The Local and the Global: Globalization and Ethnicity." In Anne McClintock, Aamir Mufti and Ella Shohat (eds.), *Dangerous Liaisons. Gender, Nation, and Postcolonial Perspectives.* Minneapolis: University of Minnesota Press, 173–87.

— (1997c). "Old and New Identities, Old and New Ethnicities." In Anthony D. King (ed.), *Culture, Globalization and the World-System. Contemporary Conditions for the Representation of Identity.* Minneapolis: University of Minnesota Press, 41–68.

— (1999). "Thinking the Diaspora: Home-Thoughts from Abroad." *Small Axe* 6, 1–18.

— (2005). "Notes on Deconstructing 'the Popular'." In Raiford Guins and Omayra Zaragoza Cruz (eds.), *Popular Culture. A Reader.* London: Sage, 64–71.

Halperin, David M. (2000). "How to Do the History of Male Homosexuality." *GLQ* 6.1, 87–124.

Hammond, Andrew (2007). "The Hybrid State: Hanif Kureishi and Thatcher's Britain." In Joel Kuortti and Jopi Nyman (eds.), *Reconstructing Hybridity. Post-Colonial Studies in Transition.* Amsterdam: Rodopi, 221–40.

Handler, Kristin (1994). "Sexing *The Crying Game.* Difference, Identity, Ethics." *Film Quarterly* 4.3, 31–42.

Haraway, Donna J. (1991). *Simians, Cyborgs and Women. The Reinvention of Nature.* New York: Routledge.

Harding, Sandra G. (1986). *The Science Question in Feminism.* Ithaca: Cornell University Press.

— (1991). *Whose Science? Whose Knowledge? Thinking from Women's Lives.* Ithaca: Cornell University Press.

— (ed.) (1993). *The "Racial" Economy of Science. Toward a Democratic Future.* Bloomington: Indiana University Press.

— (1998). *Is Science Multicultural? Postcolonialisms, Feminisms, and Epistemologies.* Bloomington: Indiana University Press.

Harris, Brent (1998). "Photography in Colonial Discourse: The Making of 'the Other' in Southern Africa, c. 1850–1950." In Wolfram Hartmann, Jeremy Silvester and Patricia Hayes (eds.), *The Colonising Camera. Photographs in the Making of Namibian History.* Cape Town: University of Cape Town Press, 20–24.

Haschemi Yekani, Elahe and Beatrice Michaelis (eds.) (2005). *Quer durch die Geisteswissenschaften. Perspektiven der Queer Theory.* Berlin: Querverlag.

Haschemi Yekani, Elahe (2007a). "'Who's the Fanatic now?' – Father-and-Son Conflicts in *My Son the Fanatic* and *East is East*." *kritische berichte* 35.4, 78–87.

— (2007b). "Transgender-Begehren im Blick: Männliche Weiblichkeiten als Spektakel im Film." In Robin Bauer, Josch Hoenes and Volker Woltersdorff (eds.), *Unbeschreiblich Männlich. Heteronormativitätskritische Perspektiven.* Hamburg: Männerschwarm Verlag, 264–78.

— (2007c). "'Enlightened Imperialism' – Der englische Gentleman-Hero als Erlös(t)er." In Sven Glawion, Elahe Haschemi Yekani and Jana Husmann-Kastein (eds.), *Erlöser. Figurationen männlicher Hegemonie.* Bielefeld: transcript, 97–109.

— (2008). "'I am often considered to be a funny kind of Englishman.' Identitätssuche zwischen queerer Polyphonie und männlicher Rezentrierung in Hanif Kureishis *The Buddha of Suburbia*." In Anna Babka and Susanne Hochreiter (eds.), *Queer Reading in den Philologien – Modelle und Anwendungen.* Göttingen: V & R unipress, 107–22.

Haschemi Yekani, Elahe, et al. (2008). "Where, When and How? Contextualizing Intersectionality." In Dorota Golańska and Aleksandra M. Różalska (eds.), *New Subjectivities. Negotiating Citizenship in the Context of Migration and Diversity.* Łódź: University of Łódź Publishing House, 19–47.

Haschemi Yekani, Elahe, Beatrice Michaelis and Gabriele Dietze (2010). "'Try Again. Fail Again. Fail Better.' Queer Interdependencies as Corrective Methodologies." In Yvette Taylor, Sally Hines and Mark E. Casey (eds.), *Theorizing Intersectionality and Sexuality.* Basingstoke: Palgrave Macmillan, 78–98.

Hawley, John C. (ed.) (2001). *Postcolonial and Queer Theories. Intersections and Essays,* Contributions to the Study of World Literature. Westport: Greenwood Press.

Hawthorn, Jeremy (1992). *Joseph Conrad. Narrative Technique and Ideological Commitment.* London: Arnold.

Head, Dominic (1997). *J.M. Coetzee.* Cambridge: Cambridge University Press.

— (2003). "Zadie Smith's *White Teeth*: Multiculturalism for the Millenium." In Richard J. Lane, Rod Mengham and Philip Tew (eds.), *Contemporary British Fiction.* Cambridge Polity Press, 106–19.

Helgesson, Stefan (2004). *Writing in Crisis. Ethics and History in Gordimer, Ndebele and Coetzee.* Scottsville: University of Kwazulu-Natal Press.

Heller, Tamar (2007). "The Unbearable Hybridity of Female Sexuality: Racial Ambiguity and the Gothic in Rider Haggard's *She*." In Ruth Bienstock Anolik (ed.), *Horrifying Sex. Essays on Sexual Difference in Gothic Literature.* Jefferson: McFarland, 55–66.

Hennessy, Rosemary (2000). "Sexual Alibis, Colonial Displacements. Materializing Myth in *The Crying Game*." In *Profit and Pleasure. Sexual Identities in Late Capitalism.* New York: Routledge, 143–74.

Henthorne, Tom (2008). *Conrad's Trojan Horses. Imperialism, Hybridity, & the Postcolonial Aesthetic.* Lubbock: Texas Tech University Press.

Hentschel, Linda (2001). *Pornotopische Techniken des Betrachtens. Raumwahrnehmung und Geschlechterordnung in visuellen Apparaten der Moderne.* Marburg: Jonas-Verlag.

Herman, David (ed.) (2007). *The Cambridge Companion to Narrative*. Cambridge: Cambridge University Press.

Hershkowitz, Robert (1980). *The British Photographer Abroad. The First Thirty Years*. London: Robert Hershokowitz Ltd.

Hever, Hannan (2002). "Facing *Disgrace*: Coetzee and the Israeli Intellectual." *Scrutiny2: Issues in English Studies in Southern Africa* 7.2, 42–46.

Hight, Eleanor M. and Gary D. Sampson (eds.) (2002). *Colonialist Photography. Imag(in)ing Race and Place*. London: Routledge.

Hillard, Molly Clark (2008). "'When Desert Armies Stand Ready to Fight': Re-Reading McEwan's *Saturday* and Arnold's 'Dover Beach'." *Partial Answers: Journal of Literature and the History of Ideas* 6.1, 181–206.

Hobsbawm, Eric J. (1989). *The Age of Empire. 1875–1914*. New York: Vintage.

Hoch, Paul (1979). *White Hero, Black Beast. Racism, Sexism and the Mask of Masculinity*. London: Pluto Press.

Holland, Michael (2002). "'Plink-Plunk' Unforgetting the Present in Coetzee's *Disgrace*." *Interventions* 4.3, 395–404.

hooks, bell (1990). "Stylish Nihilism: Race, Sex, and Class at the Movies." In *Yearning. Race, Gender, and Cultural Politics*. Boston: South End Press, 155–63.

— (1992). *Black Looks. Race and Representation*. Boston: South End Press.

Horrell, Georgina (2002). "J.M. Coetzee's *Disgrace*: One Settler, One Bullet and the 'New South Africa'." *Scrutiny2: Issues in English Studies in Southern Africa* 7.2, 25–32.

— (2008). "(White) Women and (White) Guilt in the 'New' South Africa." In Merete Falck Borch, et al. (eds.), *Bodies and Voices. The Force-Field of Representation and Discourse in Colonial and Postcolonial Studies*. Amsterdam: Rodopi, 17–31.

Horrocks, Roger (1994). *Masculinity in Crisis. Myths, Fantasies and Realities*. New York: St. Martin's Press.

Huggan, Graham (2001). *The Postcolonial Exotic. Marketing the Margins*. London: Routledge.

Huggan, Graham and Stephen Watson (1996). "Introduction." In Graham Huggan and Stephen Watson (eds.), *Critical Perspectives on J.M. Coetzee*. Basingstoke: Macmillan, 1–10.

Hunter, Allan (1983). *Joseph Conrad and the Ethics of Darwinism. The Challenges of Science*. London: Croom Helm.

Hunter, Jefferson (1982). *Edwardian Fiction*. Cambridge: Harvard University Press.

Husmann-Kastein, Jana (2006). "Schwarz-Weiß. Farb- und Geschlechtssymbolik in den Anfängen der Rassekonstruktionen." In Martina Tißberger, et al. (eds.), *Weiß – Weißsein – Whiteness. Kritische Studien zu Gender und Rassismus*. Berlin: Lang, 43–60.

Hyam, Ronald (1990). *Empire and Sexuality. The British Experience*. Manchester: Manchester University Press.

Ilona, Anthony (2003). "Hanif Kureishi's *The Buddha of Suburbia*: 'A New Way of Being British'." In Richard J. Lane, Rod Mengham and Philip Tew (eds.), *Contemporary British Fiction*. Cambridge Polity Press, 86–105.

Jakubiak, Katarzyna (2008). "Simulated Optimism: The International Marketing of *White Teeth*." In Tracey L. Walters (ed.), *Zadie Smith. Critical Essays*. New York: Lang, 201–18.

Jameson, Fredric (1992). "Modernism and Imperialism." In Terry Eagleton, Fredric Jameson and Edward W. Said (eds.), *Nationalism, Colonialism, and Literature*. 2nd ed. Minneapolis: University of Minnesota Press, 43–66.

— (1994). *The Political Unconscious. Narrative as a Socially Symbolic Act*. 1981. 7th ed. Ithaca: Cornell University Press.

JanMohamed, Abdul R. (1985). "The Economy of Manichean Allegory: The Function of Racial Difference in Colonialist Literature." *Critical Inquiry* 12.1, 59–87.

Jayasena, Nalin (2006). *Contested Masculinities. Crises in Colonial Male Identity from Joseph Conrad to Satyajit Ray*. London: Routledge.

Johnson, Robert (2003). *British Imperialism*. Basingstoke: Palgrave Macmillan.

Jolly, Rosemary Jane (1996). "Forms of Violence in J.M. Coetzee's *Dusklands* and *Waiting for the Barbarians*." In *Colonization, Violence, and Narration in White South African Writing. André Brink, Breyten Breytenbach, and J.M. Coetzee*. Athens: Ohio University Press, 110–37.

— (2006). "Going to the Dogs. Humanity in J.M. Coetzee's *Disgrace, The Lives of Animals*, and South Africa's Truth and Reconciliation Commission." In Jane Poyner (ed.), *J.M. Coetzee and the Idea of the Public Intellectual*. Athens: Ohio University Press, 148–71.

Jones, Michael P. (1985). *Conrad's Heroism. A Paradise Lost*. Ann Arbor: UMI Research Press.

Junker, Carsten (2010). *Frames of Friction. Black Genealogies, White Hegemony, and the Essay as Critical Intervention*. Frankfurt am Main: Campus.

Kaleta, Kenneth C. (1998). *Hanif Kureishi. Postcolonial Storyteller*. Austin: University of Texas Press.

Kane, Michael (1999). "Insiders/Outsiders: Conrad's *The Nigger of the Narcissus* and Stoker's *Dracula*." In *Modern Men. Mapping Masculinity in English and German Literature, 1880–1930*. London: Cassell, 120–40.

Kaplan, E. Ann (1997). *Looking for the Other. Feminism, Film, and the Imperial Gaze*. New York: Routledge.

Kaplan, Carola M. (2005). "Beyond Gender. Deconstructions of Masculinity and Femininity from "Karain" to *Under Western Eyes*." In Carola M. Kaplan, Peter Lancelot Mallios and Andrea White (eds.), *Conrad in the Twenty-First Century. Contemporary Approaches and Perspectives*. New York: Routledge, 267–79.

Kappert, Ines (2002). "Krisendiskurs ‚Mann'. Ermächtigung auf Umwegen." In Katharina Baisch, et al. (eds.), *Gender Revisited. Subjekt- und Politikbegriffe in Kultur und Medien*. Stuttgart: Metzler, 251–67.

— (2008). *Der Mann in der Krise: oder: Kapitalismuskritik in der Mainstreamkultur*. Bielefeld: transcript.

Katz, Wendy R. (1987). *Rider Haggard and the Fiction of Empire. A Critical Study of British Imperial Fiction*. Cambridge: Cambridge University Press.

Kaupen-Haas, Heidrun and Christian Saller (eds.) (1999). *Wissenschaftlicher Rassismus. Analysen einer Kontinuität in den Human- und Naturwissenschaften*. Frankfurt am Main: Campus.

Kehinde, Ayobami (2006). "African Fiction in the Service of History: Narrating Racial Dissonance in J.M. Coetzee's *Waiting for the Barbarians*." In Liliana Sikorska (ed.), *A Universe of (Hi)Stories. Essays on J.M. Coetzee*. Frankfurt am Main: Lang, 67–86.

Kemp, Wolfgang (1980). *Theorie der Fotografie I. 1839–1912*. Munich: Schirmer/ Mosel.

Kempner, Brandon (2009). "'Blow the World Back Together': Literary Nostalgia, 9/11, and Terrorism in Seamus Heaney, Chris Cleave, and Martin Amis." In Cara Cilano (ed.), *From Solidarity to Schisms. 9/11 and After in Fiction and Film from Outside the US*. Amsterdam: Rodopi, 53–74.

Kerr, Douglas (2000). "Three Ways of Going Wrong: Kipling, Conrad, Coetzee." *The Modern Language Review* 95.1, 18–27.

Kilian, Eveline (2004). *GeschlechtSverkehrt. Theoretische und literarische Perspektiven des gender-bending*. Königstein/Taunus: Helmer.

Kim, Sung Ryol (2001). "Lord Jim's Heroic Identity." *Conradiana* 33.2, 83–106.

Kimmel, Michael S. (1987). "The Contemporary Crisis of Masculinity in Historical Perspective." In Harry Brod (ed.), *The Making of Masculinities. The New Men's Studies*. Boston: Allen & Unwin, 121–53.

Kimmel, Michael S., Jeff Hearn and R.W. Connell (eds.) (2005). *Handbook of Studies on Men & Masculinities*. Thousand Oaks: Sage.

Knauer, Kris (2008). "The Root Canals of Zadie Smith: London's Intergenerational Adaptation." In Tracey L. Walters (ed.), *Zadie Smith. Critical Essays*. New York: Lang, 171–86.

Knights, Ben (1999). "Masculinity as Fiction." In *Writing Masculinities. Male Narratives in Twentieth-Century Fiction*. Basingstoke: Macmillan, 10–48.

Knopp, Eva (2009). "'There Are No Jokes in Paradise': Humour as a Politics of Representation in Recent Texts and Films from the British Migratory Contact-Zone." In Petra Rüdiger and Konrad Gross (eds.), *Translation of Cultures*. Amsterdam: Rodopi, 59–74.

Knowles, Owen (1992). *An Annotated Critical Bibliography of Joseph Conrad*. Hemel Hempstead: Harvester Wheatsheaf.

Knowles, Owen and Gene M. Moore (2000). *Oxford Reader's Companion to Conrad*. Oxford: Oxford University Press.

Koch-Rein, Anson (2006). "Passing Moments: FTM-Bodies in Contemporary Transgender Photography." *ZtG Bulletin – Texte* 32, 156–79.

Koebner, Thomas (2003). "In der Haut der anderen. Männer als Frauen – Frauen als Männer." In Christine Rüffert, et al. (eds.), *Wo/Man. Kino und Identität.* Berlin: Bertz, 45–64.

Kossew, Sue (1996). *Pen and Power. A Post-Colonial Reading of J.M. Coetzee and André Brink.* Amsterdam: Rodopi.

Kumar, Krishan (2001). "'Englishness' and English National Identity." In David Morley and Kevin Robins (eds.), *British Cultural Studies. Geography, Nationality, and Identity.* Oxford: Oxford University Press, 41–56.

Kurtén, Marina (2002). "Negotiating Identities. Expressions of 'Culture' in British Migrant Literature." *Atlantic Literary Review* 3.2, 47–55.

Laclau, Ernesto and Chantal Mouffe (1994). *Hegemony & Socialist Strategy. Towards a Radical Democratic Politics.* 1985. London: Verso.

Landry, Donna and Gerald MacLean (eds.) (1996). *The Spivak Reader. Selected Works of Gayatri Chakravorty Spivak.* New York: Routledge.

Lane, Christopher (1995). *The Ruling Passion. British Colonial Allegory and the Paradox of Homosexual Desire.* Durham: Duke University Press.

Laqueur, Thomas W. (1999). *Making Sex. Body and Gender from the Greeks to Freud.* 1990. 8th ed. Cambridge: Harvard University Press.

Leavis, F.R. (1948). *The Great Tradition. George Eliot, Henry James, Joseph Conrad.* New York: George W. Stewart.

Lebdai, Benaouda (2008). "Bodies and Voices in Coetzee's *Disgrace* and Bouraoui's *Garçon manqué.*" In Merete Falck Borch, et al. (eds.), *Bodies and Voices. The Force-Field of Representation and Discourse in Colonial and Postcolonial Studies.* Amsterdam: Rodopi, 33–43.

Ledger, Sally (1995). "The New Woman and the Crisis of Victorianism." In Sally Ledger and Scott McCracken (eds.), *Cultural Politics at the fin de siècle.* Cambridge: Cambridge University Press, 22–44.

Lee, Robert A. (1995). "Changing the Script. Sex, Lies and Videotapes in Hanif Kureishi, David Dabydeen and Mike Phillips." In Robert A. Lee (ed.), *Other Britain, Other British. Contemporary Multicultural Fiction.* London: Pluto Press, 69–89.

Lehman, Peter (2007). "Crying over the Melodramatic Penis: Melodrama and Male Nudity in Films of the 90s." In Julie F. Codell (ed.), *Genre, Gender, Race, and World Cinema.* Malden: Blackwell, 148–62.

Levine, George (1988). *Darwin and the Novelists. Patterns of Science in Victorian Fiction.* Cambridge: Harvard University Press.

Lewis, Reina and Sara Mills (eds.) (2003). *Feminist Postcolonial Theory. A Reader.* Edinburgh: Edinburgh University Press.

Liebrand, Claudia and Ines Steiner (2004). "Einleitung." In *Hollywood hybrid. Genre und Gender im zeitgenössischen Mainstream-Film.* Marburg: Schüren, 7–15.

Lindner, Silvia (2003). "The Crying Game." In *Von Tadzios zu Tootsie. Androgynie im Film.* St. Augustin: Gardez, 56–78.

Loomba, Ania (1998). *Colonialism/Postcolonialism*. The New Critical Idiom. London: Routledge.

Low, Gail Ching-Liang (1996). *White Skins/Black Masks. Representation and Colonialism*. London: Routledge.

Lyon, John (1989). "Half-Written Tales: Kipling and Conrad." In Phillip Mallett (ed.), *Kipling Considered*. Basingstoke: Macmillan, 115–34.

MacCabe, Colin and Hanif Kureishi (1999). "Interview. Hanif Kureishi on London." *Critical Quarterly* 41.3, 37–56.

MacDonald, Robert H. (1994). "The Laureate of Empire – and his Chorus." In *The Language of Empire. Myths and Metaphors of Popular Imperialism, 1880–1918*. Manchester: Manchester University Press, 145–73.

MacKenzie, John M. (ed.) (1986). *Imperialism and Popular Culture*. Manchester: Manchester University Press.

— (1987). "The Imperial Pioneer and Hunter and the British Masculine Stereotype in Late Victorian and Edwardian Times." In James A. Mangan and James Walvin (eds.), *Manliness and Morality. Middle-Class Masculinity in Britain and America 1800–1940*. Manchester: Manchester University Press, 176–98.

— (1988). *The Empire of Nature. Hunting Conservation and British Imperialism*. Manchester: Manchester University Press.

Mahood, Molly Maureen (1977). *The Colonial Encounter. A Reading of Six Novels*. London: Rex Collings.

Maisonnat, Claude (1996). "Alterity and Suicide in 'An Outpost of Progress'." *Conradiana* 28.2, 101–14.

Malik, Sarita (1996). "Beyond 'The Cinema of Duty'? The Pleasure of Hybridity: Black British Film of the 1980s and 1990s." In Andrew Higson (ed.), *Dissolving Views. Key Writings on British Cinema*. London: Cassell, 202–15.

Manalansan IV, Martin F. (2006). "Queer Intersections: Sexuality and Gender in Migration Studies." *IMR* 40.1, 224–49.

Mangan, James A. and James Walvin (eds.) (1987). *Manliness and Morality. Middle-Class Masculinity in Britain and America 1800–1940*. Manchester: Manchester University Press.

Marais, Michael (1996). "The Hermeneutics of Empire: Coetzee's Post-colonial Metafiction." In Graham Huggan and Stephen Watson (eds.), *Critical Perspectives on J.M. Coetzee*. Basingstoke: Macmillan, 66–81.

— (2001). "Very Morbid Phenomena: 'Liberal Funk', the 'Lucy-Syndrome' and J.M. Coetzee's *Disgrace*." *Scrutiny2: Issues in English Studies in Southern Africa* 6.1, 32–38.

— (2006). "J.M. Coetzee's *Disgrace* and the Task of the Imagination." *Journal of Modern Literature* 29.2, 75–93.

Mason, Philip (1975). *Kipling. The Glass, the Shadow and the Fire*. London: Cape.

Maxwell, Anne (1999). *Colonial Photography and Exhibitions. Representations of the 'Native' People and the Making of European Identities*. London: Leicester University Press.

McBratney, John (2002). *Imperial Subjects, Imperial Space: Rudyard Kipling's Fiction of the Native-Born*. Columbus: Ohio State University Press.

McCall, Leslie (2005). "The Complexity of Intersectionality." *Signs: Journal of Women in Culture and Society* 30.3, 1771–802.

McClintock, Anne (1995). *Imperial Leather. Race, Gender and Sexuality in the Colonial Contest*. New York: Routledge.

McClure, John A. (1981). *Kipling and Conrad. The Colonial Fiction*. Cambridge: Harvard University Press.

— (1985). "Problematic Presence: The Colonial Other in Kipling and Conrad." In David Dabydeen (ed.), *The Black Presence in English Literature*. Manchester: Manchester University Press, 154–67.

McCracken, Scott (1993). "'A Hard and Absolute Condition of Existence'. Reading Masculinity in *Lord Jim*." In Andrew Michael Roberts (ed.), *Conrad and Gender*. Amsterdam: Rodopi, 17–38.

McDonald, Peter D. (2002). "Disgrace Effects." *Interventions* 4.3, 321–30.

McGee, Patrick (1997). "Sexual Nations: History and the Division of Hope in *The Crying Game*." *Cinema, Theory, and Political Responsibility in Contemporary Culture*. Cambridge: Cambridge University Press, 79–160.

McLeod, John (2004). *Postcolonial London. Rewriting the Metropolis*. London: Routledge.

Meffan, James and Kim L. Worthington (2001). "Ethics before Politics. J.M. Coetzee's *Disgrace*." In Todd F. Davis and Kenneth Womack (eds.), *Mapping the Ethical Turn. A Reader in Ethics, Culture, and Literary Theory*. Charlottesville: University Press of Virginia, 131–50.

Mehlmann, Sabine (2008). "Das sexu(alis)ierte Individuum – Zur paradoxen Konstruktionslogik moderner Männlichkeit." In Ulrike Brunotte and Rainer Herrn (eds.), *Männlichkeiten und Moderne. Geschlecht in den Wissenskulturen um 1900*. Bielefeld: transcript, 37–55.

Meinig, Sigrun (2004). "'Running at a Standstill': The Paradoxes of Time and Trauma in Zadie Smith's *White Teeth*." In Stefan Glomb and Stefan Horlacher (eds.), *Beyond Extremes. Repräsentation und Reflexion von Modernisierungsprozessen im zeitgenössischen britischen Roman*. Tübingen: Narr, 241–57.

Mennecke, Arnim (1991). *Koloniales Bewusstsein in den Romanen J.M. Coetzees*. Heidelberg: Winter.

Mercer, Kobena (1994). *Welcome to the Jungle. New Positions in Black Cultural Studies*. New York: Routledge.

Messenger, Nigel (2001). "'We did not want to lose him': Jimmy Wait as the Figure of Abjection in Conrad's *The Nigger of the 'Narcissus'*." *Critical Survey* 13.1, 62–79.

Meyers, Jeffrey (1973). *Fiction and the Colonial Experience*. Ipswich: Boydell Press.

Michael, Magali Cornier (2009). "Writing Fiction in the Post-9/11 World: Ian McEwan's *Saturday*." In Cara Cilano (ed.), *From Solidarity to Schisms. 9/11 and After in Fiction and Film from Outside the US*. Amsterdam: Rodopi, 25–51.

Michaelis, Beatrice (2004). *Towards an Epistemology of a Crisis: Masculinity, Homosociality, and the Male Body in Anglo-American Fiction from the 1980s to Now.* MA Thesis. Humboldt-Universität zu Berlin.

Middleton, Tim (2002). "From Mimicry to Menace. Conrad and Late-Victorian Masculinity." In Philip Holden and Richard J. Ruppel (eds.), *Imperial Desire. Dissident Sexualities and Colonial Literature.* Minneapolis: University of Minnesota Press, 135–51.

Mignolo, Walter D. (2000). "The Many Faces of Cosmo-polis: Border Thinking and Critical Cosmopolitanism." *Public Culture* 12.3, 721–48.

Mirze, Z. Esra (2008). "Fundamental Differences in Zadie Smith's *White Teeth.*" In Tracey L. Walters (ed.), *Zadie Smith. Critical Essays.* New York: Lang, 187–200.

Mitchell, W.J. Thomas (2005). *What Do Pictures Want? The Lives and Loves of Images.* Chicago: University of Chicago Press.

Mohanram, Radhika (1995). "Postcolonial Spaces and Deterritorialized (Homo)Sexuality: The Films of Hanif Kureishi." In Gita Rajan and Radhika Mohanram (eds.), *Postcolonial Discourse and Changing Cultural Contexts. Theory and Criticism.* Westport: Greenwood Press, 117–34.

Mohanty, Satya P. (1991). "Drawing the Color Line: Kipling and the Culture of Colonial Rule." In Dominick LaCapra (ed.), *The Bounds of Race. Perspectives on Hegemony and Resistance.* Ithaca: Cornell University Press, 311–43.

Mongia, Padmini (1992). "Narrative Strategy and Imperialism in Conrad's *Lord Jim.*" *Studies in the Novel* XXIV.2, 173–86.

— (1993). "'Ghosts of the Gothic': Spectral Women and Colonized Spaces in *Lord Jim.*" In Andrew Michael Roberts (ed.), *Conrad and Gender.* Amsterdam: Rodopi, 1–16.

— (2001). "The Rescue: Conrad, Achebe, and the Critics." *Conradiana* 33.2, 153–63.

— (2005). "Between Men: Conrad in the Fiction of Two Contemporary Indian Writers." In Carola M. Kaplan, Peter Lancelot Mallios and Andrea White (eds.), *Conrad in the Twenty-First Century. Contemporary Approaches and Perspectives.* New York: Routledge, 85–100.

Montefiore, Janet (2000). "Latin, Arithmetic and Mastery: A Reading of Two Kipling Fictions." In Howard J. Booth and Nigel Rigby (eds.), *Modernism and Empire.* Manchester: Manchester University Press, 112–36.

Moor, Andrew (2006). "Beyond the Pale: The Politics of Neil Jordan's *The Crying Game.*" In Robin Griffiths (ed.), *British Queer Cinema.* London: Routledge, 157–69.

Moore-Gilbert, Bart J. (1986). *Kipling and "Orientalism".* London: Croom Helm.

— (1997). *Postcolonial Theory. Contexts, Practices, Politics.* London: Verso.

— (2001). *Hanif Kureishi.* Manchester: Manchester University Press.

Moore-Gilbert, Bart J., Gareth Stanton and Willy Maley (eds.) (1997). *Postcolonial Criticism.* London: Longman.

Morley, David and Kuan-Hsing Chen (eds.) (1996). *Stuart Hall. Critical Dialogues in Cultural Studies.* London: Routledge.

Morris, Jan (1982). *The Spectacle of Empire. Style, Effect and the Pax Britannica.* London: Faber and Faber.

Morrison, Toni (1993). *Playing in the Dark. Whiteness and the Literary Imagination.* 1992. New York: Vintage.

Moser, Thomas (1957). *Joseph Conrad. Achievement and Decline.* Cambridge: Harvard University Press.

Moses, Michael Valdez (1993). "The Mark of Empire: Writing, History, and Torture in Coetzee's *Waiting for the Barbarians.*" *Kenyon Review* 15.1, 115–27.

— (ed.) (1994). *Writings of J.M. Coetzee. The South Atlantic Quarterly* 93.1, Special Issue. Durham: Duke University Press.

Moss, Laura (2003). "The Politics of Everyday Hybridity: Zadie Smith's *White Teeth.*" *Wasafiri* 39, 11–17.

Mosse, George L. (1996). *The Image of Man. The Creation of Modern Masculinity.* Oxford: Oxford University Press.

Mulvey, Laura (1997). "Visual Pleasure and Narrative Cinema." In Robyn R. Warhol and Diane Price Herndl (eds.), *Feminisms. An Anthology of Literary Theory and Criticism.* Rev. ed. New Brunswick: Rutgers University Press, 438–48.

Muñoz, José Esteban (1999). *Disidentifications. Queers of Color and the Performance of Politics.* Minneapolis: University of Minnesota Press.

Murray, Cara (2010). "Catastrophe and Development in the Adventure Romance." *ELT* 53.2, 150–69.

Nagai, Kaori (2006). *Empire of Analogies. Kipling, India and Ireland.* Cork: Cork University Press.

Neale, Steve (1992). "Masculinity as Spectacle." In Screen (ed.), *The Sexual Subject. A Screen Reader in Sexuality.* London: Routledge, 277–87.

Newhall, Beaumont (1964). *The History of Photography. From 1830 to the Present Day.* Rev. and enlarged ed. New York: Museum of Modern Art.

Nicklas, Pascal (ed.) (2009). *Ian McEwan. Art and Politics.* Heidelberg: Winter.

Nieberle, Sigrid and Elisabeth Strowick (eds.) (2006). *Narration und Geschlecht. Texte – Medien – Episteme.* Cologne: Böhlau.

North, Michael (1994). "*The Nigger of the 'Narcissus'* as a Preface to Modernism." In *The Dialect of Modernism. Race, Language, and Twentieth-Century Literature.* New York: Oxford University Press, 37–58.

Nünning, Ansgar and Vera Nünning (eds.) (2004). *Erzähltextanalyse und Gender Studies.* Stuttgart: Metzler.

O'Hanlon, Redmond (1984). *Joseph Conrad and Charles Darwin. The Influence of Scientific Thought on Conrad's Fiction.* Edinburgh: Salamander Press.

Ochsner, Andrea (2009). *Lad Trouble. Masculinity and Identity in the British Male Confessional Novel of the 1990s.* Bielefeld: transcript.

Packer-Kinlaw, Donna (2006). "'Ain't we men?': Illusions of Gender in Joseph Conrad's *The Nigger of the 'Narcissus'.*" *Conradiana* 38.3, 247–65.

Paganoni, Maria Cristina (2003). "Zadie Smith's New Ethnicities." *Culture* 17, 113–27.

Page, Ruth E. (2003). "Feminist Narratology? Literary and Linguistic Perspectives on Gender and Narrativity." *Language and Literature* 12.1, 43–56.

Palm, Kerstin (2006). "Anti-Darwin: Biologischer Lebensbegriff und Männlichkeit um 1900." Paper presented at the conference *Produktion und Krise hegemonialer Männlichkeit in der Moderne*. Humboldt-Universität zu Berlin, Germany, December 7–12.

— (2007). "Multiple Subjekte im Labor? Objektivismuskritik als Ausgangsbasis für interdependenztheoretische Theorie und Praxis der Naturwissenschaft." In Katharina Walgenbach, et al. *Gender als interdependente Kategorie. Neue Perspektiven auf Intersektionalität, Diversität und Heterogenität*. Opladen: Budrich, 141–65.

Paproth, Matthew (2008). "The Flipping Coin: The Modernist and Postmodernist Zadie Smith." In Tracey L. Walters (ed.), *Zadie Smith. Critical Essays*. New York: Lang, 9–29.

Parker, Kenneth (1996). "J.M. Coetzee: The Postmodern and the Postcolonial." In Graham Huggan and Stephen Watson (eds.), *Critical Perspectives on J.M. Coetzee*. Basingstoke: Macmillan, 82–104.

Parry, Benita (1983). *Conrad and Imperialism. Ideological Boundaries and Visionary Frontiers*. London: Macmillan.

— (1996). "Speech and Silence in the Fictions of J.M. Coetzee." In Graham Huggan and Stephen Watson (eds.), *Critical Perspectives on J.M. Coetzee*. Basingstoke: Macmillan, 37–65.

— (1998). "Rudyard Kipling, 1865–1936." In *Delusions and Discoveries. India in the British Imagination, 1880–1930*. London: Verso, 186–224.

— (2004). *Postcolonial Studies. A Materialist Critique*. London: Routledge.

— (2005). "The Moment and After-Life of *Heart of Darkness*." In Carola M. Kaplan, Peter Lancelot Mallios and Andrea White (eds.), *Conrad in the Twenty-First Century. Contemporary Approaches and Perspectives*. New York: Routledge, 39–54.

Patteson, Richard F. (1978). "*King Solomon's Mines*: Imperialism and Narrative Structure." *The Journal of Narrative Technique* 8.2, 112–23.

Pechey, Graham (2002). "Coetzee's Purgatorial Africa: The Case of *Disgrace*." *Interventions* 4.3, 374–83.

Penner, Allen Richard (1989). *Countries of the Mind. The Fiction of J.M. Coetzee*. Greenwood.

Phillips, Richard (1997). *Mapping Men and Empire. A Geography of Adventure*. London: Routledge.

Pocock, Tom (1993). *Rider Haggard and the Lost Empire*. London: Weidenfeld and Nicolson.

Poon, Angelia (2008). "Imperial Fantasies and the Politics of Reproducing Englishness: Henry Rider Haggard's *Allan Quatermain*." In *Enacting Englishness in* the Victorian Period. Colonialism and the Politics of Performance. Aldershot: Ashgate. 125–52.

Porter, Andrew and William Roger Louis (eds.) (1999). The Nineteenth Century. The Oxford History of the British Empire. Oxford: Oxford University Press.

Poyner, Jane (2000). "Truth and Reconciliation in J.M. Coetzee's Disgrace." Scrutiny2: Issues in English Studies in Southern Africa 5.2, 67–77.

— (2009). J.M. Coetzee and the Paradox of Postcolonial Authorship. Farnham: Ashgate.

Pramaggiore, Maria (1996). "Straddling the Screen: Bisexual Spectatorship and Contemporary Narrative Cinema." In Donald Eugene Hall and Maria Pramaggiore (eds.), Representing Bisexualities. Subjects and Cultures of Fluid Desire. New York: New York University Press, 272–97.

Pratt, Mary Louise (1992). Imperial Eyes. Studies in Travel Writing and Transculturation. London: Routledge.

Procter, James (2003). Dwelling Places. Postwar Black British Writing. Manchester: Manchester University Press.

Propp, Vladimir Jakovleviéc (1973). Morphology of the Folktale. Trans. Laurence Scott. 2nd rev. ed. Austin: University of Texas Press.

Prosser, Jay (1998). Second Skins. The Body Narratives of Transsexuality. New York: Columbia University Press.

Puar, Jasbir K. (2007). Terrorist Assemblages. Homonationalism in Queer Times. Durham: Duke University Press.

Quart, Leonard (1994). "The Politics of Irony: The Frears-Kureishi Films." In Wheeler W. Dixon (ed.), Re-Viewing British Cinema, 1900–1992. Essays and Interviews. Albany: State University of New York Press, 241–48.

Ramsey-Kurz, Helga (2005). "Humouring the Terrorists or the Terrorised? Militant Muslims in Salman Rushdie, Zadie Smith and Hanif Kureishi." In Susanne Reichl and Mark Stein (eds.), Cheeky Fictions. Laughter and the Postcolonial. Amsterdam: Rodopi, 73–86.

Ranasinha, Ruvani (2002). Hanif Kureishi. Tavistock: Northcote House in Association with the British Council.

— (2009). "Racialized Masculinities and Postcolonial Critique in Contemporary British Asian Male-Authored Texts." Journal of Postcolonial Writing 45.3, 297–307.

Randall, Don (2000). Kipling's Imperial Boy. Adolescence and Cultural Hybridity. Basingstoke: Palgrave.

Raval, Suresh (1986). The Art of Failure. Conrad's Fiction. Boston: Allen & Unwin.

Ray, Sangeeta (1998). "The Nation in Performance: Bhabha, Mukherjee and Kureishi." In Monika Fludernik (ed.), Hybridity and Postcolonialism. Twentieth Century Indian Literature. Tübingen: Stauffenburg, 219–38.

Reichl, Susanne (2007). "Hanif Kureishi, The Buddha of Suburbia. Performing Identity in Postcolonial London." In Tobias Döring (ed.), A History of Postcolonial Literature in 12 1/2 books. Trier: WVT, 136–54.

Reitz, Bernhard (1996). "Der *Christian gentleman* als imperiales Konstrukt in den Afrika-Romanen Henry Rider Haggards." In Ansgar Nünning and Vera Nünning (eds.), *Intercultural Studies. Fictions of Empire*. Heidelberg: Winter, 73–90.

Richardson, Brian (2005). "Conrad and Posthumanist Narration: Fabricating Class and Consciousness on Board the *Narcissus*." In Carola M. Kaplan, Peter Lancelot Mallios and Andrea White (eds.), *Conrad in the Twenty-First Century. Contemporary Approaches and Perspectives*. New York: Routledge, 213–22.

Ricœur, Paul (1991). "Narrative Identity." *Philosophy Today* 35.1, 73–81.

Ridley, Hugh (1983). *Images of Imperial Rule*. London: Croom Helm.

Riffenburgh, Beau (1994). *The Myth of the Explorer. The Press, Sensationalism, and Geographical Discovery*. Oxford: Oxford University Press.

Roberts, Andrew Michael (2000). *Conrad and Masculinity*. Basingstoke: Macmillan.

Robinson, Sally (2000). *Marked Men. White Masculinity in Crisis*. New York: Columbia University Press.

Rogers, Katina (2008). "Affirming Complexity: *White Teeth* and Cosmopolitanism." *Interdisciplinary Literary Studies: A Journal of Criticism and Theory* 9.2, 45–61.

Rony, Fatimah Tobing (1996). *The Third Eye. Race, Cinema, and Ethnographic Spectacle*. Durham: Duke University Press.

Ross, Michael L. (2006). "'A Funny Kind of Englishman': Hanif Kureishi's Carnival of Ethnicities." In *Race Riots. Comedy and Ethnicity in Modern British Fiction*. Montreal: McGill-Queen's University Press, 228–47.

Ross, Stephen (2004). *Conrad and Empire*. Columbia: University of Missouri Press.

Rubin, Gayle (1975). "The Traffic in Women: Notes on the 'Political Economy' of Sex." In Rayna R. Reiter (ed.), *Toward an Anthropology of Women*. New York: Monthly Review Press, 157–210.

Ruppel, Richard J. (2002). "'Girl! What? Did I Mention a Girl?' The Economy of Desire in *Heart of Darkness*." In Philip Holden and Richard J. Ruppel (eds.), *Imperial Desire. Dissident Sexualities and Colonial Literature*. Minneapolis: University of Minnesota Press, 152–71.

Rushdie, Salman (1988). "Minority Literatures in a Multi-Cultural Society." In Kirsten Holst Petersen and Anna Rutherford (eds.), *Displaced Persons*. Sydney: Dangaroo Press, 33–42.

Rutherford, Jonathan and Homi K. Bhabha (1990). "The Third Space. Interview with Homi Bhabha." In Jonathan Rutherford (ed.), *Identity. Community, Culture, Difference*. London: Lawrence and Wishart, 207–21.

Ryan, James R. (1997). *Picturing Empire. Photography and the Visualisation of the British Empire*. London: Reaktion.

Sachsse, Rolf (2003). *Fotografie. Vom technischen Bildmittel zur Krise der Repräsentation*. Cologne: Deubner.

Said, Edward W. (1968). *Joseph Conrad and the Fiction of Autobiography*. 1966. 2nd ed. Cambridge: Harvard University Press.

— (1987). "Kim, The Pleasures of Imperialism." *Raritan* 7.2, 27–64.

— (1994). *Culture and Imperialism*. 1993. New York: Vintage.

— (2003). *Orientalism*. 1978. 25th anniversary ed. New York: Vintage.

Sanders, Mark (2002). "*Disgrace*." *Interventions* 4.3, 363–73.

Sandhu, Sukhdev (2000). "Pop Goes the Centre: Hanif Kureishi's London." In Laura Chrisman and Benita Parry (eds.), *Postcolonial Theory and Criticism*. Cambridge: D.S. Brewer, 133–54.

Sandison, Alan (1967). *The Wheel of Empire. A Study of the Imperial Idea in Some Late Nineteenth and Early Twentieth-Century Fiction*. London: Macmillan.

Sarasin, Philipp (2003). *Reizbare Maschinen. Eine Geschichte des Körpers 1765–1914*. Frankfurt am Main: Suhrkamp.

Saunders, Rebecca (2001). "The Agony And The Allegory: The Concept of the Foreign, the Language of Apartheid, and the Fiction of J.M. Coetzee." *Cultural Critique* 47, 215–64.

Savran, David (1998). *Taking It Like a Man. White Masculinity, Masochism, and Contemporary American Culture*. Princeton: Princeton University Press.

Schaff, Barbara (2009). "Trying to Escape, Longing to Belong: Roots, Genes and Performativity in Zadie Smith's *White Teeth* and Hari Kunzru's *The Impressionist*." In Frank Schulze-Engler, et al. (eds.), *Transcultural English Studies. Theories, Fictions, Realities*. Amsterdam: Rodopi, 281–92.

Schefold, Fabian (1999). *Koloniale Mythenbildung und ihre literarische Dekonstruktion. Britische Kolonialliteratur von Kipling zu Farrell*. Göttingen: Cuvillier.

Scherer, Joanna C. (1992). "The Photographic Document: Photographs as Primary Data in Anthropological Enquiry." In Elizabeth Edwards (ed.), *Anthropology and Photography, 1860–1920*. New Haven: Yale University Press in Association with the Royal Anthropological Institute, London, 32–41.

Schiebinger, Londa L. (1989). *The Mind Has No Sex? Women in the Origins of Modern Science*. Cambridge: Harvard University Press.

— (1993). *Nature's Body. Gender in the Making of Modern Science*. Boston: Beacon Press.

Schmidt-Linsenhoff, Viktoria, Karl Hölz and Herbert Uerlings (eds.) (2004). *Weiße Blicke. Geschlechtermythen des Kolonialismus*. Marburg: Jonas-Verlag.

Schneider, Lissa (2003). *Conrad's Narratives of Difference. Not Exactly Tales for Boys*. New York: Routledge.

Schnurbein, Stefanie von (2001). *Krisen der Männlichkeit. Schreiben und Geschlechterdiskurs in skandinavischen Romanen seit 1890*. Göttingen: Wallstein Verlag.

— (2006). "Kampf um Subjektivität. Nation, Religion und Geschlecht in zwei dänischen Romanen um 1850." In Christiane Barz and Wolfgang Behschnitt (eds.), *bildung und anderes. Alterität in Bildungsdiskursen in den skandinavischen Literaturen*. Würzburg: Ergon, 111–29.

Schoene, Berthold (1998). "Herald of Hybridity. The Emancipation of Difference in Hanif Kureishi's *The Buddha of Suburbia*." *International Journal of Cultural Studies* 1.1, 109–28.

Sedgwick, Eve Kosofsky (1985). *Between Men. English Literature and Male Homosocial Desire*. New York: Columbia University Press.

— (1990). *Epistemology of the Closet*. Berkeley: University of California Press.

— (1997). "Paranoid Reading and Reparative Reading; or, You're So Paranoid, You Probably Think This Introduction Is About You." In Eve Kosofsky Sedgwick (ed.), *Novel Gazing. Queer Readings in Fiction*. Durham: Duke University Press, 1–37.

Seeley, Tracy (1992). "Conrad's Modernist Romance." *ELH* 59.2, 495–511.

Segal, Lynne (1997). *Slow Motion. Changing Masculinities, Changing Men*. Updated and rev. ed. London: Virago.

Sekula, Allan (1986). "The Body and the Archive." *October* 39, 3–64.

Sell, Jonathan P.A. (2006). "Chance and Gesture in Zadie Smith's *White Teeth* and *The Autograph Man*: A Model for Multicultural Identity." *The Journal of Commonwealth Literature* 41.3, 27–44.

Shaffer, Brian W. (2006). "J.M. Coetzee's *Waiting for the Barbarians* (1980)." *Reading the Novel in English 1950–2000*. Malden: Blackwell, 121–37.

Shattuck, Sandra D. (2009). "Dis(g)race, or White Man Writing." In Bill McDonald (ed.), *Encountering Disgrace. Reading and Teaching Coetzee's Novel*. New York: Camden House, 138–47.

Sheils, Colleen M. (2003). "Opera, Byron and a South African Psyche in J.M. Coetzee's *Disgrace*." *Current Writing. Text and Reception in Southern Africa* 15.1, 38–50.

Sherry, Norman (ed.) (1973). *Conrad. The Critical Heritage*. London: Routledge.

Shohat, Ella (1996). "Notes on the Post-Colonial." In Padmini Mongia (ed.), *Contemporary Postcolonial Theory. A Reader*. London: Arnold, 321–34.

Showalter, Elaine (1990). "King Romance." In *Sexual Anarchy. Gender and Culture at the Fin de Siècle*. New York: Viking, 76–104.

Sielke, Sabine (2007). "'Crisis? What Crisis?' Männlichkeit, Körper, Transdisziplinarität." In Jürgen Martschukat and Olaf Stieglitz (eds.), *Väter, Soldaten, Liebhaber. Männer und Männlichkeiten in der Geschichte Nordamerikas. Ein Reader*. Bielefeld: transcript, 43–61.

Silverman, Kaja (1992). *Male Subjectivity at the Margins*. New York: Routledge.

— (1996). *The Threshold of the Visible World*. New York: Routledge.

Simmons, Diane (2007). "Rudyard Kipling: Black Sheep." In *The Narcissism of Empire. Loss, Rage, and Revenge in Thomas De Quincey, Robert Louis Stevenson, Arthur Conan Doyle, Rudyard Kipling, and Isak Dinesen*. Brighton: Sussex Academic Press, 80–98.

Simpson, Mark (1994). "A Crying Shame. Transvestism and Misogyny in *The Crying Game*." In *Male Impersonators. Men Performing Masculinity*. New York: Routledge, 164–76.

Sinha, Madhudaya (2008). "Triangular Erotics: The Politics of Masculinity, Imperialism and Big-Game Hunting in Rider Haggard's *She*." *Critical Survey* 20.3, 29–43.

Sinha, Mrinalini (1995). *Colonial Masculinity. The 'Manly Englishman' and the 'Effeminate Bengali' in the Late Nineteenth Century*. Manchester: Manchester University Press.

Sizemore, Christine W. (2005). "Willesden as a Site of 'Demotic' Cosmopolitanism in Zadie Smith's Postcolonial City Novel *White Teeth*." *Journal of Commonwealth and Postcolonial Studies* 12.2, 65–83.

Slemon, Stephen (1987). "Monuments of Empire: Allegory/Counter-Discourse/Post-Colonial Writing." *Kunapipi* 9.3, 1–16.

Solomon-Godeau, Abigail (1997). "Male Trouble. A Crisis in Representation." In *Male Trouble. A Crisis in Representation*. London: Thames and Hudson, 17–41.

Sommer, Roy (2001). *Fictions of Migration. Ein Beitrag zur Theorie und Gattungstypologie des zeitgenössischen interkulturellen Romans in Großbritannien*. Trier: WVT.

Sontag, Susan (2001). *On Photography*. New York: Picador.

Spencer, Herbert (1864). *The Principles of Biology*. London: Williams & Norgate.

Spivak, Gayatri Chakravorty (1988). "Can the Subaltern Speak?" In Cary Nelson and Lawrence Grossberg (eds.), *Marxism & The Interpretation of Culture*. London: Macmillan, 271–313.

— (1989). "In Praise of *Sammy and Rosie Get Laid*." *Critical Quarterly* 31.2, 80–88.

— (1990). *The Post-Colonial Critic. Interviews, Strategies, Dialogues*. Ed. Sarah Harasym. New York: Routledge.

— (1993a). "The Burden of English." In Carol A. Breckenridge and Peter van der Veer (eds.), *Orientalism and the Postcolonial Predicament. Perspectives on South Asia*. Philadelphia: University of Pennsylvania Press, 134–57.

— (1993b). *Outside in the Teaching Machine*. New York: Routledge.

— (2002). "Ethics and Politics in Tagore, Coetzee, and Certain Scenes of Teaching." *Diacritics* 32.3–4, 17–31.

— (2003). *A Critique of Postcolonial Reason. Toward a History of the Vanishing Present*. 1999. 4th ed. Cambridge: Harvard University Press.

Squires, Claire (2002). *Zadie Smith's White Teeth. A Reader's Guide*. New York: Continuum.

Stam, Robert and Louise Spence (1999). "Colonialism, Racism, and Representation: An Introduction." In Leo Braudy and Marshall Cohen (eds.), *Film Theory and Criticism. Introductory Readings*. 5th ed. New York: Oxford University Press, 235–50.

Stanton, Katherine (2006). "History is Larger Than Goodwill: Restitution and Redistributive Justice in J.M. Coetzee's *Age of Iron* and *Disgrace*." In *Cosmopolitan Fictions. Ethics, Politics, and Global Change in the Works of Kazuo Ishiguro, Michael Ondaatje, Jamaica Kincaid, and J.M. Coetzee*. London: Routledge, 61–77.

Stape, J.H. (1996). *The Cambridge Companion to Joseph Conrad*. Cambridge: Cambridge University Press.

Stein, Mark (2004). *Black British Literature. Novels of Transformation*. Columbus: Ohio State University Press.

Stepan, Nancy Leys (1982). *The Idea of Race in Science. Great Britain 1800–1960*. London: Macmillan.

— (1993). "Race and Gender. The Role of Analogy in Science." In Sandra Harding (ed.), *The "Racial" Economy of Science. Toward a Democratic Future.* Bloomington: Indiana University Press, 359–76.

Stepan, Nancy Leys and Sander L. Gilman (1993). "Appropriating the Idioms of Science. The Rejection of Scientific Racism." In Sandra Harding (ed.), *The "Racial" Economy of Science. Toward a Democratic Future.* Bloomington: Indiana University Press, 170–93.

Steyerl, Hito and Encarnación Gutiérrez Rodríguez (eds.) (2003). *Spricht die Subalterne deutsch? Migration und postkoloniale Kritik.* Münster: Unrast.

Stiebel, Lindy (2001). *Imagining Africa. Landscape in H. Rider Haggard's African Romances.* Westport: Greenwood Press.

Stiegler, Bernd (2006). *Bilder der Photographie. Ein Album photographischer Metaphern.* Frankfurt am Main: Suhrkamp.

Stoler, Ann Laura (1995). Race and the Education of Desire. Foucault's History of Sexuality and the Colonial Order of Things. Durham: Duke University Press.

— (2002). *Carnal Knowledge and Imperial Power. Race and the Intimate in Colonial Rule.* Berkeley: University of California Press.

Stott, Rebecca (1989). "The Dark Continent: Africa as Female Body in Haggard's Adventure Fiction." *Feminist Review* 32.1, 69–89.

Street, Brian (1985). "Reading the Novels of Empire: Race and Ideology in the Classic 'Tale of Adventure'." In David Dabydeen (ed.), *The Black Presence in English Literature.* Manchester: Manchester University Press, 95–111.

Strobel, Margaret (1987). "Gender and Race in the Nineteenth- and Twentieth-Century British Empire." In Renate Bridenthal, Claudia Koonz and Susan M. Stuard (eds.), *Becoming Visible. Women in European History.* 2nd ed. Boston: Houghton Mifflin, 375–96.

Strode, Timothy Francis (2005). "Dwelling in the Fiction of J.M. Coetzee: A Postcolonial Poetics of Exile." In *The Ethics of Exile. Colonialism in the Fictions of Charles Brockden Brown and J.M. Coetzee.* London: Routledge, 177–230.

Suleri, Sara (1992). *The Rhetoric of English India.* Chicago: University of Chicago Press.

Sulk, Kay (2005). *"Not Grace, Then, But at Least the Body." J.M. Coetzees Schriften, 1990–1999.* Bielefeld: transcript.

Sullivan, Zohreh T. (1993). *Narratives of Empire. The Fictions of Rudyard Kipling.* Cambridge: Cambridge University Press.

Swamy, Vinay (2003). "Politicizing the Sexual, Sexualizing the Political: The Crossing of Political and Sexual Orientations in Stephen Frears' and Hanif Kureishi's *My Beautiful Laundrette* (1986)." *Comparative Literature Studies* 40.2, 142–58.

Taylor, Jesse Oak (2009). "Kipling's Imperial Aestheticism: Epistemologies of Art and Empire in *Kim*." *ELT* 52.1, 49–69.

Thomas, Susie (2005). *Hanif Kureishi. A Reader's Guide to Essential Criticism.* Basingstoke: Palgrave Macmillan.

— (2006). "Zadie Smith's False Teeth: The Marketing of Multiculturalism." *Literary London: Interdisciplinary Studies in the Representation of London* 4.1, (online) 17 paragraphs.

Thompson, Molly (2005). "'Happy Multicultural Land'? The Implications of an 'Excess of Belonging' in Zadie Smith's *White Teeth*." In Kadija Sesay (ed.), *Write Black, Write British. From Post Colonial to Black British Literature*. London: Hansib, 122–40.

Tiffin, Helen (1987). "Post-Colonial Literatures and Counter-Discourse." *Kunapipi* 9.3, 17–34.

Torgovnick, Marianna (1990). *Gone Primitive. Savage Intellects, Modern Lives*. Chicago: University of Chicago Press.

Tosh, John (1999). *A Man's Place. Masculinity and the Middle-Class Home in Victorian England*. New Haven: Yale University Press.

— (2004). *Manliness and Masculinities in Nineteenth-Century Britain. Essays on Gender, Family and Empire*. Harlow: Pearson Longman.

Tredell, Nicolas (2000). *Joseph Conrad. Heart of Darkness*. 1998. New York: Columbia University Press.

Trinh T. Minh-hà (1997). "Not You/Like You: Postcolonial Women and the Interlocking Questions of Identity and Difference." In Anne McClintock, Aamir Mufti and Ella Shohat (eds.), *Dangerous Liaisons. Gender, Nation, and Postcolonial Perspectives*. Minneapolis: University of Minnesota Press, 415–19.

Upstone, Sara (2010). "9/11, British Muslims, and Popular Literary Fiction." In Jeff Birkenstein, Anna Froula and Karen Randell (eds.), *Reframing 9/11. Film, Popular Culture and the "War on Terror"*. New York: Continuum, 35–44.

Van Coller, H.P. (2006). "A Contextual Interpretation of J.M. Coetzee's Novel *Disgrace*." In Liliana Sikorska (ed.), *A Universe of (Hi)Stories. Essays on J.M. Coetzee*. Frankfurt am Main: Lang, 15–37.

Van Der Elst, Jacques (2006). "Guilt, Reconciliation and Redemption: *Disgrace* and Its South African Context." In Liliana Sikorska (ed.), *A Universe of (Hi)Stories. Essays on J.M. Coetzee*. Frankfurt am Main: Lang, 39–44.

Van Schalkwyk, Phil (2006). "Whiteman's Blues: South African English Literature." In Liliana Sikorska (ed.), *A Universe of (Hi)Stories. Essays on J.M. Coetzee*. Frankfurt am Main: Lang, 9–14.

Vance, Norman (1985). *The Sinews of the Spirit. The Ideal of Christian Manliness in Victorian Literature and Religious Thought*. Cambridge: Cambridge University Press.

Vettel-Becker, Patricia (2005). *Shooting from the Hip. Photography, Masculinity, and Postwar America*. Minneapolis: University of Minnesota Press.

Viol, Claus-Ulrich (2005). "Golden Years or Dark Ages? Cultural Memories of the 1970s in Recent British Fiction." In Christoph Ribbat (ed.), *Twenty-First Century Fiction. Readings, Essays, Conversations*. Heidelberg: Winter, 149–69.

Viola, André (1999). *J.M. Coetzee. Romancier sud-africain*. Paris: Harmattan.

— (2008). "Martyred Bodies and Silenced Voices in South African Literature Under Apartheid." In Merete Falck Borch, et al. (eds.), *Bodies and Voices. The Force-Field of Representation and Discourse in Colonial and Postcolonial Studies*. Amsterdam: Rodopi, 3–15.

Vogel, Elisabeth, Antonia Napp and Wolfram Lutterer (eds.) (2003). *Zwischen Ausgrenzung und Hybridisierung. Zur Konstruktion von Identität aus kulturwissenschaftlicher Perspektive*. Würzburg: Ergon Verlag.

Vogelsberger, Hartwig A. (1984). *"King Romance." Rider Haggard's Achievement*. Salzburg: Institut für Anglistik und Amerikanistik, Universität Salzburg.

Wachinger, Tobias A. (2003). *Posing In-between. Postcolonial Englishness and the Commodification of Hybridity*. Frankfurt am Main: Lang.

Walgenbach, Katharina (2005). *"Die weiße Frau als Trägerin deutscher Kultur." Koloniale Diskurse über Geschlecht, "Rasse" und Klasse im Kaiserreich*. Frankfurt am Main: Campus.

— (2007). "Gender als interdependente Kategorie." In Katharina Walgenbach, et al. *Gender als interdependente Kategorie. Neue Perspektiven auf Intersektionalität, Diversität und Heterogenität*. Opladen: Budrich, 23–64.

Wall, Kathleen (2008). "Ethics, Knowledge, and the Need for Beauty: Zadie Smith's *On Beauty* and Ian McEwan's *Saturday*." *University of Toronto Quarterly: A Canadian Journal of the Humanities* 77.2, 757–88.

Wallace, Elizabeth Kowaleski (2007). "Postcolonial Melancholia in Ian McEwan's *Saturday*." *Studies in the Novel* 39.4, 465–80.

Walters, Tracey L. (2005). "'We're All English Now Mate Like It or Lump It': The Black/Britishness of Zadie Smith's *White Teeth*." In Kadija Sesay (ed.), *Write Black, Write British. From Post Colonial to Black British Literature*. London: Hansib, 314–22.

— (2008). "Still Mammies and Hos: Stereotypical Images of Black Women in Zadie Smith's Novels." In Tracey L. Walters (ed.), *Zadie Smith. Critical Essays*. New York: Lang, 123–39.

Walz, Angela (2005). "Multikulturelles Erzählen in Zadie Smiths *White Teeth* und Monica Alis feministische Alternative in *Brick Lane*." In *Erzählstimmen verstehen. Narrative Subjektivität im Spannungsfeld von Trans/Differenz am Beispiel zeitgenössischer britischer Schriftstellerinnen*. Münster: LIT, 170–206.

Ware, Vron (2007). "The White Fear Factor." *Wasafiri* 22.2, 51–6.

Wartenberg, Thomas E. (1999). *"The Crying Game*: Loving in Ignorance." In *Unlikely Couples. Movie Romance as Social Criticism*. Boulder: Westview Press, 209–29.

Warth, Eva (1999). "Crossdressing im Film: *The Crying Game* (1992) und *M. Butterfly* (1993)." In Anne Koenen and Catrin Gersdorf (eds.), *Geschlechterdifferenz und Amerikastudien in Deutschland. Analysen und Interpretationen*. Leipzig: Leipziger Universitätsverlag, 125–33.

— (2003). "Eye/Identity. Blickstrukturen in Filmen der 90er Jahre." In Christine Rüffert, et al. (eds.), *Wo/Man. Kino und Identität*. Berlin: Bertz, 65–80.

Watson, Stephen (1996). "Colonialism and the Novels of J.M. Coetzee." In Graham Huggan and Stephen Watson (eds.), *Critical Perspectives on J.M. Coetzee*. Basingstoke: Macmillan, 13–36.

Watson, Tim (2000). "Indian and Irish Unrest in Kipling's *Kim*." In Laura Chrisman and Benita Parry (eds.), *Postcolonial Theory and Criticism*. Cambridge: D.S. Brewer, 95–113.

Watt, Ian (1964). "Joseph Conrad: Alienation and Commitment." In Hugh Sykes Davies, George Watson and Basil Willey (eds.), *The English Mind. Studies in the English Moralists Presented to Basil Willey*. Cambridge: Cambridge University Press, 257–78.

— (1979). *Conrad in the Nineteenth Century*. Berkeley: University of California Press.

Watts, Cedric Thomas (1983). "'A Bloody Racist': About Achebe's View of Conrad." *Yearbook of English Studies* 13, 196–209.

— (1989). *Joseph Conrad. A Literary Life*. Basingstoke: Macmillan.

Weber, Donald (1997). "'No Secrets Were Safe From Me': Situating Hanif Kureishi." *The Massachusetts Review* 38.1, 119–35.

Weeks, Jeffrey (1989). *Sex, Politics and Society. The Regulation of Sexuality since 1800*. 2nd ed. London: Longman.

Wegner, Phillip E. (1993–1994). "'Life as He Would Have It': The Invention of India in Kipling's *Kim*." *Cultural Critique* 26, 129–59.

Wells, Lynn (2006). "The Ethical Otherworld: Ian McEwan's Fiction." In Philip Tew and Rod Mengham (eds.), *British Fiction Today*. London: Continuum, 117–27.

Welsch, Wolfgang (1999). "Transculturality – the Puzzling Form of Cultures Today." In Mike Featherstone and Scott Lash (eds.), *Spaces of Culture. City, Nation, World*. London: Sage, 194–213.

Whatmore, D.E. (1987). *H. Rider Haggard. A Bibliography*. London: Mansell.

White, Andrea (1993). *Joseph Conrad and the Adventure Tradition. Constructing and Deconstructing the Imperial Subject*. Cambridge: Cambridge University Press.

White, Hayden (1976). "The Fictions of Factual Representation." In Angus Fletcher (ed.), *The Literature of Fact*. New York: Columbia University Press, 21–44.

White, Patricia (1999). *Uninvited. Classical Hollywood Cinema and Lesbian Representability*. Bloomington: Indiana University Press.

Whitehead, Stephen M. and Frank J. Barret (eds.) (2001). *The Masculinities Reader*. Cambridge: Polity.

Williams, Patrick (1989). "*Kim* and Orientalism." In Phillip Mallett (ed.), *Kipling Considered*. Basingstoke: Macmillan, 33–55.

— (2000). "'Simultaneous Uncontemporaneities': Theorising Modernism and Empire." In Howard J. Booth and Nigel Rigby (eds.), *Modernism and Empire*. Manchester: Manchester University Press, 13–38.

Williams, Raymond (1988). *Keywords. A Vocabulary of Culture and Society*. 1976. London: Fontana Press.

Wilson, Donald S. (2000). "The Beast in the Congo: How Victorian Homophobia inflects Marlow's Heart of Darkness." *Conradiana* 32.2, 96–118.

Wilson, Janet (2005). "The Family and Change: Contemporary Second-Generation British-Asian Fiction." In Irene Visser and Heidi van den Heuver-Disler (eds.), *CDS Research Report 23: The Family in Contemporary Post-Colonial Literatures in English*, 109–20.

Winkgens, Meinhard (2004). "Hybride Identitätskonstruktion zwischen einer ‚Politik kultureller Differenz' und individueller Authentifizierung in den Fiktionen Hanif Kureishis – Anmerkungen zu *The Buddha of Suburbia* und *The Black Album*." In Stefan Glomb and Stefan Horlacher (eds.), *Beyond Extremes. Repräsentation und Reflexion von Modernisierungsprozessen im zeitgenössischen britischen Roman.* Tübingen: Narr, 173–213.

Woitschig, Britta Madeleine (2002). "Irina Divina." In polymorph (ed.), *(K)ein Geschlecht oder viele? Transgender in politischer Perspektive.* Berlin: Querverlag, 93–116.

Wood, James (2005). *The Irresponsible Self. On Laughter and the Novel.* New York: Picador.

Worswick, Clark and Ainslie T. Embree (eds.) (1976). *The Last Empire. Photography in British India, 1855–1911.* New York: Aperture.

Wright, Laura (2008). "Displacing the Voice: South African Feminism and J.M. Coetzee's Female Narrators." *African Studies* 67.1, 11–32.

Wurgaft, Lewis D. (1983). *The Imperial Imagination. Magic and Myth in Kipling's India.* Middletown: Wesleyan University Press.

Young, Lola (2007). "'Nothing Is as It Seems': Re-viewing *The Crying Game*." In Julie F. Codell (ed.), *Genre, Gender, Race, and World Cinema.* Malden: Blackwell, 137–47.

Young, Robert J.C. (1990). *White Mythologies. Writing History and the West.* London: Routledge.

— (1995). *Colonial Desire. Hybridity in Theory, Culture, and Race.* London: Routledge.

— (2001). *Postcolonialism. An Historical Introduction.* Oxford: Blackwell.

— (2003). *Postcolonialism. A Very Short Introduction.* Oxford: Oxford University Press.

Young, Robert M. (1985). *Darwin's Metaphor. Nature's Place in Victorian Culture.* Cambridge: Cambridge University Press.

Young, Shannon (2006). "*She*: Rider Haggard's Queer Adventures." In Richard Fantina (ed.), *Straight Writ Queer. Non-Normative Expressions of Heterosexuality in Literature.* Jefferson: McFarland Press, 134–44.

Yousaf, Nahem (1996). "Hanif Kureishi and 'the Brown Man's Burden'." *Critical Survey* 8.1, 14–25.

— (2002). *Hanif Kureishi's The Buddha of Suburbia. A Reader's Guide.* New York: Continuum.

Zilliax, Amy (1995). "The Scorpion and The Frog. Agency and Identity in Neil Jordan's *The Crying Game*." *Camera Obscura: Feminism, Culture, and Media Studies* 35, 25–51.

Žižek, Slavoj (1993). "From Courtly Love to *The Crying Game*." *New Left Review* I.202, 95–108.

Index